ESSENTIALS OF

Educational

Research

ESSENTIALS OF

Educational

Research

Methodology and Design

CARTER V. GOOD

Dean, School of Education
University of Cincinnati

New York

APPLETON-CENTURY-CROFTS

DIVISION OF MEREDITH PUBLISHING COMPANY

PREFACE

THIS BOOK is an adaptation and updating of *Introduction to Educational Research,* to serve the purposes of a briefer edition, with a considerable reduction in bibliographical references and quotations from the literature. It may be used as a basic text in an introductory course devoted to research methods and thesis writing, or along with books on statistics and measurement in courses of larger scope. It may also serve the individual student and school worker as a handbook or manual of research methodology.

The chapters are arranged in substantially the sequence followed in problem-solving and thesis writing, although it is recognized that the movement in research is frequently shuttle-like rather than a straight line to the answer. By delimination of scope, the quantitative details of testing and measurement, statistics, and data processing are left for the many specialized texts now available.

In presenting the concepts and procedures of research methodology, there is no straining toward artificial dichotomies in problem-solving approaches, which frequently are complementary: the scientific *versus* the philosophical, the quantitative *versus* the qualitative, the mathematical *versus* the descriptive, or the statistical *versus* the case-clinical. Although this is not a "how-to-do-it cookbook" of research and graduate study, there are many hundreds of illustrations drawn from the literature and from the biographies or life histories of scientists and scholars.

The interdisciplinary interests and common investigational procedures of the behavioral sciences are now such that many illustrations have been drawn from psychology, sociology, and other social fields to supplement the examples from education. For these examples the author is indebted to the publications and achievements of hundreds of scholars and scientists.

As we read the literature and study the theory and methods of research, the conclusion is inescapable that the clear task of scientists, scholars, and teachers is to face the future, undeterred by the uncertainties of human survival in the present and future. This faith in science, scholarship, and serious study is not incompatible with or exclusive of any other kind of faith; indeed there is no inconsistency in considering the fruits of research and scholarship as one of the great instruments of higher ends. May the creative scholar and teacher have the gift of time for their work and freedom from the nervousness and brittleness of this age.

C. V. G.

University of Cincinnati

CONTENTS

1

The Scholar and Science

HALLMARKS AND OBLIGATIONS

> This chapter deals with the major characteristics of science and research, interdisciplinary cooperation in the social and behavioral fields of inquiry, role of values in science and research, hallmarks or traits of the scientist, freedom and responsibility for research, and scientific progress and social responsibility.

Characteristics of Science and Research

VARYING FRAMES OF REFERENCE

THE CHARACTERISTICS OF SCIENCE HAVE BEEN ANALYZED IN TERMS OF VARYING frames of reference. One description of science, both as substantive theory and as methodology, uses such phrasing as empirical, propositional, logical, operational, public (subject to communication to other scientists), problem-solving, abstract, tending toward a system, and on-going. Other current interpretations of the term *science,* or notions about the scientist and his work, are in relation to subject-matter fields, complicated gadgets, universal laws, systematic procedures, technical methodology, and pseudo-scientific schemes (for example, astrology, phrenology, physiognomy, palmistry, and graphology).

Such attempts to characterize or define science or research, particularly basic research, have not proved generally successful. One discussion of the problem of definition cites a list of research terms (without definitions) and concludes that, instead of futilely trying to define a long list of terms, it may seem better to relax about definitions and to concentrate on the quality of research, regardless of its setting or purpose. The terminology mentioned by way of example, in each instance preceding the word research, includes: academic, ad hoc, applied, basic, borderline, developmental, directed, experimental, theoretical, exploratory, industrial, nondirected, pot-boiling, pure, technological, long-term, and short-term.[1]

[1] Dael Wolfle, "Taxonomy of Research." *Science* 130: 1163; October 30, 1959.

ATTEMPTS TO DEFINE RESEARCH

An older description or definition of science and research during the present century was in terms of mathematical precision and accuracy, objectivity, verifiability, impartiality, and expertness, with the first letters of these five characterizations spelling out the word *movie*. We now recognize, however, that many historical, descriptive-survey, and case-clinical studies cannot be phrased or reported in mathematical terms, and that precision may be in either mathematical or verbal terms. In many instances the criteria of objectivity and verifiability can be only partially satisfied in the educational, psychological, and social areas.

As to objectivity, even tough-minded scientists, psychologists, and other scholars have been led away from facts to romance by loyalty to an ideal in the person of a "great" man. Hermann Ebbinghaus was the brilliant German originator of the experimental psychology of memory, who died in 1909 a few months before he was due to speak at Clark University. In tribute to Ebbinghaus, at the Clark meeting E. B. Titchener, the erudite, German-trained Briton, spoke as follows:

> When the cable brought the bare news, last February, that Ebbinghaus was dead, just a month after the celebration of his fifty-ninth birthday, the feeling that took precedence even of personal sorrow was the wonder what experimental psychology would do without him. . . . What characterized him was, first, an instinctive grasp of the scientific aspect of a problem . . . ; secondly, a perfect clarity of thought and language . . . ; and thirdly, an easy mastery of the facts. I say mastery, but the truth requires a stronger word. There was about Ebbinghaus a sort of masterfulness; he never did violence to facts, but he marshalled them; he made them stand and deliver; he took from them, as of right, all that they contained; and with the tribute thus extracted he built up his theories and his system.[2]

This panegyric is rather unexpected, coming from the tough-minded Titchener. Ebbinghaus has remained "great," chiefly because he was the leader in the experimental psychology of memory and learning. Psychology managed to get along without him, as it has without other great figures who have passed on, since history has a way of taking care of itself.

Although man has used other than scientific methods or sources through the centuries for arriving at answers to his questions or problems, including mythology and personification, supernatural explanation, personal experience, custom and tradition, the voice of authority, and syllogistic reasoning, it has been well said that: "The greatest invention of the nineteenth century was the invention of the method of invention. . . . One

---

[2] Edwin G. Boring, "Cognitive Dissonance: Its Use in Science." *Science* 145: 680–85; August 14, 1964.

element in the method is just the discovery of how to set about bridging the gap between the scientific ideas, and the ultimate product."[3] A striking illustration of the validity of Whitehead's statement is found in the development of instruments to explore outer space.

In recognizing the importance of "invention" and scientific method generally, we note that over the years a stereotype has developed in both the scientific and the public mind as to what constitutes serious research, especially by way of psychological investigation and scientific proof. The generally approved pattern has been as follows: crucial experiments growing out of previous findings and performed with great precision, results subjected to the closest scrutiny and alternative interpretations accepted or rejected in accordance with canons of scientific rigor, and finally, confirmed discovery inserted in a systematized lattice of already available knowledge. This type of investigation is thought to be possible only with the aid of intellectual equipment that includes logic, theory, broad and scholarly knowledge, technical proficiency in mathematics and statistics, and a background of the history and philosophy of science. This investigational stereotype, however, is only a small part of the process of active research and is more commonly found in the terminal phases, especially in controlled experimentation. The activities and the task of the individual scientist or the research psychologist are not mainly those of designing a study, collecting data, analyzing the results, and drawing conclusions, although this is probably the formal picture that many people have of the research process. Actually the process of conducting research, of creating and developing a science of psychology or of education, is a rather informal, sometimes illogical, and occasionally a disorderly-appearing affair. It includes considerable floundering around in the empirical world, and is sometimes dignified by names like "pilot studies" and "exploratory research." Somehow in the process of floundering the research worker will get an idea, or many ideas; on largely intuitive grounds he will reject some ideas and accept others as the basis for more extended work. If the idea chosen happens to be a poor one, the investigator may waste time, but if the idea proves to be a good one, he may make a significant contribution to his field of science or scholarship, the positive nature of the contribution depending on persistence, originality, intuition, and hard work. The productive investigator spends much of his time and effort on this type of activity, as compared with the more orderly and systematic phases of scientific work.[4]

While man has ordinarily found many of his answers to perplexing or

3 Quoted from Alfred N. Whitehead, *Science in the Modern World*. New York: The Macmillan Co., 1950. 296 p.

4 Donald W. Taylor and Others, "Education for Research in Psychology." *American Psychologist* 14: 167–79; April 1959.

interesting questions through other than research methods, he is engaged in research if he follows a procedure substantially as follows:

> If he questions his explanations, the stage is set for research. If he goes further and challenges the methods by which he arrived at his conclusion; if he critically and systematically repeats his observations; if he devises special tools for taking, recording, and analyzing his observations; if he tests the reliability and the validity of these tools and evaluates his data in other ways; if he scrutinizes the thought processes by which he passes from one step of his logic to another; if he gradually refines his concept of what it is he is trying to explain and considers anew the necessary and sufficient conditions for proof; if at every step he proceeds with the utmost caution, realizing that his purpose is not to arrive at an answer which is personally pleasing, but rather one which will stand up under the critical attacks of those who doubt his answer—if he can meet these criteria and steadfastly hold to his purpose, then he is doing research.[5]

STEPS OR SEQUENCE IN RESEARCH

To comment more specifically on procedural sequence, it should not be assumed that any given list (series) of steps in scientific or reflective thinking (research or investigation) follows some invariable sequence. In actuality, the steps in research or problem-solving may move backward and forward in a "shuttle-like" fashion. The investigator may go from the hypothesis to the data and, if the hypothesis proves invalid, he will return to formulation of a new hypothesis. With the possibility of this shuttle-like movement always present in research, it it helpful to identify the more important steps in problem-solving. Although the temporal order is substantially as enumerated below, we should recognize that these steps in scientific investigation represent a somewhat idealized account of how the scientist actually does his work. A brief, consolidated list of steps in research, similar to the sequence of chapters in this book, is as follows:

1. Definition and development of the problem, including the survey of the related literature and formulation of the working hypothesis
2. Selection or creation of appropriate data-gathering techniques and actual collection of data
3. Classification and analysis of data
4. Conclusions, generalizations, and applications (with due attention to reporting).

An illustration of the steps typically involved in an evaluative or experimental investigation is as follows:

---

[5] Quoted from Carter V. Good and Douglas E. Scates, *Methods of Research: Educational, Psychological, Sociological.* New York: Appleton-Century-Crofts, 1954. p. 11.

Also see William A. Brownell, "The Evaluation of Learning under Differing Systems of Instruction." *Educational Psychologist* 3: 3–7; November 1965.

1. The decision to make an evaluative study
2. Determination of the grade level at which to make it
3. Selection of appropriate subjects
4. Decision concerning the length of the period of time to be included
5. Analysis of the content and of the objectives in rival programs
6. Decision regarding the kinds of data to be collected
7. Choice of available tests or other instruments, or the making of original tests or other instruments
8. Determination of measures to assure equal quality of teaching or of means to allow for differences
9. Selection of the statistical methods best suited for the treatment of data
10. Final interpretation of the findings.

SCIENCE, THEORY, AND THE MODEL[6]

We expect of the broadly equipped educator, psychologist, or surgeon competence in the science, the theory and philosophy, and the art of his field of specialization. The able surgeon knows the latest research in his field, practices a humanitarian code of ethics, and has the skill of an artist in his fingertips. The psychologist, especially the practicing or clinical psychologist, must know the evidence in his field, must abide by a strict code of ethics for the profession, and must use the arts of interviewing and consultation effectively. Science, theory and philosophy, and art share certain common grounds. On the wall of a university physics building is the inscription: "In this philosophy propositions are based on phenomena and laws are derived by induction."

Considerable criticism and confusion are present in education generally and in the curriculum particularly, because coherent theory frequently is lacking in a field involving application of scientific method to human beings engaged in value-directed activities. It has been suggested that three stages characterize fruitful inquiry in any field, including curriculum research and the development of explanatory theory: "first, a phase embodying an analysis of the problem in which the basic elements are discerned; second, a natural history effort embracing observation, description, and classification; and third, an attempt at deductive formulation of a theory—a process in which inferences are added to facts in order to obtain concepts and testable hypotheses."[7]

Brodbeck maintains that a statement of fact, a concept, a law, a theory,

[6] N. L. Gage, "Paradigms for Research on Teaching," *Handbook of Research on Teaching*. Chicago: Rand McNally & Co., 1963. Chapter 3.

[7] F. S. C. Northrop, *The Logic of the Sciences and the Humanities*. New York: Harcourt, Brace & World, Inc. Meridian Books, 1959. 402 p.

David L. Elliott and Arthur W. Foshay, "Chart or Charter: Recent Developments in Educational Discourse." *Review of Educational Research* 33: 233–44; June 1963.

and a model are all different things.[8] A fact is a particular thing, such as Johnny's I.Q., and the statement of this fact means that a concept (I.Q.) has an instance or a number of instances.

A law is an empirical generalization, and is a statement of relations accepted as unvariable within the range of usual observations; for example, the laws of readiness, exercise, effect, contiguity, and recency.

A theory is a deductively connected set or system of related conceptions in agreement with known properties or behaviors and stated so as to guide in the search for properties or behaviors hitherto unknown; for example, culture-epochs theory, small-sample theory, identical-elements theory, field theory of learning, gestalt theory of learning, and theory of relativity.

A "model" train, if geometrically similar to a real train and if propelled in the same manner, is more complete as a model than is a toy train.

It is maintained that men who would engage in the complete act of research must of necessity be rare, since the complete act of research includes:

1. Formal theory construction, with no empirical dimension
2. Empirical theory construction, with an empirical dimension, in the sense that it could be checked out through events
3. Checking out of theory in events, which is yet another empirical dimension.

We regard theory construction as a phase of research, and men engaged in it do research. Logicians, mathematicians, theoretical scientists, and laboratory scientists are all researchers. This view answers the question of why so much talk about theory, since science *is* theory, with generalizations induced from observed particulars, and scientists in their technical writing should talk about science (or theory).[9]

It has been suggested that scientific models have at least three connotations: (1) as a noun, representation in the sense of an architect's small-scale model of a building or a physicist's large-scale model of an atom; (2) as an adjective, a degree of perfection or idealization, like a model home or model student; and (3) as a verb, to demonstrate or show what a thing is like.[10]

Psychologists and specialists in the field of experimental education talk a great deal about models, although many graduate students and readers

[8] May Brodbeck, "Models, Meaning, and Theories," *Symposium on Sociological Theory*. Edited by Llewellyn Gross. New York: Harper & Row, Publishers, Inc., 1959. p. 373–403.

Daniel E. Griffiths, "Some Assumptions Underlying the Use of Models in Research," *Educational Research: New Perspectives*. Edited by Jack A. Culbertson and Stephen P. Hencley. Danville, Illinois: Interstate, 1963. p. 121–40.

[9] Elizabeth S. Maccia, "The Complete Act of Research." *Graduate School Record* 14: 9–10; Spring 1961.

[10] Russell L. Ackoff, *Scientific Method:* Optimizing Applied Research Decisions. New York: John Wiley & Sons, Inc., 1962. p. 108–9.

of the technical journals are not very clear about the meaning of the term "model." A globe is a replica model of the earth because, in some respects, it "looks like" the earth. Today another type of model (symbolic) is what might have been called a theory several decades or more ago, and makes use of ideas, concepts, and abstract symbols to represent the object being modeled. The Helmholtz theory of hearing was a model that proved to be fact only in part. The Hering theory of vision was a speculative physiology of imaginary processes in the retinal cones that was satisfactory as a model for certain phenomena and probably not true. McDougall's drainage theory of attention and learning was a physiological speculation that now seems almost ridiculous to the sophisticated student of neurology. Physiological models always had a chance of turning out to be true; that is, a physiological explanation that accounts for conscious or behavioral phenomena might be independently confirmed by physiological observation. Today we have other kinds of models: conceptual (intervening variables), physical (electrical brain fields, the topological dynamics of life-space), mathematical (equations for the learning function).[11]

It is positive and encouraging to recognize that the model represents an habitual form of thinking, one of man's devices for bringing his enormously complex experience within the compass of his limited cognitive facilities. Science, as one such device, with a basic function of economy of thinking, uses models to reduce nature's complexity to the much lesser scope of human comprehension. In thus limiting the area of consideration, the investigator deals with the universe piecemeal; for example, the universe may be a desire to promote peace in an aggressive world. The model for a limited area of this universe may be a plan for a federalized world union, with a constitution for the union, a system of organization, a budget, and a plan to turn all arms and military forces over to it—a model of how the world would work if its peoples could be induced to want the new mechanism. This is a useful model of limited scope, even though it omits the facts of human egoism and man's need for aggression (other parts of the universe of peace in an aggressive world).[12]

To cite another example of the model, one of the methods for preparing to meet ethical issues is to develop descriptive models of the "ideal man," that is, models of what we think people should be like and what we hope they some day will be like, and perhaps expressed more simply, we might construct negative models describing the kind of people we hope will not emerge.

These models might be constructed from philosophical thinking, past and present, and scientific knowledge of man gained primarily through the social

11 Edwin G. Boring, "The Model." *Contemporary Psychology* 4: 385; December 1959.
12 Granville Clark and Louis S. Sohn, *World Peace through World Law.* Boston: Harvard University Press, 1958. 540 p.

sciences. As long as we do not have some notion of the model man and some notion of the kind of person we would not prefer, we are especially vulnerable to selling our services, unwittingly, to support endeavors which contribute to producing ends we do not wish achieved. . . .

By developing model men we should also be in a better position to enlighten the public to the dangers involved in the use of psychological power and to present the public with clearer choices in matters concerning the public welfare.[13]

Although models are useful, especially in engineering and scientific work, they are subject to important sources of error and their limitations should be clearly recognized:[14]

1. Models invite overgeneralization.
2. Models entice us into committing a logical fallacy.
3. The relationships between variables may be incorrect.
4. The constants assumed in the model may be incorrect.
5. Models are too often not validated.
6. Model building diverts useful energy into nonproductive activity.

Psychologists and other scientists and scholars should not be discouraged, however, about their models as piecemeal approaches to evidence. Although the size of a single thought or idea is relatively small, with the aid of symbolism and language a thought's implication can be enormous, and progress can be made, even though many or most of the models may not turn out to be "true."

BASIC RESEARCH, APPLIED RESEARCH, AND DEVELOPMENT

The National Science Foundation has formulated a three-fold classification of research activities—"basic research," "applied research," and "development":

Basic research includes original investigation for the advancement of scientific knowledge. The primary aim of the investigator is achievement of fuller knowledge or understanding of the subject matter under study, rather than making practical applications of new knowledge. Applied research is directed toward practical applications of scientific knowledge. Development is the systematic use of scientific knowledge for the production of useful materials, devices, systems, methods, or processes, exclusive of design and production engineering. It is evident that the sequence from research to action is in that order. An invention of a device, procedure, or method cannot be made until

13 Quoted from David B. Lynn, "A Model Man for Applied Psychology." *American Psychologist* 14: 630–32; October 1959.
14 Alphonse Chapanis, "Men, Machines, and Models." *American Psychologist* 16: 113–31; March 1961.

the key, or last essential, fact is discovered: for example, a television set coul not be produced until all the basic discoveries of electromagnetic radiation and synchronization of transmitted impulses had been made.[15]

Brief reference has been made to the "pure" or basic and to the practical or applied aspects of research. In pure research the investigator may attack any problem anywhere that appeals to his fancy. After he has selected his problem he need only apply scholarly methods to its solution and publish the results, with no concern about any practical social use of his findings. In practical (applied) research the problem is localized within practice, and the results are to be applied to the improvement of practice.

Both pure or basic and applied research should be encouraged and supported. While pure research, at the time the particular investigation was made, may have been evaluated chiefly in terms of the satisfaction afforded the research worker, at a later date the same pure research may have practical and social value. The work of Benjamin Franklin, as he played with his kite and key in studying electricity, probably would be regarded as pure research that did not take on practical and social values until Thomas A. Edison much later worked out his numerous inventions utilizing electricity. In attempting to classify pure research and practical (applied) research, we do not have a dichotomy but a continuum for the methods and values of pure and applied research. The major considerations are really the objectivity and the quality of the investigational techniques and the evidence. It may be said that research is only good or bad, not basic or applied. Any false dichotomy might develop research attitudes harmful to the graduate student. The efforts of the extreme purist and of the extreme technologist are complementary, contributing to a range of research and a diversity of attitude beneficial to society. An inscription on the wall of a university mathematics building reads: "In our most theoretical moods we may be nearest to our most practical applications." (During recent years the term *action research* has become widely accepted, as discussed in the chapter on descriptive-survey studies.)

Educational investigators are cautioned against overemphasis on the desire to solve practical problems:[16]

1. One of the most harmful effects of the overly practical emphasis in educational research is to convert education to a more or less elaborate dogma, based on experience, informal observation, and personal preference or whim.

15 Quoted from Nicholas A. Fattu, "The Role of Research in Education—Present and Future," in "The Methodology of Educational Research." *Review of Educational Research* 30: 413; December 1960.

16 Fred N. Kerlinger, "Practicality and Educational Research." *School Review* 67: 281–91; Autumn 1959.

2. Overconcern with practicality and with practical results in educational research acts as a strong social pressure on the staffs in the universities and the public schools.
3. Educational research may have a generally unscientific bias.
4. The practical investigator may have a spurious sense of adequacy.
5. Many talented workers may be channeled into such practical efforts as action research.
6. Funds from sources outside the university may be devoted largely to practical research projects.
7. Graduate students may lack competence and confidence in handling important theoretical issues and complex research designs and projects.

Expressed in other terms, in emphasizing the social usefulness and implications of science, we must recognize the need for a much larger stock of fundamental scientific information than will be used during any one limited period of time, since we cannot foresee accurately the scientific and social needs of the future. We must not overemphasize the social usefulness of science to the detriment of the internal development and extension of science. It is possible for an investigator or scholar to become so socially minded that he neglects the self-contained research activity which is a large part of the life of the working scientist—a fact of major consequence in the organization of scientific work.

Certainly scientific work should be answerable for its value to the community—but at arm's length. If a man has no sense of social responsibility, don't appoint him, but if he is known to possess such a sense, for goodness' sake don't badger him with an unceasing inquiry as to his social responsibility while he is trying to perform the work that belongs to the fulfillment of his social responsibility. Science is a tender plant, which does not take kindly to a gardener who is in the habit of taking it up by the roots to see if it is growing properly.[17]

Social and Behavioral Fields of Inquiry

In defining the scope of the behavioral sciences, we have usually included those fields dealing directly with human behavior, particularly psychology, sociology, anthropology, and education. This delimitation, however, may seem too narrow, in view of helpful comparative data resulting from study of species other than human beings. Therefore, a more inclusive view would include within the behavioral sciences the fields of ethnology, ecology, physiology, neurology, comparative psychology, and even economics and political science.

PROCEDURES IN SOCIAL SCIENCE

The physical sciences have constantly invented new methods of dealing with new sorts of data, as when the biochemists found that methods used

[17] Norbert Wiener, "Science and Society." *Science* 138: 651; November 9, 1962.

in the analysis of simple inorganic compounds would not work in dealing with complex organic substances and went on to discover methods for a respectable science of the chemistry of living beings. The biochemists invented new methods as well as new techniques for the understanding of organic part-whole relationships. "In the same manner, those who aim to be social scientists are entitled to invent their own ways of mastering their materials, and to challenge the skeptic to doubt the reliability of their results."[18] There are difficulties to be overcome, however, as we seek to develop procedures suitable for the social areas of inquiry, since the self-consciousness of science was increased when scientific study was extended vigorously to human behavior itself, and the social sciences (including psychology) posed anew questions about the range and the effects of science that had lingered since its beginnings.

1. Can science deal with human beings as it can with the rest of nature, that is, can the behavior of people be predicted?
2. Can the social sciences solve the problems besetting humanity in the same way the physical sciences deal with problems in physics and chemistry, or what is the role of the social sciences in the direction of human behavior and in controlling social changes made necessary by the progress of the natural sciences?

Mistaken Image of Social Science. In spite of encouraging progress in the several fields of social investigation, mistaken notions are common in secondary school, college, and elsewhere. Among the wrong attitudes and misconceptions concerning social science, as held by many college freshmen (and others), are six common fallacies:[19]

1. Science is techniques and gadgetry. The average student judges the merits of a particular scientific endeavor by certain superficial "techniques" which are easily grasped. He sees the scientist as a man in a white coat, working alone in a laboratory full of test tubes, gurgling retorts, and flashing electronic signals. This concept would rule out most physical scientists, more biological scientists, and all social scientists.
2. In some cases he has the stereotyped idea that a scientific law must be an algebraic equation. This would rule out many biological and social generalizations. For example, the principle of blood constancy (homeostasis) can be stated clearly in words. It applies to all human beings and has many useful applications in "life and death" problems.
3. Then there is the misconception that "it must be infallible or it isn't science." We have found that the student rejects the I.Q. test as a social

18 Harold A. Larrabee, *Reliable Knowledge.* Boston: Houghton-Mifflin Company, 1945. p. 485.
  Also see Ernest van den Haag, "Man as an Object of Science." *Science* 129: 243–47; January 30, 1959.
19 Quoted from Raymond L. Gorden, *Antioch Notes* 33: 1–8; May 1956.

invention because it has certain flaws. But he does not reject the products of the physical sciences on the same grounds. Yet anyone who has a TV set knows that it distorts reality and breaks down on occasion.

4. The social scientist is perceived as "studying people" as unique personalities and "the basic units of society"; therefore, to predict anything which will happen in society, we must know all of the unique characteristics of each individual. But to expect any social scientist to know what Mary Jones will be doing on her twenty-first birthday is as hopeless as asking the physical scientist when a cork thrown in the Mississippi River will arrive in New Orleans. Pure scientific investigation is more likely to focus on such basic variables as conformity, rumor, decision-making, role conflict, attitude, etc.

5. Another interesting belief is that, in the physical sciences, the basic theoretical concepts are more "real" and tangible than in the social sciences. For example, the majority of the freshmen classify the atom as something that has been proven beyond a shadow of a doubt, but the "subconscious mind" as having never been proven to exist—"It's just a theory." Yet, it is simpler to demonstrate the existence of the subconscious mind than the concept of the atom.

6. A large proportion of the freshmen share the misconception that "science is successful insofar as it contributes to the manufacturing of more gadgets."

INTERDISCIPLINARY RESEARCH AND COOPERATION

Understanding Between Physical and Social Scientists, and the Humanities. It has been urged that we have a broad base of mutual understanding between physical scientists and social scientists, in the interest of interdisciplinary cooperation and actually for the survival of society. What we do in a material way will be worth nothing unless we learn to live with each other. Therefore, a fair proportion of the bright young men and women must become social scientists. We do not expect the scholar to master all the complexities of today's social, political, economic, and educational problems, but we do need mutual understanding and cooperation between all physical scientists and all social scientists, with education playing the key role in achieving this understanding.[20] We are cautioned, however, that science in its several stages is both compartmentalized (or specialized) and unified. Research in its early stages may be highly particularized, seeking to answer one question to the neglect of all other questions, but in its later stages in striving toward unity it may seek to break down the very barriers that made earlier progress possible.

As the barriers between the various sciences have disappeared, so the boundaries between science and the humanities have been gradually erased. A culture of new dimensions is emerging from the interaction of

[20] Guy Suits, "Education and Science." *American Scientist* 47: 60–67; March 1959.

the arts and humanities with science. Examples of interdisciplinary co-operation are: dating through physical methods as a technique of research in history, X-ray spectra and microanalysis as tools in the study of painting, and human psychology as an aid in rewriting human history more effectively in a unified form. This teamwork between scholars and scientists representing different disciplines indicates that they do not live in different worlds and must communicate with one another. In teaching science we must remember that it involves social aspects, creativity and ingenuity, a history of ideas, and a philosophy. On their part, the humanities and social sciences must become permeated with the knowledge and spirit of science.[21]

There are urgent needs for improvement of scholarship in the humanities, including better libraries, financial aid in printing expensive books, grants for a variety of purposes, more graduate fellowships, one or more new centers of humanistic learning, and better coordination within the university to foster humanistic learning. We need a better balance in government and university support of the sciences and the humanities. It is usually erroneous to assume that government grants for science have enabled universities to use a larger fraction of their general funds to support the humanities. Better education of future scientists involves broad or at least adequate acquaintance with areas of scholarship other than science. Many future scientists, teachers, and leaders in all fields of scholarly endeavor lack the stimulation provided by humanistic scholarship. Humanists should take the lead in meeting these needs, with the expectation that scientists will lend encouragement and support.[22]

Unification of Knowledge in the Physical and Biological Sciences. Intellectual boundaries have virtually disappeared in science, especially in chemistry, physics, and biology. It is no more possible now to make a clear distinction among cytologists, geneticists, immunologists, and virologists than to make one among chemists, physical chemists, and physicists. They attend each other's meetings, present papers on related problems, and utilize common materials, techniques, and instruments. The interests and problems of science are related to politics, economics, the humanities, and the arts. The modern molecular biologist is also a chemist, a physicist, and a mathematician.[23]

Psychology and Interdisciplinary Effort. To use psychology as an illustration, we recognize that there have always been cross-currents between

[21] Albert Szent-Györgyi, "Teaching and the Expanding Knowledge." *Science* 146: 1278–79; December 4, 1964.

Bentley Glass, "The Academic Scientist, 1940–1960." *Science* 132: 598–603; September 2, 1960.

[22] Dael Wolfle, "Needs of the Humanities." *Science* 143: 1297; March 20, 1964.

[23] Warren Weaver, "The Moral Un-Neutrality of Science." *Science* 133: 255–56; January 27, 1961.

the sciences and the humanities, and it is indeed only a century since natural philosophy counted as literature. Since both breadth and depth are needed in science, modern psychology, in spite of ardent dedication to science and aggressive repudiation of anything nonexperimental in origin, may well move toward humanism, and strengthen rather than weaken its proficiency. The cultivated psychologist knows, in addition to other subjects, the psychology and psychologists of other lands, in order to think wisely in the atmosphere of other men's thinking, thus attaining wisdom as well as skill and competence. It is recognized that the dedicated experimentalist commonly would substitute, as more important tools, statistics and electronics for the languages. We need to know of other times as well as other lands, and thus get wisdom from a knowledge of the history of psychology, rather than facts as such. "One sees how thought works itself out, how human nature operates in the social institution to generate discovery and also sometimes to prevent it."[24] Science requires both objectivity and enthusiasm, and the good scientist oscillates between the two, now checking his enthusiasm with criticism, now bursting restraints in a flight of fancy.

Psychologists should not resist humanizing influences because of dedication to narrow empiricism or rigid theorizing. Psychology is really the area where the problems of the sciences and the humanities intersect. In the debate concerning the relations between science and the humanities, psychologists have been strangely silent, whereas psychological questions and modes of analysis really merit central attention in assessing the actual relations between the work of science and of the humanities. We have already heard from physicists, philosophers, literary critics, sociologists, historians, politicians, military men, and educators.

Interdisciplinary Cooperation between Sociology, Psychology, and Education. It should prove especially profitable to bridge some of the remaining gaps between sociology and psychology. Although differences in the historical roots of psychology and sociology in the realms of assumption, theory, and method have often prevented effective communication and collaboration between these two disciplines, relations are now so mature that it is profitable to make explicit some of the remaining gaps between sociology and psychology. From the beginning, sociology has considered as its central problem the question of how individuals learn to act together and to adjust to one another, while the basic question posed by psychologists about social factors is what effect they have on individual behavior. Typically the psychologist has adopted the experi-

24 E. G. Boring, "Humanizing Psychology." *Contemporary Psychology* 3: 361–2; December 1958.

Also see Sigmund Koch, "Psychological Science Versus the Science-Humanism Antinomy: Intimations of a Significant Science of Man." *American Psychologist* 16: 629–39; October 1961.

mental method as his basic research approach, and the sociologist has emphasized observation, frequently in the form of diaries and other personal documents, questionnaire responses, scales, and similar procedures, as basic techniques of gathering evidence. Psychologists and sociologists need to give further study to differences in their approaches to problems in such areas as heredity and environment, intelligence, learning, and personality.[25]

In recognizing the benefits to be derived from closer alignment between sociology and education, and in identifying the sociologist's major contribution to education, certain dangers must be avoided:

1. Overgeneralization of sociological research findings that apply to a single case or a small population so as to apply them to American education or society, when there is no logical basis for such induction
2. Uncritical acceptance of unverified pronouncements of sociologists as verified propositions
3. Acceptance of sociological research findings without critical examination of assumptions, adequacy of research methods, and conclusions.

What the sociologist has to offer is basically a series of sensitizing and analytic concepts and ideas based on theoretical and empirical analysis that will allow the practitioner to examine in a more realistic and more incisive way the multiple forces operating in his social environment. The sociologist cannot make the educational practitioner's decisions for him, nor can the sociologist's reseach findings based on one population be applied to any educational population indiscriminately. The practitioner's task is to assess the various forces that have a bearing on the achievement of his objectives, assign them relative weights, and make a decision based on these calculations. The basic sociological contribution is to add to the educator's kit of intellectual tools a set of sociological insights and concepts that will allow him to take account in his decision-making organizational, cultural, and interpersonal factors at work in his environment.[26]

By way of interdisciplinary progress, as the result of co-operative work on certain common problems, a number of theoretical concepts and propositions are now more or less the shared property of psychology, sociology, anthropology, and education, or, at least, such concepts are reasonably meaningful in theoretical discussions of an interdisciplinary nature that cross departmental boundaries. Certain interdisciplinary agreements in these fields may be found with respect to the human organ-

25 Arnold M. Rose, "The Hiatus Between Sociology and Psychology," *Theory and Method in the Social Sciences*. Minneapolis: University of Minnesota Press, 1954. p. 220-27.

26 Quoted from Neal Gross, "Some Contributions of Sociology to the Field of Education." *Harvard Educational Review* 29: 275-87; Fall 1959.

ism, human behavior, interaction, grouping, culture, social structure, personality, and symbolization and communication.

Interdisciplinary Cooperation in Behavioral Science and Human Engineering. The present national and international scene makes imperative an evaluation of the role and potential contribution of the interdisciplinary area known as behavioral science, which includes many areas concerned with human beings as individuals and in social relations: anthropology, biochemistry, ecology, economics, genetics, geography, history, linguistics, mathematical statistics, neurology, pharmacology, physiology, political science, psychiatry, psychology, sociology, and zoology, with applications to advertising, business administration, education, government, human engineering, international relations, labor relations, law, medicine, military science, operations research, personnel selection, and public relations.

Interdisciplinary cooperation is essential in the comparatively recent behavioral science of human engineering or "human factors" as a branch of modern technology that deals with ways of designing machines, operations, and work environments so that they match human capacities and limitations or, in other words, the engineering of machines for human use and of human tasks for operating machines. This rapidly growing professional specialty of "human factors" is making contributions in personnel, training, human engineering, and other areas where there is man-machine interaction. Acceptance of system concepts has made the "human part" of any system a focal point for system planning, as when a system is required to collect and input information, process this information, or display data for action or decision-making, thus involving "human factors" knowledge and techniques. The fields of specialization include experimental psychology, human engineering, computer programs, design and computer engineering, and statistics, as well as use of models, simulation, and interdisciplinary teams in seeking the optimum combination of man-machine resources. In these areas, including "operations research" (or "operations analysis" or "systems analysis"), the programs of research in business and industry have expanded rapidly. Case studies of operations research are now available.

The electronic computer and audio-visual devices have played an important role in development of the behavioral sciences. Computers have been used for large-scale data processing, data blanks and similar cumulative records, information-retrieval, and decision-making and systems-simultation approaches. Such audio-visual devices as teaching machines and programmed instruction, television, and other audio-instructional equipment have made significant contributions.[27]

27 John C. Flanagan, *Annual Report.* Pittsburgh: American Institutes for Research in the Behavioral Sciences, 1964. 36 p.

The Role of Values

During the 1950's and 1960's the interrelationships of science and public policy were recognized as increasingly important, with major efforts on the part of government, philanthropic foundations, universities, and other research agencies to help science and technology serve the best interests of the nation. This view includes a place for the great humanities, the spiritual ends of life, faith, and values, as presented in succeeding paragraphs.

SCIENCE AND HUMAN VALUES

The strength and integrity of science must be maintained in the face of varied opportunities, responsibilities, and distractions, including the involvement of scientists in social problems. Scientists are challenged to distinguish clearly between their conduct in science and behavior in dealing with issues that go beyond science alone. While the world of social and human affairs requires judgment and objectivity as essential elements in problem solving, it also weighs opinions and pressures and compromises, as well as facts, in the attempt to make value judgments.[28]

To begin with engineering as an example, and then continue with other illustrations, if American science is to continue to prosper and to attract to it an appropriate complement of creative and gifted minds, we must combat the notions that science and engineering (or other technical fields) are incompatible with the great humanities or are narrowly materialistic and destructive of human values. The clear task of men of science is to face the future, undeterred by the uncertainties of human survival in the present and future. This faith in science is not incompatible with or exclusive of any other kind of faith, and indeed there is no inconsistency in considering scientific knowledge one of the great instruments of higher ends. In a sense, any scientific theory is the best opinion or judgment of a good idea to believe, in relation to the time, place, and sometimes the group represented, which means that science is a social institution.[29]

We are reminded that a scientist, like any other human being, may hold incompatible values or views simultaneously, as illustrated by the following:[30]

[28] Alan T. Waterman, "The Changing Environment of Science." *Science* 147: 13–18; January 1, 1965.

[29] Cyril Hinshelwood, "Dreams and Visions." *Science* 132: 321; August 5, 1960.

Edwin G. Boring, "Nothing-But and Something-More." *Contemporary Psychology* 5; 124–25; April 1960.

[30] R. K. Merton, "The Ambivalence of Scientists." *Bulletin, Johns Hopkins Hospital* 112: 77; 1963.

Edwin G. Boring, "Cognitive Dissonance: Its Use in Science." *Science* 145: 680–85; August 14, 1964.

1. Publish promptly, but not prematurely.
2. Remain receptive to new ideas, but resist intellectual fads.
3. Be erudite, but do not sacrifice research to reading.
4. Teach the young researcher, but do not sacrifice research to teaching.
5. Attend to details, but ignore inconsequentials.
6. Accept tutelage from the wise, but maintain your own independence.

PSYCHOLOGY, BEHAVIORAL SCIENCE, AND VALUES

Educational research and social investigation in general, including the behavioral sciences, owe a prominent place to certain concepts that are common in our culture: purpose, motive, teleology, values, feelings, and emotions. These values are basic to human living, a view that has received greatly increased support since the 1930's. At that earlier time, there was an overemphasis in many graduate departments of education and psychology on statistical and measurement techniques, to the partial exclusion of certain other problem-solving procedures. There were even some graduate bulletins where the term *philosophy* was not permitted to appear in a course title or description. That this view has changed materially can be amply documented in the literature of education, psychology, and sociology.[31]

The "pure" scientist traditionally prided himself on his concern for fact and his indifference to value, an attitude that influenced Titchener of Cornell, who imitated the classical physicist in his zeal to make psychology scientific and excluded value, along with meaning and utility, from the then new science of psychology. It is true that some schools of psychology have centered their problems around purpose, personality, adjustment, or *Gestalten,* rather than around sensation, with at least some place for value in their world of facts, and yet other psychologists have reserved for values a central place in their system. From this varied background psychology in the 1930's developed applications of the scientific method in attacking various aspects of the problem of values. A comprehensive review of psychological studies of values, based on a bibliography of 211 items, covers the following problems:[32]

1. Measuring the values of groups of individuals and relating the results to other data concerning the groups (individual differences)
2. The origin and development of values within the individual
3. The influence of an individual's values on his cognitive life.

[31] Carter V. Good, "The Role of Values in Educational and Social Research." *Peabody Journal of Education* 33: 259–71; March 1956.

M. B. Smith, " 'Mental Health,' Reconsidered: A Special Case of the Problem of Values in Psychology." *American Psychologist* 16: 299–306; June 1961.

[32] William F. Dukes, "Psychological Studies of Values." *Psychological Bulletin* 52: 24–50; January 1955.

By way of definition and delimitation, Dukes concludes from his review that such terms as attitude, interest, motive, need, sentiment, or valence are often used interchangeably with value, or at least refer to some aspect of value, and that investigations of level of aspiration, character, or the superego almost necessarily involve evaluations.

As pointed out earlier in this chapter, in discussing the interdisciplinary aspects of research, scientists and scholars are coming to recognize that there is really no essential conflict between the problem-solving procedures of science, philosophy, logic, history, statistics, and case-clinical study, whether our concern is with values or some other major question. Therefore, in offering graduate instruction, particularly in research courses, and in our discussions of research, we should make only moderate use of the term *scientific*. The methods of science (and technology) and of philosophy (and logic) are complementary techniques, perhaps different aspects of the general purpose of a single discipline of inquiry, in the development of problem or concept and in the gathering of evidence with which to test or modify the concept. It is held that science without philosophy is blind, while philosophy without science is empty.

This point of view is in keeping with evidence of an interdisciplinary approach and of close cooperation between the different areas of behavioral and social science, as emphasized in this chapter and as found in the literature and in certain graduate programs and research centers that utilize the combined resources of psychology, sociology, anthropology, education, and a number of other social fields. This larger movement toward cooperation in all the human sciences makes it possible to develop a common pattern of research methodology (and to some extent theory, as well as background for study of values), with appropriate applications to each special field of investigation.

Today an ethical dilemma of value orientations confronts the psychologist as he plays a new role in leaving his laboratory and moving out into the world to be of practical service to mankind. As a scientist, the psychologist limits himself to *what is,* and his choice of a problem in his search for truth involves values that are chiefly personal. As a practitioner, however, the psychologist must be concerned with what *should be,* which means that his personal preferences affect the lives of others and thus become social values. It is recommended that value orientations be brought in the open, dealt with as objectively as possible, and made known to all who are personally affected by value aspects of professional behavior.[33]

33 C. Marshall Lowe, "Value Orientations—An Ethical Dilemma." *American Psychologist* 14: 687–93; November 1959.

SOCIAL SCIENCE AND VALUES

The social sciences especially are concerned with values, including social decisions, interests, desires, beliefs, prejudices, and moral implications. The "hard-nosed" or "quantitative" social scientist seeks to avoid problems of policy, value preferences, and fact-value judgments. If he deals with such problems at all, it is in terms of incidence, distribution, and intensity in a given population, with an objective and quantitative preoccupation. This value-free posture tends to blind the investigator to the really great problems of man and society, and may make social science the servant of any power elite that seeks to manipulate human behavior, regardless of goal or purpose. A value-free science is absurd in any strict sense, since science has its own norms or standards, and the search for truth or falsity is not unrelated to discovery of what is good or bad. Science may be good or bad in the degree it contributes to, or corresponds with, the basic needs and goals of human life. As both scientist and citizen, the social scientist may well seek to change those conditions of character and environment that interfere with rational choices between alternative modes of behavior. Attitudes of indifference or cynicism on the part of scientists toward moral and ethical problems of society can result in apathy and cynicism among other citizens, with resulting dangers to both science and a good society.[34]

To cite an example, four types of contributions are needed in political science, as related to problems of values:[35]

1. To project a comprehensive image of the future for the purpose of indicating how our overriding goal values are likely to be affected (if current policies continue)
2. To clarify the fundamental goal values of the body politic
3. To organize and synthesize knowledge about the past, in order to recognize and evaluate new developments
4. To originate policy alternatives by means of which goal values can be maximized.

GRADUATE EDUCATION AND VALUES

In the interest of recognizing and emphasizing meaning and values in our graduate schools and in science generally, it is urged that we effect in science a new infusion of a sense of society and human values, in social science a realistic understanding of human behavior, and in the human-

34 Peter H. Odegard, "The Social Sciences and Society." *Science* 145: 1127; September 11, 1964.

35 Harold D. Lasswell, "Political Science of Science." *Scientific Monthly* 84: 34–44; January 1957.

ities devotion to shaping a more compelling ethics and to designing better patterns for human living. These human needs are the joint responsibility of the scientist, the social scientist, and the scholar in the humanities. While it is natural that graduate education in its early stages of development historically has been concerned with the basic techniques for accurate discovery of fact and for critical study of evidence, this approach should be broadened to provide communicable understanding of the meaning and value of facts.[36]

We should not overemphasize the scientific approach in fields where problems of values are prominent. A psychologist was surprised to hear an associate in psychology say that he did not really care what a person was interested in, just so he was enthusiastic about something—anything! The first man then recalled that as a beginning graduate student he had heard with astonishment a professor's advice on selecting a thesis topic: "Pick something close to your heart." To a first-year graduate student such an unscientific phrasing seemed appalling, although he had discovered that many students wished to belong to some group which championed a theory and desired to have an enthusiastic identification with some "issue" in their chosen field, even though they remembered admonitions from some quarters "to be eclectic and sample all the points of view while remaining detached and unimpressed." It may be that a strong purpose or goal, even though extreme, is a form of dedication and a mark of professional maturity.[37]

Educational research in many graduate and postgraduate areas involves value judgments, even moral value judgments, in connection with such problems as manipulating experimental subjects appropriately and in interpretation of results as a basis for action within the profession:

> Examples are work on the "gifted" student, "adequate representation" of lower economic classes in the parentage of the high-school groups, the "appropriateness" of counseling and guidance procedures, the evaluation of colleges and high schools on a comparative or an absolute basis, the construction of effective disciplinary procedures, the introduction of automatic teaching machines, the "obligation" of the states or the federal government to finance or desegregate education, the separation of superior students into different sections and the associated acceleration procedures, and the interpretation of "creativity."[38]

[36] Roy F. Nichols, "The Stimulus of Confusion." *Graduate School Record* 12: 3–8; Winter 1959.

[37] Malcolm H. Robertson, "The Student's Need for an Issue." *Journal of Psychology* 49: 349–52; April 1960.

[38] Quoted from Michael Scriven, "The Philosophy of Science in Educational Research," in "The Methodology of Educational Research." *Review of Educational Research* 30: 422; December 1960.

Hallmarks of the Scientist

What are the major characteristics or hallmarks of the scientist and scholar? Although at a given time a particular investigator may fail to recognize urgent problems pressing for attention, may lack essential training for undertaking a particular study, may lack a full measure of singlemindedness of purpose and professional aspiration, may be short in originality and creative imagination, or may hesitate to pay the full price for an unusually time-consuming or complex investigation, most able scientists and research workers possess in some form or measure a combination of the characteristics described below. (Many additional illustrations of these traits of the scientist or scholar may be found in the chapter on the formulation and development of the problem. We recognize that science as lived by its practitioners, especially in its human and social aspects, bears but little resemblance to the stereotypes of science as described in print.)

The scientist, specifically the natural scientist, is said to be of superior intelligence, with above average ability to think quantitatively, to state problems mathematically, and to reason verbally, and in most instances he possesses a high reading speed and a useful vocabulary. The scientist has originality as an individual thinker, conceptual ability, imaginativeness, and analytic ability, plus above average manual dexterity, spatial visualization, and mechanical aptitude. To cite a specific study of the hallmarks of scientists, the lives and times of nine active scientists in the United States are described in terms of characteristics, motivation, singlemindedness of purpose in devotion to science, use of time, individuality of the creative process, and the importance of the apprenticeship role for the student scientist.[39]

THE POPULAR IMAGE OF THE SCIENTIST

The characteristics of the scientist are not well understood by the public. An executive in industry has commented on the negative image of the scientist among a sampling of high-school pupils. He goes on to refute this false impression by data from approximately half the 2,400 technically trained specialists engaged in research for the du Pont Company. These scientists received their education in 258 colleges and universities in the United States and 34 foreign institutions, 68 per cent with

[39] Paul F. Brandwein and Others, "Creativity and Personality in the Scientist," *Rethinking Science Education*. Fifty-ninth Yearbook of the National Society for the Study of Education, Part 1. Chicago: University of Chicago Press, 1960. p. 63–81.

Theodore Berland, *The Scientific Life*. New York: Coward-McCann, Inc., 1962. viii + 308 p.

doctoral degrees, with specialization chiefly in chemistry, physics, bacteriology, and biochemistry. The data from these specialists refute the negative image of the scientist among high-school pupils, as reported by a well known anthropologist.[40]

1. "A scientist should not marry. No one wants to be such a scientist or to marry him." For the sample, 88 per cent of the scientists are married, with an average of two children per family.
2. "His work may be dangerous. Chemicals may explode. He may be hurt by radiation, or may die." The injury frequency rate for the scientists was lower than the over-all company rate during the same period.
3. "He may not believe in God, or may lose his religion." 75 per cent of the research workers mentioned church in listing their activities.
4. "He is a brain; he is so involved in his work that he doesn't know what is going on in the world. He has no other interests and neglects his body for his mind. . . . He has no social life, no other intellectual interests, no hobbies or relaxations." Among 37 per cent of the scientists there was a range of 64 different civic activities.
5. "His work is uninteresting, dull, monotonous, tedious, time-consuming, and, though he works for years, he may see no results or may fail, and he is likely to receive neither adequate recompense nor recognition. He may live in a cold-water flat; his laboratory may be dingy." Only a few scientists found research dull. One out of four of these scientists decided upon his career before reaching the age of fifteen, and most of these specialists had a strong personal interest in the field of research represented.
6. "If he works by himself, he is alone and has heavy expenses. If he works for a big company, he has to do as he is told, and his discoveries must be turned over to the company and may not be used; he is just a cog in a machine." It is common for the scientist to share through a bonus system in the rewards resulting from his discoveries. Although scientists are different from ordinary people, in terms of creativity, it is this difference that contributes to the understanding of our world.

A partly erroneous image of the scientist among college students resembles in many ways the image held by high-school pupils, especially with respect to the personality of the scientist and the mode of life associated with a career in science. This image may have the effect of recruiting to science careers a certain type of person and discouraging others. The strong features of the image of the scientist are his high intelligence, driving concern to discover and extend knowledge, service to mankind, sense of satisfaction in achievement, and a fair measure of

40 Margaret Mead and Rhoda Metraux, "Image of the Scientist among High-School Students: A Pilot Study." *Science* 126: 348–90; August 30, 1957.
Samuel Lenher, *The Scientist as a Person.* Tenth Annual Management Conference, Graduate School of Business and Public Administration, Cornell University, Ithaca, N. Y., April 18, 1958. E. I. du Pont de Nemours and Co., 1958. 15 p.

success. The weaknesses of the image are disturbing: indifference to people and no success in dealing with them, indifference to art and the life of the spirit so vital to the life of the mind, noncomformist and radical attitudes, and only moderate control of impulses. Summarized in other psychological language, a definite personality pattern, including a wide range of traits, characterizes the creative scientist, as reported by a psychologist: an open attitude toward experience; indepedence of perception, cognition, and behavior; strong ego; and preoccupation with things and ideas.[41]

OPEN-MINDEDNESS AND PROBLEM AWARENESS

The chapter on development of the problem includes a variety of illustrations concerned with problem awareness or sensitivity to problems, sometimes near at hand. In discussing the importance of open-mindedness on the part of the scientist and scholar, Whitehead has expressed himself forcefully on what he terms "the fallacy of dogmatic finality."

> The Universe is vast. Nothing is more curious than the self-satisfied dogmatism with which mankind at each period of its history cherishes the delusion of the finality of its existing modes of knowledge. Sceptics and believers are all alike. At this moment scientists and sceptics are the leading dogmatists. Advance in detail is admitted; fundamental novelty is barred. This dogmatic common sense is the death of philosophic adventure. The Universe is vast.
>
> I was in Cambridge in the 1880's, first as an undergraduate, later as one of the staff. It was from two hundred to two hundred and fifty years since mathematics had had its fresh impetus from men like Descartes and Sir Isaac Newton; there were certan borderlands where affairs in that science were considered indefinable, but in the main, mathematical physics looked sound and solid. . . . By the turn of the century, nothing, absolutely nothing was left that had not been challenged, if not shaken; not a single major concept. This I consider to have been one of the supreme facts of my experience.[42]

The alert scholar or scientist has a sensitivity to problems, or a problem awareness, although at times even able scientists and inventors overlook problems and solutions close at hand. All too frequently the beginner in research suffers from the handicap of "problem blindness." In investigating his problem, the scientist may see fit to duplicate an experiment, may extend his study in time or scope, or may follow an "offshoot" of an investigation in progress that "buds out."

41 David C. Beardslee and Donald D. O'Dowd, "The College-Student Image of the Scientist." *Science* 133: 997–1001; March 31, 1961.

Anne Roe, "The Psychology of the Scientist." *Science* 134: 456–59; August 18, 1961.

42 Quoted from *Dialogues of Alfred North Whitehead*. As Recorded by Lucien Price. New York: New American Library of World Literature, Inc., 1954. p. 12, 175.

APPROPRIATE SPECIALIZATION

In modern times sound scholarship requires considerable specialization, although a caution against overspecialization is in order. It was much easier in Helmholtz's day, however, for him to consider all experimental physical science as his field and to attribute much of his success to this breadth of interest and talent: "Possessing some geometrical capacity, and equipped with a knowledge of physics, I had, by good fortune, been thrown among medical men, where I found in physiology a virgin soil of great fertility; while, on the other hand, I was led by the considerations of the vital processes to questions and points of view which are usually foreign to pure mathematicians and physicists."[43]

On the other hand, some scientists have an egocentric quality characterized by intolerance for anyone or any value not associated with a special area of intellectual activity. This attitude may have its beginnings in undergraduate studies and is strongly nourished in graduate work, where there are enormous pressures toward specialization in a limited area of science, with a thesis even more strongly focused on a narrow subject of inquiry. Such excessive concentration and specialization may cut off the young scientist or scholar from the rest of an evolving fund of knowledge and terminate in his premature obsolescence, even though leading to early establishment of a scientific reputation. Tolerance toward and interest in the work of others can make it possible for the world of learning to be a great teacher.[44]

We are also warned that, if a disproportionate number of the best minds are drawn to the physical and biological sciences for specialization, then certain other classical branches of science may suffer an irreparable loss in the form of specialized information and methodology.[45] With governmental encouragement of research in high-energy nuclear physics and, more recently, space, there may even be negative features of large appropriations in these spectacular fields of science: (1) other areas of research may suffer in support, and (2) workers may be drawn away from fields not so well supported as space and atomic research. At a time when governmental policies are shaping academic research in this country, some agency or individual should have as a primary responsibility the duty to give continuing serious thought to the effects, both positive and negative, of excessive concentration on a few areas of scientific inquiry.[46]

43 Howard Gruber and Valmai Gruber, "Hermann von Helmholtz: Nineteenth-Century Polymorph." *Scientific Monthly* 83: 92–99; August 1956.

44 Philip H. Abelson, "Bigotry in Science." *Science* 144: 371; April 24, 1964.

45 Ernst Mayr, "The New Versus the Classical in Science." *Science* 141: 765; August 30, 1963.

46 Philip H. Abelson, "Government Support of Research." *Science* 139: 377; February 1, 1963.

We are also cautioned that the scientist can lose freedom in research through excessive and unwise specialization, which can eventually leave no investigational alternatives, because of: obsolescence of a too narrow field, failure to learn newer research techniques in his area, emotional attachment to his field, too great commercial or social involvement in his specialization, and overdependence on expensive apparatus or equipment.

Relationships with associates are important in developing a field of teaching or research. In moving from the University of Michigan to the University of Chicago in 1894, John Dewey was free to pursue his work in philosophy and also in pedagogy. There was not the same opportunity in pedagogy at Michigan, since B. A. Hinsdale held the chair in the Science and Art of Teaching. At Michigan Dewey could not have offered courses in pedagogy without Hinsdale's consent or, failing that, without trespassing upon Hinsdale's academic area, and the two men did not agree on some subjects. At Chicago Dewey had a free hand to develop the field of education.[47]

ACQUAINTANCE WITH RELATED RESEARCH

In all scientific endeavor, research workers have recognized their interdependence in the identification and solution of problems. In spite of difficulties in securing the works of other scholars, even such early investigators as Roger Bacon and Leonardo da Vinci reveal an extensive knowledge of the writings of other scholars in their special fields of interest. On the other hand, it must be admitted that certain able scientists and scholars have considered it undesirable or even unwise to study closely the related literature dealing with the particular problem under study, fearing that these earlier studies would condition the investigator's mind to see the problem in the same way and thus overlook a new or more promising approach. It would seem essential and reasonable to read critically in the related literature as a stimulus to thinking.

INTELLECTUAL CURIOSITY, DRIVE, PROFESSIONAL ASPIRATION

The pages of the history of science and scholarship are filled with the names of workers led or driven to their discoveries by consuming intellectual curiosity, some compelling motivation, or single-mindedness of purpose. Historians especially have been prodigious workers with remarkable powers of concentration. Pavlov's parting advice to young investigators was to become familiar with the groundwork of the science, to become accustomed to simple scientific tools, to penetrate beneath the

47 Robert L. McCaul, "Dewey's Chicago." *School Review* 67: 258–80; Summer 1959.

surface of things, to remain modest, and to develop a compelling intellectual curiosity: "And lastly, science must be your passion. Remember that science claims a man's whole life. Had he two lives they would not suffice. Science demands an undivided allegiance from its followers. In your research there must always be passion."[48]

As to professional aspiration, even scientists with a stable, promising career at times have a feeling of comparative failure as scientists. Two major sources of this feeling of failure are inherent in the very nature of scientific work:[49]

1. In science great emphasis is placed on achievement of recognition.
2. The basic scientist usually works in a community of "great men," who serve as models for their former students and staff workers, with the result that frustration or sense of failure may follow inability to achieve at the level of the model. In this sense, a feeling of comparative failure is an evaluation resulting from a social comparison. At the same time we recognize the importance of good models in the development of high standards for training and for research. These facts are significant in the career decisions of graduate students in the sciences.

The graduate student, and even the mature scholar, need the qualities of deep motivation, self-discipline, patience, courage, and willingness to bear the frustration of disappointment or failure. It follows that scholarly and professional aspirations should be realistic and wise, that is, within the abilities and resources of the investigator.

To cite a specific study involving professional aspiration, factor analysis of the trait ratings of 239 operationally defined "eminent" psychologists and 136 "noneminent" psychologists indicates that such "eminence" is related to high research and conceptual ability and to strong professional commitments (professional aspiration), but not to a generalized concern for the welfare of others (labeled "altruism").[50]

MAGNANIMITY

One of England's distinguished novelists, who is also well known as an administrator in the field of science, considers the virtue of magnanimity essential in science and scholarly work. By way of an unusual example, three centuries ago Professor Barrow of Cambridge decided that one of his pupils, Isaac Newton, was a better mathematician and resigned his professorship on condition that Newton be immediately appointed.

48 Ivan Pavlov, *Scientific Monthly* 81: 129; September 1955.

49 Barney G. Glaser, "Comparative Failure in Science." *Science* 143: 1012–14; March 6, 1964.

50 Lauren G. Wispé, "Traits of Eminent American Psychologists." *Science* 141: 1256–61; September 27, 1963.

Turgenev was ten years older than Tolstoi, and was the most distinguished writer in Russia when he first met Tolstoi, then only a beginner, but their relative prestige or position changed fairly soon, particularly after publication of Tolstoi's *War and Peace*. Turgenev's heart was large enough to admit that he had been surpassed, and as he lay dying wrote to Tolstoi begging him to return to writing novels as the "greatest writer of the Russian land."

The English mathematician, G. H. Hardy of Cambridge, recognized the genius of Srinivasa Ramanujan, a poor clerk in Madras, India, and exerted himself financially to bring the young man to England. Thereafter Hardy for a number of years, at the peak of his own career, devoted his professional life to Ramanujan, actually teaching the young genius a considerable amount of relatively elementary mathematics, since the Indian had little formal education. Hardy had his reward in the rapidly produced volume of original contributions by the younger scholar, but unfortunately Ramanujan developed tuberculosis in a wartime winter and died in 1920 at the early age of thirty-two.[51]

WILLINGNESS TO PAY THE PRICE

Research workers frequently encounter certain costs and hazards (financial, physical, or otherwise). Wallin tells of the early difficulties of clinical psychologists in securing recognition and prestige, as compared with the M.D. In one of his early clinical positions he did all the individual and group testing, scored the papers, made the records, compiled the results, did the transcribing (as much as could be done), and the clerical work (filing, indexing, typing case reports, letters, write-ups of results, articles, and answering phone calls). He did not even have the use of a typewriter but had to purchase his own machine, on which he did all of the official typing. He paid for his own stationery and stamps. Wallin encountered serious obstacles in the early days of his clinical work, an experience that he shared with many other psychologists, in securing recognition as a professional staff member, in studying psychological phenomena of certain patients, in freedom of movement on the grounds of the institution, in association with medical members of the staff, and in freedom of publication and attendance at professional meetings.[52]

CREATIVITY, ORIGINALITY, IMAGINATION

As to technique and equipment for creativity, the most important instrument or element in research is the mind of man. Although adequate

[51] C. P. Snow, "On Magnanimity." *Harper's Magazine* 225: 37–41; July 1962.

[52] J. E. Wallace Wallin, *The Odyssey of a Psychologist: Pioneering Experiences in Special Education, Clinical Psychology, and Mental Hygiene with a Comprehensive Bibliography of the Author's Publications*. Wilmington, Del.: The Author, 1955. p. 43–51.

methods, techniques, equipment, and working conditions are important in many types of research, ornate laboratory equipment and complex measuring and recording instruments will not of themselves guarantee soundness of thinking or valid evidence. Great discoveries have been made in unexpected places and in improvised laboratories by equally great men.

Three kinds of creativity have been identified:[53]

1. When creation is clearly an expression of the inner states of the creator; for example, composers, expressionist painters, sculptors, and creative writers
2. When the creator acts largely to meet externally defined needs and goals and produces a novel and appropriate product, but adds little of himself to the result; for example, experimental physicists, engineers, inventors, and research scientists
3. When creativity cuts across the other two types, in that the product is both an expression of the creator and at the same time a meeting of the demands of some external problem; for example, architects, certain kinds of writers, representational painters, and musical performers.

Scientists commonly find beauty and esthetic joy in the creativity of their discoveries, as does the poet, novelist, or composer. The history of science provides many examples of this esthetic joy in scientific discovery.

We must avoid a stereotype that has developed over the years, which overemphasizes the formal aspects of research (designing, executing, and interpreting experimental or statistical studies) and too often overlooks the importance of the investigator's creativeness (discovery of new relationships and techniques). Expressed in other language, when psychology replaced the "arm chair," speculation, and undisciplined imagination in favor of the laboratory, experimentation, and testable hypotheses, was this freedom won from the speculative influences of philosophy and metaphysics in reality a clear gain for the new behavioral science? Is not the creative approach closely associated with the spontaneous play of ideas and love of ideas for their own sake? Graduate students especially need to be watchful that the restrictions of experimental and statistical designs do not stifle spontaneity and creativiy. In many instances creative persons are characterized by introversion rather than extroversion; for, as Wordsworth says: "The world is too much with us. Talking and visiting, we lay waste our powers."[54] To cite examples, William James and John Dewey are characterized as both scientists and philosophers, where the central

53 Creativity." *Carnegie Corporation of New York Quarterly* 9: 1–7; July 1961.

54 Irving J. Good and Others, Editors, *The Scientist Speculates: An Anthology of Partly-Baked Ideas.* New York: Basic Books, Inc., 1962. xvii + 413 p.

Calvin W. Taylor and Frank Barron, Editors, *Scientific Creativity: Its Recognition and Development.* New York: John Wiley & Sons, Inc., 1963. v + 419 p.

figure is a "man alone" engaged in solitary and individual thinking, whether he sits in an isolated cubicle or in a noisy discussion group.[55] Sometimes the truly creative person or "dreamer" has been labeled as a "crackpot" during his time, and a generation later as a genius.

Summarized briefly in other language, in the development of originality and individuality, we are urged to avoid premature publication, to take a chance on the tougher problems in the interest of intellectual honesty, to admit our mistakes as a possible source of promising problems, and to speculate on the broad implications of scientific work as a lead to further meaningful questions.[56]

THE PROPHETIC QUALITY

The modern world with its rapidity and complexity of change requires a prophetic quality of its scholars, yet this gift is too seldom found, even within our great institutions. The *prophet* of ancient times was not one who merely predicted the future, but he was concerned with action and reform. He resembles in some ways the scholar of today who deals with future projections and identification of existing trends; both seek meaning for the future from synthesis of the past and present. It has been said that the past still contains the present, just as the present (looked at deeply enough) contains the future.[57]

Freedom and Responsibility for Research

FREEDOM IN SCIENCE

Freedom is important in research to the extent that it contributes to the wise choice of problems and to the enthusiastic and successful pursuit of solutions to problems. Like food, we need enough freedom, but should not be guilty of gluttony. The research worker must be free to work on a problem that challenges him, yet is within his capabilities, rather than a problem that is dull or beyond the worker's abilities. The investigator must be free to equip himself adequately with any necessary physical apparatus, and also to equip himself intellectually, through study or through contact with other specialists.

Freedom in research does not necessarily require that a man work on his own ideas. First-rate scientists have traveled great distances to work under a particular person or with a group of specialists, and have gladly pursued problems suggested by the person or pursued by the

55 Arthur I. Gates, "Science or Sanity?" *Phi Delta Kappan* 45: 297–302; March 1964.
56 Norman H. Mackworth, "Originality." *American Psychologist* 20: 51–66; January 1965.
57 August Heckscher, "The Prophetic Quality." *Science* 137: 193; July 20, 1962.

group. The idea may come from a colleague near or far, or from an older or wiser associate. It may be that even good research workers suffer more frequently from lack of help than from lack of freedom. They need help in choosing problems wisely, in overcoming difficulties, in judging the merit of their work, in getting rid of old projects that are finished, and in starting new investigations that will prove important and attractive. Investigators also need encouragement and recognition for work well done.[58]

Freedom in research, however, is curtailed by certain forms of behavior, particularly by "snobbishness" or a sort of pecking order extending from mathematics to physics to chemistry to biology to psychology and possibly to education. The scholar certainly loses his freedom when he chooses a field of specialization and problems for study, not in terms of his interests and talents, but according to the status of the particular discipline with some person, professional group, or official journal.

The history of science includes many instances of resistance by scientists themselves to scientific discovery, with the sources of resistance varied in character: substantive concepts and theories currently prevailing, methodological conceptions currently entertained, religious ideas of scientists themselves, relative professional standing of the discoverer, pattern of specialization prevailing in science, attitudes of professional organizations and societies, rivalries of "schools" of theory or research, and relative seniority of the investigator.[59]

All over the world today people are comparing the institutions designed to assure the freedom of science with those agencies that maintain science under some form of dictatorship. It is significant, however, that at the time of the apparent triumph of Russian technology, the prestige of communism among scientists throughout the world seemed lower than in the days when Soviet science was still being discussed in largely theoretical terms. It is true that varying national patterns for support of science result from basic constitutional differences.

FREEDOM IN SOCIAL SCIENCE

Certain inhibiting conditions restrict research in the various social fields. Chapin points out that application of social-science knowledge to the solution of problems of human relations is hampered by existing habits of thought and action, with at least eight social obstacles to the acceptance of current knowledge or evidence in the social-science field, although college social scientists have reported relatively good conditions by way of freedom of inquiry and teaching.[60]

58 J. R. Pierce, "Freedom in Research." *Science* 130: 540–42; September 4, 1959.

59 Bernard Barber, "Resistance by Scientists to Scientific Discovery." *Science* 134: 596–602; September 1, 1961.

60 Francis S. Chapin, *Experimental Designs in Sociological Research.* Revised Edition. New York: Harper & Row, Publishers, Inc., 1955. p. 250–66.

1. The subject matter of social science is emotion-arousing.
2. The normative set and value-judgment approach tend to attach "praise" and "blame" to natural situations in human relationships.
3. The scientific social observer is himself a part of the social process he tries to observe.
4. The confidential and privileged character of much sociological information makes scientific or objective formulation of knowledge a difficult process.
5. "Conspiracies of silence" involve conventions that often block social research or implementation of evidence.
6. There may be unpleasant consequences to minority groups when social-science knowledge is applied.
7. Much of the subject matter of social science consists of verbal behavior, which frequently is intangible and trite.
8. Concentrated and continuous mental effort is required to know that such concepts as intangibility, relativity, and probability are basic to social understanding.

EXTERNAL FACTORS INHIBITING FREEDOM

Certain conditions external to the investigator himself many inhibit freedom for research:[61]

1. Tradition in the school or community may prove a powerful retarding influence.
2. Lack of time, energy, and resources has been a block for most teachers and administrators.
3. A climate of cooperative group work is lacking in many schools.
4. Research activity has failed significantly in one or more instances, and it has been deemed unworthy of further expenditure of time and money.
5. A particular research project is believed to have endangered the educational welfare of children.
6. Research looks so much like John Dewey's "experimentalism" that it is out of step with the prevailing educational philosophy.
7. Research procedures have been found difficult—even incomprehensible.
8. Research is considered to be the business of a few administrators.
9. Research has threatened the strongly held but vaguely supported opinions of certain supersensitive and influential teachers and administrators.

INTERNAL FACTORS INHIBITING FREEDOM

Internal factors, such as feelings of fear, threat, and uncertainty, may inhibit freedom for research on the part of school people and others:

1. They are afraid to experiment with public money and with other people's children.

[61] Ronald C. Doll, "Freedom for Research," *Research for Curriculum Improvement.* 1957 Yearbook. Washington: Association for Supervision and Curriculum Development, a Department of the National Education Association, 1957. p. 249-68.

2. They fear starting research activity in the wrong situation or in the wrong way.
3. They feel threatened when they are urged to do research concerning matters about which they are already insecure.
4. They believe they lack the necessary understanding and skill to make the end result satisfactory in their own and other people's eyes.
5. They are wanting in the adventuresome spirit that would impel them to take calculated risks in solving their problems.

To cite examples, obstacles to research or pressures have confronted even men of rare native gifts, including J. McKeen Cattell, William James, John Dewey, Charles H. Judd, and Edward L. Thorndike:[62]

1. Typical financial difficulties have been handicapping, although ultimately Dewey, Thorndike, and Judd made out quite well financially in their dedicated careers. Today there are many scholarships and research grants, and salaries have increased greatly, supplemented by writing, consultation, and speaking, with the result that the real danger may be in keeping such income-producing enterprises within reasonable bounds.
2. The pressure to follow common sense, tradition, experience, or "sanity," in contrast to the skepticism or "insanity" of such a man as Thorndike. As Gates puts it, many of our great scientists and scholars were a bit "daft," or seemed so to less able people.
3. The pressure of pedantry is illustrated by a form of professional jargon or verbal pomposity. Thorndike, Terman, Kilpatrick, Cattell, Woodworth, and Judd used technical terms, but were reasonably free of professional jargon, even though some of Dewey's writing was difficult (in a very complex subject matter).
4. The pressure of "practical" assignments and duties is like a thief in the time schedule of the scientist, research worker, and scholar, with full recognition of the fact that administrative tasks must be well done and actually make possible certain freedoms for the scientist engaged in research. Thorndike, as one of the great men of his day, was particularly successful in keeping time for his research, through very selective screening of invitations to make speeches, committee appointments, administrative posts, and doctoral advisory work.

WAYS TO PROMOTE FREEDOM IN RESEARCH

Specific ways in which school personnel can overcome obstacles to freedom in research, especially in the curriculum field, have been simply phrased, in terms of the language, principles, and procedures of action research:[63]

1. Building a feeling among potential researchers that it is all right to have problems.

[62] Arthur I. Gates, "Science or Sanity?" *Phi Delta Kappan* 45: 297–302; March 1964.
[63] Ronald C. Doll, *op. cit.*

2. Design researches that will satisfy the needs people feel.
3. Start gently, perhaps on a modified-voluntary basis.
4. Talk often about the importance of getting evidence.
5. Help people find security in groups, and help them work together successfully as group members.
6. Provide safety valves through which to "blow off steam" when things do not go well.
7. Allow for the lone researcher as well as for the researcher who wishes to work with only one or two other persons.
8. Use every legitimate means to build understanding of the research process.
9. Involve in research activities those teachers, parents, and other persons who are high in the power structure of school and community.
10. Provide all the time, resources, and help you can.
11. Attend to the climate of the school as a whole, as a valuable stimulus to research.
12. Be realistic about the limits, internal and external.
13. Resolve to press against the limits that actually exist.
14. Capitalize on growing expertness by urging its use in additional research.

RESEARCH AND UNIVERSITY OR COLLEGE TEACHING

The university staff member is generally expected to engage in research and to communicate the results to others, since it has been commonly accepted that this is a basic duty of the university to society. The faculty adviser who supervises the theses and dissertations of graduate candidates must be alive to the current problems of research in his field of specialization. Certainly the graduate faculty member must progress beyond his own dissertation stage in the intellectual adventure of scholarship. How often we hear the statement from professors many years out of the graduate school: "Now in my dissertation, I . . ." Participation in research on the part of the professor should make for an intellectually alert person and a better teacher. The obligation of the well-equipped professor to conduct the needed basic research is all the more apparent when we realize that most master's theses or projects are minor studies with local applications, while the doctor's dissertation is frequently a "one-shot" investigation to meet a degree requirement. Therefore, much of the leadership and coordination for research in a particular area remains for the university specialist, even though he is busy with teaching and advisory duties.[64]

We must remember, especially in times of large government grants for research, that the chief function of the university is to educate men and women, and at the same time discover new knowledge. During the 1950's

[64] Everett Walters, "On the Results of Research." *Graduate School Record* 8: 1, 3; March 1955.

Fletcher G. Watson and William W. Cooley, "Needed Research in Science Education," *Rethinking Science Education.* Fifty-ninth Yearbook of the National Society for the Study of Education, Part 1. Chicago: The University of Chicago Press, 1960. p. 297–312.

and 1960's the military services and the government increasingly have asked the universities to manage great programs of research and development, usually involving secrecy and often calling for discriminating business judgment. We should make certain that such programs of research in universities contribute appropriately to the instruction and development of educated men and women.[65]

During these recent years the research specialist has increased his advantage over the teacher in gaining repute outside his own institution, chiefly because of the large amounts of external money for research, the national review system for awarding grants, and the emphasis on research by federal agencies and universities. We are agreed that effective teaching may well be combined with sound research, but good teaching we must have to provide for greatly increased enrollments and to develop the talents of the next generation of teachers and researchers. The answer is clearly not in attempting to enhance the status of teaching through lowering the status of research, but in identifying and rewarding excellence in teaching.[66] In summary, our obligations for good instruction are unmistakable: scientists must meet their responsibilities as teachers; administrators must recognize and reward excellence in teaching; and federal agencies must support university research so as to contribute to, rather than compete with, educational functions.[67]

Although the place of research in the small or independent liberal-arts college is not so clearly defined as in the university, the contribution of research to education seems so clear that we wonder why research is opposed or played down in some liberal-arts colleges. While there probably are competent scientists engaged in research who are not good teachers, the competence of effective teachers certainly is increased by sound scholarship. Therefore, there is no basis for the attitude of some instructors in small colleges that research and teaching are incompatible. It is true that the overly conscientious teacher or the overworked teacher may find no time for the activities of research and scholarship. It may be that some instructors play down the importance of research and scholarship because encouragement of such activities by the college causes sharper competition for positions and promotions.[68]

RESEARCH AND EDUCATION OF GRADUATE STUDENTS

Reference has been made to the importance of research on the part of the staff member in the university and even in the small college, with

[65] "Vannevar Bush Speaks." *Science* 142: 1623; December 27, 1963.

[66] Dael Wolfle, "The Great Teachers." *Science* 146: 1421; December 11, 1964.

[67] Philip H. Abelson, "One-Sided Criticism of University Research." *Science* 148: 1177; May 28, 1965.

[68] Joseph Turner, "Small Colleges and Small Minds." *Science* 131: 171; January 8, 1960.

particular emphasis placed on the scholarly pursuits of the university professor who supervises the work of graduate students. Research and its encouragement constitute the domain and commitment of every graduate school that is fulfilling its purpose.[69] While we have understandably depended in the past on European research in certain fields, American graduate schools must depend much more upon themselves, at present and in the future. The modern graduate school serves at least two major purposes or provides two types of opportunity for the student: extending his range of knowledge and understanding in a field of special interest, and engaging in creative research. Expressed in another way, the satisfactions in graduate education may be identified in the form of its possible and desirable accomplishments as follows:

> The years in the graduate school constitute the educational period when self-responsibility asserts itself, the processes of inquiry and research in particular are learned, a subject-matter area is staked out and explored, ability to express thoughts and to write creatively is acquired, an intellectual career is anticipated, and professional responsibilities and behavior are understood.[70]

We are reminded that, in graduate education, overspecialization should not be permitted to cause a cleavage between the humanities and the sciences. Rediscovery of the humanist spirit or tradition has three aspects:[71]

1. The human being is not to be explained wholly as a mere puppet of great social forces nor as a creature of the social environment.
2. In addition to careful observation and analysis of the outer world, of both the physical universe and of society, we may well rediscover the avenue of reflection, introspection, and meditation.
3. The scientist may well recall that modern science emerged from the humanities as one aspect of careful human inquiry; emphasis on the nature of the inquiry may restore a note of humanism to the sciences.

It is recognized that a professor in a graduate professional school is called upon to meet incompatible demands in trying to be at the same time a productive scholar, a teacher, a consultant, and a spokesman for his profession:[72]

1. As a productive scholar, the professor must for substantial blocks of time isolate himself from others in order to read, to think, to analyze data, and to write.

[69] Theodore C. Blegen, "Graduate Education and Research: Problems and Prospects." *Graduate School Record* 11: 3–7; December 1957.

[70] Quoted from N. P. Hudson, "On Satisfactions in Graduate Education." *Graduate School Record* 9: 1, 3; December 1955.

[71] Paul A. Varg, "Society's Responsibility to Graduate Education." *Graduate School Record* 17: 3–8; Autumn 1963.

[72] Donald E. Super, "Scholarship in a Graduate Professional School." *Teachers College Record* 65: 391–95; February 1964.

2. As a teacher, the professor must be accessible to students and to fellow faculty members so that they may function as a community of scholars in the formulating, testing, and propagating of ideas.

3. As a consultant, the professor must be available to members of his profession and to persons from related fields who need his expert knowledge and skills in the solution of practical problems.

4. And as a spokesman for his profession and for his specialty on important issues to which his specialty can contribute, the professor in a graduate professional school must not only be available for consultation with representatives of the press and other segments of the public, but must serve on a variety of committees, speak at various kinds of gatherings and on TV, and write for semipopular and popular consumption.

An Edward L. Thorndike chooses to conduct research and to write it up for professional readers, and does this so well that he is rewarded for virtually limiting himself to one of his four possible roles; a William Heard Kilpatrick develops the twin roles of teacher and spokesman, orally and in writing, and does so with such impact that his virtual failure to contribute in research and in consultation is not considered; a Nicholas L. Engelhardt is so competent as teacher, consultant, and spokesman that his lack of research contributions goes virtually unnoticed; and it is a rare professor who, like Paul Mort, succeeds in playing all four roles with distinction.

With respect to the interrelationships between scientific progress, the universities, graduate education, and the federal government, the President's Science Advisory Committee has reached the following specific conclusions:[73]

1. Excellence deserves strong support.
2. Additional centers of excellence are urgently needed.
3. Graduate education needs expansion.
4. It is important to attract a large number of talented students to science as a career.
5. Graduate education in science needs constant modernization.
6. The financing of graduate education needs continued and flexible reinforcement.
7. The need for improved facilities is urgent.
8. New fields of research and education need particular encouragement.
9. Separate research installations should be avoided whenever possible.
10. New research laboratories for special fields should be attached to universities whenever it is practicable, and universities should make full educational use of such facilities.
11. Scientists outside universities can be fruitfully connected to graduate education.
12. Postdoctoral studies should be encouraged and their legitimate costs recognized.

[73] President's Science Advisory Committee, *Scientific Progress, the Universities, and the Federal Government.* Washington: Government Printing Office, 1960. x + 33 p.

13. University faculties must be strengthened.
14. Universities must attend to these matters and especially to their relations with the government.
15. The government must strengthen its ability to make policy in this area.
16. Increased government activity is not a good ground for lessened efforts by others.

RESEARCH BY WORKERS IN ELEMENTARY OR SECONDARY SCHOOLS

After traveling in the United States, Canada, England, Scotland, and France, inquiring into the organization and structure of educational research (especially in the United States), an Australian investigator has reported favorably, even highly optimistically, on the possibilities for research by workers in elementary and secondary schools. In determining whether teachers and other staff members in the public schools could reasonably undertake research, he asked questions as to whether the staff had the ability, time, interest, and power to participate in educational investigation. In each instance he answered in the affirmative, with the conviction that teachers in every country have the opportunity and the capacity to undertake some research, usually carried out in day-to-day work of the school and concerned directly with the problems of the particular school.[74]

A more critical survey concludes that many useful activities conducted under the name of educational research are incorrectly labeled research in the accepted meaning of the term, particularly in the research offices of large city school systems, state departments of education, and state education associations. It has been suggested that progress may be made toward meeting the need for basic research, if persons trained and experienced in investigation, such as the members of the American Educational Research Association, will increase their efforts to help teachers and administrators in the public schools realize the essential nature of research and its contribution to school practice and to education in general.[75]

Scientific Progress and Social Responsibility

Research in the physical sciences developed much earlier than in the social fields because of certain favorable factors and conditions: greater freedom of inquiry, seemingly more urgent problems, financial support,

[74] W. C. Radford, "The Function of the School, Department of Education, University, National Centre and Independent Body in Educational Research," *Report of the First International Conference on Educational Research*. Educational Studies and Documents, No. 20. Paris: UNESCO, 1956. p. 36–40.

[75] David G. Ryans, "Are Educational Research Offices Conducting Research?" *Journal of Educational Research* 51: 173–83; November 1957.

objectivity of problem and procedure, invention of instruments for recording and measuring, standardization of terminology, collection of specimens such as in museums, emphasis on scientific training, and publication of scientific materials.

A number of factors, however, have favored educational research in the United States: a democratic philosophy, decentralized schools, financial support, research departments and bureaus, teacher training and graduate work, and publication facilities.

SCIENCE AND MORAL-SOCIAL RESPONSIBILITY

In general, the accomplishments of science in our time are almost miraculous, with the rate of progress still accelerating. Research can continue to expand as long as society is friendly toward this form of progress. There is evidence of stress and strain, however, between the great accomplishments of the physical sciences and the much slower development of the social sciences (which provide the controls for human behavior). At times an impossible course of action has been suggested, to the effect that physical research should take a holiday until social science catches up, since certain discoveries (as in the domain of atomic energy) involve the potential for great harm to, or even destruction of, society when wrongly applied. Scholars and scientists have a grave social obligation to see that scientific and technological (and social) discoveries are used for the benefit of society and that appropriate controls of human behavior are developed, with the aid of knowledge in social science, psychology, education, and religion. We constantly ask ourselves the haunting question: Can science aid in the search for sophistication in dealing with order and disorder in human affairs, not only to enrich individual lives but to prolong the survival of the human species in an acceptable form of society?[76]

Scientists and Ethical Neutrality. Scientists occasionally have adopted the doctrine of the ethical neutrality of science, based on invention of comfortable categories of specialization, which would assign responsibility for discovery to the research worker and for implementation to others (for example, the politician). Scientists ultimately cannot escape the consequences of their own knowledge and should show themselves disposed to good use of their discoveries.[77]

Another parallel view of the social responsibility of science, rather than a posture of neutrality, points out that science from its beginning has had important effects outside the realm of pure science itself, although

[76] Van Rensselaer Potter, "Society and Science." *Science* 146: 1018–22; November 20, 1964.

[77] Charles P. Snow, "The Moral Un-Neutrality of Science." *Science* 133: 256–59; January 27, 1961.

scientists have differed as to their own responsibility for such effects. The view that the function of the scientist is to supply knowledge, without concern for the use made of such knowledge, is no longer tenable in our time. The scientist also is a citizen with an obligation to use his skill in the public interest. More specifically: "What is the social responsibility of science?" This question rephrased is: "What contribution can scientists make to the social and political process of our society?" We recognize, however, that scientists, as compared with other experts and specialists, have no peculiar or exclusive social responsibility. There may even be a form of hypocrisy when laymen ask of scientists special things by way of social responsibility, beyond the obligations necessarily required of any human being today, scientist or not. Probably any doctrine of the ethical neutrality of science will diminish and disappear when all scientists come to agree completely that ultimately science belongs to all mankind.

Scientists and Military Technology. Since science supports an ever expanding military technology and, therefore, acquires moral properties, many people wonder to what extent American scientists should assume responsibility for the uses to which the government puts their discoveries and talents. There are three positions relating to the social obligations of the scientists, with the preferred position probably somewhere between too little and too much responsibility for the social consequences of research.[78]

1. The scientist's responsibility ends with his willingness to do work directly or indirectly for the government, including work on weapons.
2. The scientist should consider the possible social consequences of any research project before it is begun and determine his participation accordingly.
3. A middle position between too little and too much responsibility for the social consequences of military research.

Science and National Policy. Science and technology have been of particular concern to the federal government in times of national crisis, when deficits in our knowledge were revealed, as in the Civil War, with the threat of grave epidemics during the great period of immigration in the 1880's, in World War I, and in World War II. More recently science, technology, and the general welfare in a democracy have involved three major developments, each of which alone has changed or will change civilization: (1) the destructive and constructive effects of atomic energy, (2) computers and automation, and (3) discoveries in molecular biology. We will need to apportion funds among the different fields of science and research for a balanced program of investigation, facilities, and teaching,

[78] Joseph Turner, "Between Two Extremes." *Science* 131: 1013; April 8, 1960.

which will include consideration of how much is justified for high-energy physics.[79]

Science must cooperate with other disciplines and professions in meeting the great responsibility which rests upon science today, in the light of its extraordinary opportunities to participate in the formulation of national policy. The increasingly strong linkage of science and technology with government requires of science a new order of poise, steadiness, and statesmanship, and demands of scientists who serve in advisory capacities a deep understanding of the role and the limitation of the adviser.

A similar view of the need for cooperation between the scientist and non-scientist points out the human, political, and traditional complexities of policy making.

> On the whole, the verdict seems to be that the scientist is indispensable to policy making but that he has much to learn about a game which has so many human and political complexities and so much social tradition behind it. At the same time, those who have studied the subject at close hand concede that the point of view of scientists is valuable, even apart from their technical knowledge, and that the non-scientist should make a more determined effort to meet the scientist half way.[80]

The problems of finding and training persons to develop appropriate cooperative relationships between science and public policy present major difficulties.

> Who in the future will man the frontiers at the many interfaces between science and public policy? Where will these people come from? What should their training be? The scientific and technical skills and knowledge and judgment that are brought to the service of the nation at the governmental level are multiple in the points at which they enter and the avenues through which they serve. They are also multiple in kind. In the realm of policy one can distinguish at least four general kinds of function: the execution of policy involving matters of science and technology on the domestic front; the corresponding function in relation to foreign policy; the formulation of foreign and domestic scientific policy; and the integration of scientific policy with the wider formulation of a general foreign policy. There is also the fundamental task of scientific planning at the substantive level—the task, essentially, of scientific creativity. The several levels of scientific planning have their counterparts in the kinds of background and talents required of those who would discharge these functions.[81]

79 Philip H. Abelson, "Science and the General Welfare in a Democracy." *Science* 144: 957; May 22, 1964.

80 Quoted from review by Alan T. Waterman, "Scientists and the Making of National Policy." *Science* 144: 1438–39; June 19, 1964, of Robert Gilpin and Christopher Wright, Editors, *Scientists and National Policy-Making.* New York: Columbia University Press, 1964. 315 p.

81 Caryl P. Haskins, "Interfaces between Science and Public Policy." *Science* 144: 801; May 15, 1964.

It is not necessarily true that professional scientists are always the best persons for appointment to policy-making positions in government, since policy-making (even in science) has its own problems and techniques, which are not the restricted province of scientists as a profession. It is true that the scientist must always participate in the policy-making process, along with the economist, the military man, the public official, and others (including the educator). The professional policy maker must be skillful in dealing with the issues that affect science, must be scientifically literate and be able to sift good from bad scientific advice, and must function as a communications link between the professional scientist and the professional politician. The difficult task of policy making for science requires the close cooperation of public officials, professional scientists, scholars in general, and educators especially.[82] In considering the relation of the scientist to national policy, however, there is nothing in his experience, training, and discipline as such that should cut him off from *any* responsible activity in government. It is nonsense to emphasize the political neutrality of scientists or to say that scientists should give advice only on scientific subjects, and keep away from military, political, social, and economic problems, for scientists are *people* with deep concern for the values and welfare of a human world.[83]

Federal Support of Research in Universities. In administering large amounts of money for research, government agencies have avoided control of higher education, but at the same time government officials and scientists have fostered a type of external control over universities through the screening or evaluating panels of experts who recommend research awards. While both scientists and government officials see advantages in having teams of scholars recommend grants in their own fields of specialization, there is the danger of lessening university responsibility and of shifting faculty loyalty toward the agency making the award. Plans have been developed during recent years for grants to support major university improvements and developments rather than specific projects or programs of individual staff members or departments, thus strengthening the universities in exercising responsible judgment in administering and supporting a balanced program of research activities.[84]

It has been urged that the government support scholarly work in both the humanities and the sciences through a single agency or foundation intended to foster advanced scholarship and education of high quality, not by segments but as a whole. Such a single foundation for governmental support of all fields of university scholarship would center faculty loyalties

[82] Emmanuel G. Mesthene, "Can Only Scientists Make Government Science Policy?" *Science* 145: 237–40; July 17, 1964.

[83] McGeorge Bundy, "The Scientist and National Policy." *Science* 139: 805–9; March 1, 1963.

[84] Dael Wolfle, "University Responsibility." *Science* 140: 861; May 24, 1963.

on the university itself rather than on a number of agencies and organizations that have served individual fields of science, particularly if grants are made in the future to the corporate university, in contrast to departments and individual investigators.[85]

There is danger that federal support of research for predoctoral and postdoctoral fellows may stifle their initiative when the grants are for specific objectives under the direction of the principal investigators. These predoctoral and immediate postdoctoral years are crucial in the lives of scientists and scholars, since they are making the change from absorbers to creators of knowledge, with a drastic change in viewpoint and development of a new set of value judgments. It is difficult to achieve independence and creativity when the young worker finds himself a member of a large "team" whose purposes are determined by the principal investigator. A promising alternative in awarding fellowships is to make the grant to institutions rather than to individuals.[86]

Failure of scientists to evaluate or criticize in any real way federal grants and programs for research and development involves their own self-interest, even though the long-term interest of science dictates that unwise expenditures be avoided. The scientist, in questioning the wisdom of the granting establishment, usually fears that he will pay a price or incur certain hazards in the form of distraction from his professional activities, the enmity of powerful foes, and reprisals against himself or his institution. He may fear only shadows, but federal funds are so important to research institutions that prudence seems to dictate silence.[87]

It should be said, however, that some scientists are coming to wonder whether large grants and success will spoil basic research. It is argued that scientists become involved in projects that have little to do with basic research, however important these projects may be in terms of military security or international good will. It is further argued that many scientists involved in these projects spend their time in administrative duties rather than creative efforts. It should be noted, however, that further progress in some of our most fundamental and interesting scientific investigations involves the construction of extraordinarily expensive and complicated equipment, which makes government support essential. Therefore, our defense of bigness is that in some areas of research it may be a necessary condition for further progress. One reason for the large role of the government in support of science is that science is playing such a large role in the prestige and power of nations. Possibly scientists will come to say of some of our huge projects that the resulting gains in our

85 Dael Wolfle, "Fields of Scholarship." *Science* 147: 1091; March 5, 1965.

86 Philip H. Abelson, "Predoctoral and Postdoctoral Fellowships." *Science* 144: 1181; June 5, 1964.

87 Philip H. Abelson, "Only One Side of the Question." *Science* 145: 347; July 24, 1964.

understanding of nature fully warranted the effort, even though hope of such gains was not the only reason for supporting particular projects.[88]

Science, International Relations, and Human Welfare. In considering the problems of international competition and cooperation in research, some ventures are so global in character, so extreme in cost, and of such critical social implications that we may well take the lead for collaboration among nations. Examples are large-scale experiments that might involve the risk of altering the earth's environment, as in some aspects of space exploration and research into weather modification.[89] Beyond our own borders we see that science and technology have had a dramatic effect on international relations and foreign policy in four ways:[90]

1. The political importance to a nation of having the appearance of world scientific leadership
2. The effect of international scientific activities on the relations between nations
3. The importance of the technical component of some prospective arms-control measures
4. The relation of science to technical aid for less-developed countries.

Another international view of science agrees that it is impossible in the modern world for a man of science to say with any honesty: "My business is to provide knowledge, and what use is made of the knowledge is not my responsibility," because knowledge that a scientist provides may fall into the hands of men or institutions devoted to utterly unworthy objects. It is not suggested that a man of science, or even a large body of scientists, can altogether prevent this, but they can diminish the magnitude of the evil. As Russell says, now life for the scholar and scientist in an ivory tower becomes increasingly impossible, and many authorities argue for popularization of science, based on the belief that any distinction between the man of science and the ordinary man is no longer admissible, any more than a form of segregation based on an inequality of knowledge.[91]

As to international cooperation in psychological research, four categories of projects have been suggested:[92]

1. Cross-national involvement in general psychological problems
2. Comparative cross-national or cross-cultural research; for example, institutional patterns, social mechanisms, values and attitudes, language structure,

[88] Joseph Turner, "Bigness Has Its Place." *Science* 129: 1709; June 26, 1959.

[89] Alan T. Waterman, "International Competition and Cooperation." *Science* 145: 1261; September 18, 1964.

[90] G. B. Kistiakowsky, "Science and Foreign Affairs." *Science* 131: 1019–24; April 8, 1960.

[91] Bertrand Russell, "The Social Responsibilities of Scientists." *Science* 131: 391–92; February 12, 1960.

[92] Herbert C. Kelman and E. P. Hollander, "International Cooperation in Psychological Research." *American Psychologist* 19: 779–82; September 1964.

decision-making processes, cooperation and competition, role behavior, and child rearing

3. Universal human problems; for example, stimulus deprivation in infancy, effect of prenatal and paranatal influences on development, mental retardation, institutional care of young children, automated teaching, eradicating illiteracy, and communication with illiterates

4. International tensions; for example, development of indices of international tension, so as to permit periodic accumulation of data on tension level.

SOCIAL SCIENCE AND RESPONSIBILITY

Scientists can help overcome the uncertainty, confusion, and fear generated by the crises of war by presenting objectively and calmly the necessary facts to the public. The same call of duty that has placed science at the command of warfare now requires scientists to serve with equal devotion the social need for peace and find a means of protecting society that does not run the risk of destroying it. Governmental agencies are now placing more reliance on social science in determining public policy and in improving communication between social scientists and public officials.

We are reminded that in the past man's basic problems were concerned with the complexities of his physical environment, but now in our time the focus of the basic problem has changed from the external to the internal environment. Our primary need is now to learn rapidly how to cope with ourselves and with each other, particularly with regard to intergroup and international conflicts, so that we can preserve freedom in peace. Does our future security depend as much upon priority in exploring outer space as upon our wisdom in managing the space in which we live?

Much has been said about the social responsibility of the scientist, frequently meaning the physical scientist. The rapid increase of knowledge about the control of the physical world has posed the question of whether society will be able to direct this knowledge, applying it for the benefit of mankind rather than for the destruction of man and his civilization. The social responsibility of the social scientist is equally great in the sense of discovering enough knowledge about society so that society can, if it wishes to employ this information, control the use of physical knowledge. The next question logically follows: Once the social scientists gain the social knowledge that is needed to control physical knowledge and society, how will this social evidence be controlled and what is to prevent a social scientist from taking advantage of such social knowledge to expedite the enslavement or the destruction of society? What is there to prevent one group in society from exploiting this social knowledge for the purpose of controlling another group? Examples of this problem may be found in the fields of market research, public opinion, industrial relations, and economic control (as in price and monetary controls). The social scientist's activities should be an asset to democratic society and he should be continually conscious of his obligation as a member of society.[93]

PSYCHOLOGY AND RESPONSIBILITY

Physicists, by releasing the might of the atom, were forced to face the ethical issues concerning use and control of this potentially destructive force, while lacking both training and temperament to deal with such problems of ethics. Psychologists, particularly applied and clinical psychologists, also inevitably meet ethical issues because of the nature of their subject matter and techniques. In addition to the relationships of psychotherapy, ethical judgments are involved in giving advice or information concerning methods of child rearing, depth motivational methods and subliminal stimulation in advertising, and the personal or private life of a subject or client.

A sharp comment on the "social indifference" of psychology maintains that workers in such disciplines as sociology, anthropology, political science, and economics are too often disappointed when they turn to psychology for help, following the admonition "to see the psychologist, he deals with people." The reason cited is that the major areas of social activity are commonly the *place* where psychologists study interesting problems, rather than the *focus of inquiry*.

If someone is interested in social behavior he ought not to rely upon or even trust the analysis that a psychologist makes of most of it. I am impressed with how naive and conventional my colleagues and I are when confronted with most social phenomena. We are ignorant of the historical dimensions of most social activity, we do not see the complex interweaving of institutions and arrangements, when we think of social meanings and facts we tend to deal with them in terms of their possessors, we substitute fancy for fact, preference for actuality—not, to be sure, that political scientists and sociologists do not do this too often, too. In general, psychologists tend to be like laymen when they confront social phenomena, particularly those that involve large scale patterns. And the reason for all of this is that the main areas of social activity are only the *place* where psychologists study interesting sorts of things, rather than being the *focus of inquiry*.[94]

To cite a specific positive example in the field of psychology, Edward Tolman, following his death in November, 1959, was characterized as

[93] Arnold M. Rose, "The Social Responsibility of the Social Scientist," *Theory and Method in the Social Sciences, op. cit.*, p. 179–92.

[94] Richard A. Littman, "Psychology: The Socially Indifferent Science." *American Psychologist* 16: 232–36; May 1961.

one who led a life of both scientific and social purpose. He was described as a gentle and humane teacher of psychology, capable of instilling permanent scientific enthusiasms in his students. Beyond his major contributions as a respected scientist and rare teacher, Tolman was a citizen with a social conscience who sought in many ways to understand the psychological sources of warlike behavior, to protect civil rights and academic freedom, and to promote individual justice.[95]

Concluding Statement

It is both logical and functional to discuss research in terms of the characteristics and sequence of scientific method and problem-solving. In attempting to classify pure research and practical (applied) research, we have a continuum rather than a dichotomy for methods and values. It has been well said that the greatest invention of the nineteenth century was the invention of the method of invention and that the most important instrument or element in research is the mind of man.

Interdisciplinary research and professional collaboration in the social and behavioral fields of inquiry have led to the development of certain theoretical concepts and propositions that are regarded as the common property of education, psychology, sociology, and anthropology. We need a broad base of mutual understanding between physical scientists, social scientists, and scholars in the humanities, with education playing the key role in achieving this understanding.

Values are inescapably present in research, in the form of such factors as purpose, motive, aspiration, interest, need, attitude, feeling, emotion, and sentiment, with a proper place for the great humanities, the spiritual ends of life, and faith. Without such a philosophy of values, science is blind or lacks direction. Science may be good or bad in the degree it contributes to, or corresponds with, the basic needs and goals of human life.

The hallmarks of the scientist are typically problem awareness, appropriate specialization, intellectual curiosity and professional aspiration, magnanimity, willingness to encounter hazards in research, creativity and originality, and something of a prophetic quality. Great scholars and scientists have been compared with torches shining at long intervals, to guide the advance of science.

Although certain external and internal factors may inhibit freedom for research, there are definite ways in which the investigator, including school personnel, may overcome obstacles to freedom in research. We cannot tolerate any pecking order of priority in the fields of scholarship

[95] Richard S. Crutchfield, David Krech, and Robert C. Tryon, "Edward Chace Tolman: A Life of Scientific and Social Purpose." *Science* 131: 714–16; March 11, 1960.

and research. Like food, we need enough freedom in research, but should not be guilty of gluttony. Development of self-responsibility and freedom of inquiry in graduate education may well serve the two purposes of broadening and deepening the student's knowledge in a particular field, and of creative investigation.

Federal grants to university research programs should be so managed as to develop and maintain an appropriate balance between effective instruction and significant research projects.

It is not enough to emphasize the social responsibility of the physical scientist. Social scientists, psychologists, and educators have equally great obligations (and inevitably meet ethical issues) as they seek to use their knowledge for the benefit of democratic society. It has been suggested that our future security may depend less on priority in exploring outer space than on our wisdom in managing the space in which we live.

SELECTED REFERENCES

ACKOFF, Russell L. *Scientific Method: Optimizing Applied Research Decisions.* New York: John Wiley & Sons, Inc., 1962. xii + 464 p.

BENJAMIN, A. C. *Science, Technology, and Human Values.* Columbia: University of Missouri Press, 1965. x + 296 p.

BERELSON, Bernard. *Graduate Education in the United States.* New York: McGraw-Hill Book Co., 1960. vi + 346 p.

BOGARDUS, Emory S. *The Development of Social Thought.* Fourth Edition. New York: Longmans, Green and Co., 1960. x + 689 p.

BONNEY, Merl E. "Sociometric Methods," *Encyclopedia of Educational Research.* Edited by Chester W. Harris. Third Edition. New York: The Macmillan Co., 1960. p. 1319-23.

BRODBECK, May. "Logic and Scientific Method in Research on Teaching," *Handbook of Research on Teaching.* Edited by N. L. Gage. Chicago: Rand McNally, 1963. Chapter 2.

BRODE, Wallace R., Editor. *Science in Progress.* Vol. 13. New Haven, Conn.: Yale University Press, 1963. 319 p.

BROWN, Laurence D., and SLATER, J. Marlowe. *The Doctorate in Education: An Inquiry into Conditions Affecting Pursuit of the Doctoral Degree in the Field of Education.* Vol. 1, The Graduates. Washington: American Association of Colleges for Teacher Education, 1960. ix + 110 p.

CARMICHAEL, Oliver C. *Graduate Education: A Critique and a Program.* New York: Harper & Row, Publishers, Inc., 1961. ix + 213 p.

EIDUSON, Bernice T. *Scientists: Their Psychological World.* New York: Basic Books, Inc., Publishers, 1962. xvi + 299 p.

EISERER, Paul E. *The School Psychologist.* New York: Center for Applied Research in Education, 1963. ix + 115 p.

GAGE, N. L. "Paradigms for Research on Teaching," *Handbook of Research on Teaching.* Chicago: Rand McNally & Co., 1963. Chapter 3.

GILPIN, Robert, and WRIGHT, Christopher, Editors. *Scientists and National Policy-Making.* New York: Columbia University Press, 1964. 315 p.

GLASER, Barney G. *Organizational Scientists: Their Professional Careers.* Indianapolis: The Bobbs-Merrill Co., Inc., 1965. xix + 140 p.

GOOD, Carter V. *Introduction to Educational Research: Methodology of Design in the Behavioral and Social Sciences.* Second Edition. New York: Appleton-Century-Crofts, 1963. Chapter 1.

GRAY, Susan W. *The Psychologist in the Schools.* New York: Holt, Rinehart and Winston, Inc., 1963. v + 406 p.

HAMMOND, Phillip E., Editor. *Sociologists at Work: Essays on the Craft of Social Research.* New York: Basic Books, Inc., Publishers, 1964. x + 401 p.

HANDY, Rollo. *Methodology of the Behavioral Sciences: Problems and Controversies.* Springfield, Ill.: Charles C Thomas, 1964. xi + 182 p.

HARMON, Lindsey R., and SOLDZ, Gerbert. *Doctorate Production in United States Universities, 1920-1962: With Baccalaureate Origins of Doctorates in Sciences, Arts, and Professions.* Washington: National Academy of Sciences, 1964. viii + 215 p.

HOROWITZ, Irving L. *Philosophy, Science, and the Sociology of Knowledge.* Springfield, Illinois: Charles C Thomas, 1961. 192 p.

KAPLAN, Abraham. *The Conduct of Inquiry: Methodology for Behavioral Science.* San Francisco: Chandler Publishing Co., 1964. xix + 428 p.

KNAPP, Robert H. *The Origins of American Humanistic Scholars.* Englewood Cliffs, N.J.: Prentice-Hall, Inc., 1964. xvi + 172 p.

LAZARSFELD, Paul F., and SIEBER, Sam D. *Organizing Educational Research: An Exploration.* Englewood Cliffs, N.J.: Prentice-Hall, Inc., 1964. ix + 113 p.

LAZARSFELD, Paul F., and THIELENS, Wagner, Jr. *The Academic Mind: Social Scientists in a Time of Crisis.* New York: Free Press of Glencoe, Inc., 1958. xiii + 460 p.

LITTLE, J. Kenneth. "Graduate Education," *Encyclopedia of Educational Research.* Chester W. Harris, Editor. Third Edition. New York: The Macmillan Co., 1960. p. 593-602.

LUNDBERG, George A. *Can Science Save Us?* Second Edition. New York: Longmans, Green and Co., 1961. 150 p.

MECHANIC, David. *Students under Stress: A Study in the Social Psychology of Adaptation.* New York: Free Press of Glencoe, Inc., 1962. v + 231 p.

TAYLOR, Calvin W., Editor. *Creativity: Progress and Potential.* New York: McGraw-Hill Book Co., 1964. xiii + 241 p.

TAYLOR, Calvin W., and BARRON, Frank, Editors. *Scientific Creativity: Its Recognition and Development.* New York: John Wiley & Sons, Inc., 1963. v + 419 p.

THOMPSON, Albert S., and SUPER, Donald E., Editors. *The Professional Preparation of Counseling Psychologists.* Report of the 1964 Greyston Conference. New York: Teachers College, Columbia University, 1964. x + 165 p.

2
Problem and Hypothesis

ADVISER AND STUDENT

This chapter discusses problem awareness or sensitivity to problem situations; identification of problems through advanced study and critical reading, analysis of trends and needs, and repetition or extension of investigations; factors important in selection of the problem—novelty and importance, curiosity and drive or motivation, background of scholarship and personal traits or characteristics, technique and working facilities, sponsorship and cooperation, risks and costs, and time requirements; initial statement and fuller definition of the problem; and development and testing of hypotheses.

Awareness or Identification of Problems

MANY BEGINNERS IN RESEARCH AND GRADUATE STUDENTS ARE PRONE TO CONclude that most of our educational problems have been solved. They may be overawed by the large number of research studies in print. At the time the first edition of the *Encyclopedia of Educational Research* was published in 1941 it was estimated that if research was liberally interpreted and unpublished studies were included, the total number of studies was near 100,000. Since that time, an estimate based on the bibliographies appearing in the *Review of Educational Research* indicates that by the middle 1960's the total had reached approximately 175,000. The number of doctoral dissertations and studies per year in education was about 2,500 by the middle 1960's. To these figures should be added a considerable number of master's theses and projects, although many master's degrees are awarded without a thesis requirement.

SENSITIVITY TO PROBLEMS

The difficulty for many beginners in research lies in an insensitivity to problems or "problem blindness." Later chapters of this book will present many examples of studies essential to future progress in education. Historical sources accumulate with each passing event, making necessary the extension of earlier historical narratives and sometimes a reinterpretation of older accounts. Descriptive-survey studies are soon out of date and must be repeated, as in the annual school census for a local system. Controlled experiments are repeated to test the validity of earlier investigations.

It may seem surprising that, early in the development of public schools in the United States, some educators mistakenly concluded that most of our educational problems had been solved, as expressed by the writer of more than a century ago in the *Ohio Journal of Education* (1856). He said that interest in all areas of education had "prompted inquiry into all departments of the subject" to such a degree that it was difficult "to find a point of space unoccupied, or at least unnoticed," by way of investigation.

The poet at times has recognized the human tendency to overlook problems close at hand or even in one's "backyard." Lowell, in his "The Vision of Sir Launfal," tells of the young knight who scornfully tossed the leper a piece of gold as he left the castle gate to seek the Holy Grail. Later the knight, returning old and broken after a fruitless search, found in this same beggar and in the woden bowl the object of his quest.

> In many climes, without avail,
> Thou hast spent thy life for the Holy Grail;
> Behold, it is here,—this cup which thou
> Didst fill at the streamlet for me but now.

It may be that the investigator who is sensitive to problems nearby understands rather well the meaning of the lines in Shakespeare's *As You Like It.*

> Finds tongues in trees, books in the running brooks,
> Sermons in stones, and good in everything.

Social scientists have been chided for failure to take better advantage of major social changes to study the processes and effects involved; for example, a tax reduction program, a "war on poverty," or integration in their natural settings. Possible explanations for neglect of research on these complex social problems may be inexperience in tackling such large issues or even lack of interest and motivation. Lessons may be learned from the natural scientists.

Natural scientists are more forehanded. A solar eclipse is preceded by elaborate preparation in order to gain the maximum possible amount of new information during the fleeting moment of the event itself. The International Geophysical Year included arrangements for a world-wide warning system so that observations of solar flares and other particularly significant events could be coordinated on a world-wide basis. The U.S. Geological Survey maintains an observatory on the rim of Kilauea to study the forewarnings, the active processes, and the subsidence of volcanic eruptions.[1]

More recent reports indicate that the record for the social sciences is not entirely a negative one, since certain studies have been made of changes in the federal income tax, presidential elections, trends in consumer behavior, psychological and social factors associated with changes in the birth rate, space efforts in relation to society, "disaster studies," and integration and urban renewal. It should be noted that private foundations and government agencies have been reluctant to support studies of politically sensitive social changes (as represented by the status of a particular minority group) or when changes are slow in developing (as in the impact of automation on worker satisfaction).

It is also true that a study of the consumers' responses to the 1964 tax cut was initiated promptly, but we should remember that an uncertain legislative situation makes it awkward to approach governmental or foundation agencies in advance of enactment of the particular legislation involved. It is likewise true that large-scale projects in the social sciences command only a small fraction of the large sums available for research in the natural sciences, and that the launching of studies in the social fields is relatively slow and time-consuming.[2]

Physical scientists, too, have had their blind spots.

The synthesis of xenon tetrafluoride and related compounds . . . makes necessary the revision of many chemistry textbooks. For about 50 years, students taking elementary courses in the subject have been taught that the noble gases are nonreactive. Millions of pupils have absorbed this dogma and faithfully parroted it back at examination time.

There is a sobering lesson here, as well as an exciting prospect. For perhaps 15 years, at least a million scientists all over the world have been blind to a potential opportunity to make this important discovery. All that was required to overthrow a respectable and entrenched dogma was a few hours of effort and a germ of skepticism. Our intuition tells us that this is just one of countless opportunities in all areas of inquiry. The imaginative and original mind need not be overawed by the imposing body of present knowledge or by the complex and costly paraphernalia which today surround much of scientific activity. The great shortage in science now is not opportunity, manpower, money, or laboratory space. What is really needed is more of that healthy skepticism which generates the key idea—the liberating concept.[3]

1 Dael Wolfle, "Lost Opportunities." *Science* 143: 999; March 6, 1964.
2 Joseph A. Pechman, "Timing of Research on Social Change." *Science* 145: 8; July 3, 1964.
3 Philip H. Abelson, "The Need for Skepticism." *Science* 138: 75; October 12, 1962.

So great was Kettering's wish to know and so keen his awareness of how little we do know, that often he spoke after the following fashion: "We have great libraries all over the country which contain the books of things we know. But I want to build libraries . . . to hold the books that we don't know anything about—the unwritten books. That would be a great library as I see it. . . . Someday it is going to be filled."[4]

The insight essential to recognition of research problems differs from the background necessary for sensing and doing practical or routine tasks in the school. Frequently the answers to these practical questions are provided in terms of judgment or experience, without resort to an investigational approach. The beginner in research may have to reorient his thinking to achieve the research perspective or may even find it necessary to undertake a more difficult task, an intellectual reorganization so as to interpret his educational world in the form of problems to be solved. The graduate student or field worker may make his choice with respect to investigating problems close at hand or more distant in time or space.

Some experienced professors have recommended assignment of important thesis problems to students by graduate advisers, although other research advisers argue that such assignments would limit the development of originality and creativity.[5]

Sources for Identification of Problems

ADVANCED STUDY AND CRITICAL READING

The background of scholarship resulting from thorough training in a particular field of specialization and research should identify both the available evidence and the unsolved problems. Helpful related activities may include instruction, administration, reading, writing, and investigation. It has been typical for the graduate student to select a thesis problem in his major field of concentration and quite common for the more mature research worker to follow up the area of interest represented in his doctoral dissertation. As a caution against too narrow specialization, however, we are reminded of the current interest in interdisciplinary training and research, as described in Chapter 1.

The Senior Scholar and the Younger Worker. Stimulating contacts between professor and student inside and outside the classroom or seminar, or between the senior scholar and younger worker, frequently have been profitable in selection and development of problems for investigation and

4 Quoted from T. A. Boyd, *Professional Amateur: The Biography of Charles Franklin Kettering.* New York: E. P. Dutton and Co., Inc., 1957. p. 214.

5 Thomas H. Briggs, "Research in Education." *Phi Delta Kappan* 46: 99–103; November 1964.

in encouragement of creativity. Well-known examples are the influence of William James on Dewey, Thorndike, and Woodworth; Wundt on Cattell, Stanley Hall, Judd, and Titchener; and Dewey, Thorndike, and Judd on many educational and psychological investigators active in the mid-twentieth century and later.

As an example of early influence on doctoral students, Wilhelm Wundt sponsored a long list of doctoral dissertations by candidates from Europe and the United States between 1875 and 1919, a total of 186 (70 on philosophical and 116 on psychological problems), although at least 86 of these doctoral graduates did not become well known and could not be found at a later date. To summarize a philosopher's influence:

> In tracing the influence of the senior scholar or teacher on his students, we find Dewey's case to be an interesting one. Some persons have thought that Dewey derived his educational ideas from Rousseau and Froebel, although Dewey told Kilpatrick explicitly that he had not read the works of either man until after he had formed his educational outlook. Dewey said that he got help in his educational thinking from Francis W. Parker and his psychology from William James; both Dewey and James were greatly indebted to Darwin's *Origin of Species*. As to Dewey's comparative place in the history of philosophy, Kilpatrick places him next to Plato and Aristotle; first in the history of philosophy of education; and in his current influence on education, in the company of William James, Francis W. Parker, and Edward L. Thorndike.[6]
>
> Dewey is an example of a scholar whose great influence on his students far exceeded his skill as a teacher and lecturer. Many dozens of his students became pivotal figures in the intellectual life of our country, yet by all the usual criteria of effective instruction Dewey was a poor teacher. Many of these students tell tales of Dewey's dullness as a lecturer and in the next breath say that Dewey's teaching fundamentally changed their thinking. His appearance was farmer-like, weather-beaten, and unpretentious. He remained seated throughout the hour, seldom seemed to be looking directly at his audience, often would turn in his chair and glance sideways, as if half-looking out the window and half-absorbed in his private thoughts. There is the standard legend of Dewey's lecture on "Interest in Education," which put many of his hearers to sleep. An inspired understatement concerning his style is to the effect that "Professor Dewey was a quiet talker." Dewey's quiet temperament was apparent as early as completion of his doctoral program at Johns Hopkins in 1884, when President Gilman called him to the office and, after warning him not to remain so "seclusive and bookish," offered a loan for study in Europe.[7]
>
> Kilpatrick (1871-1965) says that he got little from his first personal contact with John Dewey through an 1898 summer course in education at the Uni-

[6] William H. Kilpatrick, "Personal Reminiscences of Dewey and My Judgment of His Present Influence." *School and Society* 87: 374–75; October 10, 1959.

[7] Harold A. Larrabee, "John Dewey as Teacher." *School and Society* 87: 378–81; October 10, 1959.

versity of Chicago, chiefly because he was not ready for Dewey's thinking and method of teaching. Dewey's practice was to come to the class with a problem on his mind and sit before the class thinking out loud as he sought a solution. Two years later Kilpatrick studied Dewey's monograph, *Interest as Related to Will*, under Charles DeGarmo, which did have a deep and lasting effect. In 1907 Kilpatrick received a scholarship which permitted him to study at Columbia University under Dewey for the next three years. Later Dewey read and approved Kilpatrick's manuscript for the 1912 book, *The Montessori System Examined*. In turn Kilpatrick suggested problems for inclusion as chapters in Dewey's book, *Democracy and Education*.[8]

James R. Angell had studied with Dewey at Michigan (and also with James and Royce at Harvard), and later became a colleague at Chicago. Angell, a psychologist, became one of the most influential proponents of a functional psychology, a carrier of the thinking of James and Dewey conjoined.[9]

As in the case of Dewey, the senior scholar has not always been a "great teacher" in terms of craftsmanship. Gardner Murphy tells what it meant to him as a young psychologist to sit in a course taught by Woodworth at Columbia in 1919–20, under the title of "Physiological and Genetic Psychology."

Entering the classroom in an unpressed, baggy suit, and wearing army shoes, Woodworth would make his way to the blackboard, not quite sure how to begin. He would numble; then stop dead; fail to find the phrase he wanted; turn and look at the class in a helpless sort of way; go back to the blackboard, and then utter some inimitable word of insight or whimsy, which would go into our notebooks to be remembered in the decades that followed.[10]

At the age of nearly ninety, when Woodworth gave his last Columbia lecture, he was overwhelmed for many minutes by thunderous applause. When at last he could make himself heard, Woodworth in his characteristically modest manner said: "I know I'm not really such a very good teacher. But I'm still trying; I'm still learning."

Gates, recognized especially for his work in reading and educational psychology, speaks of the early influences on his background of professional preparation:[11]

1. The "savage" brilliance of James McKeen Cattell, in illuminating the educational significance of both the experimental and statistical approaches, who said: "Science is what good scientists do."

8 William H. Kilpatrick, *op. cit.*

9 Maxine Greene, "Dewey and American Education, 1894–1920." *School and Society* 87: 381–86; October 10, 1959.

10 Gardner Murphy, "Robert Sessions Woodworth, 1869–1962." *American Psychologist* 18: 131–33; March 1963.

11 Arthur I. Gates, "Science or Sanity?" *Phi Delta Kappan* 45: 297–302; March 1964.

2. William James, regarded by many as the greatest psychologist (chiefly theoretical) of all times, despite the fact that he made but one experimental study (of quite faulty design).
3. John Dewey, trained for and inventive in psychology, who began early to attack the most complex social problems with slow, deep persistence.
4. Charles H. Judd, the able and "brusque" Chicago leader in laboratory experimentation, especially as applied to educational problems.
5. The brilliant and versatile Edward L. Thorndike, the most prolific worker in the early scientific movement.

The relationship between Binet and Simon is a striking example of the influence of a senior scholar on a younger associate. Terman guaranteed that Alfred Binet would be remembered by calling his revision of the scale Stanford-Binet, but Théodore Simon (trained as a physician) became almost a forgotten figure. While Binet died in 1911, Simon was found active as late as 1959–60 in Paris, serving as long-time president (since 1912) of the Société Alfred Binet, housed in Simon's study. In his eighty-seventh year, the slight old man, bearded and bent, walked with shuffling steps. Originally Binet was slow to accept Simon's offer of assistance by way of subjects and advice, but later Simon did provide some needed subjects for testing and proved an intelligent, professionally oriented, loyal research associate, with a mixture of admiration and hero worship for Binet. Shortly before his death, Binet is reported to have said:

I have had many students and collaborators, but I have never had any as sincere and as loyal as Simon. And another thing, never would he say "yes" to me when he thought "no." How I regret going so soon! Now I shall never see Simon at the height of the scale.[12]

It is interesting to summarize in further detail the training and influence of a number of other psychologists. John B. Watson, self-styled "the behaviorist," died September 25, 1958, at the age of 80, although his scientific life as such had come to a close a third of a century earlier, and he was unknown personally to a whole generation of younger men in psychology. In dispensing with mentalistic explanations of behavior, Watson cleared the way for a scientific analysis. He has acknowledged his indebtedness to Lloyd Morgan, Edward L. Thorndike, George H. Mead, John Dewey, James R. Angell, Jacques Loeb, H. S. Jennings, Adolph Meyer, Knight Dunlap, Robert Yerkes, Curt Richter, and K. S. Lashley. From this exceptional variety of strong stimulation, Watson emerged with a pressing recognition of the needs for a science of behavior.[13]

[12] Quoted from Theta H. Wolf, "An Individual Who Made a Difference." *American Psychologist* 16: 245–48; May 1961.
[13] B. F. Skinner, "John Broadus Watson, Behaviorist." *Science* 129: 197–98; January 23, 1959.

In 1904 Herbert Sidney Langfeld resigned his position as Secretary to the Naval Attache of the American Embassy in Berlin, in favor of graduate study in psychology at the University of Berlin. While this decision was a loss to American foreign service, at the same time it was an important gain for American education in general and psychology in particular. Langfeld was the last American to study under the first generation of German psychologists (who were also philosophers with a breadth of imagination that partially offset their lack of knowledge of the experimental techniques and statistical analyses possessed by the psychologists of today). Throughout his long professional career as teacher, lecturer, administrator, and editor, Langfeld served as a valuable link between psychology in America and in other countries.[14]

In his autobiography Wallin cites a number of examples of the influence of able psychologists on their students. He describes Stanley Hall as a genial, stimulating, and helpful teacher, but one who knew how to "put the heat" on graduate fellows if they appeared to be loafing on the job or if they failed to produce research results. This may explain in part why the Clark fellows majoring under Hall were so productive, although an important cause was also the fact that Hall was an inspiring teacher and writer with a brilliant, retentive, and encyclopedic mind. Wallin speaks of Hall as having enormous breadth of erudition, fertile imagination, catholicity of view, effective presentation, untiring industry, and prodigious productivity.[15] During the early days of psychology in the United States, Hall was the great graduate teacher. By 1893 eleven of fourteen Ph.D. degrees had been sponsored by him, and by 1898 the number had increased to thirty out of fifty-four.

Great teachers at times are dramatic in the classroom, as illustrated by certain techniques of the sociologist, Lester F. Ward. On the other hand, great men in sociology (as in other fields) sometimes have been dull in their class-lecture presentation. Albion W. Small's lectures in sociology were occasionally very monotonous. At times his graduate students developed a plan to break the monotony of these presentations. A student was assigned each day to ask questions for the purpose of interrupting the lecture. The questions would stimulate Small to lay down his sheaf of papers, step forward, and launch into an interesting discussion of the point concerning which he had written rather ponderous notes in preparation for the lecture. In general, Small was an able teacher and author, with a dynamic personality.

[14] Carroll C. Pratt, "Herbert Sidney Langfeld." *Psychological Review* 65: 321–24; November 1958.

[15] J. E. Wallace Wallin, *The Odyssey of a Psychologist: Pioneering Experiences in Special Education, Clinical Psychology, and Mental Hygiene with a Comprehensive Bibliography of the Author's Publications.* Wilmington, Del.: The Author, 1955. p. 19, 24, 39.

Franklin H. Giddings of Columbia University (1855–1931) found time to encourage younger workers in sociology. When a young teacher in a small western community reported a local study in the village newspaper, with some wider publicity, he received a long-hand letter from Giddings, suggesting continuation of the study, some advice about publication, and ideas for future investigations. For several years, whenever this young teacher published anything, Giddings wrote to him, giving advice and suggestions. A long list of Ph.D. candidates completed their work under Giddings' guidance, and scattered throughout the United States and to foreign lands. In most fields the influence of the senior scholar is reflected in the work of his doctoral graduates.[16]

During his senior year at Indiana University, 1890–91, Ellwood P. Cubberley had an unusual opportunity to become well acquainted with David Starr Jordan, the president of Indiana University. Jordan had gained wide recognition as a speaker and was accustomed to traveling and speaking on a variety of subjects, illustrating his lectures at times with slides projected by a stereopticon lantern. Cubberley accompanied Jordan on these tours and operated the lantern. The long hours together on slow trains, the prolonged stay at stations between trains, and occupancy of the same hotel room provided opportunities for conversation and exchange of ideas that influenced the younger man throughout his long career in education.[17]

Harold Rugg speaks of his long association with John Dewey as his "credentials" for appraising Dewey and his contemporaries from the perspective provided by the centennial of Dewey's birth and by a common interest in certain phases of educational philosophy. Rugg was born the year Dewey's first book, *Psychology*, was published, 1886. In his professional career, Rugg was a colleague of Dewey at Columbia for twenty years, worked closely with him for two winters in the 1930's, went with him to the Union of South Africa for the New Education Fellowship in 1934, and was a fellow editor with Dewey for the *Social Frontier* in the middle 1930's.[18]

Frederick J. Turner was the most important teacher in Carl Becker's life, and imparted to Becker an enthusiasm for history by encouraging him to do research in it and by discouraging Becker from thinking that Turner or anyone could give him final answers about history or anything

[16] M. C. Elmer, *Contemporary Social Thought: Contributors and Trends*. Pittsburgh: University of Pittsburgh Press, 1956. p. 12, 16–17, 25.

Emory S. Bogardus, *The Development of Social Thought*. Fourth Edition. New York: Longmans, Green and Co., 1960. p. 451–61.

[17] Jesse B. Sears and Adin D. Henderson, *Cubberley of Stanford: And His Contribution to American Education*. Stanford, Calif.: Stanford University Press, 1957. p. 15–16.

[18] Harold Rugg, "Dewey and His Contemporaries," *John Dewey in Perspective*. Bulletin of the School of Education, Indiana University, Vol. 36, No. 1. Bloomington, Indiana: Indiana University, January, 1960. 42 p.

else. Turner gave Becker "freedom" and with it self-confidence to become a historian and writer.[19]

There are even instances when the college attended and the professors heard have seemingly had little significance as preparation for future educational work. Horace Mann attended Brown University, 1816–1819, at a time when it was common to eulogize one's alma mater and the venerable sages on the staff who supposedly provided a philosophy of life to launch the student on a career of prominent public service. Mann, however, thought of his years at Brown as "a heroic struggle to obtain an education, plagued by poor health, overwork, poverty and limited preparation." If some "Mark Hopkins" was there, Mann never found him or at least never acknowledged him. Where the classroom and the rule book had failed, however, the debating society and the dormitory as socializing processes had, almost inadvertently, succeeded in causing Mann and his fellows to think of themselves as "the new leaders of a chosen generation whose foreordained triumph over ignorance, poverty, and greed seemed just beyond their outstretched grasp."[20]

Extensive and Critical Reading. With respect to wide reading, in all scientific endeavor the interdependence of research workers is recognized in the identification and solution of problems. In spite of difficulties in securing the works of other scholars, even such early investigators as Roger Bacon and Leonardo da Vinci relied on extensive knowledge of the writings of others in their special fields of interest. The inspiration for many of Bacon's experiments may be found in the work of other scholars. The 5,000 manuscript pages of Leonardo's notebooks disclose his indebtedness to other workers and his wide reading (he quotes from 72 medieval and classical authors).

Charles H. Judd had exceptional opportunities for extensive reading in his undergraduate training in the United States and in his graduate work in Germany; his advice to beginning students is that they select teachers with broad interests and read widely. Although Edward L. Thorndike considered himself an investigator or experimenter rather than a scholar, in the sense of devoting his time to books and the literature, he estimated in 1936 that he had spent well over 20,000 hours reading and studying scientific books and journals. The extensive reading, erudition, and range of information of William James may well explain his success in bringing together the work of the Scottish, English, French, and German schools of psychology.

John Dewey grew up an omnivorous reader, and the habit seems to have grown on him in college, which he entered in 1875. His record of

---

[19] Burleigh T. Wilkins, *Carl Becker: A Biographical Study in American Intellectual History.* Cambridge, Mass.: M.I.T. Press and Harvard University Press, 1961. p. 36–48.

[20] Jonathan C. Messerli, "Horace Mann at Brown." *Harvard Educational Review* 33: 285–311; Summer 1963.

withdrawals from the library of the University of Vermont includes 114 entries—novels, histories, poems, essays, translations from the Greek and Latin authors, works on political and social science, treatises on philosophy, and volumes of English and American journals. Possibly he read more, because he was ill at ease in social groups, poor at sports, bashful in the presence of girls, and suffering from vague dissatisfactions and dim yearnings, and could find success and recognition through mental effort and abstract thinking. Although on graduation seriously disturbed by the cleavages he felt within himself and observed about him, Dewey began his long search for the principles of unity that could satisfy him intellectually and emotionally.[21] As an example of his later professional reading, Dewey's early book on psychology (written in 1887, when he was only twenty-eight years of age) was based largely upon his extensive reading, including the American, British, French, German, and Italian authors. For example, in his chapter of fifty-three pages on "Elements of Knowledge," Dewey refers to seventy-eight sources, and in his chapter, "Processes of Knowledge," of seventy-three pages he cites fifty-four sources.[22]

Cubberley's meticulous habits of work and extensive reading are illustrated by the manner in which he prepared for the teaching of a new course. He began immediately to develop syllabus outlines with references for reading. For his history of education course, the syllabus developed in the direction of a history of culture. For his first course in school administration he drew upon collections of documents. A typical scene was that of Cubberley leaving his office after class in the evening with an armful of school laws and reports. Next morning he would lug them back to their shelves in the library. Night after night he read, made notes, and kept his syllabus growing. Sometimes when he had left the campus for lectures at institutes, his notes were not far ahead of the class. Even after retirement in 1933, Cubberley did a great deal of reading on a wide variety of subjects. After each title he placed a rating such as he was accustomed to do in his entries of stocks or bonds—double "A" if excellent, etc. He left notes on 25 books read in 1934 and 46 in 1935.[23]

As background for his major contributions to philosophy, Whitehead had the benefit of extensive reading in the classics (Latin and Greek), mathematics, science, theology over a period of some eight years, and philosophy. His varied experience and teaching at Cambridge University, London University, and Harvard University profoundly affected the development of his philosophy. In view of the size of Whitehead's library,

[21] Robert L. McCaul, "Dewey in College, 1875–79." *School Review* 70: 437–56; Winter 1962.

[22] Junius L. Meriam, "John Dewey in History." *School and Society* 87: 376–78; October 10, 1959.

[23] Jesse B. Sears and Adin D. Henderson, *op. cit.*, p. 69, 83.

his remark to a friend about not having read a great quantity of books should be taken relatively.

"I read very slowly," said Whitehead. "Sometimes I see myself referred to as 'a well-read man.' As a matter of fact, I have not read a great quantity of books; but I think about what I read, and it sticks."

"Speed is not for me. On the other hand, some of my reading is 'skippy.' Last night, for example, I was reading that book in your lap on the Jesuits, but finding, at the beginnings of successive chapters that he was still on the same aspect of a subject whose point I had already grasped, I did not hesitate to skip."[24]

The youthful reading of Thomas Huxley, the scientist, foreshadowed his later interests. He read popular novels, histories of Europe, works on science, philosophy, religion, and a large, illustrated Bible that delighted him.[25]

It should be pointed out, however, that some scholars and scientists have not been interested in making a study of the earlier writings or related literature in their fields of specialization and research. Agassiz found the study of things themselves more attractive than what was printed in books about the particular subject; he usually was satisfied with paging through the volumes of natural history, so that he might later identify the objects he examined in nature. Comte, in the latter part of his life, practiced what he called "cerebral hygiene," that is, he refrained from reading the books of other social thinkers, which meant that he was not always abreast of the times, although in his synthetic thinking and encyclopedic work Comte borrowed ideas from many predecessors. W. G. Sumner, the sociologist, paid little attention to the work of other writers in his field, not even mentioning in bibliography or index the names of Comte, Ward, and Giddings, although he did draw upon the ideas of other scholars.

Some of these scientists and scholars have considered it undesirable or even unwise to study closely the related literature, fearing that the research worker's mind might be conditioned to see the problem in the same way or in a traditional manner and thus overlook a new or more fruitful approach. It has been said that every laboratory needs one "crackpot" who doesn't know yet what you can't do. Charles Kettering, a research specialist in industry, believed that, as a result of studying conventional textbooks, we fall into a rut, escape from which may take as much effort as the solution of the specific problem. He chided men of science

24 Quoted from *Dialogues of Alfred North Whitehead*. As Recorded by Lucien Price. New York: New American Library of World Literature, Inc., 1954. p. 140, 320.
25 Charles S. Blinderman, "Thomas Henry Huxley." *Scientific Monthly* 84: 171–82; April 1957.

who "create obstacles to their progress by referring to theories which say certain matters cannot be accomplished." Kettering's unorthodox advice to specialists is "to throw away the books and work toward the objective," based on his opinion that "the smaller the library the less chance to find excuses that it can't be done."

> We know that there is no absolute knowledge, that there are only theories; but we forget this. The better educated we are, the harder we believe in axioms. I asked Einstein in Berlin once how he, a trained, drilled, teaching scientist of the worst sort, a mathematician, physicist, astronomer, had been able to make his discoveries. "How did you ever do it," I exclaimed, and he, understanding and smiling, gave the answer: "By challenging an axiom!"[26]

Sometimes even able men in their college days (and later) have not always sought and cited evidence or documentation, as compared with using oratory and rhetoric to establish a position. With his facility in using language, Horace Mann, as a student at Brown University, 1816–1819, wrote with apparent authority on problems for which he had little understanding. He denounced English critics of American literature without mentioning a single critic by name or any specific American object of criticism. He also denounced fiction in general, without listing a single novel he thought "harmful." In his senior year Mann delivered an oration on the Congress of Vienna, with a scathing attack on its leading figures and their political maneuvers, but without identifying a single individual by name.[27]

As to the related literature, the poet, Byron, has aptly expressed the dilemma of creative workers: "To be perfectly original one should think much and read little, and this is impossible, for one must have read before one has learnt to think." It would seem that for most graduate students and research workers the solution of this dilemma does depend on critical reading as a stimulus to thinking.

ANALYSIS OF EVIDENCE, PRACTICES, TRENDS, OR NEEDS IN A PARTICULAR AREA

When a field of knowledge is being analyzed to identify problems for study, the particular research area should be sufficiently limited to serve effectively as sources of specific problems for investigation; for example, physical growth, mental development, or reading readiness rather than child psychology or abnormal psychology. On the other hand, the research area under analysis should be large enough to permit development of meaningful, integrating concepts of interpretation; for example,

---

[26] Lincoln Steffens, Quoted in *Contemporary Psychology* 5: 105; March 1960.
[27] Jonathan C. Messerli, "Horace Mann at Brown." *Harvard Educational Review* 33: 285–311; Summer 1963.

language development rather than the phonetic range of the one-year-old. Much of the background for separating a subject into its constituent parts and for identifying the research problems in each subarea is derived from the programs of reading and instruction described in the preceding section of this chapter.

Beginners in research frequently are not sensitive to problems, practices, trends, and needs close at hand, as illustrated earlier in this chapter. To cite another example, even as early as 1915, when a young sociologist went to teach at the University of Kansas, Frank W. Blackmar asked, "Young man, what do you know about the people of Kansas?" When the new staff member admitted his ignorance, Blackmar said, "You can't teach young people without knowing something about their background." He handed the new teacher a copy of the *Kansas City Star*, with the question, "Do you see anything about Kansas that interests you?" When the young man replied that he saw the name of a city, Beloit, Kansas, Blackmar answered: "All right, I have arranged for a fund of $900. You will teach five hours a week this semester. Next week, you go to Beloit, spend a couple of days there, talk with anyone and everyone until you have an idea of what people around Beloit do and think."[28]

REPETITION, EXTENSION, OR "BUDDING OUT" OF PROBLEMS: SERENDIPITY

In this chapter we have already indicated that history is never complete, that descriptive-survey studies are accurate only for the time and sample represented, and that many experiments should be repeated under the same or different conditions for purposes of verification. The scientist favors duplication of experiments under various conditions, lest some uncontrolled factor be present in the original experiment. At times, however, even the experienced investigator has failed to follow up a discovery in the direction of even more important conclusions or applications.

In 1754 Horace Walpole proposed adding a new word to our vocabulary, "serendipity," which means "the happy faculty, or luck, of finding unforeseen evidence of one's ideas or, with surprise, coming upon new objects or relations which were not being sought." Pasteur by chance discovered his method of immunization, when he used an old and forgotten bacterial culture to inoculate fowls, which became ill but did not die. He decided that, by first using cultures with little virulence and then repeating the injections with cultures of greater virulence, the animals could be made to develop gradually a resistance to infection. Thus, he became able to immunize sheep against anthrax and human beings against rabies. Pasteur recognized, however, that a favorable "accident"

28 M. C. Elmer, *op. cit.*, p. 48.

must be met by sharp insight: "In the field of observation, chance favors only the prepared mind." Even earlier, the American physicist, Joseph Henry, said: "The seeds of great discoveries are constantly floating around us, but they only take root in minds well prepared to receive them."[29] Expressed in other language, the scientist and scholar get no more from their studies than they invest by way of thought, preparation, performance, and analysis. Serendipity sometimes is a bonus to the perceptive, prepared research worker, but is not a satisfactory substitute for scientific or scholarly background and hard work. Furthermore, a psychoanalyst has demonstrated by clinical examples that serendipity is not, as is commonly supposed, a happy adjunct of genius whereby important scientific or scholarly discoveries are made, but on the contrary may prove to be a crippling neurotic symptom and may constitute an impairment of the ability to learn.[30]

A few examples, such as Perkin's discovery of an artificial dye, have dramatic value and hence are overemphasized. Perkin's discovery, while important to the course of development of chemistry at the time, plays only a minor role in the structure of science today. Organic chemistry, one of man's greatest intellectual triumphs, was built as a cumulative result of answers to a series of closely directed questions. Occasionally a chance observation has led to unexpected enlightenment. In general, however, progress has come because experimenters were seeking it.

Consider advances in another field—nuclear physics during the 1930's. This was an area where, to the highest degree, a kind of serendipity entered in. The discoveries of the neutron, artificial radioactivity, and uranium fission were unexpected. Yet in each instance the experimenters involved were extraordinarily competent. They had posed clear-cut questions. Chadwick in 1932 was attempting to study the physics of interaction of alpha particles on beryllium when he noticed that a "hard" gamma ray accompanied the reaction. On exploring the matter further he found that he was dealing not with gamma rays but with neutrons. The Joliot-Curies were studying the reaction of aluminum with energetic alpha particles. They observed that when the source of particles was removed, the aluminum target continued to emit radiation.

The most unexpected and far-reaching discovery in nuclear physics was that of uranium fission, reported by Hahn and Strassmann in 1939. In this case the discovery was more a result of careful work than anything else. Earlier, Fermi and his group had irradiated uranium with neutrons, and they thought they had discovered transuranic elements. Hahn and Strassmann were following up this work and found what they believed might be radium, presumably arising from neutron-stimulated emission of alpha particles from uranium. A first step in the isolation of radium is coprecipitation of radium and a barium salt. Later the mixture is recrystallized and the two elements can be separated. But in

[29] Walter B. Cannon, *The Way of an Investigator.* New York: W. W. Norton and Co., Inc., 1945.

[30] W. N. Evans, "Serendipity." *Psychoanalytic Quarterly* 32: 205–14; 1963.

the products from uranium the radioactivity precipitated with the barium could not later be separated from it. When this was confirmed, Hahn and Strassmann were forced to conclude that they had produced barium from uranium. In a sense the discovery involved luck, but only in part. The experimenters had posed an interesting, clear-cut question, "Is radium a product of irradiation of uranium?" They devised an appropriate set of experiments to answer the query. The result was certain to be important, whatever it was. If they had proved that radium was a product, the result would have been considered very important, though not so significant as what they actually found.

Other developments in nuclear physics, such as the discovery of carbon-14 and other radioactive tracers, were sought, as was the understanding of nuclear forces. Indeed, most of the structure of nuclear physics is a product of carefully planned research rather than a series of happy incidents.[31]

To cite another example, in 1928 a spore of a green mold drifted into the laboratory of Alexander Fleming, a Scottish scientist, and "spoiled" a culture of bacteria. When Fleming returned from a short vacation he noticed the mold growing in the culture dish of bacteria and was ready to discard the "spoiled" culture when he saw a transparent ring around the mold. Outside the ring bacteria thrived, but there was none inside it, for something was killing the germs. Fleming then began his research leading to the discovery of penicillin, following up what has been termed a "chance" discovery. Although the discovery was a fortunate "accident," it should be remembered that Fleming had the training and ability to recognize the significance of the accident. It should be added that, although Fleming described crude preparations of penicillin in 1929, he left this work, after a time, without developing a therapeutic agent, and it remained for Florey to complete this task.

To comment further on so-called "chance" discovery in science and research, we know that Roentgen was already a scientist of some repute before he made his "accidental" discovery of x-rays.

The reader will be quite impressed with Roentgen's experimental ability and logical mind, particularly in his three papers on x-rays (December 28, 1895, March 9, 1896 and March 10, 1897). . . . The x-ray expert and the lay reader both will be amazed at the wide scope, completeness, carefulness and significance of his measurements. He practically "cleaned out the field," there being very few further important advances in x-rays until 1912 when x-ray diffraction was discovered. He was not famous by a chance discovery, he was a superior scientist. Not only was Roentgen great in science but he was great in humility for he refused to accept nobility.[32]

[31] Philip H. Abelson, "Serendipity in Research." *Science* 140: 1177; June 14, 1963.
[32] Quoted from review by Leonard Muldawer, *American Scientist* 47: 86A; March 1959, of Otto Glasser, *Dr. W. C. Roentgen.* Second Edition. Springfield, Ill.: Charles C Thomas, 1958. 169 p.

In 1912, nearly a decade before the discovery of insulin by Banting and Best, one of Anton J. Carlson's graduate students isolated a crude extract of insulin which mitigated the effect of diabetes in dogs. Carlson freely admitted to what he called his "stupidity" in not following up his promising line of investigation.

In many instances an "offshoot" of a problem under study or of a technique in use leads to more fruitful results than the original problem or approach; for example, the idea of the delayed-reaction experiment, as a method of studying animal mentality, came to Edward L. Thorndike after two years of work with animals. Willis R. Whitney's apt statement concerning the "budding out" of problems is: "We found nature easy to follow and difficult to drive. We usually wanted what she gave for our seeking, but we could seldom get exactly what we thought we wanted at the time. We wanted light. She gave us rectifiers."[33]

Sometimes the "bypath" in an investigation proves to be a blind alley, but careful reporting of this fact may prevent other research workers from wasting time on the same project. By way of illustration, when an enthusiastic but immature student proposed a research project dealing with attempts to standardize an aspect of social research, he first sought assistance from two professors in sociology, without success. As a last resort, the graduate student went to a third sociologist, Albion W. Small, and received the following reaction:

> Young man, I believe you are on the wrong track. I believe that you will find your search for research methods leading you into a blind alley. That, however, is perfectly satisfactory. Do your job so well that no one need ever waste any time on that project again. I spent three years of hard work on a study of the Cameralists. I think it was largely futile. But I covered the ground completely enough that no one needs to go over it again. Therefore, I consider it three years well spent.[34]

Factors in Selection of the Problem

The investigator usually considers a number of external factors in choosing a problem for study: novelty, significance, sources, technique, equipment, working conditions, sponsorship, and cooperative relationships. He also evaluates such internal or personal factors as interest, motivation, intellectual curiosity, background of scholarship and training, temperament and personal characteristics, costs, risks, and timing.

NOVELTY, COOPERATIVE STUDIES, AND SIGNIFICANCE

The next chapter describes the library guides or keys for determining the research completed in a particular sphere of investigation. As pointed

33 T. A. Boyd, *Research*. New York: Appleton-Century-Crofts, 1935. p. 270.
34 Quoted from M. C. Elmer, *op. cit.*, p. 24.

out earlier in the present chapter, when it seems desirable to repeat or extend earlier experiments or investigations, what is implied is deliberate and systematic planning rather than accidental or random duplication of earlier studies through ignorance of the research literature. We have already noted that even able scientists and scholars sometimes have been negligent or indifferent to the literature in their particular fields of specialization.

In view of the number and complexity of problems in education, and of the relatively recent application of research methods to such problems, the question of uniqueness may be less important than the ways in which studies are comparable or related, or fit into a pattern of investigation and results. One view maintains that duplication is vital and invigorating to research, in the sense that competition and constructive rivalry may spur the imagination, develop ingenuity, and stimulate hard work. To draw a parallel from competition in the business world, rarely do monopoly situations lead to optimal progress.[35]

A strong argument for the gradualness and continuity of the progress of science is in the occurrence of multiples (simultaneous discovery) in research and invention. Discovery and new insight tend to be independent but synchronous in the minds of unassociated contemporaries, and frequently have a long history of less specific or less well publicized anticipation. Boring refers to an analysis of 264 multiple discoveries by R. K. Merton and Elinor Barber, finding 179 doublets, 51 triplets, and so on up to two discoveries (each of which was made independently nine times).[36]

The question of overlapping of dissertation problems or novelty sometimes arises when two or more graduate students engage in a cooperative program of research, which is a type of investigation that has come into increasing use on the part of commissions, survey teams, and research agencies (often with the assistance of graduate students). Many teams of scholars or inventors have found it profitable to work cooperatively in seeking answers to their problems.

To cite a specific example of cooperation in the graduate field at the University of Texas, team studies have been undertaken, in order that broader research problems may be studied than is usually possible when the responsibility is carried by one person. Four doctoral candidates have cooperated in attacking the problem of class size, two such candidates have worked together to discover what happens to children whose parents insist that they enter the first grade below the age of six, and four students have been investigating methods of reporting to parents at the elementary-school level.

35 Philip H. Abelson, "Waste and Duplication." *Science* 142: 625; November 8, 1963.
36 Edwin G. Boring, "Cognitive Dissonance: Its Use in Science," *Science* 145: 680–85; April 14, 1964.

While recognizing the value of team work, Kettering did not want to suppress originality in any way. When another man who was doing much to support research on cancer suggested to Kettering that, in order to get better coordination in cancer research and to avoid duplication of effort, the two of them go together and try to organize all the cancer studies in the nation and get them under one common head or guidance, Kettering said he would not favor the proposal.

> I'm afraid of a single direction in such things. It is too likely to steer the endeavor down one road, which may turn out to be the wrong road. I'm not worried about the duplication of effort in research. Such duplication is sometimes a good thing. It is not what two groups do alike that matters. It's what they do differently that is liable to count.[37]

The trend toward teamwork and cooperation in education, psychology, and other fields is resulting in multiple authorship, especially when working with the sponsorship or support of large research organizations and with large funds available for attacking complex and difficult problems.

It should be recognized that some contributions to the literature are valuable for purposes other than novelty or creativity; for example, Charles A. Ellwood (1873–1946) did not produce particularly new ideas in especially brilliant style, but he wrote in such a clear, logical manner that his work was readily understood and easily translated. Ellwood's discussion of methods in sociology vigorously criticized the tendency to overemphasize objective and statistical methods, and did much to revive interest in nonstatistical procedures.[38]

The criterion of significance or importance for the field represented and for the individual involves the realm of values. The discussions of the role of values in research and of the social responsibility of the scientist in Chapter 1, as well as certain topics of the present chapter, deal with values that frequently play a prominent part in the selection of problems for study. The literature includes a large number of analyses of problems for research, frequently with an indication of the importance or significance for the field represented, as illustrated in the chapter bibliography.

CURIOSITY, DRIVE, MOTIVATION

Much of the strength of science and scholarship is in attracting individuals who love knowledge and its creation. The research worker's rewards and satisfactions are in growing recognition of a new truth, the

---

37 Quoted from T. A. Boyd, *op. cit.*, p. 184–85.
38 M. C. Elmer, *op. cit.*, p. 35.
Emory S. Bogardus, *op. cit.*, p. 590–604.

approbation of professional colleagues, publication, and communication of the findings at scientific meetings.[39] Many scientists and scholars have been urged forward by an insatiable curiosity, driving interest, or other powerful motivation, sometimes to extremes in concentration, withdrawal from social contacts, or neglect of health. One scientist has suggested that our ideas need to be jostled about so that we do not become intellectually sluggish, or that we need a certain amount of "dither" in our mental mechanisms. When a professor who does research teaches elementary courses, the contacts with young students may jostle his mind or even put him in a dither, but that is good for him.

> When working, early in World War II, on antiaircraft computing and gun-laying devices, I learned from British colleagues a new use of an old word. When building such devices, they often included a small eccentric or vibrating member which kept the whole mechanism in a constant state of minor but rapid vibration. This they called the "dither."
>
> The purpose, once one thinks a moment, is perfectly clear. Kinetic friction is less than static friction. If the parts are constantly in slight motion, then the whole device is alert, is on the jump, is ready to respond promptly to the earliest beginnings of forces seeking to move the gun, the little dither gimmick preventing any sluggish delay caused by static friction. The same phenomenon arises in other connections. For example, the types of flight instruments which are dependably responsive in an aircraft with reciprocating engines and a good deal of resulting general vibration might tend to stick or respond tardily in jet aircraft with their almost vibrationless flight.[40]

Intellectual Curiosity, Drive, and the Scientist. Thomas Jefferson probably knew more than any single man of his age, and in the breadth of his interests has been compared with Leonardo da Vinci. He produced inventions, books, and new ideas, and was an expert in agriculture, archeology, architecture, and medicine. He was also an educator, mathematician, musician, politician, scientist, and world traveler. Although Jefferson seemed in appearance an untidy philosopher rather than a President, he was actually quite disciplined, rising at dawn to write and read, then breakfast, then another hour of reading. After a day of work he would burn the midnight oil, reading in Latin, Greek, French, Spanish, Italian, and Anglo-Saxon, laboriously taking notes on everything he read. The works of this good and tireless writer would fill more than 50 volumes, and he wrote at least 50,000 letters. By the incessant process of writing Jefferson forged his own thought and evolving ideas, and developed the

[39] Philip H. Abelson, "The Roots of Scientific Integrity." *Science* 139: 1257; March 29, 1963.

[40] Quoted from Warren Weaver, "Dither." *Science* 130: 301; August 7, 1959. Reprinted from *Science* by permission.

masterful skill displayed in the drafting of the Declaration of Independence, and the Statute of Virginia for Religious Freedom.[41]

As another example of great drive, Alexander von Humboldt, 1769–1859, was a notable explorer and scientist, as well as a confidant of kings. He spent five years (1799–1804) exploring northern South America and Mexico with Bonpland; in these explorations he covered six thousand miles, mostly on foot. "He kept diaries, plotted route maps, collected and described plants, recorded plant and animal assemblages, determined rocks and geological structures, made excellent sketches, and carried out hundreds of determinations of latitude, longitude, barometric pressure, and geomagnetic orientation and intensity."[42]

As a youth, Agassiz was a model of industry; he led in his studies and soon mastered the classical learning that was available to him in the Collège de Bienne in his native Switzerland, but this was not enough.

> He wanted to become a naturalist, and without the entire approval of his family, he extended his studies and his field researches. Even as a boy he revealed both his ambition and his determination. He decided to become the greatest naturalist of his generation, and he determined that no person, no hardship, and no obstacle should deter him.
>
> He was remarkably well equipped for his chosen career. He learned easily and quickly, and he retained great masses of facts almost automatically and without effort. He also understood what he learned and he could organize his knowledge and recognize the underlying principles in his accumulated data, as he showed when he classified the fishes of the world and when he devised his theory of continental glaciers.[43]

An example of early assumption of responsibility for a heavy load of teaching and editing, and of a compelling drive to achieve, is found in the life and work of Charles J. Herrick, the neurologist, who died at the age of 91, before he had completed all he had planned to do. At one time he served as editor, business manager without a secretary, proofreader, and supervisor of the printing of engravings for the *Journal of Comparative Neurology*, paying the deficits of the journal from his own salary. When invited to the University of Chicago as professor of neurology in 1907, Herrick hesitated to make so radical a change because of

[41] Bruce Bliven, "Our Legacy from Mr. Jefferson." *Reader's Digest* 42: 160–68; March 1963.

[42] Quoted from review by A. O. Woodford, *Science* 140: 973; May 31, 1963, of L. Kellner, *Alexander von Humboldt*. New York: Oxford University Press, 1963. viii + 247 p.

[43] Quoted from review by Conway Zirkle, *Science* 132: 1655–56; December 2, 1960, of Edward Lurie, *Louis Agassiz: A Life in Science*. Chicago: University of Chicago Press, 1960. 449 p. Reprinted from *Science* by permission.

his health, but his wife's question decided the issue: "Would you rather go to Chicago and burn out or stay here and rust out?"[44]

Motivation and the Historian. The accomplishments of Douglas Southall Freeman in his 67 years, as editor, historian and biographer, educator, and broadcaster and lecturer are attributed to discipline and hard work through almost incredible hours. In his own words, "Outside writing by a newspaperman is primarily a matter of forgetting other things. He cannot do his day's work, share all the social activities that others enjoy, and still have time for historical research or literary work. If he wants the leisure that unhurried composition and painstaking revision demand, he must pay the price." With iron discipline, Freeman cheerfully paid the price through a daily working schedule that stretched over 17 hours, usually rising at 3:15 A.M. and retiring at 8:00 P.M.[45]

Historians frequently have been prodigious workers with remarkable powers of concentration. Ranke continued incessantly busy at work until the age of ninety-one, driving his assistants to the point of exhaustion. He lived a long life, during which he produced some 50 volumes of history. Lord Acton tells of his last meeting with Ranke, who at that time, in 1876, was past eighty. Acton says of him: "He was feeble, sunken, and almost blind, scarcely able to read or write. He uttered his farewell with a kindly emotion, and I feared that the next I should hear of him would be the news of his death." However, Ranke produced another group of volumes before his death in 1886, including a *World History,* which was broken off somewhere in the late Middle Ages.[46]

Compelling Drive and the Psychologist. It is not strange that strong motivation should play a prominent role in the life and work of psychologists. Edwin G. Boring attributes his achievements in research and writing to certain irresistible compulsions, to a capacity for hard work, and to a persistent sense of insecurity during the earlier decades of his life. He says that his compulsive temperament drove him hard, especially during the 1920's, on an eighty-hour week, fifty-week year, which he found near his physiological limit. Somehow Boring had persuaded himself that he was not as bright as most of his colleagues and could make up for the deficiency by working harder. This decade produced his *History of Experimental Psychology,* a major work, although Boring feared for a time that psychologists would regard history as less important than laboratory experimentation. In 1934–35 Boring spent 168 sessions, $1680 at the

44 George W. Bartelmez, "Charles Judson Herrick, Neurologist." *Science* 131: 1654–55; June 3, 1960.
45 Charles H. Hamilton, "The Most Unforgettable Character I've Met." *Reader's Digest* 77: 149–54; July 1960.
46 Pieter Geyl, *From Ranke to Toynbee: Five Lectures on Historians and Historiographical Problems.* Northampton, Mass.: Smith College Studies in History, 1952. p. 3.

special reduced rate, in psychoanalysis with Hanns Sachs, because he felt himself insecure, unhappy, frustrated, afraid, and unproductive, and for many years thereafter continued his search for maturity, although most psychologists have envied Boring for his achievements as experimentalist, teacher, critic, theorist, administrator, popular expositor, and editor.

Lewis M. Terman had tremendous drive and persistence that lasted in his pursuit of knowledge all through his life, in spite of setbacks with tuberculosis, being burned in a fire, breaking a hip, and other disabilities.

When Lewis M. Terman died, near the end of his 80th year, he was working on the manuscript of volume 5 of *Genetic Studies of Genius* and was simultaneously planning the next 3 years' research on his group of 1500 "gifted children." No other facts could mark the man so well. From 1903, when he arrived at Clark University to begin graduate work, until his death, his career was a continuous sequence of research and writing, broken now and then by illness and accident but never interrupted in its main course.[47]

Motivation and the Sociologist. Illustrations of the driving force of intellectual curiosity and of related types of motivation are available in the field of sociology. The sociologist, Lester F. Ward (1841–1913), was the youngest of ten children, whose mechanic father had a tendency to drift from place to place in his work. When Ward was sixteen his father died, and the boy went to Pennsylvania to live with a brother, where he worked on a farm and in a sawmill for his board and room. In his spare time he made wagon hubs, which were traded for books, articles of clothing, and other things that he needed. Ward picked up a scattered education, largely undirected, although he attained some proficiency in French, German, Greek, and Latin. Later in Washington, while an employee of the government, he was able to earn the A.B., LL.B., M.A., and LL.D. degrees. When Ward left government service in 1906 and went to teach sociology at Brown University at the age of sixty-five, he had achieved a full lifetime of outstanding work in botany, geology, and paleontology, and was regarded as the leading sociologist in America. Ward was characterized by an impressive command of his subject and by a "terrific mental drive."[48]

Another example of delay in beginning collegiate academic work and subsequent high purpose is found in the life of the sociologist Howard Becker (1899–1960), who left school at the age of 14, worked as a laborer in the West, later became an industrial engineer, and then in 1922 turned

---

[47] Quoted from Robert R. Sears, "L. M. Terman, Pioneer in Mental Measurement." *Science* 125: 978–79; May 17, 1957. Reprinted from *Science* by permission.
[48] Emory S. Bogardus, *op. cit.*, p. 305–23.
M. C. Elmer, *op. cit.*, p. 11, 127–28.

to academic pursuits, receiving the A.B. degree in 1925, the A.M. in 1926, and the Ph.D. in 1930.[49]

A rugged physique and dogged determination helped George Lundberg accomplish tasks that others thought very difficult. One night in Wisconsin, when driving with another professor, the car stopped because of carburetor trouble. Lundberg walked eight miles to the next town, found a place to buy repair parts, then walked back to the car and put it in running order. His philosophy of work was: "When anything needs to be done—do it." Lundberg considered large-scale studies and quantitative methods important, but said: "I sometimes wonder whether the most important research done in the world is not what people steal time from the regular employment to do, rather than what they are paid and honored for doing."

Other Examples of Compelling Motivation. Strong motivation impelled Ellwood P. Cubberley to draw up careful plans for retirement, with his projects scheduled by years and the achievements checked against the calendar. He expected his program of writing to continue after retirement, including the editing of his series of professional textbooks in education. As early as 1913, Cubberley estimated what his income would be that year, at the age of forty-five, again for 1915, and at five-year intervals to the age of seventy-five.[50]

The years as Commissioner of Education in Rhode Island were probably the happiest and most successful in Henry Barnard's career. His educational statesmanship and prodigious work were reflected in numerous reforms, almost countless addresses and visitations, and his famous annual reports. A trait that became habitual was to outline carefully in advance whatever he planned to do.[51]

Seeking to explain such extraordinary manifestations of concentration and intensity in the form of powerful driving impulses or compulsions, we enter the realm of depth psychology.

What is the significance of this extraordinary concentration and intensity? What powerful impulses are driving their way at such moments? For there is every reason to suppose that men of genius are characterized by possessing exceptionally strong emotions and usually a correspondingly strong capacity for containing them. The tension induced by the preceding efforts to find a solution gradually mounts until it reaches a climax. The great mathematician of genius, Henri Poincaré, in describing how he made his own discoveries, said: "One is struck by these appearances of sudden illumination, obvious indications of a long course of previous unconscious work. . . . These sudden

---

[49] Hans H. Gerth, "Howard Becker, 1899–1960." *American Sociological Review* 25: 743–44; October 1960.
[50] Jesse B. Sears and Adin D. Henderson, *op. cit.,* p. 229–30.
[51] Richard K. Morris, "Parnassus on Wheels: A Biographical Sketch of Henry Barnard, 1811–1900." *Teacher Education Quarterly* 18: 45–57; Winter 1960–61.

inspirations are never produced except after some days of voluntary efforts which appeared absolutely fruitless." Einstein has given a very similar description, and in the Fliess correspondence there are numerous allusions to the exhausting stress and strain Freud experienced in the continuously hard work of attaining his various pieces of insight. Kretschmer speaks of the great scientists' "passionate emotions developing which drive their thought constantly in the same direction, producing the utmost tension until at last a short-circuit occurs: somewhere a spark leaps to a new spot where up till then no human thought had ever passed."[52]

BACKGROUND OF SCHOLARSHIP AND PERSONAL CHARACTERISTICS

The analysis of the hallmarks of the scientist and scholar in Chapter 1, and the earlier section of the present chapter dealing with advanced study and reading, are pertinent to a discussion of criteria for selection of the problem for investigation. Illustrations of the part played by training and certain personal or temperamental characteristics in choice and development of research problems will be drawn from such fields as psychology, sociology, history, education, and other areas of scholarship and research. Frequently, training or scholarship in other (cognate) fields (for example, physics, mathematics, physiology, biology, medicine, philosophy) has provided important background for the early development of psychology and psychologists, and later through psychology for the field of education.

Besides great scholarship, Thomas Aquinas also became a Christian saint, having been dedicated to a religious life as a member of the Dominican Order. When Thomas was twenty, in 1245, he went to Paris to study under Albert the Great. After further study in Cologne, and again in Paris, he was so accelerated as a student that, instead of having to await his thirty-fourth birthday, as regulation required, a papal dispensation granted him his Magistrate (doctorate) in theology in 1256 at the age of thirty-one.[53]

As to breadth of scholarship and service, the biography of a Nobel Peace Prize winner appropriately carries the title, *The Three Worlds of Albert Schweitzer;* he was an eminent organist and author of musical studies, a scholarly theologian and author of religious works, and an heroic physician in Africa.[54]

Scholarship in Education. Harold Rugg (1886–1960) was versatile and talented and was at the forefront of many significant movements in edu-

[52] Quoted from Ernest Jones, "Nature of Genius." *Scientific Monthly* 84: 75–83; February 1957.

[53] Robert I. Watson, *The Great Psychologists.* Philadelphia: J. B. Lippincott Co., 1963. p. 107–11.

[54] Robert Payne, *The Three Worlds of Albert Schweitzer.* New York: Thomas Nelson & Sons, 1957.

cation. He first taught engineering, wrote one of the first books in educational statistics, did extensive work in test development during World War I, wrote social studies textbooks, pioneered in progressive education, played a major part in developing the "foundations" courses in education, and explored aesthetics and creativity in relation to education. The fact that he sometimes stammered in speaking did not lessen his effectiveness and influence in conveying a challenging message to his audience or class.[55]

William C. Bagley (1874–1946), characterized as a stalwart educator, had the advantage of graduate study in psychology under Joseph Jastrow at Wisconsin and E. B. Titchener at Cornell, and of early association with William T. Harris in St. Louis. In spite of his competence in the various professional activities of surveys, editing, writing, lecturing, and teaching, Bagley showed evident signs of nervousness before he entered a classroom or mounted a platform to speak, but once started, usually with a slight nervous cough, he went forward with clarity and conviction to the end. Bagley's claim to a prominent place in the history of American education is not based on a reputation as a reformer or innovator, but on his balanced point of view and steady sense of direction in the midst of a succession of innovations relating to educational aims, methods, and content.[56]

An example of productive activity is found in the life and work of Ellwood P. Cubberley, who made early contributions to educational history, administration and school surveys, and textbook editing. Early in his career Cubberley learned certain elementary but useful concepts of research, at a time during the first decade of the twentieth century when the field of education was just beginning to develop. Cubberley had studied some phases of the method of historical research while preparing his syllabus in the history of education. During his graduate work at Columbia University he secured what was then an acceptable introduction to statistical method, a new field being developed by Edward L. Thorndike. In the course of his doctor's dissertation he learned useful procedures of a descriptive-survey type, as he found his way factually into the then unexplored field of school administration.[57]

Cubberley's long and busy life was spent in building a small department of education into a school of wide reputation, developing his own field of work, carrying a full-time schedule of teaching, writing and editing books, and serving as consultant and adviser. Of the 106 books in the professional series that Cubberley edited, he wrote ten, fifteen others

55 B. O. Smith, "Harold Rugg: A Memoir." *Educational Theory* 10: 176–78; July, 1960.

56 I. L. Kandel, *William Chandler Bagley: Stalwart Educator.* New York: Bureau of Publications, Teachers College, Columbia University, 1961. ix + 131 p.

57 Jesse B. Sears and Adin D. Henderson, *op. cit.*, p. 87–88, 97–98.

bore the names of his colleagues, and a number of others were prepared by his former students. Cubberley's ten books in this series sold to the number of 341,000 copies, and the figures for the entire series of 106 books amounted to "approximately 3,070,000 copies."

In summary, Cubberley contributed to five areas of activity: as teacher, educational historian, writer in school administration, investigator and consultant, and editor and author of textbooks. His insight in developing and editing the series of professional textbooks in education is significant, especially as viewed against the background of the undeveloped status of education when plans were first made for the series in 1911.

> School administration was scarcely recognized as a field of study. The curriculum, as a field, had hardly been thought of. The psychology was at most only partly applicable and parts of it were being questioned as to their validity. The literature on methods and management and on supervision was little more than armchair opinion. Educational theory was vague and general at best. There were books promoting special systems of arithmetic or of reading but the systems had been conjured from successful experience, not from careful observation and experiment.[58]

Scholarship in Psychology. Alfred Binet (1857–1911), destined to become a psychologist, received a law degree in 1878, studied the sciences and medicine, took a degree in the natural sciences in 1890, and a doctorate in sciene in 1894 with a thesis on the nervous system of insects.

The versatility of Francis Galton, born in 1822, is illustrated by studies of spectacles for divers, the breeding of rabbits, gregariousness in cattle, a statistical analysis of the efficacy of prayer, visualized movement, composite portraitures, color blindness, outfitting an anthropometric laboratory, the Australian marriage system, dice for statistical experiments, arithmetic by smell, and the speed of trotting horses. He pioneered in bringing about a union between psychological methods of measurement and the theory of evolution.

William James (1842–1910) is regarded as the first great psychologist in the United States, although prior to the awarding of an honorary degree at the 1903 Harvard Commencement he went about for days, half in jest and half in earnest, insisting that he was a philosopher, dreading to hear President Eliot's citation pronounce him "psychologist."

Terman's long lifetime of research and writing followed up the pioneer area of his doctoral dissertation.

> The half-century since Terman finished his doctoral training is almost coincident with the history of mental testing. So is Lewis Terman. From the first, there was something provocative and exciting to him in the very idea of

[58] *Ibid.*, p. 191–94.

measuring complex psychological qualities. His doctoral dissertation was a comparison of seven bright and seven dull schoolboys. He gave each child a battery of more than 40 hours of individual tests, probably the most overwhelming test-assault inflicted on any child up to that time. Nothing much came of the study, but it did give Terman a chance to try his hand at making up tests. He loved it, and he went right on loving it to the end of his life. He built test after test for 40 years, all of them good (technically) and nearly all of them useful.[59]

Terman and Merrill—that means, since Terman has gone, Maud Merrill James—have now come out with the 1960 revision of the Stanford-Binet Intelligence Scale. . . . It is a thread through Terman's lifetime, with a prenatal phase fixed in the Binet-Simon scale of 1908 and now this postmortem by Maud Merrill.

In a way Stanley Hall was the godfather, much as he disapproved of tests. His Clark Ph.D.'s, when he was being so deeply concerned with psychology in education, tended to turn up teaching at normal schools. Stanford wanted an educational psychologist. It got Bergström, a Hall man, who unexpectedly died in 1910. Then Stanford invited Huey, another Hall man, who refused in order to stay at Hopkins, and who recommended Terman, a third Hallian, then at the Los Angeles State Normal School, at the same time advising Terman to take the job and to make the development of Binet-Simon intelligence testing his main endeavor in his new post. The result presently was the Stanford Revision of the Binet scale in 1916, introducing the IQ as a practical concept. Then ten years of testing the tests, in association with Maud Merrill, and the Terman-Merrill revision of 1937, improved, extended at the ends, with two forms. Then more years of criticism and now the third distillate, carried through to completion by Dr. Merrill after Terman's death in 1956. It is a single form that keeps the "best" items and continues to push the concept measured, "intelligence," over toward the Binet type of general functioning, "mental adaptability to new problems," "intelligence in action," away from the more manipulative abilities.

So that is one strand in psychology's warp, 57 years long if you start with Binet's *L'étude expérimentale de l'intelligence* of 1903 and come right on up to now. For 46 of those years Lewis Terman was weaving the weft on the warp, and for 30 of them Maud Merrill.[60]

Arnold Gesell (1880–1961), in a remarkably single-minded effort, concentrated his life on scientific investigation and guidance of child behavior, serving from time to time as school teacher and principal, graduate student in psychology, professor of psychology, medical student, clinical psychologist, physician, investigator, author, and teacher.[61]

59 Quoted from Robert R. Sears, *op. cit.*
60 Quoted from E. G. Boring, "Revised Revision Revised." *Contemporary Psychology* 5: 187; June 1960.
61 Louise B. Ames, "Arnold L. Gesell: 'Behavior Has Shape'." *Science* 134: 266–67; July 28, 1961.

To cite specific instances of the contributions of other fields of scholarship to the background of psychologists, Wundt, physician and physiologist, accepted a chair of philosophy at Leipzig in 1875, although his place is that of a founder in the history of psychology. Stanley Hall came into psychology with a diversified background of theological preparation, European study, college teaching, and physiology. The broad training and experience of Edward B. Titchener covered music, collection of coins, classical languages, half a dozen modern languages, linguistics and philology, biology, physiology, and anthropology.

Although many of the founders of modern psychology came from philosophy or other basic disciplines, it is also true that a number of modern psychologists have entered the field as graduates of other areas of specialization: Edwin G. Boring, L. L. Thurstone, and Edward C. Tolman from engineering, Godfrey Thomson from physics, Jean Piaget from natural science. Tolman speaks of a number of sources that influenced his psychological points of view: the Gestalt psychologists, a year's stay in Vienna (involving both the academic and psychoanalytical traditions of European psychology), war experiences that developed points of view relating to personality psychology, and contacts with a group of workers interested in sociology, anthropology, personality, and social psychology. Walter Bingham's interest in music as a hobby led to a topic for his doctoral dissertation dealing with the nature of melody.

Scholarship in History. Many historians have drawn on an exceptional background of training and scholarship. Barthold Niebuhr at the age of eighteen knew 18 European languages, as well as Hebrew, Persian, and Arabic. His phenomenal memory was an enormous asset as he went on to master philosophy, mathematics, physics, chemistry, natural history, history, Roman law, and practical politics and administration. The great German scholar, Theodore Mommsen, published 1,513 different titles, and was a scholar in at least six fields of knowledge: epigraphy, numismatics, history, law, archaeology, and early Italian philology. Adolf von Harnack published at least 1,800 titles of books and articles, a record that invites comparison with Mommsen.

Scholarship in Sociology. Examples from sociology indicate the varied training, broad scholarship, and wide reading of the pioneers in this field. Lester F. Ward studied and read philosophy, medicine, law, botany, geology, and anthropology. William G. Sumner had at his command a dozen languages in studying cultural-anthropological problems, and did extensive reading in history, theology, metaphysics, and general literature. Franklin H. Giddings read extensively in European philosophy and sociology, and had six years of experience in journalism and six years of teaching in experimental school situations.

Although officially classified as a sociologist, William F. Ogburn (1886–

1959) had far-reaching interests that carried him through all the social sciences for almost 50 years of research and teaching. He wrote in 1932 about the death of the great German psychologist:

> When Wilhelm Wundt died in 1920 it was remarked that the last of the great men who knew it all had passed away. Seventeen years earlier when Herbert Spencer died he took with him a greater range of knowledge than Wundt had possessed. . . . Previous to Spencer there were many great intellects that covered the whole field of human knowledge. . . . Wundt was the last of the old men of our modern civilized tribes.[62]

> Ogburn, in his interests and works, must be called the last of the great social scientists who wished to know it all. It is a tribute both to the man who was able to foresee events and to the social sciences that the field has become so diversified and the total volume of knowledge so large that no one man can any longer expect to know all the social sciences.[63]

In his wide travels, Ogburn revealed his interests in the arts and natural history, as well as social life, with special knowledge of the dances of Indonesia, the music of India, the bird life of Burma, the vegetation of the Alps, the textiles of Guatemala, and the marine life of the Florida Coast. From 1910 to 1918 he taught economics, politics, history, and sociology. At one time he served as Chairman of the Psychoanalytic Institute of Chicago.[64]

Personal Traits, Special Talents, and Achievement. The earlier discussions of advanced study, critical reading, and creative scholarship, as well as the illustrations just presented, remind us that classroom instruction and the library are only part of the background and setting for the accomplishments of scientists and scholars. Able scientists sometimes have not appeared to good advantage in meeting formal examination requirements. The examiners recognized the special talents of Paul Ehrlich, German scientist and physician, and somewhat reluctantly passed him on his final medical examinations. History records that Einstein failed at the entrance examinations to the Polytechnic School. It is possible that the inventive scientist or creative scholar may even be at a disadvantage in accumulating the factual information frequently tested on formal examinations, in contrast to the bright student with a good memory who accepts uncritically what he is told or what he reads. Graduate students sometimes quote with appreciation the reply of George

[62] Quoted from W. F. Ogburn, "Volume of Knowledge." *Journal of Adult Education* 4: 26–29; January 1932.

[63] Quoted from A. J. Jaffe, "William Fielding Ogburn, Social Scientist." *Science* 130: 319–20; August 7, 1959. Reprinted from *Science* by permission.

[64] M. F. Nimkoff, "William Fielding Ogburn, 1886–1959." *American Sociological Review* 24: 563–65; August 1959.

Lyman Kittredge, American philologist and author, when he was asked why he did not qualify for a Ph.D. degree: "Who would give me the examination?"

Although Alfred Binet's intelligence scale has been considered as probably the most important development in all the history of psychology, in the first decade of his own professional development Binet encountered failures and made serious errors of judgment and methodology. He began in 1880 as an armchair psychologist, stating categorically that all problems in psychology could be solved by appropriate application of the laws of association of ideas by contiguity and similarity, accepted wholeheartedly belief in mental images as the basis for thought, and went astray in the field of hypnotic phenomena and methodological controls. These facts may prove comforting, or even encouraging, to others who encounter difficulties or make errors in their investigations.[65]

Such examples appear to be contradictions in the traits and training of a great man. Winston Churchill could get nowhere in mathematics at school, yet became Chancellor of the Exchequer and put together the extremely complicated budget of Great Britain. He could make little sense of Latin or Greek, never graduated from Harrow, and never went to a university, yet received dozens of honorary degrees from some of the world's major universities and produced historical works read the world over. While at Harrow, Churchill's dislike of Latin and mathematics did result in intensive instruction in English grammar and English literature, which served him well later in becoming a famous speaker and author.

A high grade record may be evidence of high intelligence, but it may also be evidence of a tendency to social conformity which may be undesirable for research. Indeed, many types of deviant behavior may be assets in a research man. For example, rejection of authority, perseveration on "pet" ideas, unwillingness to commit energy in subject areas of low interest, and general independence of thinking are all probably desirable characteristics for research. These same characteristics, however, may result in an appearance of undesirable deviation from the norm—for example, in a spotty grade record. Evidence of high intelligence is important, but this need not be in the form of a high grade average. Even more important, evidence must be sought of those characteristics such as independence of thought and creativity without which high intelligence is of little use in research.[66]

The greatness of George Washington is not obscured by the fact that he possessed quite human and personal characteristics: a strong vocabulary (although he once issued an order that banned any swearing throughout

    [65] Theta H. Wolf, "Alfred Binet: A Time of Crisis." *American Psychologist* 19: 762–71; September 1964.
    [66] Quoted from Donald W. Taylor and Others, "Education for Research in Psychology." *American Psychologist* 14: 167–79; April 1959.

the U. S. Army), a poor speller, difficulty in getting the names of even close friends right, something of a hypochondriac, unsmiling, solemn, moody, sensitive, and easily hurt by criticism.

For some scientists and scholars certain traits of personality or temperament have helped at times; others have been hindered in their work and influence on advanced students. The personal factor manifests itself in the very structure of science, as in any act of choice, appraisal, or accreditation.

Personal Traits and Psychology. Psychologists have been cautioned that overemphasis on factual materials and formal requirements in graduate work may actually inhibit development of creativity, scholarship, and individual talents. It is agreed that knowledge of facts is important for research, but much of the factual knowledge of the mature scientist has been accumulated during the course of his career rather than through specific graduate instruction. More attention should be given to methods of individual study and development as tools for use whenever additional knowledge may be needed. Statistical competence, scholarship, and theoretical sophistication are important as means toward the end of contribution to knowledge, but not as ends in themselves as part of a formal or rigid graduate program.[67]

From a long life of direct contacts with psychologists, Wallin sketches many interesting pictures of personalities.[68] For example, Ladd is described as a scholar of profound erudition, an indefatigable worker, and an amazingly productive author. Wallin draws a picture of Ladd as a somewhat aloof person, with a coldly analytical mind, endowed with the rare power of systematically pursuing a sustained line of thought in his class lectures without recourse to, or with very little dependence on, notes, and with the same inexorable logic, precision of verbal expression, and freedom from rambling that characterized his textbooks. Ladd's sentence structure was so exact that it gave the impression he was reading chapters verbatim from one of his books. He was the author of some 33 books, including revisions but exclusive of articles, at least 28 of which were in the fields of psychology, philosophy, ethics, religion, and education. Unfortunately, his style of writing was ponderous and involved, which robbed him of the recognition from his colleagues he so richly deserved, and he was not accorded the acclaim by psychologists at large that was his just due by virtue of outstanding ability and accomplishments. One of Ladd's anecdotes was to the effect that one day on the campus a former student accosted him and said about one of Ladd's most recent books: "Professor, that was a corking book you issued recently, but it is way above my head." Ladd's quick retort was: "The book

67 Donald W. Taylor and Others, *op. cit.*
68 J. E. Wallace Wallin, *op. cit.*, p. 12–24.

may be above your head, but God understands it, and so does Ladd, and possibly President Hadley [of Yale] also."

William James' work reveals both his early exposure to his father's therapeutic Swedenborgianism and his incipient awareness of psychoanalysis, with the latter culminating in the walk he took with Sigmund Freud in 1909, when Freud made his only visit to America.

> Commenting on that visit in one of his letters, William James noted the intellectual tenacity of his companion—"a man obsessed with fixed ideas" but insisted characteristically that no impediment be placed in the way of his working out the full implications. Freud in a corresponding comment recalled James' remarkable courage in the face of an attack of angina pectoris which he suffered during the walk; the victim asked his companion to walk ahead and leave him to his recovery. James did recover and continued the walk, but the following year he was dead.[69]

Personal Traits and Anthropology and Sociology. We have been reminded that anthropology, as a scholarly profession, has drawn more than its share of nonconformists who are comforted by its findings that each culture has its own values and standards of behavior, and that the demands of our own society are no more right in an absolute sense than those of any other culture. Although Ruth Benedict seemed to be an exception, with a good adjustment to her world, her published writings reveal a nonconformist individual (in effect a private self and a social self) who finally found a creative outlet, and possibly relief, in anthropology.[70]

Although Gillin's interest in sociological theory and history of social thought was active and productive, his reputation rested mainly on his critically constructive work and extensive writings in criminology and penology, and on his equally important role as adviser, consultant, and administrator in Wisconsin.

> Within Wisconsin, Professor Gillin was known to many people who were relatively unfamiliar with his scholarly achievements; what he meant to them was immediate, direct, and personal. It was mainly his interest in social reforms which touched their lives closely. Many a prisoner was grateful that Professor Gillin not only launched programs looking toward his betterment but also took a warm and friendly interest in him as a human being. . . .
>
> It may well be that this combination of honesty, simplicity, warmth, and firm principle accounts for his remarkable influence in advancing many social reforms in Wisconsin. It would be a stubborn legislator or administrator who

---

[69] Quoted from review by Saul Rosenzweig, "The Jameses' Stream of Consciousness." *Contemporary Psychology* 3: 250–57; September 1958, of Frederick W. Dupee, Editor, *Henry James: Autobiography.* New York: Criterion Books, Inc., 1956. xiv + 622 p.

[70] Margaret Mead, *An Anthropologist at Work: Writings of Ruth Benedict.* Boston: Houghton Mifflin Company, 1959. xxii + 583 p.

could not be brought to see the wisdom of the proposals that Professor Gillin took the trouble to recommend.[71]

At times, traits of personality or temperament (or a feeling of self-sufficiency) have influenced able scholars to disregard the work of their fellows or to disagree sharply among themselves. Lester F. Ward had a feeling of self-sufficiency and finality about his own views and statements, and was outspoken in his rejection of other points of view. Another sociologist once commented on certain of Ward's conclusions as follows: "It appears to me that Ward's conclusions are not correct. However, I may not be a competent critic since Ward has stated that, because of my different point of view, I am not a sociologist."[72]

William G. Sumner (1840–1910) was one of the first teachers of sociology in the United States. He was never quite accepted by Small, Ward, or Giddings as a sociologist, but neither did Sumner accept them. Small expressed surprise when Sumner was elected president of the American Sociological Society: "It came to me consequently as a surprise and a shock that he was thought of as second president of the American Sociological Society. At that time (1907) he was not within my field of vision as even nominally a sociologist."

Personal Traits and Other Fields of Science

Newton had a markedly irritable and suspicious temperament, and much of the controversy that disfigured his life arose from his credulous belief in the statements of overcandid friends. In later life these qualities deteriorated for a while into paranoic delusions of persecution; perhaps in this connection it is not irrelevant to remark that Newton never fell in love and never married.

Faraday, the supreme physicist of the 19th century, had also his vein of credulousness. He said: "In early life I was a very imaginative lively person who could believe in the *Arabian Nights* as easily as in the *Encyclopedia,* but facts were important to me and saved me." Throughout his life he was an adherent of the obscure sect of Sandemanians, followers of the religious prophet Robert Sandeman, and for 3 years regularly preached sermons before them. One must place this in contrast with Faraday's exceptional intelligence in other spheres, since it would be commonplace otherwise.

Darwin was a man of far more placid temperament, and it is probable that any turmoil of emotions found their expression in the psychosomatic afflictions to which he was a martyr. But his skepticism was tempered by a credulous attitude toward other authorities. Even after his great discovery of the operation of evolution through natural selection he still believed in Lamarck's doctrine of evolution through the inheritance of acquired characters, a doctrine his own work had rendered superfluous and indeed erroneous.

[71] Quoted from Howard Becker and Neal B. DeNood, "John Lewis Gillin, 1871–1958." *American Sociological Review* 24: 562–63; August 1959.

[72] M. C. Elmer, *op. cit.,* p. 16, 21–22.

Emory S. Bogardus, *op. cit.,* p. 305–51.

His friend and contemporary Huxley offers a very interesting contrast to the genius Darwin. Although possessing a wider knowledge than Darwin, and gifted with more originality and a greater intellectual daring, Huxley's actual achievements are of a different order. On first reading Darwin's theory he exclaimed: "How extremely stupid of me not to have thought of that." Now, Huxley was endowed with any amount of skepticism, of indeed a rather pugnacious brand. It has been said of him: "He allowed himself no prejudice, no sentimentalities, no illusions." But there is no record in his life of any evidence of credulousness to match it and, according to my view, to enable him to make really great discoveries.[73]

Many scientists have been extremely modest people. Stating that the number of men widely recognized as possessing the attributes of genius is very small (Newton, Darwin, and Einstein), Jones speaks of Freud's disclaimer:

"The genius of Freud" is a phrase that has been used so widely that I think we must subscribe to a truth contained in it. Characteristically enough, Freud himself vehemently dissented from its being applied to him. Even as far back as 1886, when he was 29, he wrote to his betrothed: "There was a time when I grieved that Nature had not, in one of her gracious moods, impressed on me that stamp of genius as she sometimes does. Since then I have long known that I am no genius, and I no longer understand how I could have wished to be one. I am not even very talented; my whole capacity for work probably lies in my character attributes." On one occasion in later life when it was applied to him he burst out with the protest: "Geniuses are unbearable people. You have only to ask my family to know how easy a person I am to live with. So I cannot be a genius." This disclaimer, however, was based on a very partial definition of genius, so we need not take it too seriously.[74]

Pavlov urged modesty in seeking obstinately for the explanations of facts. "Never think you know it all. Though others may flatter you, retain the courage to say, 'I am ignorant.' Never be proud. And lastly, science must be your passion."[75]

SOURCES, TECHNIQUE, EQUIPMENT, AND WORKING CONDITIONS

Procedure and Equipment. The problems in selection of sources and method are closely related to the scholar's background of training and personal characteristics. The several methodological chapters of this book provide appropriate orientation for selection of a suitable technique for the problem at hand, although we should remember that investigators vary in their degree of devotion to highly formalized methods. When

[73] Quoted from Ernest Jones, *op. cit.*
[74] Quoted from Ernest Jones, *op. cit.*
[75] Quoted from Ivan Pavlov, *Scientific Monthly* 81: 129; September 1955.

a group of young sociologists, over-impressed by the rigors of formalized approaches in gathering data, quizzed Edward A. Ross about his methods of research, he smiled and replied:

> I am not a research man, I just write what I think best explains a process or a situation. For example, a number of years ago I decided to spend some time in China. I told everybody I was going to China and asked if they knew anybody there. By the time I left for China I had three thousand names and addresses of people: Chinese officials, Chinese scholars, coolie brothers of laundry men, beach combers, missionaries, teachers, relatives. I made up a list of five things I would like to know about changes taking place in China. I contacted, wherever possible, the names I had and countless others. When I talked with them at first our general conversation might lead to the person expressing himself on one or more of these five questions. If the answer did not come up naturally, I asked him questions. After the interview I would sit down on the side of the road on a stone or back in my room and write up, as nearly as possible, an exact account of what had been said to me. I returned to Wisconsin with many boxes full of notes and with the aid of some intelligent assistants classified these notes and put them in the form of a little book, *The Changing Chinese*. Nothing scientific about it, it was just what I had gathered from hundreds of sources.[76]

Ross traveled widely in the United States and abroad; he was a keen observer and recorder of social life.

As illustrated in the later chapters on research methods, special equipment or tools must be devised or adapted for certain types of investigation. Favorable working conditions are usually helpful, but not an absolute prerequisite to successful research or productive scholarship. The quality of scientific work depends much less on the complexity of the equipment or instruments than on the soundness of the thinking and the validity of the evidence, since the most important instrument or element in research is the mind of man. Work in improvised laboratories sometimes has produced remarkable results. There are many examples of great discoveries outside the laboratory or study.

> With John MacGillivray, son of the famous ornithologist, Huxley improvised dredging nets, often finding his specimens kicked off the deck by sailors; nevertheless, the lack of scientific instruments, the necessity of lashing his microscope to the mast, the paucity of scientific literature, and the presence of unsympathetic mates merely threw him upon his own resources.[77]

Appropriate illustrations may be drawn from the field of psychology. William James began instruction in experimental psychology at Harvard

[76] Quoted from M. C. Elmer, *op. cit.*, p. 33–34.
Emory S. Bogardus, *op. cit.*, p. 523–39.
[77] Quoted from Charles S. Blinderman, *op. cit.*

in 1875 with equipment described by Stanley Hall as a "tiny room under the stairway of Agassiz Museum . . . with a metronome, a device for whirling a frog, a horopter chart, and one or two bits of apparatus." However, as early as 1879 Stanley Hall exposed the fallacy of theatrical methods and "brass-instrument" psychology, insisting that curves, instruments, and flashing charts of themselves would not insure the accuracy of a doubtful generalization, and objecting to the fad of reducing everything to mechanics and motion (a movement that was spreading even in the 1870's). Lewis M. Terman was inept with apparatus just when American psychology was becoming brass-instrument conscious, but he found in Stanley Hall (not an apparatus man) an erudite interpreter of the mind, fitted himself into the Hall pattern, took his doctor's degree at Clark, and went on to the top in psychology, with specialization in mental testing and the gifted child.

Edward L. Thorndike modestly underrates his background in mentioning an extreme ineptitude and distaste on his part for using machinery and physical instruments. He regrets the absence in his training of a systematic course in the use of standard physiological and psychological apparatus for exposing, timing, and registering, and of extended preparation in mathematics. Yet William James once said of his pupil Thorndike that, more than any other contemporary, Thorndike had the quality most essential to a scientific man—the ability to see things apart from acquired perspective and personal reference. Thorndike, together with Charles H. Judd of the University of Chicago, revolutionized the techniques of educational investigation through emphasis on fact-finding, statistical, and experimental procedures.[78]

The work of many other psychologists has benefited from their considerable ingenuity in devising equipment or apparatus. Clark L. Hull conceived the idea of building a machine that would do nearly all of his correlation work automatically. Although Hull could not make mechanical drawings and his assistant could not read such drawings, they achieved their purpose by making marks free-hand on bits of paper at the mechanic's work bench; both had an idea of how the wheels should go around to do certain things.

An experimental geologist began graduate study with an extraordinary range of techniques and skills.

Skilled in observation, both by eye and with a camera; possessed of unusual ability to visualize lines, planes, and curved surfaces in three dimensions, thanks to superb training in geometry; master of the slide rule and possessing the engineer's knowledge of the mechanics of solids; of original bent and adept

[78] Merle Curti, *The Social Ideas of American Educators*. Revised Edition. Paterson, N.J.: Littlefield, Adams and Co., 1959. p. 459-60.

in the use of machine tools; and keenly interested in determining the how and why of natural phenomena and in developing ways and means of demonstrating and applying these phenomena, Warren Mead was exceptionally well equipped to attack both quantitatively and experimentally the whole broad front of physical geology as he entered Wisconsin's graduate school in 1906.[79]

Important as apparatus is, we are warned that too great dependence on expensive or elaborate equipment may actually restrict freedom in research if the investigator proves reluctant or unwilling to leave his apparatus to do research in other important fields.

Another thing that we can't do without is apparatus. Some ideas, some projects call for lots of expensive equipment. If a man has acquired a large-scale accelerator, a big radio telescope, or a large-scale computer, or if he has set to work on a large-scale experimental system of some sort, he is not likely to walk out on it because an attractive idea in some other field occurs to him. If a systems experiment is shackling him, he can abandon it if it is bad or complete it if it is good, but if he has an accelerator, a radio telescope, or a computer around his neck, he may be stuck in a field for life. This isn't fatal, of course; he can direct his thoughts to the field in question and have and pursue ideas in that field only. But he has lost freedom in that there is little chance that he will actually do something else, however much he may daydream about it. If he wants to recover his freedom, he can perhaps find a substitute, put him in charge, and leave him holding the bag.[80]

Working Conditions and Environment. Varied conditions of work and environment have contributed to the solution of important problems, depending in part on the temperament of the scientist or scholar. Helmholtz has said that, after working on a problem for some time, happy ideas for a solution frequently came to him at some place other than his working table. Some scientists have claimed that an unexpected insight or intuition, at times in sleep, produces the answer to a problem, although these solutions probably do not take place spontaneously in the absence of adequate preparation; rather, such "insights" come from a mind with a rich background of knowledge. Scientists and scholars have reported certain conditions or environmental settings are favorable to the emergence of solutions to problems: freedom from competing problems or worries, periods of relaxation or sleep, and recovery from fatigue. In so far as Helmholtz offers an explanatory theory, it is based on fatigue associated with development of the problem and procedure, and recovery

[79] Quoted from Robert R. Shrock, "W. J. Mead, Experimental Geologist." *Science* 132: 1235–6; October 28, 1960. Reprinted from *Science* by permission.

[80] Quoted from J. R. Pierce, "Freedom in Research." *Science* 130: 540–42; September 4, 1959. Reprinted from *Science* by permission.

from fatigue. In 1896, at a dinner in honor of his seventieth birthday, Helmholtz spoke of his methods of work on original problems as follows:

> I must say that those fields of work have become ever more agreeable to me in which one need not depend on lucky accidents and "happy thoughts." But as I have found myself pretty often in the uncomfortable position of [waiting for thoughts my story is useful to others]; . . . they never came to a fatigued brain and never at the writing desk. It was always necessary, first of all, that I should have turned my problem over on all sides to such an extent that I had all its angles and complexities "in my head" and could run through them freely without writing. To bring the matter to that point is usually impossible without long preliminary labor. Then, after the fatigue resulting from this labor had passed away, there must come an hour of complete physical freshness and quiet well-being, before the good ideas arrived. Often they were there in the morning when I awoke, just according to Goethe's oft-cited verses, and as Gauss also once noted. But they liked specially to make their appearance while I was taking an easy walk over wooded hills in sunny weather. The smallest amount of alcohol seemed to frighten them away.[81]

A characterization or analysis of the nature of genius takes cognizance of examples of intuition or spontaneity in problem-solving, but recognizes that this feature is not always present in research and scholarly activity.

> This seems to accord with the frequency with which geniuses often receive their inspiration in a sudden flash that startles the recipient himself. It is a feature that has always been recognized. Both Plato and Aristotle commented on it, and they associated it with the divine source of the inspiration. The description of Apollo in the third book of *Hyperion* seemed to Keats to have come by chance or magic—to be, as it were, something given to him. He said also that he had often not been aware of the beauty of some thought or expression until after he had composed and written it down. It had then struck him with astonishment and seemed rather the production of another person than his own. Alfred Russell Wallace wrote: "Finally both Darwin and myself, at the critical period, had our attention directed to the system of *positive checks* as expounded by Malthus in his *Principles of Population*. The effect was analogous to that of friction upon the specially prepared match, producing that flash of insight which led us immediately to the simple but universal law of the 'survival of the fittest.' " This is, however, a feature by no means always present. The flash of insight which Wallace described did presumably happen to him, but Darwin himself seems to have reflected on the suggestion more calmly. No one can have accepted revelation more tardily and gradually, even cautiously and very timidly, than Darwin, whose dawning vision came only as the result of many years of hard work.[82]

81 Quoted from Robert S. Woodworth and Harold Schlosberg, *Experimental Psychology*. Revised Edition. New York: Holt, Rinehart and Winston, Inc., 1954. p. 838.
82 Quoted from Ernest Jones, *op. cit.*

We do not know the optimum of gregariousness needed for creativity. Is the ideal university really a student on one end of a log with Mark Hopkins on the other end? We can hardly imagine a scientist contributing to knowledge without any social stimulus at all. Group interaction and stimulation frequently aid scientists and scholars in exchange of information, understanding, making judgments, and in developing creativity. The stimulus may come from another individual, a small group, a larger group, or from the general community. The national meetings of scientific and scholarly societies are now so large, however, that they may provide only limited intellectual satisfaction, as compared with the stimulation derived from small closed symposia. The effective small group probably needs members of different background and temperament—a skilled experimenter or research specialist, an enthusiast full of ideas, a judicious scholar equally sensitive to promising leads and sterile ideas, and a compromiser or peacemaker.[83] We know that many creative individuals work best with constant stimulation from small groups with common interests —disciples, or peers, or students; for example, the psychologist, Clark Hull, received great support from his "in-group," which came to extend far beyond the Yale campus. Both the dedicated individual and the cohesive small group with a purpose may contribute to science and scholarship.

While constructive interaction among colleagues does provide a stimulating atmosphere for realization of the full creative capacity of the scientist, too many nonprofessional assistants may prove distracting, although such helpers are needed by the scientist who is doing routine development work or is administrative head of a large laboratory or department. If the major purpose of the investigator is fundamental research, however, too many aides may require so much supervision as to rob the scientist of precious time, particularly when he becomes the equivalent of a straw boss in a factory.[84]

To cite examples of the desire of scholars to study in peace, René Descartes, born in 1596, had unusual habits of work. During his early years of study in the College of La Flèche he was in frail health, and was allowed to stay in bed in the mornings, where he did his lessons and developed the habit of long-sustained reflection and analysis-practices that he continued through most of his life. Although Descartes preferred to live quietly, his thinking attracted considerable attention, and during the twenty most productive years of his life he moved frequently from one

83 Philip H. Abelson, "Group Interaction among Scientists." *Science* 148: 447; April 23, 1965.

84 Philip H. Abelson, "A Favorable Environment for Research." *Science* 139: 875; March 8, 1963.

Edwin G. Boring, "The Social Stimulus to Creativity." *Science* 142: 622–23; November 8, 1963.

to another of his 24 Dutch hideouts, in order to avoid the distractions of friends and personal contacts. Although he sought solitude for meditating and writing, he corresponded with his peers, got into controversies, and cultivated the acquaintance of some persons whom he admired.

Simplicity of living and study arrangements is illustrated in the case of Immanuel Kant (1724–1804), who was never more than sixty miles from his birth place in East Prussia, never married, took a walk at the same hour each day, habitually gazed at a church steeple while meditating, and when fame came to him had to change restaurants for his noonday meal in order to avoid sightseers. He devoted his entire life to ideas—never did anything except "think."[85]

Wilhelm Wundt (1832–1920), son of a Lutheran pastor, was a solitary child, never close to his parents, played little, absorbed himself in study, and even as a young child stayed in the home of a Lutheran vicar who served as his tutor. Wundt grew up to be a quiet, unassuming person whose life followed a totally regulated pattern. He wrote during the morning, then had a consultation hour, in the afternoon paid a formal visit to the laboratory, followed by a walk during which he cast his lecture in rough form, then delivery of the lecture without notes, and a second informal return to the laboratory. It is not surprising that from this background came the hard-driving author of so many books in so many editions, at times so very dry.[86]

At times conditions of enforced absence from academic or professional life, or even circumstances of public or personal calamity, may illustrate the truth of the old proverb: "It's an ill wind that blows nobody good." During the plague years of 1665–66 Isaac Newton, having just graduated and having been appointed junior fellow at Trinity College, Cambridge, retired to his mother's home with a mind full of speculative ideas on the current problems in astronomy, mathematics, and optics. In the two years of enforced retirement because of the plague he discovered the law of gravitation, the concept of fluxions, and the color of light. Upon his return to the College he continued his studies, particularly in gravitation and the spectrum of light, and also experimented in alchemy, undoubtedly seeking the law of affinity, and later on became an excellent scholar in theology and chronology.

Although the diverse and powerful forces of the Chicago environment contributed greatly to ten productive years in creating Dewey's philosophic system, with a metaphysics, a logic, an ethics, and a psychology, the accompanying stresses eventually led to his move to Columbia University. Here was a mild, diffident philosopher who confessed that "ad-

---

[85] Robert I. Watson, *The Great Psychologists*. Philadelphia: J. B. Lippincott Co., 1963. p. 203–207.

[86] *Ibid.*, p. 244–54.

ministrative work is not just in my line." Although possessed of great inner strength and a superior mind, he did not have the physical and temperamental attributes of leadership for a complex administrative position. Dewey and President Harper became estranged, his faculty split into hostile factions, and his wife was dropped from her school post. In 1904 Dewey went to Columbia University as professor of philosophy, where he spent the remainder of his long and eminent career. It is possible that, had Dewey remained at Chicago to work out more fully his theory in an empirical setting of experience, such a mature educational theory and methodology might have prevented much of the bickering and controversy that hampered educational progress during the first half of the twentieth century.[87]

In contrast to the notion that we need a certain amount of "dither" in our mental mechanisms in order to avoid intellectual sluggishness, the autobiography of Mark Van Doren is the story of a man who worked almost all his life under favorable and tranquil conditions. Van Doren has expressed a theory about teaching which suggests that the more abundant a man's life is, the better he will teach, and the story of his own life of nearly forty years of teaching at Columbia University deals everywhere with abundance. The autobiography is a record of the many-sided life of a distinguished professor and poet, and the tale of a happy man. Although the story sounds like a leisurely and reflective life, the fact is that Van Doren taught uninterruptedly through the years until his retirement, and he wrote and edited more than forty volumes. Certainly he worked long and hard at his poetry, which in the end reveals only the harmony in his life and something of the secret of his quiet serenity and content.[88]

Some critics have asked whether increased federal subsidies and generous scholarship programs for graduate students have been reflected in a higher quality of student and excellence in research. Do relatively relaxed conditions of work and freedom from financial worry necessarily produce a high quality of research and scholarship among graduate students? Is there sufficient motivation if one works in comfort and leisure?

Some graduate students in more than one eastern school are on the job only 40 hours a week. A desirable standard is more like 70 to 90 hours. This development indicates lack of motivation. A gifted individual has nothing if he is without drive and a sense of direction. A man of moderate endowment may show flashes of genius if he struggles hard enough. Some of the great scientists of the

87 Robert L. McCaul, "Dewey's Chicago." *School Review* 67: 258–80; Summer 1959.
88 Condensed from review by Helen Bevington, *AAUP Bulletin* 45: 295–97; June 1959, of Mark Van Doren, *The Autobiography of Mark Van Doren*. New York: Harcourt, Brace & World, Inc., 1958. 371 p.

past were comparatively free from financial pressures; others were creative in spite of adversity. Most individuals seem to need a hardening experience to bring out their best. Giving such people financial security is as likely to hurt them as to help them. The Great Depression was a valuable experience for some scientists who were in their formative years at the time. Turning away from the negative aspects of lack of money, they emphasized the search for truth, the love of knowledge, the joy of discovery, the esteem of colleagues. Will these values seem important to the additional students who are lured into graduate school by increased subsidies?[89]

SPONSORSHIP AND COOPERATION

In selection of a thesis or research adviser, it is essential to reflect carefully on the availability and personality characteristics of the particular professor or staff member under consideration; among the important factors are leave of absence, a heavy teaching schedule, a large number of advisees, concentration on writing or research, numerous speaking engagements, ill health, or temperamental difficulties. For certain types of studies sponsorship, cooperation, or special permission from responsible school officers may be necessary; for example, to administer tests to pupils, to interview employees, to distribute questionnaires, to observe pupils and teachers at work, to evaluate buildings or equipment, to try out innovations in curriculum or method, or to make case studies of pupils.

The present chapter and other sections of this book identify directly or indirectly many instances of helpful cooperation between professor and student. It is only honest to say that graduate students and others sometimes have suffered from lack of intelligent advising, appropriate sponsorship, or administrative cooperation. To cite an example, Wallin believes that the dissension caused by the ouster of certain psychologists from Yale University in the first decade of this century proved especially disastrous for Yale psychology graduates over a number of years, with respect to securing major positions in philosophy or psychology. He speaks of the young Yale graduates in psychology of those early days as a "lost generation," in terms of finding or being recommended for attractive positions in psychology.[90]

Scripture's sudden severance from Yale University made it impossible for him to do the editorial work on Wallin's thesis, which had been accepted for publication in the Studies from the Yale Psychological Laboratory (Scripture was the editor). Wallin himself had to do all the editorial work at a time when he had no experience in scientific publication. The one suggestion Scripture had made was that the copy for publication

89 Philip H. Abelson, "Manpower or Mind Power." *Science* 139: 79; January 11, 1963.
90 J. E. Wallace Wallin, *op. cit.,* p. 12, 15–16.

should be boiled down about 50 per cent, not by eliminations but by condensing the sentences and by packing them brim full of content. (Scripture said that he scarcely recognized his own thesis when Wundt, the great German psychologist and founder of the world's first psychological laboratory in 1879, got through with it.)

To cite an example of either extreme independence in working out the dissertation or of an authoritarian adviser (possibly both), E. G. Boring says that in his thesis research at Cornell he conferred with Titchener only twice, once when the problem was planned and once eighteen months later when Titchener had gone over the finished manuscript.

RISKS AND COSTS

In the selection and development of certain types of problems there are sometimes special risks, penalties, handicaps, or costs of a physical, financial, personal, social, or professional character. Fortunately the costs of graduate study and research have been considerably eased during recent years through a variety of financial resources.

Risks and Ethics. The risks in educational research, where human relationships usually are involved, may include problems of professional ethics.

To what extent is the investigator free to tamper with complex organisms and their relationships to one another?

To what extent is he free to set up conditions which are strictly his—conditions with which the subjects of research may not even be familiar and which are not of their making?

Are the proposed risks in research legitimate? For example, to what extent does one have the right to use an untried method of instruction? On the other hand, to what extent is one obligated to try out new methods of instruction in order that progress might be made?

Do the child and his parents have the right to expect that the school will make use in its instructional program of those methods and procedures which have been found somewhat productive, or is the child's school experience to be a testing ground for untried, albeit promising hypotheses?

What is the effect on the learner whose opportunity to learn has been impeded by the research process (the process to produce the information that the procedure in question was not efficacious)? Would the deprived learner have legitimate grounds for complaint, and would his parents?

To what extent does the learner bear a part of the burden of extending knowledge as to how learning takes place?

To what extent is the research worker free to disregard the expectations of the learner in a given situation?

If a deficiency discovered in a survey has been corrected, should the results of the survey be published?

Should we be as assiduous in trying to find external factors which might cause substantially better performance than was anticipated, as we are in seeking such explanations for performances which are not up to our expectations?

If the unfortunate personal traits of a staff member in a school system have created a barrier to research, to what extent should he be informed of the effects of his own personal idiosyncrasies?

To what extent are we justified in using students and faculty members as unwitting guinea pigs? Can we excuse this type of procedure on the grounds that their awareness of the nature of the research would invalidate the findings and make these less generally applicable? Or can we justify giving full information with the general conclusion that people will do better and behave more intelligently if they know what they are doing and why they are doing it?[91]

[An affirmative answer represents the philosophy of action research.]

Physical or Health Hazards and Costs. The hazards of research in the field of medicine and health are well known to the doctors, scientists, interns, medical students, research workers, patients, and others who test new treatments for disease, new drugs, or new scientific equipment. Selected research volunteers for service in this field have formed the Walter Reed Society, named after Major Walter Reed of Spanish-American War fame, who dramatized the use of human volunteers in medical experience and helped to solve the riddle of yellow fever.

Men of high achievement have often accomplished their work in spite of physical or health handicaps. Sir Walter Scott was lame as a result of a childhood attack of polio and was ill for much of his life. At times he dictated while racked by pain from gallstone and stomach cramps.

Samuel Johnson achieved greatness in spite of lifelong suffering from a compulsive neurosis, the distorting convulsions of his severe tic, and his attacks of depression. It has been suggested that, had Johnson lived at a later date, science would have been able at least to name his oddities, if not to cure them. His habits with respect to eating, drinking, and personal cleanliness should be viewed in the perspective of the eighteenth century rather than in terms of standards or customs two hundred years later.[92]

Although George Washington had great physical strength and endurance, he was subjected to a number of diseases in his lifetime, including at least ten serious illnesses that on several occasions brought him near the brink of death. These ailments included malaria (at that time called ague), smallpox, acute pleurisy, a febrile disease (apparently of the influenza type), dysentery, what was probably typhoid fever, and his last fatal illness, probably a streptococcic laryngitis. The great man's

91 Quoted from James A. Hall, "Some Ethical Problems," *Research for Curriculum Improvement.* 1957 Yearbook. Washington: Association for Supervision and Curriculum Development, a Department of the National Education Association, 1957. p. 269–77.

92 Edward Hitschmann, *Great Men: Psychoanalytic Studies.* New York: International Universities Press, 1956. p. 176.

cheeks were sunken because of ill-fitting dentures, his complexion was sallow and pock marked (as the result of smallpox), and he was flat-chested and somewhat hollow in the center of the chest (probably from rickets).

John Stuart Mill (1806–1873) was a child prodigy, and was dominated throughout life by a celebrated father, James Mill. The son learned Greek at the age of three and by eight was reading Herodotus and Plato in the original. He was without boyhood friends and never learned to play. John Stuart Mill so admired and feared his father that his first book, on logic, was delayed in publication until the father had been dead seven years, but once the spell of the elder Mill was broken the son published voluminously.

Gustav Theodor Fechner (1801–1887) during his seventy productive years was successively physiologist, physicist, psychophysicist, experimental estheticist, and philosopher. He founded psychophysics, which was instrumental in founding experimental psychology. Fechner broke under the strain of a tremendous work load and became, in the language of his day, a "nervous invalid," with a serious eye disorder that forced him to spend many hours in contemplation as a method of study. Although in 1844 he received a small university pension, for nearly another forty-four years he studied and wrote.[93]

Psychologists have had their share of physical and health problems. William James took years to decide upon the work for which he was best fitted, with training in painting, science, philosophy, medicine, and after interruptions in study finally taking his medical degree in 1869. At times James felt that he did not have the stamina to carry the arduous work of preparation for medicine, decided against practice of medicine, and finally through disciplined reading and speculation made a gradual recovery of his health to accept an offer in 1872 to teach physiology at Harvard. In 1875 James gave his first course in psychology, on the relation between physiology and psychology.[94] His earlier illnesses over a period of nearly five years included a neurotic depression with insomnia, eye trouble, digestive disorders, severe back pain, and other symptoms. His nervous disorder may have contributed indirectly to his intellectual development, since it gave him psychological insight into abnormal conditions and took him abroad in search of a cure, with profitable visits to the intellectual and artistic centers of Europe.[95]

The tic (blinking) of Edward B. Titchener may have struck the young student as a strange flaw in a famous psychologist, but Titchener's personality was so natural and spontaneous that in the course of the seminar or lecture the tic was disregarded and forgotten. Clark L. Hull

93 Robert I. Watson, *op. cit.*, p. 211–16.

94 *Ibid.*, p. 320–30.

95 Merle Curti, *The Social Ideas of American Educators*. Revised Edition. Totowa, New Jersey: Littlefield, Adams and Co., 1959. p. 430–31.

was handicapped by a severe attack of typhoid fever that left him with a generalized bad memory for names; an attack of polio left one leg badly paralyzed and crippled; and his earlier years of psychological study were made much more difficult because of his weak eyes. James R. Angell, near the end of his college course, considered medicine as a career, but weak eyes caused him to believe that he could not do the exacting microscopic work required as part of the medical program.

For sixteen years at Cambridge University, Whitehead had a constant struggle with insomnia, and each September, after a summer's vacation in the country or by the sea, he would wonder whether he could endure another year of teaching. However, the insomnia never seemed to affect his work, and when he moved to London University it diminished and finally ceased.[96]

The sociologist, Charles H. Cooley (1864–1929), spent seven years as an undergraduate student at the University of Michigan because of ill health. We do not know how much effect his ill health, and the influence of his able jurist father, may have had on his quiet, effective thinking and writing. Most of his work assumed the form of digesting and interpreting the writings of others, and in applying the conclusions to life around him.[97]

When Clyde Kluckhohn (1905–1960) was forced, because of ill health, to delay his college education, he retired to a ranch in New Mexico to recuperate. This event played a large part in shaping his subsequent career in anthropology. From the ranch he made pack trips through the adjacent Navaho country and, after recovery of his health, frequently revisited the Southwest during the summers. As an ethnographer Kluckhohn devoted most of his life to the Navaho Indian. He spoke fluent French and Spanish, as well as German and Navaho, and traveled in Mexico, Australia, Japan, and India in following his wide-ranging interests.[98]

During the 1920's and 1930's, behind the mental fatigue of Carl Becker, the historian, lay a physical fatigue brought on by painful, prolonged stomach disorders and a number of seemingly endless visits to the hospital. To a friend visiting him in the hospital, Becker exclaimed wearily in effect: "They talk a lot about a sound mind in a sound body; *any* kind of mind in a sound body." Becker also commented that his illness made him feel like Gulliver tied down by the Lilliputians. For many years he was doomed to a kind of apathy, compounded of emotional dejection and physical fatigue, and twice sought escape through travel

[96] *Dialogues of Alfred North Whitehead.* As Recorded by Lucien Price. New York: New American Library of World Literature, Inc., 1954. 320 p.

[97] M. C. Elmer, *op. cit.*, p. 36.
Emory S. Bogardus, *op. cit.*, p. 492–504.

[98] George P. Murdock, "Clyde Kluckhohn (1905–1960)." *Behavioral Science* 6: 2–4; January 1961.

from moodiness and discouragement. Drastic stomach surgery in 1940 relieved Becker from ill health for the rest of his life, until his unexpected death of uremic poisoning in 1945. During these few remaining years he resumed his creative work and wrote three books.[99]

David Starr Jordan, the naturalist and educator, turned a physical handicap into an advantage. He had such farsighted vision that his eyes were almost telescopic, which made reading difficult, but led him to develop such fast reading habits as to absorb a book in half an hour. This was not mere scanning, but a technique of picking out the new information on each page and of skimming lightly over what he already knew.

Ellwood P. Cubberley produced a large volume of published material and edited works, in spite of colds, stomach ulcers, and sinus disturbances that caused him frequent discomfort for many years. His notebooks record the symptoms and the treatment, often including a record of temperature and blood pressure together with the physician's diagnosis. Later he was hospitalized a number of times, and underwent several serious operations, the details of which he set down in his notebooks. His major illnesses included surgery for an ulcer in 1918, removal of his appendix in 1934 and of a kidney in 1935, and the handicap of a serious heart ailment.

Graduate students of the latter part of the past century, including those at Johns Hopkins in the 1880's, voiced complaints all too familiar today about cramming for examinations, long hours, too little recreation, loss of sleep, eyestrain, and the drudgery of copying materials for reports and dissertations.

> Worse than cramming was the unavoidable drudgery of copying. Cyrus Adler's transcribing of his dissertation of over six hundred pages in two weeks was herculean. Excepting the Sabbaths, his daily regimen allowed time for meals, an hour's walk, and two hours' sleep; the rest of each day he spent copying. Students paid a physical price for their intellectual excesses in headaches, strained eyes, and nervous dyspepsia.[100]

Financial Risks, Costs, and Resources. Scientists and scholars frequently have encountered financial difficulties or have sacrificed their personal resources. Sir Walter Scott's badly managed ventures in printing and publishing failed, with debts of 130,000 pounds charged against him. Refusing bankruptcy, during the last six years of his life Scott produced a nine-volume life of Napoleon and in two years turned over 40,000 pounds to his creditors. He continued writing best sellers until his frail

---

[99] Burleigh T. Wilkins, *Carl Becker: A Biographical Study in American Intellectual History.* Cambridge, Mass.: M.I.T. Press and Harvard University Press, 1961. p. 141–73.
[100] Quoted from Hugh Hawkins, *Pioneer: A History of the Johns Hopkins University, 1874–1889.* Ithaca, New York: Cornell University Press, 1960. p. 283–84.

health cracked, and he died at the age of sixty-one. Later, the sale of Scott's works settled the last of the debts that helped kill him.

Herbert Spencer was an invalid most of his life, with an uncertain income. He invested more in his early books than he received from them, since he usually employed an amanuensis. In the early days of the *American Journal of Psychology*, Stanley Hall had to spend $8,000 of his own money on the publication, in order to keep it going.

Henry Barnard devoted a considerable part of his long life, 1811–1900, to the thirty-one volumes of the *Journal of Education*, not merely as editor, but later as promoter and publisher.[101] His financial sacrifices for the *Journal* included the mortgaging of his home, personal savings, and generous gifts of copies to persons who could not afford the purchase price. At one time the financial status of the *Journal* was so shaky that Barnard considered the melting of the plates in order to sell the metal to meet his indebtedness. In reply to this proposal, the English educator Robert H. Quick said, "I would as soon hear that there was talk of pulling down one of our cathedrals and selling the stones for building material.[102] These financial difficulties probably were due in part to mismanagement and poor record-keeping, which were a matter of concern to Barnard's wife, who closed her letter written to him in 1856, "I am lonesome and cross at being left so much alone, the evenings are too dismal to live through. Love to all but the Journal to whom (*sic*) I have sworn eternal enmity."[103]

In many instances scientists have disregarded monetary costs and returns, particularly when their work was supported by educational institutions and agencies. Pasteur declared, "I could never work for money, but I would always work for science," and Agassiz said, "I have no time to make money." On the other hand, early in life Agassiz exhibited a characteristic that we are only now beginning to appreciate fully—he was always able to raise money.

> When his father's resources for financing his extended education in Germany proved insufficient, he found a maternal uncle whom he persuaded to take over. His teachers were also uniformly helpful. Later, in France, Cuvier did his part and made it possible for Agassiz to remain a while in Paris. Baron Alexander von Humbolt contributed to Agassiz from his personal funds and used his political influence to get Agassiz grants from the Prussian state. Later, at Harvard, Agassiz routinely and conscientiously ignored all budget limitations and overspent his funds almost as a matter of principle, but he was always able to raise enough money to cover the deficits. He could always rehabilitate

[101] Richard K. Morris, "Parnassus on Wheels: A Biographical Sketch of Henry Barnard, 1811–1900." *Teacher Education Quarterly* 18: 45–57; Winter 1960–61.

[102] Reprinted in the *Journal of Education* 14: 7; August 25, 1881.

[103] Quoted in R. E. Thursfield, *Henry Barnard's American Journal of Education*, p. 47. From a letter in the Monroe Collection, New York University, dated June 8, 1856.

his own personal finances by giving a few public lectures. Such talents we can appreciate.[104]

In some instances the scientist may even have religious or moral scruples about accepting money for research or consultation:

Faraday was an active member of a very strict sect of the Nonconformist Church. His lofty religious ideals and his urge to pursue as far as possible the spiritual implications of his scientific work led him to abandon all industrial consultation work and to renounce the monetary and social advantages that he could have derived from his immense fame. Yet, while he properly emphasized the usefulness of science in the practical affairs of man, he rarely voiced his inner conviction that science is an attempt to understand the universe as much as it is a technique to exploit nature; that—to use an expression of which he was fond—science is above and beyond everything else, "natural philosophy."[105]

Some scientists have had the benefit of large personal resources for conducting their research. Roger Bacon was a member of a wealthy family and probably earned substantial fees for lecturing. He spent 10,000 pounds, in modern money, on the purchase of books, experiments and instruments, journeys to meet scholars, and secretaries. Charles Darwin was an English gentleman of wealth and leisure, with favorable conditions for making his scientific studies.

The grandfather of William and Henry James had left a fortune of three million, a huge sum for pre-Civil War America. This wealth profoundly influenced the lives of his grandsons through rich cultural opportunities in the form of special schools, foreign travel, and favorable living conditions. William James was able to spend ten years in higher studies as preparation for his life work, trying his hand at painting, science, philosophy, and medicine. He could comment to his banker about his lack of anxiety concerning money, "beyond wishing not to live on capital."[106]

Occasionally a professional risk and related financial costs are involved in a disagreement between graduate student and professor. Hugo Münsterberg disagreed with Wundt in setting up a dissertation problem in the Leipzig laboratory and was shifted to another (less important) problem which was accepted. Although Münsterberg later adapted the rejected dissertation for another purpose, he lost the favor of Wundt and as a result was handicapped in securing a position. On the other hand, Wundt's

104 Quoted from review by Conway Zirkle, *Science* 132: 1655–56; December 2, 1960, of Edward Lurie, *Louis Agassiz: A Life in Science*. Chicago: University of Chicago Press, 1960. 449 p. Reprinted from *Science* by permission.

105 Quoted from René Dubos, "Scientist and Public." *Science* 133: 1207–11; April 21, 1961. Reprinted from *Science* by permission.

106 Merle Curti, *op. cit.*, p. 430–31.

treatment of Münsterberg won James' sympathy for the young psychologist and led to a Harvard appointment for Münsterberg.

Wundt was strongly opposed to the application of psychology and was severely critical of any of his students who entered an applied field. When the gifted Meumann turned to educational psychology, Wundt treated it as though a case of desertion. Kraepelin fared somewhat better when he applied psychology to psychiatry and was advised by Wundt to leave psychology for psychiatry.

James McKeen Cattell was an exception to Wundt's usual custom of assigning problems to his graduate students. Cattell worked on his own problems in reaction time, in keeping with his spirit of independence and firm convictions. He worked out some of his experiments at his lodging rather than in the laboratory, since Wundt would not permit subjects in his laboratory who could not profit from introspection. Although professor-student relationships were somewhat strained, they never reached the breaking point, and Cattell took the Ph.D. at Leipzig in 1886, then in 1888 was appointed at the University of Pennsylvania to the first professorship in *psychology,* not just in the United States but anywhere in the world.

When the academic dynamo, Cattell, at the age of 31 was head of Columbia's Department of Psychology, many of his colleagues confidently expected him to leap to first place in the new and characteristically American science of pragmatic psychology. Instead, Cattell chose to divert some of his remarkable energies to founding a publishing and business empire, which eventually included seven scholarly periodicals (each edited on a different day of the week from the Cattell home, with the entire family at work), as well as *American Men of Science* and the Psychological Corporation. Cattell apparently had a nonacademic gift for both psychology and financial management, and thus he began his tenure as publisher of *Science* in January, 1895.[107]

When John Dewey was offered a head professorship in 1894 by President Harper of the University of Chicago, the philosopher asked for $5,000 a year, $2,000 more than his salary at the University of Michigan. Dewey said that the proposed salary of $4,000 per year was inadequate to meet the needs of his family in a city like Chicago, but he finally accepted the offer, expressing the hope that in due time an increase would be provided. Thus it appears that problems of cost of living in relation to salary have been with us for a long time. Possibly Dewey left his well established position at the University of Michigan at a salary less than he thought adequate in order to work in the stimulating atmosphere of a large city.[108]

[107] "Our 81-Year-Old Weekly." *AAAS Bulletin:* 1–4; July 1961.
[108] Robert L. McCaul, "Dewey's Chicago." *School Review* 67: 258–80; Summer 1959.

Occasionally a specialist in psychology or education has made himself financially independent. Edward L. Thorndike made it a rule early in his career to spend so little and earn so much that he would be free from financial worry, and in so doing became a person of considerable means. Ellwood P. Cubberley was able to accumulate a fortune, derived chiefly from royalties on books and fees for editorial services, with smaller sums from services as consultant, investigator, and lecturer. These sums were increased greatly through investments that proved sound. The gifts by Cubberley and his wife to Stanford University totaled more than three quarters of a million dollars, including more than a half million dollars for a new School of Education building.[109]

There are usually problems of securing financial support for research, when the worker lacks university or institutional sponsorship and proper laboratory facilities. The world of scholarship and science probably is the poorer because of the formalities involved in securing grants for research. It is said that such persons as Koch and Jenner were fortunate that their studies did not depend on the approval of grant applications under modern conditions.

> Suppose Robert Koch had needed a research grant to study the cause of anthrax. An obscure district physician, without university or research institute affiliation, he wished to develop original techniques to explore a new field. He worked, not in a laboratory, but in his own house. It seems obvious that he would have been brushed off quickly by almost any foundation or fund-granting agency operating according to current practices.
>
> Suppose Edward Jenner had applied for a grant. He was a country practitioner, without university or research institute affiliation. He proposed to investigate an old wives' tale, that cowpox would prevent smallpox. He planned to test his postulation on human beings, without prior trial on animals. He had no statistically sound plan. Would any respectable voluntary foundation or government agency give such a crackpot funds?[110]

TIME REQUIREMENTS FOR RESEARCH

The variables of worker, problem, technique, adviser, sponsorship, and working conditions are such that it is extremely hazardous to predict the length of time required to complete a specific investigation. Beyond a certain point additional money, equipment, and personnel resources will not shorten the period of development and maturation essential for successful research. Charles F. Kettering once estimated that a certain project would require a year for completion. When urged to double his

109 Jesse B. Sears and Adin D. Henderson, *op. cit.*, p. 267, 280.
110 Alvan G. Foraker, "If Robert Koch Had Applied for a Research Grant." *Science* 142: 11; October 4, 1963.

force and reduce the time to six months, he made a characteristic, homely reply.

Pressure for development of the drawer-operated cash register was made stronger by the circumstance that President Patterson was soon to leave on a trip to Europe. Kettering was asked whether he thought the development could be finished before the date of his departure. Yes, he thought it could.

"We ought really to have the job completed sooner," said Patterson. So he directed that Kettering be given more help. "Give him twice as many men," he said, "so he can finish it up in half the time."

At that, Kettering protested that he could not use so many helpers to advantage.

"Why can't you?" Patterson asked. "If ten men can dig a rod of ditch in an hour, then surely twenty men can dig two rods."

"This is more a job of hatching eggs than digging ditches, Mr. Patterson," was the reply. "Do you think that if two hens were put on a nest a setting of eggs could be hatched out in less than three weeks?"[111]

A neurophysiologist and philanthropic foundation adviser expresses the hope that science may pursue its course free from pressure for quick results.[112]

Finally it should be said that it makes no sense to criticize a science for not knowing more than it does. This would seem to be particularly true of psychology. Everybody else, prophets, priests, philosophers, doctors, lawyers, the man in the street—ever since the time when there were no streets—has tried to understand the behavior of man. And it is now more true than it ever was that man's greatest mystery is man himself. Why should not science have its chance? May it pursue it free from pressure for quick results.

And just in case you feel like brushing off these comments as those of a philanthropoid who should never have been allowed out of his Ivory Tower, let me quote a practical politician, Theodore Heuss, President of the German Republic: "We have the obligation to free the scientist from the nervousness of this era and to put the gift of time again at his disposal."

With painstaking German thoroughness, Paul Ehrlich made his great discovery of a syphilis cure by wading without success through 605 organic arsenic compounds in search of a chemical that could destroy a disease-producing organism without harming the victim of the disease; he finally was dramatically successful with the next drug, named "606."

In 1807 Noah Webster wrote of the painstaking effort and time required to produce a dictionary.

I hope to be able to finish my Complete Dictionary. . . . It will require the incessant labor of from three to five years." In 1812 he moved to Amherst,

111 Quoted from T. A. Boyd, op. cit., p. 57–58.
112 As quoted from Robert S. Morison, "Gradualness, Gradualness, Gradualness." American Psychologist 15: 187–97; March 1960.

Massachusetts, where for ten years he labored from point to point about the large circular table that held the dictionaries and grammars of twenty languages. In 1824 he sailed to spend a year in the libraries of Paris, London, and Cambridge in order to consult books that could not be had in America. In 1828, at the age of seventy, he at length published the *American Dictionary of the English Language* in an edition of 2500 copies. . . .

Webster brought out a revised edition of the Dictionary in 1841, just before his death.[113]

The need for relatively long periods of sustained effort in research is aptly expressed by Cannon.

An investigator may be given a palace to live in, a perfect laboratory to work in, he may be surrounded by all the conveniences money can provide; but if his time is taken from him he will remain sterile. On the other hand, as the history of science abundantly shows, an investigator may be poverty-stricken, he may be ill-clothed, he may live in a garret and have only meager appliances for his use; but given time he can be productive.[114]

It is unusual to have as exact (and surprisingly short) a time schedule for completion of a dissertation as that left on record by Ellwood P. Cubberley, who made a study of state school laws on finance under the title, "School Funds and Their Apportionment." This dissertation was the beginning of many years of study by Cubberley of the financing of public-education administration. He began the research for his dissertation on January 24, 1905; Mrs. Cubberley began the typing on March 17, and Cubberley presented the dissertation to his adviser on April 14. In his diary he entered the comment: "Handed it to Dr. Perry, returned borrowed sections of Teachers College Library, and breathed a sigh of relief—Done!" He took his oral examination on May 19 and received the Ph.D. degree on June 14, 1905, at Columbia University.[115]

The idealized picture for completing a Ph.D. in science is of a student who had his program of study well charted in advance, and was aided by assistantships or fellowships to earn the doctorate in approximately four graduate years, but only about one student in ten finishes so quickly. Typically in the field of science the Ph.D. comes nearly eight years after the Bachelor's degree. Suggestions have been made for reducing this time lapse, in the form of changes in organization and planning, earlier counseling, and more systematic program planning, although too much guidance, structuring, and detailed program planning would change the

---

113 Quoted from *Webster's Third New International Dictionary of the English Language, Unabridged.* Springfield, Mass.: G. and C. Merriam Co., 1961.

114 Quoted from Walter B. Cannon, *op. cit.,* p. 87.

115 Jesse B. Sears and Adin D. Henderson, *op. cit.,* p. 81.

character of the Ph.D. and interfere with the development of scholarly independence on the part of the student.[116]

William James was relatively slow in his development and program of writing; he required considerable persuasion to complete a textbook in psychology, his famous *Principles of Psychology* (1890), after twelve years of hard work. On the other hand, John Dewey was only 26 years of age when he produced his *Psychology*, which means that he was engaged in writing this book at the age of 24 or 25 (an unusual accomplishment for so young a man).

One aspect of timing involves historical or research perspective—the ability to evaluate one's work or the efforts of others in the contemporary setting and also in relation to changed conditions or new evidence after a period of time. For example, Edward A. Ross (1866–1952) was outspoken in criticism, even of his own works, when conditions changed or new evidence appeared.

> In the thirty-five years since the book left my anvil, I have scrutinized society in many countries and a society which "controls" does not look so global to me now as it did to me in 1900. . . . I doubt if "lessons from history" will have much to do with shaping humanity's future. Basic conditions are changing so rapidly that most of the old techniques of control are junk. . . . Science and invention—together with applied psychology open vistas into a wondrous new age with its own problems of control, in which control devices will be employed that the past never heard of.[117]

Ross, speaking of his 1920 book on *Principles of Sociology*, stated that when published he thought it sound, but "even then sensed that certain parts were labored and foggy." He sad that almost every month fresh shortcomings had appeared and that, if by 1960 it should prove forty to fifty parts sound, he would be content.

Extensive travel and too many commitments eat up the time of scholars. Shortly after he had settled in the United States, Einstein plaintively commented on the unquiet atmosphere of academic life, even in Princeton, and the resulting deleterious effect on scientific productivity. Certain well-known scientists have compared their travel schedules for a year with the miles logged by an international airline pilot. While there *is* a shortage of able people, this shortage is aggravated by the continued "spinning" of the able, creative scholars and scientists we have, by way of extensive travel, too many commitments, and overextension of activi-

116 Kenneth M. Wilson, *Of Time and the Doctorate.* Atlanta, Georgia: Southern Regional Education Board, 1965. ix + 212 p.
Dael Wolfle, "Of Time and the Doctorate." *Science* 148: 1045; May 21, 1965.
117 Quoted from M. C. Elmer, *op. cit.,* p. 29–30.
Emory S. Bogardus, *op. cit.,* p. 523–39.

ties in general. The motivation for participating in these distractions is varied.

A man's reputation, his power, his prestige are very much conditioned by his being "on the inside." Only those who circulate, who circulate in the right circles, who have the right connections are likely to be called on to give advice to be remembered when funds are distributed, to be elected when an opening occurs.

It is not easy to turn one's back on possible appointments, on other opportunities, and to stay put in a laboratory or library to struggle with one's problems and possibly to fail. Fortunately, however, some men are not suited to the life of the academic "operator." And a few others are able to withstand the temptations.

The size of our country adds to the difficulties. It is not easy to know the good people in a field where this requires an overview of 60 or 160 institutions scattered over an area of 6 million square miles. And so the good men who are identified are sought out again and again, until their scientific careers become a part of the past. As a consequence, many younger men who could help share the load—for we do need many to serve on committees and to do the other chores that need doing—remain unrecognized and are unable to enjoy opportunities that could add an important dimension to their development.

Many years ago, Wesley Clair Mitchell, great empiricist that he was, took out his appointment book to review what had happened to him during the preceding ten months. He calculated that he had been able to devote only about 30 percent of his total time to his research. And Mitchell was a most disciplined scholar.

We chew up the best people in this country. We do it for good or bad reasons, but we do it. The most important lesson that we have to learn is the importance of one word—no. For creative work requires time and repose. The nation is not suffering from a shortage of talent. It is suffering from a shortage of talented people who know how to preserve and protect their time.[118]

Initial Statement of the Problem

FOCUSING TOPICS FOR RESEARCH

The importance of the doctoral dissertation in the graduate program is emphasized by this anecdote. One student said that all he lacked was his dissertation. Another graduate student replied: "You said that wrong; you should say it this way, 'All I have got off are my courses.'"[119]

After the title of a thesis or investigation has been phrased within one or two lines, the next step is to provide an adequate statement of the

118 Eli Ginzberg, "Time and Talent." *Science* 138: 1305; December 21, 1962.
119 "The Good Dissertations Live Longer." *Peabody Journal of Education* 40: 257–58; March 1963.

problem in one or more paragraphs in the introductory chapter of the report. Certain errors in the phrasing of thesis or research topics should be avoided:

1. Naming a broad field or area of study instead of a specific problem for investigation; for example, "the effect of various factors on learning," which might be delimited as "the effect of three thirty-minute periods of practice versus five eighteen-minute periods on learning silent reading in the fifth grade"; or the history of music the world over for all time, which was delimited by one student to present a history of a particular conservatory of music.
2. Narrowing or localizing a topic to such an extent that it may prove a "pinpoint" problem; for example, a proposed history of a one-room school might be broadened to deal with the history of the school district or even the history of the county school system in which the one-room school is located.
3. Wording of a hortatory or biased character, or citing undigested data without identifying a problem; for example, "an argument for free textbooks in the public schools" might better be phrased as "the practices of public schools in a particular area in providing free textbooks." "Fifty tape recordings of home room programs" might become "an analysis of the content of home room programs, based on tape recordings."

To cite additional illustrations, which in some instances return to the criteria analyzed early in this chapter, proposals for thesis and other research purposes are faulty not so much because of the investigational method advocated, but more commonly because of the following shortcomings:[120]

1. Lack of general significance to education, because the problem is trivial, is not likely to produce widely applicable generalizations, or is too vast, as when one investigator proposed with the help of one graduate assistant over a nine-month period to sudy the educational impact of all the significant inventions from the Stone Age to the present.
2. The objectives are too broadly stated; for example, "the broad hypothesis is that a procedure can be followed which will lead to the initial formulation, revision, and final development of a broadly conceived theory of education based upon psychological and other relevant research findings."
3. The study is poorly designed, usually because the investigator fails to recognize the complexity of the task involved. One proposal sought to provide a program of mathematics and English instruction for an experimental group of high school graduates during the summer before they entered college and to compare their achievement during the freshman year with that of a comparable group that had no instruction. This study

[120] Francis A. J. Ianni, "USOE Cooperative Research." *School Life* 46: 26–27; March-April 1964.

said, in effect, that a group which has had instruction in math and English will be better prepared to cope with college math and English than a comparable group which has received no instruction. The intergroup analysis not only compares "something" (the instruction) with "nothing" (the lack of instruction), but it also completely obscures the complexity of the problem. In reality, one would expect some students—those who are highly motivated but who lack certain math and English skills—to show significant improvement, and others—those who lack the motivation for academic work—to show little improvement.

4. Lack of convincing evidence that the project will be economically efficient, in terms of cost and probable service to the educational community.

BRIEF STATEMENT OF THE PROBLEM

The problem may be stated in the form of a question (or series of questions) or as a declarative statement (or series of statements). The question form may have an advantage in sharpening or focusing the issue, but the declarative statement probably is more common. The following example combines the two ways (question and declarative statement) of phrasing the problem.[121]

The purpose of this study, broadly stated, was to investigate the effectiveness of a method of teaching arithmetic in which children's immature procedures in dealing with number are accepted as normal and valuable steps toward their achievement of competent, mature behavior with reference to number. More narrowly, the objective of the investigation was to determine the effect upon the arithmetical development of children of their temporary use of certain immature procedures, when careful guidance is given by teachers. These procedures are designated as "intermediate," since they occur between the initial awareness of number and the achievment of mature modes of dealing with number relationships. The study was limited to the development of understanding in the four fundamental processes, on the part of the second-grade children.

Preliminary Problems.—Two preliminary problems which were basic to the major purpose of the study may be stated as follows:

1. The discovery of the intermediate procedures that were being used by children at the beginning of the study.
2. The selection of those intermediate procedures which showed promise as aids to more mature understanding of number ideas by pupils.

Sub-problems.—In the evaluation of a teaching technique in which the immature or intermediate procedures of children are regarded as of central im-

121 Quoted from Edwina Deans, "The Effect of Certain Immature Procedures on the Learning of Arithmetical Processes by Second-Grade Children," *Abstracts of Graduate Theses in Education,* 1944–54, Vol. 5. Cincinnati: Teachers College, University of Cincinnati, 1955. p. 129–47.

portance, a number of pertinent questions arise. Such questions, which may be regarded as sub-problems, include the following:

1. In what ways can experience be provided for all children on the selected intermediate procedures?
2. Is it possible for some children to bypass some intermediate procedures without jeopardizing understanding?
3. Do some children tend to move to more advanced procedures before understanding is present?
4. How can readiness for a more advanced intermediate procedure be determined?
5. Do children willingly discontinue the use of immature procedures?
6. Under what circumstances are less mature methods dropped and replaced by more mature methods?
7. What steps can be taken by the teacher to encourage children to discontinue the use of immature methods?
8. As children are taught intermediate procedures, to what extent is their later thinking characterized by increasingly higher levels of maturity in dealing with number situations?
9. What problems do teachers encounter as they attempt to guide children through succeeding maturity levels in dealing with number situations?

Fuller Definition of the Problem

The brief introductory statement of the problem usually is followed by a fuller definition and development of background concerning sub-problems, scope, related literature, sources of data, method, significance, terminology, assumptions, and hypotheses. Of course it may not be appropriate for a particular study to include all of these items of background as part of the fuller development of the problem, which means that the candidate has certain options.

CONSTITUENT ELEMENTS AND SCOPE

The preceding illustrative study of arithmetical processes by Deans also shows how the major problem is divided into subproblems, constituent elements, or questions to answer. A statement of the limits or scope of the investigation well may provide information concerning "who, what, when, where, and how many."

To cite another example, thoughtful analysis of problems for action research (discussed at length in Chapter 5) involves answers to such questions as the following:[122]

1. What conditions need to prevail both to allow and to invite teachers to state problems of importance to them?

[122] Hilda Taba, "Problem Identification," *Research for Curriculum Improvement.* 1957 Yearbook. Washington: Association for Supervision and Curriculum Development, a Department of the National Education Association, 1957. p. 42–71.

2. In what context do problem identification and analysis produce the maximum of identification, allow for varied levels of involvement depending on the capacity and the insight of individuals, and permit significant problems to emerge?
3. What is the sequence in opening up a problem for research with teachers?
4. What is the timing factor? How is one to gauge how fast or how slowly to proceed, at which point to introduce which considerations?
5. What is a team pattern in guiding action research which yields the greatest possible combined competence? What is the role of the research consultants? of the supervisor? of teachers?

RELATED LITERATURE AND TERMINOLOGY

We have already noted the importance of the literature in the selection of problems for investigation. The next chapter presents the keys to the related literature, from which may come explanatory hypotheses, techniques for gathering evidence, and comparative data for purposes of interpretation. The orientation provided by a survey of the related research is helpful in making a straightforward statement of the need for the investigation, avoiding the two extremes of an apologetic attitude and exaggerated claims or boastfulness. Chapters of the *Encyclopedia of Educational Research, Review of Educational Research,* and the *Annual Review of Psychology* may serve as useful examples of summaries of the research literature on specific topics.

Certain specialized terms in the technical report or in the related studies may require definition. Comprehensive dictionaries are available for the fields of education, psychology, and sociology.[123]

SOURCES OF DATA AND METHOD

An introductory section of the technical report should include appropriate information concerning sources of evidence and techniques of data-gathering, including a frank admission of any weaknesses or shortcomings. Detailed discussions of sources and methods are found later in this book in the several chapters on research methodology. The following illustrative statement of sources and method involves an analysis of the attitudes of junior high school pupils toward police officers.

This study was limited to 971 junior high school pupils in four Cincinnati public junior high schools and to officers of the Cincinnati Division of Police. Classification of pupil subjects was limited to: (1) age in

[123] Carter V. Good, Editor, *Dictionary of Education.* Second Edition. New York: McGraw-Hill Book Co., 1959. xxx + 676 p.

Horace B. English and Ava C. English, *Comprehensive Dictionary of Psychological and Psychoanalytical Terms.* New York: Longmans, Green and Co., 1958. xiv + 594 p.

H. P. Fairchild, Editor, *Dictionary of Sociology.* New York: Philosophical Library, 1944. viii + 342 p.

years, (2) sex, (3) race, either Negro or white, (4) grade level, (5) course of study, either basic, general, or academic, as grouped by the Cincinnati public schools, (6) participation in school-sponsored activities, (7) church attendance, and (8) socioeconomic level, as determined by parent occupation and home ownership.

A normative-survey method of research was employed, utilizing three data-gathering techniques. The measurement of student attitudes toward the police was by means of an attitude scale. This scale construction and the scoring of the scale were based on Thurstone scaling methods and Likert scoring techniques. The meaning of the measurements was determined by a series of interviews with selected pupil-subjects. Additional data were secured by means of direct observation of police-juvenile contacts. Classification data were supplied by the pupil-subjects.

A twenty statement Attitude-Toward-Police Scale was developed by Thurstone judging techniques, using the statements of approximately one hundred pupils and ninety-four judges. This scale was then administered to 971 junior high school pupil-subjects and scored by the Likert technique of summated rating. Means were computed for the total group and for all sub-group classifications. To determine the meaning of the mean scores and to define the attitudes toward police held by the large middle group scoring between plus and minus one standard deviation from the mean, fifty-nine pupils whose scale scores were judged to be representative were interviewed. These interviews had the additional purposes of providing a check on the validity of the scale, the honesty of responses to the scale, and background information for the creation of the fictional material. Following the completion of the interview phase of the research, direct observation was made of police-juvenile contacts over a period of approximately three hundred hours of participation in police activities. A statistical analysis of all pertinent data was conducted through the facilities of the university computing center, to test for significance of variation of the means of scores on the attitude scale. Bartlett's test for homogeneity of variance, an F-test, and t-tests of all combinations of pairs in each grouping were made. Finally, drawing on the information, concepts, episodes, and conclusions, the junior novel was written.[124]

Investigators are sometimes frustrated in searching for the original data of a research project. It appears that few authors of articles in even such scholarly journals as the A. P. A. group store their data for future reference. Availability of data would serve several useful purposes:[125]

[124] Robert G. Portune, "An Analysis of the Attitudes of Junior High School Pupils toward Police Officers, Applied to the Preparation of a Work of Juvenile Fiction." Doctoral Disseration, University of Cincinnati, 1965.

[125] Richard W. Johnson, "Retain the Original Data!" *American Psychologist* 19: 350–51; May 1964.

1. Checking the statistical analysis and possible cross-laboratory replication
2. Reanalysis of the data from a different point of view
3. Comparison with additional data collected on the same subjects at a later point in time
4. Loan of data to other investigators for research use.

BASIC ASSUMPTIONS

In social investigations and in school and community life, certain premises or assumptions are generally accepted, frequently without identification in the technical or research reports; for example, in a democracy we assume that cooperation rather than strife and respect for the individual rather than rigid regimentation are desirable. We accept the premise that schools and education are necessary, and that transportation of pupils in rural areas is desirable.

The scientist typically accepts two basic assumptions:[126]

1. That there is lawfulness in the events of nature as opposed to capricious, chaotic, or spontaneous occurrences (in other words, determinism)
2. That every natural event or phenomenon has a discoverable and limited number of conditions or factors which are responsible for it (an assumption of finite causation).

To the extent that basic assumptions are open to question, the results of the particular investigation are subject to challenge. Even great scientists have encountered difficulties in understanding the basic assumptions of other scientists or in defending their own postulates.

That Agassiz failed to become the greatest naturalist of his time was due to a development he could never quite understand. He was equipped with almost unlimited industriousness and ambition. He was exceptionally intelligent and attractive. As a youth, he worked with the leading scientists of his time, and they one and all liked him, admired him, and advanced his fortunes in every way they could. He had also prepared himself in the best possible ways. He had mastered *Naturphilosophie* in Germany but had also learned, by studying in France with the hard-headed and practical Cuvier, to prefer the factual to the speculative aspects of science. He had mastered and practically dominated ichthyology and was credited with establishing the glacial theory. For a time he dominated biology in America, all the while remaining a very potent force in Europe. He and his work were universally respected, but something went wrong.

In 1859, Charles Darwin hit him in his postulates, and he found his basic assumptions under attack. That Agassiz did not know at first what had happened to him is clear from his reactions. Later on, when he began to suspect,

[126] Benton J. Underwood, *Psychological Research*. New York: Appleton-Century-Crofts, 1957. p. 3–6.

he was dazed and puzzled. He made an honest effort to understand the newer developments and to evaluate the evidence on which the theory of evolution was based, but he failed completely, as he showed by a paper he wrote just before his death.[127]

Many assumptions or premises in the social areas involve the realm of values and are not subject at present to validation through any known scientific procedure. Underlying assumptions should be stated as part of the definition and development of the problem, and also in connection with the conclusions of the investigation.

Development and Testing of Hypotheses

CHARACTERISTICS AND FUNCTIONS OF HYPOTHESES[128]

If only the precise results of observations had been incorporated into science, scientific knowledge would have developed into a gigantic and unmanageable mass of isolated items of information. Science owes its unity and fertility to subordination of the precise details of each individual case to simplification, in the form of assuming common uniformities and explaining irregularities as due to accidental factors. The explanatory and predictive power of science is enhanced through useful theories and hypotheses, which represent a form of simplification in dealing with detailed items of information.

A hypothesis is an informed or shrewd guess or inference, with a reasonable chance of being right, formulated and tentatively adopted to explain observed facts or conditions and to guide in further investigation, in other words, to serve as the investigator's "eyes" in seeking answers to questions. The scientist's hypothesis parallels the common man's personal opinion or hunch.

Expressed in other language, Charles Darwin said in an 1857 letter to his contemporary Alfred R. Wallace, "Without speculation there is no good and original observation." Speculation, or intuitive contemplation guided by past discoveries, led Darwin to his famous observations, as set forth in *Origin of Species*.

Hypotheses may serve the following functions: They may contribute as explanations, stimuli to research, sources of methodology, criteria for evaluating experimental and other techniques, and as organizing principles. In thus limiting the area of investigation, sensitizing the worker to pertinent data and relationships, and providing a unifying concept,

---

[127] Quoted from review by Conway Zirkle, *Science* 132: 1655–56; December 2, 1960, of Edward Lurie, *Louis Agassiz: A Life in Science*. Chicago: The University of Chicago Press, 1960. 449 p. Reprinted from *Science* by permission.

[128] Clarence W. Brown and Edwin E. Ghiselli, *Scientific Method in Psychology*. New York: McGraw-Hill Book Co., 1955. p. 157–59.

the single hypothesis should not blind the research worker's observation of all pertinent data, even though some facts may not contribute to validation of the chosen hypothesis. As emphasized later, it is common for a particular study to involve formulation and testing of more than one hypothesis.

Factors that contribute to the emergence of hypotheses include generalizing beyond the results of previous investigations, analyzing factual conditions requiring explanation, intellectual equipment and resources of the scientist, and inspiration. Expressed otherwise, hypotheses originate from substantially the same background as that which serves to identify problems: the insight and imagination that should result from a sound instructional program, extensive and critical reading, knowledge of existing practices and needs, and meaningful contact with pertinent data.[129]

There is no sharp line of demarcation between hypothesis and theory, since the basic difference is one of complexity and the extent of testing against the evidence. In its early stages of testing, a theory usually has been called a hypothesis but, as the hypothesis is checked against the data and their logical implications toward a successful conclusion, it may become known as a theory. A law represents an order or relation of phenomena that is invariable under the given conditions and permits of no exception in its operation.

The working hypothesis, when checked against the data, may emerge as a central explanatory theme for purposes of interpretation, although the hypothesis, as a tentative supposition, shrewd guess, conjecture, inference, or "if-then" statement, is not always stated explicitly in the graduate thesis, particularly the descriptive-survey study. In many reports of investigations of status or current conditions, a formal expression of the hypothesis is omitted in favor of a direct question or declarative statement of purpose, as illustrated earlier in this chapter.

TESTING HYPOTHESES AND REPORTING
FALSE HYPOTHESES

The hypothesis may be evaluated in terms of agreement with and explanation of the evidence, absence of conflict with satisfactorily proved generalizations, success for purposes of prediction, simplicity and clarity of statement, and logical consistency.[130] Although a specific investigation usually involves the development and testing of more than one hypothesis, many scientists and scholars have been reluctant to describe their rejected hypotheses or failures. This means that it is frequently impossible to learn

[129] *Ibid.*, p. 162–63.
[130] Morris R. Cohen and Ernest Nagel, *An Introduction to Logic and Scientific Method*. New York: Harcourt, Brace & World, Inc., 1934. p. 207–15.

about the blind alleys traveled by earlier investigators. Since the technical report is usually prepared at the conclusion of the study, the author commonly tells a simple story of "smooth sailing." If research workers are overly cautious about making and reporting mistakes, they are not likely to make either errors or discoveries. As Whitehead says, "Panic of error is the death of progress." According to Humphrey Davy, "The most important of my discoveries have been suggested to me by my failures." It may be surprising that so able a scientist as Charles Darwin could not recall a single first-formed hypothesis, with the exception of the Coral Reefs, which had not after a time been given up or greatly modified.[131] We also know that the scientist, like any other human being, frequently holds views that are inconsistent with one another.

This reluctance to describe the scientist's mistakes to the reader is aptly described by Helmholtz, in commenting on his work during 1891, including the solution of certain problems in mathematics and physics over which great mathematicians had puzzled in vain.

> But any pride I might have felt in my conclusions was perceptibly lessened by the fact that I knew that the solution of these problems had almost always come to me as the gradual generalization of favourable examples, by a series of fortunate conjectures, after many errors. I am fain to compare myself with a wanderer on the mountains, who, not knowing the path, climbs slowly and painfully upwards, and often has to retrace his steps because he can go no farther—then, whether by taking thought or from luck, discovers a new track that leads him on a little, till at length when he reaches the summit he finds to his shame that there is a royal road, by which he might have ascended, had he only had the wits to find the right approach to it. In my works I naturally said nothing about my mistakes to the reader, but only described the made track by which he may now reach the same heights without difficulty.[132]

A similar view concerning the development and testing of hypotheses has been expressed by Cannon, a research worker in medicine and physiology.[133]

> Investigators do not march straight to their goal with ease and directness. In their imagination they see a possible fact and they set forth to learn whether their foresight can be realized. Or they come upon something which is puzzling and challenging and which they wish to explain; then they try in various ways to relate it to other phenomena that would solve the riddle. Obstacles and

131 Allen Johnson, *The Historian and Historical Evidence.* New York: Charles Scribner's Sons, 1926. p. 166–67.

Edwin G. Boring, "Cognitive Dissonance: Its Use in Science." *Science* 145: 680–85; August 14, 1964.

132 Quoted in William H. George, *The Scientist in Action: A Scientific Study of His Methods.* London: Williams and Norgate, 1936. p. 229–30.

133 Quoted from Walter B. Cannon, *op. cit.,* p. 22.

difficulties are sure to be encountered. The search for understanding is an adventure or, more commonly, series of adventures. If an attempt in one direction fails, the failure is not discouraging to an eager explorer. There are other possible approaches to the end in view and relentlessly, one after another, these are tried.

Kettering expressed the opinion that he could teach young men to be inventors, provided they could overcome fear of failure. He reminds us that in research and invention one major success may be preceded by hundreds of failures. "You must learn how to fail intelligently! . . . Once you've failed, analyze the problem and find out why . . . The only time you don't want to fail is the last time you try."[134]

It has even been suggested that a journal should be established for publication of negative results.

> The usual first step in an experimental study is a search of the literature for previous work relevant to the proposed research. Certainly no problem exists if the researcher finds the work has been done. Unfortunately, the only studies that are likely to appear in any journal are those which come up with "publishable results" (i.e., results that are statistically significant). If an experiment yields "negative results" (i.e., results which fail to confirm the tested hypothesis), the findings are usually relegated to the experimenter's filing cabinet and are likely to remain there. This approach can hardly be thought of as extending scientific communication.
>
> It is suggested that the value of negative results has been underestimated. Negative findings can add to our knowledge by indicating unfruitful aspects of a given problem, thereby eliminating wasted research time and energy. In building up the empirical foundation of a science, it is important to know not only what *does* exist, but what does *not* exist as well.
>
> A way of coping with this problem would be to have a place to publish these findings. This could be done by establishing a *Journal of Negative Results*.[135]

EXAMPLES OF HYPOTHESES

To cite an example of the working hypothesis, an investigation of the correlates of daydreaming expresses its general hypothesis as follows:

> The general hypothesis of this study is that subjects who indicate a greater frequency of daydream behavior are also characterized by greater reported frequency of night dreams, social introversion, and creativity in their spontaneous reports of daydreams or storytelling activity. They are, in addition, more likely to be identified with their mothers (on the basis of measures of assumed similarity of interests); those who report less daydreaming, on the

[134] Quoted from T. A. Boyd, *Professional Amateur, op. cit.*, p. 209–10.
[135] Quoted from Marvin R. Goldfried and Gary C. Walters, "Needed: Publication of Negative Results." *American Psychologist* 14: 598; September 1959.

other hand, are expected to show greater evidence of repression or denial of problems and a lesser tendency toward identification with their mothers.[136]

To use another example, a dynamic hypothesis in social psychology may be formulated by restating Hamilton's principle of physics, to the effect that, "In a system of particles subject only to their own gravitational forces, any particle will move, over a period of time, on a path such that the difference between the kinetic and potential energies of the system will be minimized." The restatement of Hamilton's principle for investigation in social psychology would be:

An individual S in a social group G behaves, over a period of time, in such a way as to minimize the difference between
  A. the ability of G to accomplish its work by virtue of its position, prestige, status or reputation among other groups; and
  B. the ability of G to do its work by virtue of its interaction, conflict, etc., with other groups.
Many predictions of what S will do in G, if the restatement be true, are obvious. For example, if $A < B$, the members S_i should then behave, on the average, in such ways as either to raise A or lower B or both. Or if $A = B$, the S_i will behave in such ways as to preserve the balance within certain limits, etc.[137]

Other illustrations of hypotheses may be found in the chapter on history and historiography. In summary and by way of further example, thinking analytically involves not only thinking in terms of what is actual, as illustrated by the data of many descriptive-survey studies, but also thinking in terms of what is possible.

Thinking what is possible is hypothetical thinking. Such thinking is characterized in part by the employment of conditional propositions which are of the form, "if p then q." A proposition of this form is suppositional.

In the sciences conditional statements are often about inferred entities— e.g., statements about molecules or atoms or electrons. Consider the following statement: "If the kinetic energy of a gas is increased then molecules travel at a higher rate of velocity." The inferred entity, molecule, which is talked about in the preceding statement differs from an actual entity. It is derived, not observed. Thus, the statement is suppositional rather than actual.

Hypothetical thinking also employs the contrary-to-fact statement which differs from the conditional statement in being expressed in the subjunctive mood. For example, the chemist states: "If the temperature were to fall to $-273°C$ there would be zero volume." This statement does not relate directly

---

[136] Quoted from Jerome L. Singer and Rosalea A. Schonbar, "Correlates of Day-dreaming: A Dimension of Self-Awareness." *Journal of Consulting Psychology* 25: 1–6; February 1961.

[137] Quoted from Harold Webster, "Dynamic Hypotheses in Psychology." *Psychological Review* 59: 168–71; March 1952.

to what is actual. All known substances solidify at a temperature above
−273°C, thereby fixing observable volume at some definite value greater than
zero. Every schoolboy and every physical scientist uses the concept of Absolute
Zero, a concept which is derived from the proposition just stated. Although
the schoolboy may be, the scientist is not disturbed by the obvious discrepancy
between his thinking and his experience of the actual. The scientist knows
that he can describe the actual with greater certainty by considering what is
possible, rather than by solely considering what is actual.[138]

Concluding Statement

The investigator is aided in identifying significant problems through
advanced study and critical reading, analysis of practices and needs, and
repetition or extension of earlier studies. Insensitivity to problems near
at hand sometimes has been called problem blindness in our own "back-
yards." It is customary for students to pay tribute to their professors,
but there are some instances when the colleges attended have had little
influence as preparation for future educational work or research. For
most scholars and scientists, critical reading of the related literature
serves as a stimulus to thinking and creativity, although it has been said
that every laboratory needs one "crackpot" who doesn't know yet what
you can't do. Serendipity sometimes is a bonus to the perceptive worker,
but is not a satisfactory substitute for scholarship and hard work. The
chapter bibliography includes references dealing with trends, prophecies,
and needed research.

Important factors in selection of the problem include: novelty and
significance, intellectual curiosity and drive, scholarship and personal
characteristics, sources and technique, sponsorship and cooperation, risks
and costs, and timing. A famous inventor said that he was more interested in what investigators do differently than what they do alike, and
did not worry about duplication of effort in research. A scientist has
suggested that our ideas need to be jostled about or that we need a certain
amount of "dither" to prevent intellectual stagnation. Overemphasis on
factual materials and formal requirements in the training of research
workers may actually inhibit development of creativity. We are warned
that too great dependence on elaborate equipment may even restrict
freedom in research. It has been said that we have an obligation to "free
the scientist from the nervousness of this era and to put the gift of time
again at his disposal."

The initial statement and fuller definition of the problem involve
appropriate focusing of the topic, constituent elements and scope, related
literature and terminology, sources of evidence and methodology, and

---

[138] Quoted from George S. Maccia, "Hypothetical Thinking in Education." *Educational Theory* 10: 182–86; July 1960.

basic assumptions. As a rule the graduate student avoids both "global" and "pinpoint" problems.

The hypothesis may serve the purposes of explanations, stimuli to research, sources of methodology, criteria for evaluating research techniques, and organizing principles. In other words, speculation, or intuitive contemplation guided by past discoveries, should lead to careful observations as a basis for testing hypotheses. Great scientists and inventors have urged beginners in research to overcome fear of failure and to analyze their mistakes, since the overly cautious investigator is not likely to make either errors or discoveries.

SELECTED REFERENCES

ABELSON, Philip H. "Trends in Scientific Research." *Science* 143: 218-23; January 17, 1964.

BARDEN, John. "The 1984 Look." *Journal of Higher Education* 34: 324-29; June 1963.

BERTHOFF, Rowland. "The American Social Order: A Conservative Hypothesis." *American Historical Review* 65: 495-553; April 1960.

CARMICHAEL, Leonard, and Others. "Child Development Research: The Next Twenty-Five Years." *Child Development* 31: 191-208; March 1960.

CARROLL, John B. "Neglected Areas in Educational Research." *Phi Delta Kappan* 42: 339-46; May 1961.

CARTWRIGHT, William H. "The Teacher in 2065." *Teachers College Record* 66: 295-304; January 1965.

CHANSKY, Norman M. "Problems of Research in Reading." *Journal of Developmental Reading* 7: 102-19; Winter 1964.

Educational Television: The Next Ten Years. Stanford, Calif.: Institute for Communication Research, Stanford University, 1962. xi + 375 p.

EURICH, Alvin C. "A Twenty-first Century Look at Higher Education." *Current Issues in Higher Education, 1963.* Washington: Association for Higher Education, NEA, 1963. pp. 39-46.

GOOD, Carter V. *Introduction to Educational Research: Methodology of Design in the Behavioral and Social Sciences.* Second Edition. New York: Appleton-Century-Crofts, 1963. Chapter 2.

GUTEK, Gerald. "Unsolved Educational Problems of the 1960's—A Legacy of the Depression of the 1930's." *Peabody Journal of Education* 43: 13-17; July 1965.

JOHN, M. E. "Rural Sociology in the Years Ahead." *Rural Sociology* 27: 107-15; June 1962.

KNOX, Alan B. "Current Needs in Adult Education Research." *Journal of Education* 147: 21-31; February 1965.

LEMESHOW, Seymour. "Teacher Education in 2015: A Projected Outline." *Journal of Teacher Education* 16: 229-31; June 1965.

LEONARD, Regis J. "Guidance in 1975." *Journal of Educational Sociology* 36: 229-36; January 1963.

LIEBERMAN, Myron. "Education for Tomorrow: 67 Theses." *School and Society* 88: 34-38; January 16, 1960.

MACCIA, George S. "Hypothetical Thinking in Education." *Educational Theory* 10: 182-86; July 1960.

MILES, Matthew B. "Education in the '70s: Some Predictions." *Teachers College Record* 65: 441-54; February 1964.

MURPHY, Gardner. "The Psychology of 1975: An Extrapolation." *American Psychologist* 18: 689-95; November 1963.

PATTEN, Thomas H. "Directions of Research in Industrial Sociology." *American Catholic Sociological Review* 24: 316-32; Winter 1963.

RYANS, David G. "Possible Directions for Teacher-Behavior Research." *Theory into Practice* 2: 105-12; April 1963.

SANFORD, Nevitt. "Will Psychologists Study Human Problems?" *American Psychologist* 20: 192-202; March 1965.

"The School of the Future—1985." *Educational Leadership* 17: 470-508; May 1960.

SHEATS, Paul H., and Others. "Extension Education Views the Next Fifty Years." *NUEA Spectator* 30: 4-25; April-May 1965.

"A Symposium on Teacher Education: Significant Developments, Unsolved Problems, Looking Twenty-five Years Ahead." *Journal of Teacher Education* 14: 9-50; March 1963.

TROW, William C. "Predictions Twenty-Years After." *University of Michigan School of Education Bulletin* 35: 17-19; November 1963.

VANDER WERF, Lester S. "Needed Research in Vocational Education." *Phi Delta Kappan* 46: 405-10; April 1965.

WASHBURNE, Carleton. "An Eighty Years Perspective on Education." *Phi Delta Kappan* 45: 145-50; December 1963.

WATSON, Robert I. "The History of Psychology: A Neglected Area." *American Psychologist* 15: 251-55; April 1960.

WEBB, Wilse B. "The Choice of the Problem." *American Psychologist* 16: 223-27; May 1961.

WEBER, Eugen. "The Right in France: A Working Hypothesis." *American Historical Review* 65: 554-68; April 1960.

WINDLE, Charles, and VALLANCE, T. R. "The Future of Military Psychology: Paramilitary Psychology." *American Psychologist* 19: 119-29; February 1964.

3

Integration of the Related Literature

LIBRARY KEYS

The importance of the related literature as background for problem-solving has already been emphasized in Chapter 2. The present chapter describes the guides or keys to the vast storehouse of research (books, periodicals, and theses) now available in education, psychology, sociology, and cognate social fields, as sources for integration of the related literature. This chapter also presents certain problems closely related to library technique, such as information retrieval, note-taking, and synthesis of published findings, although the topic of documentation and bibliographical form is reserved for the last chapter, dealing with the technical report. The present chapter can do no more than mention briefly a few of the most generally used library tools (including extensive bibliographies, exhaustive summaries of research, and research handbooks), leaving for the comprehensive guides to reference works the detailed information concerning several hundred helpful titles of reference books.[1] In the brief description of the guides to the literature, it will be helpful to identify major subdivisions or the larger subheadings in education, psychology, and sociology, under which the related studies usually are classified or indexed.

---

[1] Carter Alexander and Arvid J. Burke, *How to Locate Educational Information and Data.* Fourth Edition. New York: Bureau of Publications, Teachers College, Columbia University, 1958. xvii + 419 p.

I. G. Mudge, *Guide to Reference Books.* Sixth Edition. Chicago: American Library Association, 1936. xii + 504 p. Also see earlier editions and the informal supplements.

Constance M. Winchell, *Guide to Reference Books.* Seventh Edition. Chicago: American Library Association, 1951. xvii + 645 p.

Constance M. Winchell and O. A. Johnson, *Guide to Reference Books.* Seventh Edition Supplement, 1950–52. Second Supplement, 1953–55. Third Supplement, 1956–58. Fourth Supplement, 1959–62. Chicago: American Library Association, 1954, 1956, 1960, 1963. 140 p., 134 p., 145 p., 151 p.

Louis Shores, *Basic Reference Sources.* Chicago: American Library Association, 1954. ix + 378 p.

THE COMPREHENSIVENESS OF ONE MAJOR HANDBOOK FOR SEARCHING THE educational literature and of the library resources is indicated by the following chapter topics:[2]

General Suggestions for Library Searching
Procedures in Library Searching
Selecting Headings before Searching for References
Locating Books through the Library Card Catalog
Locating Books Outside the Library Used
Locating Periodicals and Other Serials
Making the Most of the Education Index
Making a Bibliography
Securing a Guide to the Professional Literature of One's Field
Library Reading
Note-Taking in Work with Library Materials
Reference Books
Evaluations of Books and Other References
Publications of Educational Associations
United States Office of Education Publications
Government Documents
Instructional Materials and Aids
History of an Educational Problem or Topic
Legal Aspects of Education
Biographical Information
Names and Addresses
News Items
Quotations and Proverbs
Educational Researches
Statistics and Statistical Methodology.

Integration or Synthesis of Published Findings

It is generally recognized that a field of knowledge makes progress as a scientific discipline through the activities of the worker who is engaged in conducting and interpreting research. There is another function, however, that involves important activities of integration and assimilation of the bodies of data and published findings in the many sub-areas of such fields as education and psychology. Unless the research findings from many thousands of individual studies are incorporated within appropriate theories, it is virtually impossible for graduate students and others to assimilate the knowledge in a particular field of specialization. It is possible that data and published studies are accumulating more rapidly than they can be integrated or summarized effectively, as witnessed by difficulties in securing qualified persons to prepare summarizing

2 Carter Alexander and Arvid J. Burke, *op. cit.*

articles for the *Review of Educational Research, Encyclopedia of Educational Research,* and *Annual Review of Psychology.*

Therefore, it seems appropriate to give due recognition to the scholar who does his work in the library, sorting research findings according to an integrating scheme, summarizing sound empirical findings, noting contradictory results, identifying needed research, and noting the status of explanatory efforts. This type of assimilating or integrating work may prove more valuable to the profession as a summary of several hundred research reports than for a scholar to spend the same amount of time in collecting original data on a single limited problem.[3] It has even been recommended that some scientists may well "commit themselves deeply to the job of sifting, reviewing, and synthesizing information," since research workers and scholars rather generally consider critical reviewing, writing of scholarly books, and insightful synthesizing as much a part of science as is more traditional research. It has been urged that the technical or scientific community accord such evaluating and synthesizing individuals an esteem commensurate with the importance of their services and reward them well.[4]

To illustrate more specifically at the graduate level the importance of finding and comprehending the literature, we know that it is common practice in the elementary schools, secondary schools, and undergraduate colleges to rely on the textbook for instructional purposes, although many teachers make good use of supplementary sources. In the graduate school, however, the student is expected to go direct to a variety of sources for the evidence on his topic or problem for special study—to articles in professional journals, original documents, reports of investigations, and other pertinent sources.[5]

It is here that the basic techniques of graduate study become most clearly indispensable. The student must be able to gather, to analyze, to evaluate, to synthesize, and to report the primary literature on a topic chosen or assigned. With moderate proficiency in these skills as a common "first level," to be gained at the outset by all beginning graduate students, a great deal of time now wasted could be used to good advantage.

When the fundamental ability—to find and comprehend the literature—is the common offering at the beginning of graduate work, the student can move from humble depedence on the source of authority to an increasing independence in scholarship. Courses can be devoted less to indoctrination, exchange of experience, and audiovisual aids, and more to finding out what is

3 Benton J. Underwood, *Psychological Research.* New York: Appleton-Century-Crofts, 1957. p. 290–91.

4 Philip H. Abelson, "Science, Government, and Information." *Science* 139: 1015; March 15, 1963.

5 Warren R. Good, "The Essentials in Technique for Graduate Study in Education." *University of Michigan School of Education Bulletin* 33: 119–22; May 1962.

already known about issues or problems. Not knowing the literature can be responsible for wasting many hours in "discussion" that consists chiefly in exchanging ignorance, or for treating the panacea of homogeneous grouping as a novel suggestion or solemnly accepting the old wives' tales about lefthandedness as the basis for educational treatment of the problems. Most of this paragraph, incidentally, seems to have an application to committee work.

A competent survey of the literature requires several abilities that are needed throughout the pursuit of scholarship. One is the ability to find and inspect what promises to be the pertinent literature, which is done mostly on the basis of tricks of the trade that can be taught rather easily. But without specific training and directed practice on this job the student is a rudderless vessel on a murky sea.

Next is the ability to analyze what remains of the "literature" as the useless items are discarded. But the useful remainder may vary from a series of opinions on some unexplored topic to clusters of meticulous experiments on aspects of a recognizedly complex problem. The analysis demands, of course, that the student understand what he reads. And with regard to technical preparation, this means especially methods of research and methods of statistical analysis. Both areas are background also for a collateral reaction, the *evaluation* of quantitative literature; which involves criticism of conditions and techniques, and particularly of the relation between evidence and conclusions or recommendations.

The student makes notes on each study or other item that he is to report, being sure to get such basic research information as (1) the purpose, date, place, and conditions of the study, (2) the name of the investigator and the citation of the published report, (3) the number and kinds of subjects, (4) the basis on which the subjects were chosen, (5) the initial tests or other measures used to determine ability at the beginning of the study, (6) methods used in choosing or equating groups, (7) the experimental or investigational procedure followed, (8) the tests or other instruments used for final measurement, (9) the methods used in analyzing the data, (10) the results obtained, expressed in figures from the study, and (11) the main conclusions drawn by the investigator. Aside from the background needed in order to take such notes, collecting the summary of information is in itself a new skill; and this, too, needs practice under the guidance of an experienced hand.

Synthesis of the notes from source materials is the next job, to make a coherent account of what is known, so far, about the topic. The reporting is so different from the creative writing for English courses that the student needs help with the problems of organization, precise and appropriate statement of fact, quotation, condensation, documentation, technical standards in the production of manuscript, and so on.

It must be clear that the student, before he can review the literature, must have some knowledge of the fundamental logic of scientific method, its application in methods of research, and methods of collecting and analyzing data.

As to end results, the survey of the related literature may provide guiding hypotheses, suggestive methods of investigation, and comparative data for interpretative purposes. Sometimes textbooks and subjective critiques of a problem area provide important insights and hypotheses that may well have a place in the summary of the related literature. The summarizer of research always has before him the problem of striking a balance between tedious detail and superficial sketchiness. One technique is to group similar studies, with a representative investigation analyzed in some detail. The weaknesses of unsound studies and the merits of outstanding investigations should be indicated in a constructive manner, but without the ordinary adjectives of denunciation or praise as such.

The review of related research should be an integral part of the total report rather than an appendage or a loosely related supplement. The purpose of this review is not primarily to produce a relatively complete annotated bibliography. A number of existing agencies have much better facilities than the graduate student for exhaustive bibliographical work; for example, the *Encyclopedia of Educational Research, Review of Educational Research, Psychological Abstracts, Annual Review of Psychology,* and *Sociological Abstracts.*

> Another, and perhaps even more common, misconception is the idea that the review is presented to show that the candidate's research has not been done previously by someone else. But any necessarily limited review cannot provide this proof of originality. At best it can only show that no piece of research reviewed by the candidate is exactly the same as his study. With educational research being carried on at a multitude of educational institutions and by numerous other agencies, it is extremely doubtful that any candidate can even discover references to any considerable portion of the studies that have been carried out in his area of interest. Also, in an area such as education where problems are so numerous and so complex and where the application of scientific methods is relatively new, it is doubtful that the question of the uniqueness of research is nearly as important as many other questions. It might be suggested that finding the ways in which studies are comparable and in which they are related to one another is a more important problem. . . .
>
> . . . It is this fitting of a particular project into a broader scheme, enabling one to see its importance and to relate it to many other studies, that is the real purpose of the review of related research. Through this study of existing research, the candidate locates and defines his exact problem. Then in writing up this review, he so organizes these previous findings that the reader can see just why the problem is important and how it is going to fit into a wider pattern of research results.
>
> This purpose of the review of research may also be viewed in another manner. It may be considered as a small contribution to the building of research theory.[6]

[6] Quoted from C. M. Lindvall, "The Review of Related Research." *Phi Delta Kappan* 40: 179–80; January 1959.

As early as 1851 the secretary to the Smithsonian Institution observed that the scholar or scientist should be acquainted with what had previously been done on his problem, but feared that the "pile" of 20,000 additions to knowledge published annually would begin to totter under its own weight, and that literature and science would be overwhelmed by their own unwieldy truth.[7]

As to the present size of the job of integrating the literature, it is estimated that in 1960 alone, 212 core psychological journals published 1,500 articles, mostly in English, representing a floodtide of materials for colleagues in many lands. "While there has been growing concern about communication across language barriers, psychologists have given relatively little attention to new techniques of selective electronic dissemination of scientific papers, micropublication, and mechanized retrieval of stored information."[8]

To cite another illustration, the problem of reporting and disseminating evidence is especially urgent in medical research, which has moved so rapidly into new fields that doctors are faced by an ever-growing mountain of new facts, theories, and procedures, as reported in some 900 medical journals published in the United States alone. For example, among the few truly effective drugs early in this century were morphine and digitalis, but by 1960 there were some 500 pure and potent therapeutic substances, marketed in at least 20,000 forms and combinations.

Careful handling of references is imperative in relation to effective summarizing. In the matter of bibliographical work, even as experienced and prolific an author as Ellwood P. Cubberley encountered criticisms that seemed merited. A reviewer of Cubberley's *Syllabus of Lectures on the History of Education* thought the bibliographies were useful but complained of the defective or incomplete references, having found 39 on a single page. The number of such faulty references throughout the book caused the reviewer to wonder whether much of the bibliographical work had not been done by students. For the careless reference work, Cubberley could have no excuse, except that he had only a master's degree at that time, with no record of bibliographical training. His later reference work evidenced improvement.[9]

Information Retrieval and Automation

With respect to information retrieval, we are challenged to decide which tools and procedures are the most efficient for providing the

[7] J. W. Asher and Marvin Kurfeerst, "The Computer and Information Retrieval: School Law a Case Study." *Harvard Educational Review* 35: 178–90; Spring 1965.

[8] Henry P. David and William M. Swartley, "Toward More Effective International Communication in Psychology." *American Psychologist* 16: 696–98; November 1961.

[9] Jesse B. Sears and Adin D. Henderson, *Cubberley of Stanford: And His Contribution to American Education.* Stanford, Calif: Stanford University Press, 1957. p. 119–20.

information desired at the level of quality and speed required. If computers can retrieve information more efficiently than can be done by other methods, we should be using them more widely. Improvement of information services may be approached through simultaneous operation of three programs:[10]

1. Better support of basic library and dissemination functions that use conventional means
2. Development of a science upon which a better information technology may be built, rather than to depend so heavily on purely empirical foundations
3. Rigorous investigation of technological proposals to determine their merits, as compared with known methods for attaining the same objective.

We are cautioned, however, to avoid a stampede into information retrieval systems designed to recover factual information from the printed mass, that is, to disinter a book, article, review, or report, which will then be read by someone to retrieve its information content. The prior question always is: What are we looking for? If we are looking for a new field theory or a scientific approach that will open up new lines of research, factual retrieval systems will not suffice. In other words, when we are looking for new scientific knowledge that does not necessarily fit present ground rules, which is in advance of its time and may be obscured among the mass of current publications, the scientist himself must look, since the librarian typically does not have the background, learning, and attitude of mind to recognize and grasp the meaning of the scientific information when it comes along.[11]

To illustrate from the field of psychology the problem of an efficient method for storage and selective retrieval of the results of research, it has been generally assumed in the past that the need is satisfied by printed archives in the form of journals, monographs, books, summaries, abstracts, and bibliographies, and that the technique of retrieval depends on the initiative and skill of the individual scholar. This traditional emphasis, by way of a storage function for libraries, has continued in psychology (and in many other areas). The problems of scientific communication that must be solved include:

(a) an overloading of the various channels of publication; (b) a stereotyping of publications so as to fit a standardized mold of reporting; (c) an excessive amount of reporting in archival journals of fragmentary findings, of "first steps" of research which are often never followed up, and too little integrative reporting of "firm" conclusions; (d) an overloading of the programs of regional and national conventions with "bit-by-bit" reports of research; and (e) a failure to use the conventions as an occasion for the exchange of important ideas

[10] Ralph R. Shaw, "Information Retrieval." *Science* 140: 606–09; May 10, 1963.
[11] Phyllis A. Richmond, "What Are We Looking For?" *Science* 139: 737–39; February 22, 1963.

and information or for the stimulation of quality and originality in psychological research.[12]

Language Skills

Although the traditional acceptance of the basic position of foreign languages in the qualifications for the doctoral degree has been considerably modified since the 1930's, especially for professional degrees, a reading knowledge of one or more modern foreign languages should prove helpful in canvassing the related literature on a problem for investigation. It has been typical to stress the "tool" aspect of the foreign language, supporting the view that a doctoral candidate should be able to read German or French, so that he can translate the most recent technical articles relating to his special field or problem. This use of a foreign language is similar to the study of statistics in psychology, education, sociology, or economics, as a necessary or practical tool or technique. On the other hand, many graduate students and some professors maintain that all the important literature has been translated into English or is being translated, so that there is no longer a need for the foreign-language requirement in the doctoral program. One answer to this view is that it smacks of provincialism, and that something usually is lost in translation. Many scientists and scholars still take pride in the ability to translate for themselves, supporting the adage, "Never read a book about a book, read the book," although this is an extreme position. However, there is now a growing recognition that English has become the language of science, and there is an increasing demand for the scientific publications of the U. S. As these great changes take place in the distribution and use of scientific literature, we are making important contributions to other nations capable of utilization of our publications.

Another important advantage of foreign-language facility as a tool is its practical employment by the scholar or scientist who travels abroad. With an increasing number of overseas fellowships and scholarships available, and more American specialists in demand as technical advisers to foreign governments and American overseas financial enterprises, more academic people now are enabled to travel abroad. When such persons have been able to converse directly with men in their own fields, the value of a foreign language has been demonstrated, not only on the practical grounds of communication, but also as a means of better understanding of another nationality, with some lessening of the narrow provincialism of which our nation and our higher institutions have sometimes been guilty.[13]

---

12 Quoted from Board of Scientific Affairs, "Technical Communication in Psychology: A Statement of the Problem." *American Psychologist* 14: 267–71; June 1959.

13 Everett Walters, "Foreign Languages: Benefit or Barrier?" *Graduate School Record* 9: 1, 3; January 1956.

To return to a specific problem of translation, with respect to different editions of a book, the timing of the translation may prove difficult. In the early days of psychology, Edward B. Titchener found it hard to keep up with the different editions of Wundt's *Principles of Physiological Psychology*. When Titchener had finished translating the third edition, he found that the indefatigable Wundt had written the fourth edition, which in turn was translated, only to find that the prolific Wundt had turned out the fifth edition. After translating six of the twenty-two chapters of the fifth edition, Titchener took no chances and went to press.[14]

To use the field of psychology as an example, the "language requirement" too frequently has been perfunctory rather than functional in terms of the particular field or problem for specialization or research.[15]

> If knowledge of one or more foreign languages is important to an individual's research, then he will need to achieve much higher proficiency than is presently typically attained; and such proficiency should be required in those fields where language competence is critical. However, for some fields of research endeavor, knowledge of other tool subjects may be far more critical than knowledge of a foreign language. For example, thorough competence in mathematics is of vital importance to those attempting to contribute to statistical behavior theory. Similarly, new developments in research in learning, taking place largely in the United States, place a high premium on competence in electronics and relay engineering.
>
> Given the development of adequate translation services, as well as the somewhat unpredictable shifts in major research activity in some specialities from one language area to another, substantial foreign language proficiency, as any other tool competence, should be required selectively for those individuals to whose interests and plans it is relevant, and not as a *rite de passage* for all.

Note-Taking[16]

It is essential, especially in summarizing the literature and in historical studies, to collect the material systematically, with a well-arranged plan of note-taking. A note system should be flexible, to permit addition of

14 Robert I. Watson, *The Great Psychologists*. Philadelphia: J. B. Lippincott Co., 1963. p. 360.

15 Quoted from Donald W. Taylor and Others, "Education for Research in Psychology." *American Psychologist* 14: 167–79; April 1959. Also see: Philip H. Abelson, "Distribution of U. S. Scientific Literature." *Science* 149: 589; August 6, 1965.

16 Carter Alexander and Arvid J. Burke, *op. cit.*, p. 52–56, 168–80.

Jacques Barzun and Henry F. Graff, *The Modern Researcher*. New York: Harcourt, Brace and Co., 1957. p. 18–39.

William W. Brickman, *Guide to Research in Educational History*. New York: New York University Bookstore, 1949. p. 191–200.

Homer C. Hockett, *The Critical Method in Historical Research and Writing*. New York: The Macmillan Co., 1955. p. 89–142.

new material, without disarranging the older notes, and with the possibility of rearranging the notes as desired. To make this possible, it is necessary that the notes be taken on separate sheets of paper, slips, or cards.

Three kinds of notes are regularly made by historical workers and are also appropriate, with some adaptations, for summarizing studies. The bibliographical note includes the standard data, author, title, pages, place and date of publication, and other formal facts about the document or study. The subject note contains one item of information about a specific topic, with the source indicated; most notes collected by the summarizer or historian usually are of this type. The "method" notes include suggestions or ideas useful in interpreting the facts.

Some preliminary reading and note-taking probably have taken place before the major topics of the outline begin to stand out in relief, and in turn the tentative outline and its headings serve as a guide for further reading, study, and note-taking. Expansion of the bibliography, analysis of content, and gathering of notes probably continue until the actual writing of the report begins and even later.

Although able historians like George Bancroft, J. B. McMaster, James Ford Rhodes, and Edward Gibbon used bound notebooks instead of a flexible system, it can only be said that they succeeded in spite of their notebooks in calendar form. During the 1840's Bancroft had a number of quarto-size blank books, in which one or more pages were allocated to the successive days of the years, and the data were entered on the page corresponding to the day and year when the event occurred. Even as late as the 1890's, Rhodes used blank books for his notes, since the card system at that time was something of a novelty.

William G. Sumner, the sociologist, had no financial assistance for research and little help, yet his files of notes compared favorably with many later research workers supported by relatively large financial grants. Sumner filled 52 drawers and boxes of notes, averaging 3,000 sheets each.

Soon after Clark Hull, the psychologist, began graduate study, he initiated a permanent notebook system of the original ideas on psychological subjects that came to him on reading a new book, agreements or disagreements with the author, and views on subjects discussed in class or seminar. Near the end of his career, this series of notebooks totaled 27 volumes. To his surprise Hull discovered that the notes were valuable not so much as aids to memory, but as stimuli to systematic thinking. Hull confesses that he had little success in persuading promising graduate students in his seminars to keep similar notebooks, even when he presented notebooks to the students.[17]

[17] Herbert S. Langfeld, Editor, *A History of Psychology in Autobiography.* Vol. 4. Worcester, Mass.: Clark University Press, 1952. xii + 356 p.

Throughout his life Ellwood P. Cubberley kept notes on a wide variety of subjects which interested him, particularly matters revealing significant trends (by studying data in series). Cubberley left an unusual record for his biographer: a long series of pocket calendar notebooks which he kept with regularity through the years from 1905 to 1940. These booklets were filled with facts about home, work, travel, accounts, attendance at operas and concerts and dinner meetings, illnesses, books he was working on as author or editor, trips for business or pleasure, expenses for clothes, lecture dates and topics, life-insurance policies with dates when premiums were due, library interests, his college program of study and reading, notes on the weather, and other memoranda of items he liked or wanted to remember or think about. Although Cubberley said that he did not want to be run by a card catalogue and seemed to dislike the thought of a system of formal records, in his notebooks there is evidence of care and considerable labor in recording a mass of detail, but detail dictated by his own personal interests and tastes rather than by any schemes of logic or plan of systematic accounting.[18]

Classification Systems in the Library

The reader who uses such documentary materials as books is indebted to the workers who have given their attention to classification for the purpose of affording order and system, without which library work would be virtually impossible. The two principal systems of library classification in the United States are that worked out by Melvil Dewey and published in 1876, commonly referred to as the "Dewey decimal" system, and the Library of Congress system (devised because developments in certain fields seriously crowded the older Dewey scheme). In addition to the basic systems, many special rules are necessary to cover detailed questions that arise, and some libraries have issued their own rule publications.

These classification schemes or systems are supplemented from time to time by efforts toward classification in special fields, as in education,[19] psychology, and sociology. The first extensive list of subject headings in education was prepared by Voegelein, *List of Educational Subject Headings*, 1928, which influenced the *Education Index*, first published in 1929. A latter list by Pettus, *Subject Headings in Education*, 1938, was arranged in classified rather than dictionary (alphabetical) form, and included definitions of various heads and subheads. Other sources that indicate the scope of a particular field or discipline are the *Review of Educational*

18 Jesse B. Sears and Adin D. Henderson, *op. cit.*, p. 82.

19 L. Belle Voegelein, *List of Educational Subject Headings*. Columbus: The Ohio State University Press, 1928. xiv + 338 p.

Clyde Pettus, *Subject Headings in Education: A Systematic List for Use in a Dictionary Catalogue.* New York: H. W. Wilson Co., 1938. 188 p.

Research, Encyclopedia of Educational Research, Dictionary of Education, Psychological Abstracts, Annual Review of Psychology, and *Sociological Abstracts,* as illustrated by the lists of subtopics later in this chapter. If librarians, professors, and graduate students will learn to think outside the limitations of the Dewey decimal system and the Library of Congress system, there is opportunity for a much closer relationship between bibliographical organization in the social fields and its physical implementation in libraries, thus furthering an interdisciplinary approach to problems in the behavioral and human sciences.

Whatever the classification systems and mechanisms or tools involved, library service should be so organized as to provide each research worker or scholar what he needs when he needs it, and in the form most useful to him. The individual scientist should have access to at least five classes of services:[20]

1. He needs to have access to as broad a file for browsing as he feels he can use; the size of this file will vary from scientist to scientist, from field to field, and from time to time.
2. He needs to be able to browse in bibliographical and abstracting journals which may give him leads that he may or may not be looking for.
3. He needs "current-awareness" service to the extent that his field calls for it and that he can use it.
4. He needs retrospective approaches to literature, through annual reviews, or reviews of the state of the art, or special bibliographic searches.
5. Above all, he needs access to material that he wants when he wants it, regardless of where it is housed, and he needs some screening service, so that, in searches of older or of current material, at least the obviously redundant and nonpertinent can be deleted.

To comment more specifically on "current awareness" of related studies, the investigator interacts with his immediate colleagues through correspondence, visits, professional meetings, conferences, and membership and participation in small, special interest groups. Through such media, the scholar or scientist secures *contemporary* findings for planning and interpreting his own research, whereas information retrieval services typically wait for "public" information (from or in archival sources).

The Card Catalog in the Library

The card catalog of the library is of major importance, as illustrated by a description of this tool in a particular university library.[21]

20 Ralph R. Shaw, "Documentation and the Individual." *Science* 137: 409–11; August 10, 1962.

21 Quoted from Arthur Hamlin, *News Notes from the Library* (University of Cincinnati) 6: 1–5; May 1961.

Judged by almost any standard the card catalog in the main library is the most valuable single possession of the University of Cincinnati. What other tool, machine, computer or instrument is insured for one and a third million dollars, or costs, in annual maintenance, over $75,000? What other instrument is comprised of nearly two million pieces, each precision-made by skilled craftsmen? If, as most educators claim, the library is the heart or center of the university, certainly the catalog is the heart *and* center of the library. Those who have been using it merely as a means of getting the call number of main library books are missing a great deal. It performs many services for those who are sufficiently sophisticated to use them. In analogy, some of us would have difficulty in using the university's computer to add two and two, while our more knowledgeable colleagues use it to compute orbits. So it is with the catalog which must be both an abacus and an electronic brain, equally useful to the most naive freshman and the senior scholar. There are not more than a handful here, or on any other campus, sufficiently sophisticated to utilize the card catalog to its maximum potential.

Coverage: In theory any main catalog records the book and manuscript holdings of a university. Actually, it seldom does all this, and it does not do so here. It records most of these, but not all. It also records much that is not owned by the University of Cincinnati.

Most, but by no means all, American university library catalogs are dictionary catalogs, so-called because the author, title, subject, and other entries are filed in one alphabet. So it is at Cincinnati. We depart from this only when the sheer bulk requires further breakdown. Thus U.S. History is subdivided by periods and George Washington precedes John Adams in this file in spite of alphabet. As most users are aware, cards called "added entries" are often made for translators, joint authors, illustrators, and other individuals or corporate bodies which have played important roles in the preparation of a publication.

If the card catalog is the heart of the library, there are a number of important related organs which are just as vital to the body corporate as the liver, the lungs, or the stomach to the human body, and very, very useful to faculty and students as well as to librarians.

The Shelf-list: In simplest terms, the shelf list is a record of the university library holdings by call number, regardless of physical location. The mathematician can easily look in the card catalog for a subject such as Permutations or Vector Analysis, but he would never find, under mathematics, or journals, or anything else, a list of the serials in mathematics. This the shelf list provides.

A few American research libraries no longer make subject cards and require all subject approach to the collection to be made through a very much expanded shelf-list. Scholars who have become experienced with this approach generally approve of it. This, combined with an index on cards, is called a "classed catalog."

The shelf list is extremely valuable for many needs of readers as well as librarians. It is easily available for public use.

The Serial record: Another key file is the list of our holdings of periodicals or journals. The card catalog merely tells when our file of a serial began and does not attempt to state how complete the holdings are. Instead it states "See Serial Record." Many of us assume, quite rightly, that holdings of a standard periodical, like *Harpers,* will be complete, and send for the volume needed with confidence. But the situation is different under a heading like *Royal Society of London.* The brief moment it takes to consult the adjacent Serial Record is well spent. The reasons for maintaining this separate record are complex and involved. Suffice it to say that an official of the Library of Congress spent several days here this very month in a search for certain material they did not have, and wanted. Our Serial Record caused an admiring comment that this was one library which "had everything listed—no more, and no less."

Contents file: This is a minor and possibly unique organ of the body corporate. It is not essential to existence, but serves a worthy purpose. There are many numbered series, like the *Publications* of the Harvard Graduate school of Engineering, which are kept as a series but must include, under that entry, the author and title of each number. Some of these series run into many hundred separate numbers and monographs and therefore take several score cards to list all the parts. In such cases the main catalog includes a single card for the series and refers the occasional student, who wishes to look over the various monographs included, to the Contents File.

Each departmental library catalog contains the same author, subject and some title cards, but of course only for the books in that collection.

Let us now look at the catalog for its function in providing an approach by subject. Obviously we must use indexes and bibliographies to dig out periodical articles. No library makes subject cards for issues of the *New Yorker* or even the *Transactions of the American Philosophical Society.* A Festschrift may contain many really significant contributions, but libraries cannot and should not spend ten times the purchase price in preparing 50-100 subject cards for an individual issue or volume. On the other hand there are hundreds of series in which each volume consists of several scholarly monographs. For each of these individual contributions a full set of author and subject cards should be made. These are called "analytics." Every library must decide for itself which series it will analyze. The limitation is, of course, the expense.

The Cincinnati catalog has gone extensively into "analytics." We are now cautiously revising this policy. For example the *Bulletin of the U. S. Geological Survey* was analyzed until very recently. This one series is represented in the main and geology library catalogs by well over five thousand cards. Important as this series is, the advanced student has subject access to the individual numbers through the *Bibliography of North American Geology.* Similar economies are regularly considered.

Returning now to the catalog as a whole, what does it attempt to do? First, it is a record of ownership, an inventory of what we have. Then it is a record of location, the key which tells where or how to get any item. It is also a subject bibliography which tells the student what material is available on his subject. Finally, it provides some physical description of every book as well as very scholarly, detailed description of selected material.

Educational and General Guides

Before beginning a systematic examination of the titles in the library guides, it may prove desirable to secure certain background concerning the problem by reading the kind of overview treatment commonly found in textbooks and general reference works. From this more general reading should come at least an initial list of subtopics for use in examining the library guides.

The beginner in research or graduate student probably will start with the *Education Index* (1929–   ), which has listed virtually all the educational materials in published form in the United States, except elementary and high-school textbooks, but after 1960 reduced considerably its scope and usefulness. For research materials the summaries in the *Encyclopedia of Educational Research*[22] (published in 1941, and revised in the 1950 and 1960 editions) are useful. A fourth edition is in progress. For current research studies and to supplement the *Encyclopedia of Educational Research*, the *Review of Educational Research* is the chief summarizing guide (beginning in January, 1931). The *Review* originally planned to cover fifteen major subdivisions of education within a three-year cycle, but as the years passed the number of topics increased and the appearance of a particular topic once in three years was not always possible or desirable. It is of interest to examine the following list of selected topics covered in the *Review,* noting the appearance of a particular subject at three-year intervals during recent years.

REVIEW OF EDUCATIONAL RESEARCH

ADMINISTRATION: XXII:4 (October 1952); XXV:4 (October 1955); XXVIII:4 (October 1958); XXXI:4 (October 1961); XXXIV:4 (October 1964).

EDUCATIONAL MEASUREMENT: XX:1 (February 1950); XXIII:1 (February 1953); XXVI:1 (February 1956); XXIX:1 (February 1959); XXXII:1 (February 1962); XXXV:1 (February 1965).

GUIDANCE AND COUNSELING: XXI:2 (April 1951); XXIV:2 (April 1954); XXVII:2 (April 1957); XXX:2 (April 1960); XXXIII:2 (April 1963).

MENTAL AND PHYSICAL DEVELOPMENT: XXII:5 (December 1952); XXV:5 (December 1955); XXVIII:5 (December 1958); XXXI:5 (December 1961); XXXIV:5 (December 1964).

The *Handbook of Research on Teaching*[23] probably will be kept up to date through later editions.

[22] Douglas E. Scates, "Unlocking for the Profession a Wealth of Educational Research." *Journal of Teacher Education* 11: 558–62; December 1960. Describes the *Encyclopedia of Educational Research.*

[23] N. L. Gage, Editor, *Handbook of Research on Teaching.* Chicago: Rand McNally & Co., 1963. xiv + 1218 p.

The *Bibliographic Index* is really a cumulative bibliography of bibliographies dealing with a wide range of subjects. The first number, published in 1938, includes 4,400 references.

The monthly *Book Review Digest* takes the form of a specialized periodical index, in the sense that it provides excerpts from the reviews that appear in some eighty book-review periodicals. In the course of a year it lists approximately 4,000 books, and cumulates at intervals.

The inclusive term *serials* has been defined as any publication issued serially or in successive parts more or less regularly. The Ayer list[24] is a bibliography of newspapers and periodicals, but it includes much additional information. The Gregory union list[25] of serials indicates the extent to which more than 75,000 different serials are found in the more important libraries in the United States and Canada. Ulrich's directory of periodicals[26] lists the titles published in the United States and in foreign countries that have proved most useful in American collections.

The *United States Catalogue* lists virtually all books in print in this country on a specific subject. It is kept up to date by the monthly *Cumulative Book Index*, which cumulates at irregular intervals during the year, annually into a supplement, and after several years into a large supplement. The *Publishers' Weekly* is regarded as a supplement to the *Cumulative Book Index*, in the sense that it describes and indexes new books in a convenient reference and buying list.

Guides are available for current graduate theses[27] and dissertations in education, although a research master's study is no longer generally required for the awarding of the first graduate degree. Since many graduate institutions publish abstract volumes or lists of their graduate theses, it is helpful that we have available an older basic guide[28] to such summaries.

24 *Directory of Newspapers and Periodicals.* Philadelphia: N. W. Ayer and Sons, 1880–. See recent supplements.

25 Winifred Gregory, Editor, *Union List of Serials in Libraries of the United States and Canada.* Second Edition. New York: H. W. Wilson Co., 1943. 3065 p. Also see supplements.

Also see *New Serial Titles: A Union List of Serials Commencing Publication After December 31, 1949.* Washington: Library of Congress, 1959. vii + 1275 p. 1963 Cumulation, 1964. xii + 2035 p.

26 Eileen C. Graves, Editor, *Ulrich's Periodicals Directory: A Classified Guide to a Selected List of Current Periodicals, Foreign and Domestic.* Ninth Edition. New York: R. R. Bowker Co., 1959. xvi + 825 p. Tenth Edition, 1963. xii + 667 p.

27 Herbert M. Silvey, Editor, *Master's Theses in Education, 1962–63.* No. 12. Cedar Falls, Iowa: Research Publications, 1963. 196 p. Also see later numbers.

28 Thomas R. Palfrey and Henry E. Coleman, *Guide to Bibliographies of Theses— United States and Canada.* Second Edition. Chicago: American Library Association, 1940. 54 p.

Also see Willard Brehaut, "An Analysis of Dissertations (English) in Education Accepted by Canadian Universities, 1930–1955." *Ontario Journal of Educational Research* 2: 109–222; April 1960.

Starting with 1952, Phi Delta Kappa has sponsored an annual list of doctoral dissertations completed in education and a list of doctoral dissertations under way in education, classified under the following headings for current numbers:[29]

AREAS OF EDUCATION

Philosophy of Education; Educational Principles and Trends

International Education; Intercultural Education; Minority Education

Religious Education; Religion and the Schools

Educational Administration and Organization; Team Teaching

Educational Administration—Local and State

Educational Administration—School Boards; Trustees; Regents; Reorganization

Supervision

Public Relations; School and Community Relations

Recruitment

Finance

School Plant (Construction; Space Allotment; Maintenance); Pupil Transportation

Educational Legislation; School Laws; Court Decisions

Educational History; Biography

Child Study; Child Psychology

Educational Psychology; General Psychology

Studies in Adolescence; Youth Groups and Problems

Measurement and Evaluation; Research; Statistics

Teacher Education; In-Service Training

Audio-Visual Education

Programmed Instruction; Teaching Machines

Curriculum; CoCurriculum Activities; Camping

Methods of Teaching; Teaching Aids; Libraries

Desegregation

Pre-School; Kindergarten; Elementary Education

Secondary Education; Junior High School; High School; Accreditation

Language Arts (Speech, Writing, Communication, Grammar)

Reading; Literature

Foreign Language Instruction

English in High School; Journalism

English in the University

Science

Arithmetic; Mathematics

Social Studies

Art; Music

Theater; Dance

[29] Mary L. Lyda, Harold Anderson, Joseph L. Mapes, and Carter V. Good, *Research Studies in Education, 1964: A Subject-Author Index and Research Methods Bibliography.* Bloomington, Indiana: Phi Delta Kappa, 1965. 203 p. Also see later numbers.

Vocational Education; Industrial Arts Education
Business Education
Vocational Agriculture
Guidance and Counseling
Student Problems—General
Student Problems—Kindergarten to Twelfth Grade
Student Problems Beyond the High School
Health
Physical Education
Safety Education; Driver Education
Recreation; Athletics; Sports
Special Education: Classroom, the Handicapped
Juvenile Delinquency; Rehabilitation
Home Economics; Family Life Education; Consumer Education
Rural Education; Conservation
Teachers' Problems—Personal and Personnel
Teachers' Problems—Professional; Certification
Undergraduate Education; Accreditation
Graduate Education; Accreditation
Junior College; Community College
Adult Education
Professional Education.

At one time it was possible to borrow typewritten graduate theses or dissertations by interlibrary loan, although occasionally it was difficult or even impossible to secure one of the older studies. John Dewey's doctoral dissertation (1884) at Johns Hopkins University, dealing with the psychology of Kant, was never published and no copy is available, since the Johns Hopkins Library apparently did not preserve the manuscript.[30]

The *List of American Doctoral Dissertations* (covering 1912 through 1938, Library of Congress) and *Doctoral Dissertations Accepted by American Universities* (1933–34 through 1954–55, sponsored by the Association of Research Libraries) overlapped some 5½ years. The successor to these two series of dissertation lists appears under the title *Index to American Doctoral Dissertations,* published annually by University Microfilms, beginning in 1957. The same publisher also issues *Dissertation Abstracts* monthly and for each abstract makes available a microfilm of the entire manuscript.[31] This microfilm service is now generally used for inspecting dissertations.

[30] A. A. Roback, *History of American Psychology.* New York: Library Publishers, 1952. p. 98.
[31] Douglas E. Scates, "Changing Sources of Information about Thesis Research." *Journal of Teacher Education* 8: 210–13; June 1957.
Index to American Doctoral Dissertations, 1961–62. Ann Arbor, Mich.: University Microfilms, 1963. xiii + 258. Also see later numbers.
Also see Bert Kaplan, "Dissemination of Primary Research Data in Psychology." *American Psychologist* 13: 53–55; February 1958. With the development of microcopy

Educational Literature and National Agencies

It is informative to note the major contributions to the literature made by selected organizations or agencies in education.

N.E.A.

Since 1922 the Research Division of the National Education Association has performed the two functions of providing current information on education, and of undertaking investigations expected to be helpful in solving future problems in education. The major fields of study are: (1) teacher welfare (salaries, retirement, evaluation, tenure, personnel policies), particularly economic status; (2) pupil welfare, including class size, court decisions, and curriculum; and (3) miscellaneous statistics, such as current estimates of enrollment and expenditures. Each month the Division answers 1,200-1,500 letters from teachers, administrators, and others seeking information on professional problems, and prepares hundreds of short papers and bibliographies to send to these inquirers. The Division annually publishes 20-25 Research Reports on its major studies, and a quarterly *NEA Research Bulletin* that presents in brief, illustrated articles the highlights of its major studies. Staff members serve as consultants to individuals and committees of laymen and teachers and to national, state, and local professional conferences. Through its continuing studies, the Division contributes to other educational agencies new technical knowledge of sample design for educational surveys.[32]

AMERICAN COUNCIL ON EDUCATION

The American Council on Education has served as a clearing house for the exchange of information and opinion, has conducted numerous inquiries into specific educational problems, and has secured the cooperation of appropriate agencies (especially higher institutions) for the solution of such problems.[33]

The Educational Record, the quarterly journal of the Council, has been issued regularly since 1920. It is a general educational periodical of considerable circulation.

A second periodical, widely distributed, is the bulletin, *Higher Education and National Affairs,* about 40 issues a year, which reports and

---

as a medium of scholarly publication, the financial barriers to publication are partly eliminated, although the cost of a good microcard reader still presents a problem. On a 3 × 5-inch microcard, up to 60 pages of material can be reproduced.

[32] *NEA Handbook, 1965-66.* Washington: National Education Association, 1965. p. 84-85. Also see later numbers.

[33] *A Brief Statement of Programs and Activities of the American Council on Education.* Washington: The Council, 1965. 48 p. Also see later numbers.

interprets significant federal developments and other activities of concern to educational institutions and organizations.

As the end result of its research, special studies, and conferences, the Council publishes some 15 books a year. About 200 titles are currently in print and on sale.

Two standard directories inaugurated by the Council are the only directories composed exclusively of *accredited* institutions of higher education. They are: *American Universities and Colleges,* first issued in 1928, and the companion volume *American Junior Colleges,* first issued in 1940. These volumes are issued every four years. *Accredited Institutions of Higher Education* is an annual supplement to these directories.

A monthly *Special Report on Federal Programs* provides college and university administrators with detailed information concerning federal programs affecting higher education.

A *Bulletin on International Education,* published approximately eight times a year, reports significant programs and developments in international education involving U. S. colleges and universities, the federal government, national associations in higher education, foundations, and the Council itself.

A newsletter, *Expanding Opportunities,* published approximately eight times a year, reports activities in colleges, universities, and foundations in providing greater opportunities in higher education for Negroes and other "disadvantaged" persons.

Report on Questionnaires is a monthly bulletin dealing with current research conducted by questionnaires addressed to colleges and universities.

U. S. OFFICE OF EDUCATION[34]

In performing its three major functions, the United States Office of Education has an extensive program of publication in the fields of educational research, educational services, and administration of grants. The Office carries on its work through publishing its research studies and survey reports, participating in conferences, speaking and writing, consultation and field work, contracting with higher institutions and state departments of education to conduct research, and administering grant funds as stipulated by the Congress. Through its publications and otherwise, the Office interprets the educational needs of the nation and promotes a general understanding of educational objectives, collects and disseminates information on education in the states and territories to make possible intelligent comparison and wise decisions on programs and operations, presents proposals for improving practices and the adoption

[34] See the current *Handbook* of the Office of Education for a particular year.

of educational standards (arrived at by cooperative planning and research), and with the aid of authentic information seeks to stimulate improvement in educational leadership.

The Office is organized in several staff offices and four Bureaus:

1. Office of the Commissioner, with Office of the Associate Commissioner for International Education, Office of the Associate Commissioner for Federal-State Relations, National Center for Educational Statistics, Office of Equal Educational Opportunities, Office of Programs of Education for Disadvantaged and Handicapped, Office of Legislation and Congressional Relations, Contracts and Construction Services, Office of Program Planning and Evaluation, Office of Administration, and Office of Information.

2. Bureau of Elementary and Secondary Education, with Division of Plans and Supplementary Centers, Division of Program Operations, Division of State Agency Cooperation, Division of School Assistance in Federally Affected Areas, and Division of Education Personnel Training.

3. Bureau of Adult and Vocational Education, with Division of Vocational and Technical Education, Division of Library Services and Educational Facilities, and Division of Adult Education Programs.

4. Bureau of Higher Education, with Division of Student Financial Aid, Division of Foreign Studies, Division of Graduate Programs, and Division of College Programs.

5. Bureau of Research, with Division of Elementary-Secondary Research, Division of Adult and Vocational Research, Division of Higher Education Research, Division of Laboratories and Research Development, and Division of Research Training and Dissemination.

Through its statistical services, the Office of Education:

Collects, verifies, analyzes, and publishes educational statistics of wide interest and national significance.

Prepares analytical models of the educational system of the United States to assist in the evaluation of Federal programs in education.

Provides technical statistical services to the divisions of the Office, including consultation and advice on research methods, as well as operational assistance in data collection, tabulation, calculation, and analysis.

Responds to requests for information in the field of educational statistics.

Maintains liaison with other departments or agencies, especially the Office of Statistical Standards of the Bureau of the Budget.

Through its information services, the Office of Education:

Plans and directs its over-all program of information and publications.

Maintains liaison with educational and information groups and individuals outside the Office.

Assists authors in planning individual publications, and edits, designs, and handles the technical production and distribution of all publications issued by the Office.

Plans, edits, and distributes *American Education,* published 10 times a year.

Prepares official statements, messages, articles, scripts, speeches, and news releases, and acts as a clearinghouse for information requested by the Congress, the White House, other government agencies, communications media, the educational profession, and the public.

Psychological Guides

For the field of psychology, the major guides to the literature are *Psychological Abstracts,* founded in 1927, and the *Annual Review of Psychology,* initiated in 1950. The *Abstracts* journal typically has only a few lines (at times a dozen) for each reference, while the *Review* is an integrated summary of the research on particular topics. The major areas covered in *Psychological Abstracts* are as follows:

PSYCHOLOGICAL ABSTRACTS

General
Experimental Psychology
Physiological Psychology
Animal Psychology
Developmental Psychology
Social Psychology
Personality and Abilities
Therapy and Guidance
Abnormal Psychology
Educational Psychology
Industrial and Military Psychology.

Social Science Guides

For the social fields the classic fifteen-volume *Encyclopedia of the Social Sciences*[35] covers the fields of anthropology, economics, education, history, law, philosophy, political science, psychology, social work, sociology, and statistics. In order to include the numerous advances and most recent development in the social sciences, a new work rather than a revision of the original encyclopedia was tentatively scheduled for simultaneous publication of the twelve to fifteen volumes in 1965. The contents are distributed fairly evenly among the various social sciences: anthropology, economics, political science, psychology, and sociology.

[35] Edwin R. A. Seligman and Alvin Johnson, Editors, *Encyclopedia of the Social Sciences.* New York: The Macmillan Co., 1930–34. 15 vols. New work scheduled for 1965.

Other useful guides in the social sciences include the *Dictionary of American Biography*,[36] *Dictionary of American History*,[37] and recently the *Guide to Historical Literature*,[38] *Sources of Information in the Social Sciences*,[39] *Dictionary of the Social Sciences;*[40] and the periodicals *Biography Index* and *Sociological Abstracts,* with the major headings of the latter as follows:

SOCIOLOGICAL ABSTRACTS

Methodology and Research Technology
Sociology: History, Theory, and the Sociology of Knowledge
Social Psychology
Group Interactions
Culture and Social Structure
Complex Organizations (Management)
Social Change and Economic Development
Mass Phenomena
Political Interactions
Social Differentiation
Community Development and Rural Sociology
Urban Structure and Ecology
Sociology of the Arts
Sociology of Education
Sociology of Religion
Social Control
Sociology of Science
Demography and Human Biology
Family and Socialization
Sociology of Health and Medicine
Social Problems and Social Welfare.

Historical Abstracts summarizes articles on political, diplomatic, economic, social, cultural, and intellectual history relating to the period 1775-1945, published in the periodical literature (some 800 journals) the

36 Allen Johnson and Dumas Malone, Editors, *Dictionary of American Biography.* New York: Charles Scribner's Sons, 1928–37. 20 vols. and index, plus supplements.

Also see *Biography Index: A Cumulative Index to Biographical Material in Books and Magazines.* New York: H. W. Wilson Co., 1946—.

37 James T. Adams and R. V. Coleman, Editors, *Dictionary of American History.* New York: Charles Scribner's Sons, 1940. 5 vols. and index. Additional volume, 1961.

Wayne Andrews, Editor, *Concise Dictionary of American History.* New York: Charles Scribner's Sons, 1962. viii + 1156 p.

38 George F. Howe and Others, *Guide to Historical Literature.* New York: The Macmillan Co., 1961. xxxv + 962 p.

39 Carl M. White, Editor, *Sources of Information in the Social Sciences.* Totowa, N. J.: Bedminster Press, 1964. xiii + 498 p.

40 Julius Gould and William L. Kolb, Editors, *A Dictionary of the Social Sciences.* New York: Free Press of Glencoe, 1964. xvi + 761 p.

world over. The publication also includes general articles on historiography, bibliography, and research methods.

Concluding Statement

In relation to a survey of the related literature, the question of uniqueness or originality may prove less important than the ways in which studies are comparable, or related, or fit into a pattern of investigation and results. We now recognize the important contributions of the scholar engaged in assimilating and integrating the results of research as reported in numerous and varied sources. We are challenged to make effective use of computers and automation in information retrieval.

In addition to the bibliographic and summarizing guides, important tools or aids are foreign languages, note-taking systems, and classification schemes. If a foreign language is essential for a particular field of research, the "language requirement" should be in functional terms rather than perfunctory. Careful notes may prove valuable not only as aids to memory, but also as stimuli to systematic thinking, just as extensive and critical reading serves as a stimulus to thinking. Improved and expanded classification systems for the literature may identify closer relationships between the social, educational, and psychological areas and may further an interdisciplinary approach to problems in the behavioral and human sciences.

The keys to the vast storehouse of published literature may open doors to sources of significant problems and explanatory hypotheses, and provide helpful orientation for definition of the problem, background for selection of procedure, and comparative data for interpretation of results. The major reference works and guides since the 1920's have greatly simplified the canvass of related literature and have appeared just in time to help the graduate student and investigator explore the greatly increased volume of research. The numerous bibliographic and documentary guides and sources suggest that there has been a trend toward use of such aids as an ally of the scientific and experimental movement.

SELECTED REFERENCES

ALEXANDER, Carter, and BURKE, Arvid J. *How to Locate Educational Information and Data.* Fourth Edition. New York: Bureau of Publications, Teachers College, Columbia University, 1958. xvii + 419 p.

BUROS, Oscar K., Editor. *The Fifth Mental Measurements Yearbook.* Highland Park, N. J.: Gryphon Press, 1959. 1,292 p. *Sixth Yearbook,* 1965.

BUROS, Oscar K., Editor. *Tests in Print: A Comprehensive Bibliography of Tests for Use in Education, Psychology, and Industry.* Highland Park, N. J.: Gryphon Press, 1962. xxix + 479 p.

"Doctoral Dissertations Newly Started in 1964." *American Journal of Sociology* 71: 94-101; July 1965. Also see later numbers.

"Doctor's Degrees in Sociology, 1964." *American Journal of Sociology* 71: 87-93; July 1965. Also see later numbers.

DREVER, James, Editor. *A Dictionary of Psychology.* Baltimore: Penguin Books, Inc., 1964. 315 p.

"Educational Books of 1964." *Educational Horizons* 43: 93-118; Spring 1965. Also see later numbers.

ENGLISH, Horace B., and ENGLISH, Ava C. *Comprehensive Dictionary of Psychological and Psychoanalytical Terms.* New York: Longmans, Green and Co., 1958. xiv + 594 p.

FARNSWORTH, Paul R., Editor. *Annual Review of Psychology.* Palo Alto, Cal.: Annual Reviews, 1965. ix + 571 p. Also see later numbers .

GOOD, Carter V., Editor. *Dictionary of Education.* Second Edition. New York: McGraw-Hill Book Co., 1959. xxx + 676 p.

GOOD, Carter V. *Introduction to Educational Research: Methodology of Design in the Behavioral and Social Sciences.* Second Edition. New York: Appleton-Century-Crofts, 1963. Chapter 3.

GOULD, Julius, and KOLB, William L., Editors. *A Dictionary of the Social Sciences.* New York: Free Press of Glencoe, 1964. xvi + 761 p.

HARRIS, Chester W., Editor. *Encyclopedia of Educational Research.* Third Edition. New York: The MacMillan Co., 1960. xxix + 1,564 p. Fourth edition in progress.

HOWE, George F., and Others. *Guide to Historical Literature.* New York: The Macmillan Co., 1961. xxxv + 962 p.

LYDA, Mary L., ANDERSON, Harold, MAPES, Joseph L., and GOOD, Carter V. *Research Studies in Education, 1964: A Subject-Author Index and Research Methods Bibliography.* Bloomington, Ind.: Phi Delta Kappa, 1965. 203 p. Also see later numbers.

SHORES, Louis. *Basic Reference Sources.* Chicago: American Library Association, 1954. ix + 378 p.

TROTIER, Arnold H., and HARMAN, Marian, Editor. *Doctoral Dissertations Accepted by American Universities 1954-1955.* No. 22. Compiled for the Association of Research Libraries. New York: H. W. Wilson Co., 1955. 298 p. Also see earlier numbers.

WHITE, Carl M., Editor. *Sources of Information in the Social Sciences.* Totowa, N. J.: The Bedminster Press, Inc., 1964. xiii + 498 p.

WINCHELL, Constance M. *Guide to Reference Books.* Seventh Edition. Chicago: American Library Association, 1951. xvii + 645 p. Also see later supplements.

WINCHELL, Constance M., and JOHNSON, O. A. *Guide to Reference Books.* Seventh Edition Supplement, 1950-52. Second Supplement, 1953-55. Third Supplement, 1956-58. Fourth Supplement, 1959-62. Chicago: American Library Association, 1954, 140 p.; 1956, 134 p.; 1960, 145 p.; 1963, 151 p.

4

The Seamless Web of History

INTEGRATED NARRATIVE OF PAST EVENTS

This chapter considers history as a field of knowledge and then presents the major steps, processes, or aspects of historical research and historiography: collection of data, with consideration of sources as documents and remains, and as primary and secondary; evaluation of data, including external and internal criticism; and presentation of the facts in readable narrative form, including problems of organization, composition, and interpretation.

History as a Field of Knowledge and Research

DEFINITION AND SCOPE OF HISTORY[1]

VIEWED AS RESEARCH, HISTORY MAY BE DEFINED AS AN INTEGRATED NARRATIVE or description of past events or facts, written in the spirit of critical inquiry, to find the whole truth and report it. A newspaper or journalistic report of some current event, or a debate in Congress or a state legislature, is not history, because it is not typically an inquiry into the *whole* truth. The campaign book of a political party summarizing the events and activities of the party for the four years preceding the election is not history, since it was not written as a *critical* inquiry into the truth. The historical novel is not history, even though incorporating certain events and threads of historical truth, but rather it seeks to entertain the reader. Biography or autobiography becomes history when adequate historical perspective enables the author to see the individual in relation to the society and events of his time, but is not history when the account is limited to a single life in isolation. Antiquarian research or writing

---

1 Jacques Barzun and Henry F. Graff, *The Modern Researcher*. New York: Harcourt, Brace & World, Inc., 1957. p. 3–17, 43–56.

Homer C. Hockett, *The Critical Method in Historical Research and Writing*. New York: The Macmillan Co., 1955. p. 237–54.

Allan Nevins, *The Gateway to History*. Boston: D. C. Heath & Co., 1938. p. 22–23. Revised 1962.

does not become history merely through the process of preserving material or records in almanac or museum-like fashion.

As to scope, history embraces the entire field of the human past and is as broad as life itself. Our human past includes many areas of social experience and activities that frequently have proved more significant than political history or military campaigns; for example, culture, ideals, institutions, law, religion, literature, art, travel, engineering, industry, technology, medicine, science, philosophy, economics, education, psychology, anthropology, and sociology. There is general agreement among modern historians concerning the richness of the content of history, including social, cultural, economic, and intellectual developments, and on a broad view of past events, extending far beyond the study of politics, diplomatics, constitutions, and "drum and trumpet" war materials. To comment specifically on genuine world history, it is a fascinating story of man and how he rose to his present elevation, including a limited number of creative men (heroes) who produced new knowledge, new moral or ethical values, or new beauty. The negative, destructive phases of history include the names of kings, generals, and dictators who fought battles and wars, in search of riches and power, thus destroying what others had built. Preoccupation with both of these types of "heroes" tends to produce a lopsided history and omits the lice, rats, malnutrition, and epidemics (with the accompanying stench, dirt, callousness, and misery) that have had more to do with the course of things than generals and kings.[2]

It is a basic characteristic of history that the historian is concerned with human beings, not primarily as individuals (as in psychology, biography, or the novel), but in groups—religions, cultural, ideological, interest, occupational, or social. Frequently the historian deals with people in national groups, which usually coincide with a political state, but it is too restrictive to say that the national group is simply a political group, since the historian often is not concerned with the political aspects of the history of the group.[3]

INTERRELATIONSHIPS OF HISTORY AND SCIENCE

It is without profit to argue the question of whether history is science or art. History qualifies as science in the sense that its methods of inquiry are critical and objective, and that the results are accepted as organized knowledge by a consensus of trained investigators. The research aspects of history in dealing with sources are scientific in approach, while narra-

2 Albert Szent-Györgyi, "Teaching and the Expanding Knowledge." *Science* 146: 1278–79; December 4, 1964.

3 David M. Potter, "The Historian's Use of Nationalism and Vice Versa." *American Historical Review* 67: 924–50; July 1962.

tion and historiography commonly involve the art of expression and philosophy of the author. The historian thinks of the method of investigation as scientific, and of the manner of presentation as belonging to the realm of art.

Until recent years the natural sciences and the cultural sciences were generally regarded as far apart, yet these two fields of research are parts of a meaningful whole when we think of scientific knowledge not merely as a finished product but as a historical development, with a dimension of historic depth. On the other hand, the unique or disparate events of human history may fit into a unified, integrated pattern or process, if we view the gradual advance of man's knowledge as a central theme of historical development. Science makes history, in the sense that growth of knowledge is a compelling force in historical events and that intellectual development brings about historic changes in the life of man. Our life is affected profoundly by what the scientists and philosophers of the past two centuries have thought and said. These interrelationships of history and science make it important that the modern historian be well grounded in the sciences.[4]

The history of society and ideas now has joined the history of kings and generals as part of the study of the past in what has been called the new history of science and technology. This new history does not prove that the progress of mankind is necessarily guaranteed, but does show the ever present possibility of progress in human affairs and provides us with some hope for the future through the methods of reason, imagination, and ingenuity in solving our complex and disturbing problems.[5]

History differs in method from the natural sciences, since it is not a discipline of direct observation or experimentation, but utilizes reports of observations that cannot be repeated; the historian cannot recall the actors of the past to reproduce the famous scenes of history on the stage of today. Instead of the direct observations used in science, the historian usualy must depend on the observations of others (often untrained observers). Therefore, the historical method involves a procedure supplementary to observation, a process by which the historian seeks to test the truthfulness of the reports of observations made by others. Both historian and scientist examine data, formulate hypotheses, and test the hypotheses against the evidence until acceptable conclusions are reached. A number of historians, in emphasizing the interpretation and meaning of facts, have sought to identify tendencies, themes, patterns, and laws of history, while some of these investigators have dealt with such philosophical or theoretical problems in history as discovery of laws, unity and continuity,

4 Pascual Jordan, *Science and the Course of History*. Translated by Ralph Manheim. New Haven: Yale University Press, 1955. p. vii–viii, 3–4.

5 Melvin Kranzberg, "The Newest History: Science and Technology." *Science* 136: 46–68; May 11, 1962.

possibility or impossibility of prediction, and oversimplification growing out of the search for clues or keys.

HISTORY IN RELATION TO OTHER SOCIAL FIELDS

History and Economics. History hase close interrelationships with other social fields. The economists have introduced a quantitative emphasis into modern history; for example, citing numerical data such as the United States census for a given year, or basing certain computations upon such data, in calculating by decades the rate of increase of the population of the United States. Handling of quantitative material is important in economic history, in sound social history (with its dependence on knowledge of population movement, inheritance, and social mobility), and sometimes in military history.

History and Sociology. As another example of close interrelationships between the social fields, history and sociology are complementary, in the sense that both areas seek to explain the past, although the sociologist is interested primarily in generalized descriptions and in types of societal evolution, without the historian's concern with time-and-place relationships and unique events. It is true that American sociologists by choice ignore the bulk of historical findings by restricting themselves to a single culture and to the short time span they consider relevant to contemporary conditions. Even within the present, the interests of sociologists are normally narrower than those of historians, who deal with the contemporary national scene in relation to foreign, political, legal, and economic issues, as well as the rise and decline of communities, corporations, families, ideologies, and the fortunes of ethnic groups. When it serves its purpose, to clarify an argument or exposition, the historian does introduce new elements of explicit theory (economic, social, political, or legal). Specific ways in which history and sociology can learn from each other involve questions of the observation, selection, and organization of factual evidence or data.

The dependence of sociology on history may be expressed in other terms as follows:

1. History provides a greater variety of social forms and problems than does the contemporary world.
2. Contemporary forms are themselves historical products, and can be understood neither singly nor comparatively without attention paid to their historical dimension.
3. As soon as the sociologist wishes to consider "long-term" factors, he must turn to history.
4. Any given society can be understood only in terms of the "specific period" in which it exists.[6]

[6] Asa Briggs, "Sociology and History," *Society: Problems and Methods of Study.* London: Routledge & Kegan Paul, 1962. p. 91–98.

History and Literature. History may serve to link literature with social science, whereas it once linked philosophy with poetry.

> History has always thought of itself as an inclusive, a mediating discipline. Once it linked philosophy with poetry. Now it is linking literature with social science. History's new consciousness of its debt to social science need not mean a weakening of its artistic ties. Indeed, the contrary is the case. For it is history that can lead social science itself along the path of imagination and bold hypothesis toward literature—back to the realms in which it dwelt and prospered in the century and three quarters of great achievement that began with Montesquieu and ended with Weber.[7]

Comparative Education and Educational History. Comparative education is an aspect of educational history—an extension of the past into the present and the substance of tomorrow's history of education. While the historian must reach the elusive past through documents and relics, the student of comparative education has the advantage of coming in direct touch with the subject under scrutiny, as in tracing the movement of a current educational idea or practice from one culture to another, although the literature is soon out of date. Many things done by historians are cross-cultural and comparative, and comparative studies of movement of ideas or practices from one country to another reach into the past, which means there is no sharp line drawn between historical and comparative investigations. (At this point a cross-reference should be made to the discussion of cross-cultural studies in the chapter on developmental and growth investigations and to the chapter on descriptive-survey studies.)

Many of the writings in comparative education are of limited usefulness, because of such factors as subjectivity, obsolescence, ethnocentrism, limited and derived source materials instead of extensive primary sources and scholarly monographs in the original languages, and the narrow framework of many writings to the partial neglect of exploration of the sociocultural and historical contexts of educational problems. Sound descriptive studies in comparative education are important, but they are only preliminary to new studies of depth that seek rational explanations for individual differences among countries.[8] Better research in comparative education may discourage the casual commentator, the returning tourist with a manuscript or speech, and others who feel that their

[7] Quoted from H. Stuart Hughes, "The Historian and the Social Scientist." *American Historical Review* 66: 20–46; October 1960.

[8] William W. Brickman, "Comparative Education," in "Philosophical and Social Framework of Education." *Review of Educational Research* 34: 44–61; February 1964.

George F. Kneller, "Comparative Education," *Encyclopedia of Educational Research.* Edited by Chester W. Harris. Third Edition. New York: The Macmillan Co., 1960. p. 316–22.

opinions on problems of comparative education are as good as those of the specialist. The problem of evaluation in comparative education is difficult, since there are at present no comparable standards by which the quality of an educational system can be measured, and such evaluative criteria will not be available until comparative standards are developed for assessing the quality of a culture in general.

For some seventy-five years before the middle of the twentieth century the history of American education had a promising future that was not fulfilled, although Herbert Baxter Adams in the Johns Hopkins seminar on historical and political science pointed out the relationships of the history of education with the churches, charities, industries, economics, municipal reform, and labor laws. The historian may well ask how education has come to take the shape it has or how a constellation of institutions has influenced the life of society.

Much of the existing educational history consists of institutional biographies in the form of histories of single schools, colleges, or universities, but we must remember that behind these actual centers of instruction stand the historically significant associations of teachers, librarians, and youth leaders; philanthropic foundations; accrediting organizations; and certification agencies. Points of departure for the historical study of education include the following:[9]

1. The building of new communities on the frontier
2. The adjustment of the foreign policy of the United States to its growing responsibilities as a world power
3. The utilization of the immensely rich material resources of the nation
4. The transformation of the immigrant into an American
5. The fulfillment of the promise of American life
6. The growth of distinctively American political institutions
7. The transformation of American society
8. The growth of a distinctive American culture over a vast continental area.

In other words, the new educational historian uses broader historical references; has a wider, more humanistic and professional commitment; relates the educational institution to its social setting and to other cultural institutions; exposes the complexity of ideas and movements; and reveals how men and events control, or are guided by, educational themes and organizations. We are cautioned, however, to guard against certain dangers of interpretation in writing educational history.

One must not read back, must not interpret the past in contemporary terms, must not see the forms of an imperfect past as unfolding inexorably into the more nearly perfect forms of today, and must not use history for missionary or

[9] Committee on the Role of Education in American History, *Education and American History*. New York: Fund for the Advancement of Education, 1965. 24 p.

propagandist purposes. But this should not blind one to the complementary realization that history must be *relevant,* must be *useful,* must be concerned with issues that are important *today.* Furthermore, history must make a *difference;* it must be concerned with *action,* in the sense that its study should make one's judgments, choices, decisions, and actions wiser, more profound, more sophisticated than they have been.[10]

In summary, as to the literature of the history of education, the middle of this century has proved fruitful, including textbooks, guides to historiography, biography, and treatments of geographical or regional areas, school levels, and particular movements or problems in education. Major historical contributions have been made to psychology and related social disciplines. Sharp criticisms, however, have appeared with an underlying assumption that somewhere education took the wrong turn, thus centering the great educational debate in part on America's educational history. As in other periods of crises, when people have turned to their history for guidance and a sense of direction, educational historians are challenged to a sober reappraisal of our educational tradition.[11]

USES AND FUNCTIONAL NATURE OF HISTORY

Historians of the twentieth century have commonly emphasized the immediate usefulness of history in dealing with contemporary problems. They have stressed the importance of a social consciousness for the historian, use of history to throw light on the present, inquiry into the past for solutions to contemporary problems, and avoidance of the charge of antiquarianism. Modern historians, like economists, political scientists, sociologists, and psychologists, have maintained that they too have answers to contemporary social problems. History may enable communities to grasp their relationship with the past and to plan more intelligently for the future; it may give to people a sense of continuity and a consciousness of unity in their efforts and achievements. "Seated at the roaring loom of time, for six thousand years man has woven a seamless garment. But that garment is invisible and intangible save where the dyes of written history fall upon it, and forever preserve it as a possession of generations to come."[12]

History of Education. To cite another example, in order to understand education as a social process with a long history, and to evaluate school theories and plans, we need to know the historical evidence or approach in the form of origins that have influenced the present state of educa-

10 Paul Nash, "History of Education," in "Philosophical and Social Framework of Education." *Review of Educational Research* 34: 5–21; February 1964.
11 Merle L. Borrowman, "History of Education," *Encyclopedia of Educational Research, op. cit.,* p. 661–66.
12 Allan Nevins, *op. cit.,* p. 3, 5.

tion and of the schools, serial or temporal data for identification of significant causal factors, and the insights of educational thinkers in appraising panaceas, half-truths, and fads or frills. Specific competencies to be developed through instruction in the history of education have been listed as follows:[13]

1. Understanding the dynamics of educational change
2. Increased understanding of the relationship between education and the culture in which it operates
3. Increased understanding of contemporary educational problems
4. Understanding the functions and limitations of historical evidence in analyzing educational problems
5. Development of elementary ability in locating, analyzing, and appraising historical evidence
6. Development of a sense of the dignity and responsibility of the teaching profession.

Among the modern problem areas of functional value in educational history are the non-school educational agencies and their influence on man's behavior, including newspapers, popular journals, novels, drama, radio, and television, which will give clues about what the image of child, school, or teacher has been through the years. Other problems relate to the school as the moulder or "container" of national and regional character, academic freedom (especially at elementary and secondary levels), pupil dropout, relation between political and educational patterns, shifts in educational leadership, and purgation of vague and confusing concepts commonly found in education. Certain problem areas of educational sociology frequently involve historical sources and approaches: longitudinal analysis of the socialization process in educational institutions, changes in student and faculty value systems, emergence of educational institutions, and the impact of social-class background upon educational motivation and achievement.

Specific applications of the historical approach extend beyond the general field of educational history to comparative education; to legal research in education, with the statutory law and the case or common law as the sources; to thorough bibliographical and summarizing studies, as illustrated by the *Encyclopedia of Educational Research* and *Review of Educational Research;* to psychology, as illustrated by biographical and autobiographical narratives, general histories of psychology, and the *Annual Review of Psychology;* and to the biographical, case-history, and

[13] Committee on Historical Foundations of the National Society of College Teachers of Education, R. Freeman Butts, Chairman, *The Role of the History of Education in the Professional Preparation of Teachers.* Ann Arbor, Mich.: The Society, 1957. p. 19–29, 65–66, 84–98, 123–29.

life-history materials and other historical approaches of sociology and certain related social disciplines.

History of Psychology. Especially during the second quarter of the present century and later, historical studies have made important contributions to psychology, as illustrated in a five-fold classification:[14]

1. Topical surveys, dealing with specific psychological concepts, such as Greek theories of cognition
2. Surveys of periods, and expositions of the views of particular men or groups, such as the history of Greek psychology
3. Source books, sometimes making available important materials in foreign languages
4. Biography, providing accounts of the lives of men who have made significant contributions to psychology
5. General histories of psychology, some devoted to the late modern period, and others purporting to cover the entire scope of psychological history.

In the field of psychology many genetic, biographical, autobiographical, case, and clinical studies are essentially historical in approach. One of the areas for further development in psychology is the training of specialists to do research and to give instruction in the history of psychology. If psychologists remain ignorant of their history, some of their efforts will take the form of discoveries that are truisms or that repeat the errors of the past. Knowledge of psychology and an interest in its history will not guarantee competence in historiography. Professional historians have properly been critical of the scientist who thinks that his specialization of itself provides the essential equipment for historical research. The historian in psychology needs basic knowledge of the methodology of history or historiography and the appropriate historical backgrounds from philosophy, science, and sociology.[15]

The professional historian urges the preservation of historical materials in the field of psychology. The records (especially personal papers) of the heroic age of American psychology between 1890 and World War II have been neglected and are fast disappearing. Exceptions are the William James papers at Harvard and the J. McKeen Cattell papers in the Library of Congress. John B. Watson left no personal papers. It is urged that the following types of materials be preserved and ultimately deposited in a responsible archive:[16]

1. Letters from major and secondary figures in psychology and other sciences
2. Notes on unpublished lectures of such figures

14 Knight Dunlap, "The Historical Method in Psychology." *Journal of General Psychology* 24: 49–62; January 1941.
15 Robert I. Watson, "The History of Psychology: A Neglected Area." *American Psychologist* 15: 251–55; April 1960.
16 John C. Burnham, "Preservation of Historical Materials." *American Psychologist* 14: 655–56; October 1959.

3. Personal recollections of historical occurrences, such as the founding of SPSSI and of the American Psychological Association itself
4. One's own personal files of correspondence, private memoranda, unpublished lectures.

Problem and Process

The selection and development of the problem for study, and the chief library guides, have been discussed in earlier chapters. As in other fields, the beginner in historical research frequently chooses too broad a topic. As examples of delimitation of an overly large topic, a history of political parties in the United States became a treatment of a presidential campaign in one state, and a study of one-time Negro land-grant colleges in the United States became the story of a particular land-grant college. Less frequently the historical problem is broadened as a study progresses, as when the history of a small church-related college became a history of the program of higher education supported by the specific church denomination. In the background program of reading for development of the problem, the investigator may proceed from the best general treatises to specialized volumes and printed collections of sources, then to calendars of documents, expert bibliographies, and reviews in historical and other appropriate journals. Specialized and detailed advice for selection and development of the historical problem is available.[17]

Some years ago the greatly increased number of psychological manuscripts forced editors to eliminate or drastically curtail what at one time was an essential part of the research report—the historical introduction. Thus, a valuable source of historical perspective was lost, although some attempt is still made in the master's thesis and doctoral dissertation to place the research problem in its historical context. This editorial policy with respect to historical introductions, and the attitude of many psychologists, are negative factors in providing appropriate historical training and background for students of psychology.[18]

Historical research and historiography involve three major steps, processes, or aspects:

Collection of data, with consideration of sources as documents and remains or relics, and as primary and secondary

[17] Jacques Barzun and Henry F. Graff, *op. cit.*, p. 18–27.

William W. Brickman, *Guide to Research in Educational History*. New York: New York University Bookstore, 1949. p. 1–8.

Louis R. Gottschalk, *Understanding History*. New York: Alfred A. Knopf, Inc., 1950. p. 62–70, 174–78.

Homer C. Hockett, *op. cit.*, p. 86–89, 184–86.

[18] Arthur J. Bachrach, Editor, *Experimental Foundations of Clinical Psychology*. New York: Basic Books, Inc., Publishers, 1962. p. 1–2.

Criticism of the data, including the process of external criticism (questions of authorship, time, place, genuineness, and actual language or text of the original document) and the process of internal criticism (questions of accuracy and value of the statements made)

Presentation of the facts in readable narrative form, including problems of organization, composition, exposition, and interpretation.

Historical Sources

A classification of sources appropriate for history, as well as other social fields, is as follows:

1. Physical remains: historic sites, roads, aqueducts, pyramids, fortifications, buildings ruined or whole, furniture, human remains, clothing, food, utensils, pottery, implements, weapons, machinery, industrial processes, and fine arts and museum pieces of many kinds
2. Orally transmitted material (sometimes in writing), such as folklore, legends, ballads, tales, anecdotes, sagas, traditions, customs, manners, burials, ceremonials, social institutions, and language
3. More elementary and durable kinds of representative or artistic materials, not written in the ordinary sense, such as inscriptions baked upon clay, chiselled stones, monuments, stamped coins, woven tapestries, vases, scenic or portrait sculptures, historical paintings, and portraits
4. Hand-written materials (sometimes in print), including papyri, bricks bearing cuneiform writing, vellum or parchment manuscripts, and such more recent documents as chronicles, annals, biographies, memoirs, diaries, and genealogies
5. Printed books, papers, and literature
6. Motion-picture film, microfilm, and recordings, including radio and television
7. Personal observation (by the writer or by people whom he interviews).

Systematic oral history is a comparatively recent development. An important part of the Ford Archives was oral history, under the general direction of Allan Nevins, who interviewed leading figures in the early history of the automotive industry. A single interview often went into weeks of testimony, was taped, typed in the rough, revised by the subject, and retyped in final form for posterity. Nevins actually began this type of historical archives in 1948 as the Oral History Collection of Columbia University, including such persons as architects, mariners, artists, geneticists, professors, police officers, clergymen, missionaries, and librarians, and covering such subjects as business, labor, law, medicine, journalism, music, literature, art, sociology, and pure science. The Columbia collection grows at the rate of forty volumes of typescript a year, with proper indexing.[19]

19 Arthur T. Hamlin, *News Notes from the Library, University of Cincinnati* 8: 4–5; May 1963.

The work of the Woodrow Wilson Foundation illustrates the large volume of work required in dealing with the papers of an important historical personage. The number of control cards typed and arranged in the files of the Foundation was near a half million in 1964. The number of items on photocopy and arranged in the files was more than 175,000 and the pages photocopied well beyond a half million. As part of its work in the editing and publishing of the papers of Wilson, the Foundation employed a shorthand expert to transcribe Wilson's shorthand materials. Even Wilson's books were searched for shorthand notes and comments. Transcription of these shorthand materials has made it possible to determine Wilson's first thoughts on important problems and to trace the development of his thinking as he worked on major speeches and state papers.[20]

DOCUMENTS AND REMAINS

The preceding classification of sources suggests that certain of the earlier simple categories have become more complex and probably will continue to expand in the future. In illustrating the varied sources in educational history, it is reasonably satisfactory to use two broad divisions: documents and remains or relics. Documents are reports of events, consisting of impressions made on some human brain by past events and consciously or deliberately recorded for the purpose of transmitting information. The observer's or eye-witness's impression of the event is illustrated by such documents as the opinion of a judge, minutes prepared by the secretary of a board of education, a superintendent's annual report, the director's report of a school survey, a college catalogue prepared by a dean, or a course of study transmitted to the superintendent by the chairman of the particular curriculum committee. Relics are physical objects (sometimes written materials of historical value) produced without the conscious intention of imparting connected information. Through documentary sources one sees not the event of the past, but what the eye-witness thought the act was. In remains or relics one sees the actual objects as handed down from the past. Sometimes man more nearly reveals the truth unconsciously through these physical objects or remains than through the documents that he deliberately records. For example, a schoolmaster may write in his annual report or diary (documentary source) of the humane and kindly methods of discipline employed, whereas the remains in the form of his devices for physical punishment (bundle of switches, iron-bound ruler, and whipping post) may reveal the truth and the inaccuracy of the documentary source.

As sources, government publications cover almost every field of human

[20] *Two-Year Report and Forty Years in Retrospect: Report for the Years, 1961–1963.* Princeton, New Jersey: Woodrow Wilson Foundation, 1963. 71 p.

knowledge and endeavor and have become increasingly important tools for investigators and educators; these publications include: catalogs and indexes, bibliographies, congressional publications, federal and state constitutions, federal laws, state laws, court decisions, administrative regulations and departmental rulings, presidential papers, foreign affairs, reports on operations, organization and personnel, maps, technical and other department publications, periodicals, and microfacsimile editions of government publications.[21]

The preceding classification of historical sources suggests that many types of materials have not been fully utilized, especially remains or relics. In the writing of history, physical remains usually have been considered more valuable for social and economic history than for political history, and more useful for descriptive than analytical phases of history. Some remains or relics are called "memorials," with the characteristics of both remains and documents. A gravestone including only a name is a relic, but with the addition of dates of birth and death, and possibly other information, it becomes a "memorial." The cornerstone or dedication plaque of a school building, including identifying dates, architect, or school board, has the characteristics of both remains and documents. The significance of educational remains has not been fully recognized, and space for housing bulky collections of remains has not been so commonly provided as for documents.

As an indication of comparatively recent interest in relics or remains, among other things the Fine Arts Committee has collected for the White House a tufted chair from Lincoln's bedroom, Dolley Madison's empire sofa, James Madison's medicine chest, James Monroe's bellange armchair and piertable, a bust of Martin Van Buren, a sheraton sofa on which Daniel Webster once rested, and an early nineteenth century sofa owned by Nellie Custis.

The same source at different times may be classified as either a document or a remain, when used for different purposes; for example, when letters written by George Washington and others (before Noah Webster's efforts toward standardization of spelling) are studied to determine variations in spelling, rather than the messages deliberately recorded in the letters, these sources would serve the purposes of remains and would be so classified. If the historian searches the same letters to identify attitudes toward education, his interest is in the recorded messages, which means that the source serves the purposes of a document and is so classified. A printed diploma or report card in blank is a remain, but when the name of a pupil and his attainments are entered in the proper blanks, the source presents a message and becomes a document. School textbooks are

[21] Laurence F. Schmeckebier and Roy B. Eastin, *Government Publications and Their Use*. Revised Edition. Washington: Brookings Institution, 1961. 476 p.

remains, since they do not deliberately or consciously record information concerning school practice or teaching procedure, although they do throw considerable light on such problems for a particular period of time. As a rule, the author's preface in a textbook comments on certain curricular, teaching, or learning problems and as such is a documentary source. The school textbook in some instances illustrates the relative values of documents and remains in the search for truth; in the preface the author may deliberately or consciously lay claim to modern curriculum materials and methods, but the discussion and exercises in the body of the textbook, serving as a silent witness, may testify that the materials and methods are obsolete.

PRIMARY AND SECONDARY SOURCES

An earlier section of this chapter has characterized sources as documents and as remains or relics. Another possible classification of sources is as primary or secondary, and even tertiary or a greater number of times removed from the eye witness or direct observer of the event. Primary sources are the original documents or remains, the first witnesses to the event, with only the mind of the observer or eye witness coming between the original event and the user of the source. The preceding lists of documents and remains provide numerous examples of primary sources. The secretary's minutes of a school-board meeting are primary, but the newspaper editor's comment on the meeting of the board, even though based on the minutes of the meeting, is secondary, since both the secretary and the editor have come between the event and the person who reads the newspaper comment. If the editor is present in person at the meeting of the school board, then his comments are primary.

The primary sources for writing the history of equipment in the science laboratories of secondary schools would include the equipment itself as preserved in storerooms or museums, pictures of apparatus, state or local manuals specifying laboratory equipment, written records by science teachers describing their laboratory apparatus or procedures, order blanks for requisitioning science materials, and the oral testimony of pupils and teachers who worked in the science laboratories of the past. Secondary sources for the same topic would include such materials as portions of histories of education, special bibliographies, and parts of books on the teaching of science, which usually are several times removed from the original event or have several minds between the laboratory equipment described and the user of the source.

The official registration cards for students in a school are a primary source for analyzing age, sex, and geographical distribution, but a newspaper report based on this analysis is a secondary source.

The nature of the problem and its purpose sometimes determine whether a particular source is primary or secondary. For most purposes, textbooks in the history of education are secondary sources, with most chapters and sections of the book many times removed from the original event; the author actually witnessed only a few of the events during the modern period in writing a history of education in the United States. If the problem and purpose of the historical study should change to the organization of materials, philosophy of interpretation, and style of writing employed by certain authors, then their books become primary sources; the author's book is as close as one can come to his philosophy of interpretation and style of writing. In the initial stage of a particular problem, a secondary source (such as a history of education) may prove more helpful and even more accurate than a primary source, if the educational historian has been successful in evaluating primary sources, interpreting meaning, and writing the narrative. As a first step in writing a history of reading instruction in the elementary school for a stipulated period of time, it probably is desirable to begin with such secondary sources as historical chapters in books on the teaching of reading.

The vitality of history is enhanced not only through reading the original sources but also through visitation of place of origin of events (personal contact with the setting). Aristotle says that a Libyan, when asked to name the best manure, replied: "The land-owner's footprints." When asked about the best feed to fatten a horse, a Persian answered: "His master's eye." If Livy had paid more attention to factors of geography and topography, and had he visited Lake Trasimenus, only some thirty miles from his birthplace, he would have written differently about that famous battlefield.[22]

Preservation of Sources. An interesting example of modern literary scholarship and extensive travel in the recovery of a large quantity of manuscripts involves the papers of James Boswell, the biographer of Samuel Johnson. Through painstaking efforts an American professor became acquainted with Boswell's descendants and located the Boswell manuscripts in Ireland, after which the papers were purchased and brought to the United States.

Today valuable source materials are being destroyed at an alarming rate. Modern living quarters do not have attics or storerooms for housing heirlooms, photograph albums, diaries, notebooks, and papers, and this generation of children does not carry on a long family tradition. It is not enough to preserve the papers of an Einstein, but to keep primary source materials for the many hundreds of outstanding men engaged in important creative work in the several fields of science and scholarship. The heroic age of American science between the Civil War and World

[22] Thomas Woody, "Of History and Its Method." *Journal of Experimental Education* 15: 175–201; March 1947.

War II is of unique interest to the future historians of science and scholarship, but much of this rich source material has disappeared. The scientist himself needs a more sensitive awareness of the importance of preserving personal and professional records for our future historians. The successor to Agassiz as director of the Museum of Comparative Zoology at Harvard expressed surprise that Agassiz had kept so few records of the museum and its early workers.

The manuscripts of social welfare present special questions about the preservation and use of the files of social agencies. These working files are among the most valuable sources of information on modern social welfare, but they involve complex problems of preservation, availability, and confidentiality. Even though social agencies are considered "hard for the outsider to reach," in terms of use of records, careful protection of the client is essential. Archivists should remember that records as far back as the latter part of the past century may reveal facts concerning adoption and aid that would prove embarrassing to grandchildren or even children of today. To publicize relief roll lists may prove a needless opening of the private lives of obscure people. Since the ultimate goal of the social worker is rehabilitation of individuals and families, the research worker must follow the guiding criterion of data-gathering that *to count* is one thing, but *to name* is quite another thing.

A recent president of the American Historical Association has analyzed at length the needs, services, and facilities for a national center of historical scholarship, preferably in the Nation's Capitol.[23]

Importance of Nonofficial Documents. Both historians and sociologists are agreed on the importance of such nonofficial documents as personal letters, autobiographies, diaries, life histories, and similar records. Especially of late, a keen public interest in such historical sources has developed, as witnessed by accounts in popular magazines of collections relating to Lincoln, the Lewis and Clark explorations, Boswell, and works of art.

Collections of private letters have certain limitations when published by the writer himself or by a literary executor, since damaging passages or even entire letters may be omitted; an editor without personal relations with the author of the letters is much more likely to present an unbiased treatment. Diaries and autobiographies edited and published by the author are subject to the same limitations mentioned for letters. It is only natural that many self-centered persons who write letters, diaries, and autobiographies will describe themselves and their motives, and edit their collections, as they wish to appear to the public rather than as they actually are. An exception to this characterization is Samuel Pepys, who

[23] Julian P. Boyd, "A Modest Proposal to Meet an Urgent Need." *American Historical Review* 70: 329–49; January 1965.

presumably wrote with candor and honesty in his diary, since he probably did not expect anyone to decode his special system of shorthand. Although James Boswell was almost ideally qualified to write the *Life of Johnson,* in view of his close relationships with his subject, Boswell omitted interesting details in following what he considered the dictates of good taste in biography.

External Criticism: Authenticity

The historian is obligated to determine the authenticity and meaning of sources. Many writers on the historical method and on historiography have labeled these processes of criticism and evaluation as external criticism and internal criticism, while other historiographers have avoided the formality or logic of such a classification of the aspects of criticism. For present purposes it seems helpful to employ the terms *external* and *internal criticism.*

External criticism deals with the genuineness of the document, whether it is what it seems to be and reads true to the original. It is concerned with form and appearance of the document rather than meaning of the contents, although external criticism at times may employ internal evidence from the document through a study of its contents, in an attempt to establish questions of authorship. Problems of external criticism, in testing the genuineness of a document or remain, involve questions about the characteristics of the author and his qualifications as a reporter; factors or conditions that may have influenced the production of the document, such as time, place, purpose, and circumstances of composition; and the extent to which the document and its parts read true to the original.

The work of external criticism has been greatly facilitated through the development of a number of auxiliary sciences, and of printing and photography, especially in dealing with older sources. A partial list of the important auxiliary aids or fields includes: anthropology, archaeology, astronomy, cartography, chemistry, chronology, diplomatics, economics, education, epigraphy, exact sciences, genealogy, geography, geology, heraldry, historical method and philosophies, languages, law, literature, military affairs, natural history, numismatics, paleontology, paleography, philately, philology, philosophy, politics, prehistory, and psychology.

THE PROBLEM OF ERROR

Before the invention of printing, when manuscripts were copied by hand, there were frequently inadvertent errors in the form of unintentional omissions or insertions, and sometimes deliberate changes in the text. During recent years microphotography has made it possible to reproduce and transmit entire books, bulky records, newspapers, and other manuscripts for projection in some distant library or research center, thus obviating the type of error that arises in copying.

Even today, however, the problem of error in transmitting messages is still with us. There are differences in wording with respect to the cable of October 29, 1918, sent by Woodrow Wilson to Colonel House in Paris, when the text written on the President's own typewriter is compared with the cable or message actually received by House. One change is quite important.

> The meaning of Wilson's words "too much success or security on the part of the Allies" is significantly different from the meaning of the message House received saying "too much severity on the part of the Allies." The latter thought is on the character of the terms to be imposed on the Germans. It does not contain some of the elements in the mind of Wilson. His thinking was focused on the Allies, on their security and his desire for some insecurity so that they could be coerced by an American threat of a separate peace.[24]

It may be added that Wilson personally typed many historic documents now on file in the Library of Congress. The precision of his mind and his effectiveness in typing and shorthand were such that he seldom made a mistake in either wording or typing. Before Wilson became ill in 1919 he did not use "ghost" writers and frequently composed declarations and diplomatic communications at his typewriter, recently placed on exhibition at the White House along with facsimiles of historic documents typed on it. It is probable that some of Wilson's state documents contained technical material prepared for him by Cabinet officers and after 1919 his messages to Congress were prepared by various members of the Cabinet.

HONESTY OF SCIENTISTS AND SCHOLARS

As a group, scientists have an outstanding record for morality and honesty in seeking and reporting the truth, with relatively few exceptions deviating from the search for truth. However, the great emphasis on original discovery does create stress in the behavior of some scientists, as analyzed in a sociological interpretation of the frequently puzzling aspects of conflicts over priority or originality in scientific discovery. Merton's interpretation is that, like other social institutions, science has its characteristic values, norms, and organization, including emphasis on the value of originality. As emphasis upon originality and its recognition is stepped up, the greater becomes the involvement of the scientist in the successful outcome of inquiry and his emotional vulnerability to failure.

---

[24] Quoted from W. Stull Holt, "What Wilson Sent and What House Received: Or Scholars Need to Check Carefully." *American Historical Review* 65: 569–71; April 1960.

This cultural and social background can lead scientists to develop an extreme concern for recognition, which is in turn the validation by peers of their work, and can lead to reprehensible conduct on the part of individual scientists. The history of science reports instances of deviant behavior in the form of contentiousness, self-assertive claims, secretiveness lest one be forestalled, reporting only the data that support a hypothesis, false charges of plagiarism, even the occasional theft of ideas and, in rare cases, the fabrication of data. This misbehavior is in response to a discrepancy between the great emphasis in the culture of science upon original discovery and the actual difficulty many scientists experience in making an original discovery, with the result that, in a situation of stress and strain, various forms of questionable adaptive behavior are adopted.[25]

To cite a positive illustration, a notable facet of Carl Brigham's personality was his intellectual honesty and integrity, as illustrated by his rejection of the "native intelligence" hypothesis in 1930, when he retracted his conclusions about mental differences as published in a 1923 book, *A Study of American Intelligence*. In 1930 Brigham said that scores on intelligence tests were a composite of schooling, family background, familiarity with English, and other factors or conditions. He also concluded that comparative studies of racial and national groups could not be made with existing tests, and thus scrapped his major scholarly publication (1923)—a gallant exhibition of scientific integrity.[26]

It is true that students in education and other social fields do not often encounter problems of actual genuineness in dealing with modern documents, especially printed sources. There is little temptation to forge a modern arithmetic textbook, a course of study, or school-board minutes. Even though there may not be any great incentive to perpetrate frauds or forgeries in the modern literature of the social fields, there is still the question of authorship (external criticism) in determining the extent to which a city superintendent has written his annual report rather than his assistant superintendents and supervisors, and the part played by a university president in preparing his annual report as compared with contributions by the deans of his several component colleges.

Typical motives for deception in the preparation of older documents were: use of a well-known name to increase the sales or prestige of a manuscript, enhancement of the reputation of prominent persons through employment of "ghost" writers, and use of pseudonyms to stimulate the curiosity of the public. Types of invention or forgery that have appeared in the past include: witty sayings of famous persons, invented speeches

25 Robert K. Merton, "Priorities in Scientific Discovery: A Chapter in the Sociology of Science." *American Sociological Review* 22: 635–59; December 1957.

26 Matthew T. Downey, *Carl Campbell Brigham: Scientist and Educator*. Princeton, New Jersey: Educational Testing Service, 1961. p. 26–27.

placed in the mouths of famous personages by the older historians, insertion of applause in the written record of legislative speeches never delivered, genealogies and family trees, interpolations or insertions for deceptive purposes by copyists or others, and business documents, works of art, and antiques.

ILLUSTRATIONS OF FRAUDS AND FORGERIES

Forgery was practiced even thousands of years ago. The Egyptian pharaohs often claimed for themselves the deeds of their ancestors by erasing the name of the hero on the wall and by chiseling in their own names. Sometimes the pharaohs reproduced on another slab or monument the record of the hero's achievements, with their own names inserted to receive credit.

Interesting examples of hoaxes, frauds, and forgeries from a number of fields may be cited to illustrate the range and complexity of problems of genuineness in external criticism. For example, a painting is brought to the United States labeled as a self-portrait done by a great Dutch artist. The authenticity of the painting is challenged by the artist's nephew, and a battle develops between art experts in the United States, in Europe, and the U. S. Treasury Department. The customs officers are interested because original works of art are duty-free, whereas copies and reproductions are not. One group of experts on art, handwriting, pigment, and language decides that the picture is genuine, so it is admitted to this country duty-free, but another group of specialists is unwilling to accept the painting as an original work by the Dutch artist.

The Metropolitan Museum of Art in New York sadly reported that three sculptures of Etruscan warriors, supposedly dating from 500 B.C., were twentieth century forgeries. One of the museum's experts had discovered that the black glaze on the statues was produced by the modern dyeing agent, manganese dioxide, and not by the ancient Greek oxidizing method. The credentials of the three sculptures had seemed impressive when they came to the museum in fragments, seemingly worn by the centuries and with a glaze like the ancient Greek black, but a retired art expert living in Rome later became suspicious of the statues stylistically. He discovered that three men, specialists in mending ancient pottery for Italian antique dealers, decided they could create as well as mend ancient works of art. In 1914 they began work on the three Etruscan figures and on completion painted the unfired creations in the Etruscan manner, broke them into pieces, fired the fragments, smeared them with mud, and turned over the pieces to a dealer. In 1961, when the museum sent an art expert to Rome with a plaster cast of one of the warrior's hands from which the thumb was missing, the chief forger produced a thumb of baked pottery that he had been keeping for years. When placed together, thumb and hand fitted perfectly.

Although Abraham Lincoln has proved to be the greatest figure of his period, he was not appreciated in his own time and no engravings of him were made in his lifetime. Suddenly, after his assassination in 1865, there was an enormous public demand for such engravings, and to meet it, the hasty expedient was adopted of creating "grafted" or "hybrid" engravings by placing photographs of Lincoln's head on the bodies of other statesmen (for example, John C. Calhoun and Martin Van Buren) whose plates were already available in stock. Recently, years of detective work have revealed these century-old deceptions or frauds.

The public interest of recent years in antique furniture has made the manufacture of fakes a profitable business. Tests of genuineness are based on certain facts and conditions. A new pine table may have been smoked (with a resulting odor) to give it a smudgy color or aged effect, or may even have been left in the hot sun to let it "mellow." The "joiners" or carpenters of the early American period did not make four-poster double beds. Circular saw markings on the bottom of cabinet drawers cannot date back to Queen Anne's days of 1710. The old joiners chose their wood with care; pine and oak furniture was made of carefully matched boards and rarely had knots. The early carpenters made dowels or pegs by hand which were never perfectly round like the later machine-made pegs. Hand-made chair legs are not perfectly round, and diameter varies slightly on the length of the leg. If the glass in the doors of a cupboard is perfectly smooth, flat, and transparent, the claim of antiquity is open to serious question.

Art experts tell us that forgery follows the market. When English portraiture was popular it was also forged relatively frequently, whereas at present there probably is little forgery taking place in the Michelangelo period. Certain artists left many unfinished works, some of which forgers obtained and completed; for example, a skillfully finished Renoir could bring a larger price and detection of the forgery would prove difficult. In some cases the forgery is so excellent a likeness that it is almost impossible to say whether the original is "better," which involves an aesthetic problem or value. Most forgery, however, is too crude to involve aesthetic values and is simple fraud. Detection of art forgery today is greatly simplified by the rapidity of communication throughout the world.

In modern times the forger has little chance of deceiving the handwriting expert or "questioned document examiner." The forger must attempt to disguise or suppress every revealing characteristic of his own handwriting, and at the same time must include all the telltale traits of the handwriting he is trying to imitate. It may be that the ink or paper used actually was not available on the purported date of the forged instrument. Typewriters develop idiosyncrasies, in that type may be knocked askew or tiny bits of letters are chipped off. Design or size of type sometimes varies with the model of the machine, which may mean that the type used for the forged document was not even in existence on the purported date.

Ultraviolet rays and fluorescence photography have been developed as new methods of examining documents, especially in detecting alterations and erasures. Through such techniques it has been discovered that numerous changes were made in the personal journals of Nathaniel Hawthorne by Mrs. Hawthorne after her husband's death. By reading even heavily blacked out portions of Hawthorne's journals, the scholar has found him a man of real vigor and some bluntness of expression, although Hawthorne's widow had toned down his writing to sound more genteel or inoffensive.

The problem of original or authentic transcripts, however, is always with us, whether for high school graduation, advanced undergraduate or graduate standing, certification of degrees, or appointment to positions. Photostatic copies made by the student's agent are not acceptable for these purposes; only the original coming direct from the registrar's office, with the proper seal and signature, is satisfactory. One such instance of forgery of transcripts sounds fantastic. A telephone call from a state university in Illinois inquired about a job applicant who claimed an Ed. M. degree in 1963 from a particular municipal university, with a dissertation title, "Problems and Solutions of Educational Supervision and Administration." Investigation revealed that the forger of the transcript had only a Bachelor's degree in radio and TV from a music school in 1950, which later became a part of the municipal university. The forger had manufactured a transcript with a complete listing of courses for the two graduate degrees. The internal evidence relating to the transcript was especially revealing. The original transcript, with the registrar's official seal, included only three courses, but the forger filled in the remaining spaces with fake entries in India ink, then made photostatic copies. It is true that the registrar's seal then became only a photostatic copy and, therefore, invalid for official transcript purposes. Other internal evidence revealed that the forger had assigned himself far more hours of credit for the Master's thesis and the Doctor's dissertation than the regulations of the university permitted.

News agencies have reported a secret forgery factory of world importance in an obscure corner of a run-down district of East Berlin, established for the purpose of producing faked documents calculated to embarrass the West. Ingenious techniques of criticism have been employed to expose the forgeries. A faked letter with State Department engraving was addressed to "Dear Clare," whereas this Ambassador has been called "Tim" since boyhood. One purported United States document, supposedly a highly secret paper, used the British spelling, "defence," instead of "defense." A glaring linguistic error in a forged memorandum was a reference to the "National Safety Agency," whereas in American usage the phrasing is "National Defense Agency."

In a letter under an 1834 date, attributed to Lincoln, is an expression "that North East quarter of Section 40" of which Lincoln as an experienced surveyor could hardly have been guilty, since he knew quite well that a Congressional township was made up of 36 sections. The same letter included the geographical term *Kansas;* the territory of Kansas was not organized and open for settlement until 1854, and the term probably was not in use as early as 1834. The fact that the handwriting bore no resemblance to Lincoln's authenticated style helped establish the letters as forgeries. One of the spurious letters attributed to Ann Rutledge mentions a Spencerian copybook not in use until 1848; Ann died in 1835.

In its crudest form, falsification of personal documents is conscious, deliberate deceit, with the possible motives of material gain or malice, or as a practcal joke or literary exercise. An impressive example in the psychological literature is a very skillful forgery of the diary of an adolescent girl, which deceived even Freud. After several years the critics discovered the falsification, concluding that the style was too mature for a girl between 11 and 14 years, that erroneous references were made to the weather on particular days, and that a place mentioned was nonexistent at the date on which the entry appeared in the diary.

INVENTIONS AND DISTORTIONS

Thucydides, the Greek historian, created elaborate speeches or orations for his leading characters, intended not merely for rhetorical effect but also to set forth the politics and diplomacy of his philosophy of history. The Roman dictator, Sulla, after his retirement from public life wrote a fabulous autobiography, pointing to a series of miraculous occurrences coincident with his public work, for the purpose of showing that the hand of the Goddess Tyche was visible throughout his activities. In marked contrast, Caesar's Commentaries present at least an external illusion of impartiality and self-restraint, although we should remember that Caesar wrote primarily to justify himself before the Roman people. When Alexander the Great was listening to an account of how he slew his opponent's elephant with a single blow of his spear, the young conqueror's sense of historical accuracy could not condone such exaggerated hero worship, and he snatched the book and threw it into the water with the comment that the author of such untruth also should be ducked. In the writing of Thucydides, rhetorical speeches had served a genuinely dramatic purpose, but many of his successors made these inventions occasions for dramatic flourishes and illustrations of their command of style.

Parson Weems' rhetorical *Life of George Washington* includes many inventions in the form of dialogues, speeches, and anecdotes. The pioneer historian, Jared Sparks, edited the everyday language of George Washington and corrected his spelling, in order to picture Washington as a character of almost superhuman traits. Sparks has been accused of omitting materials that did not support his purpose of exalting some individual, and even of manufacturing a source or narrative as needed.

Belated appearance of a tradition, especially after the death of the person involved, may give rise to doubt. Captain John Smith's second version of his adventures in Virginia describes dramatically how Pocahontas saved his life, whereas she was barely mentioned in the first version. The story of Ann Rutledge and Abraham Lincoln is thought to be mainly legendary, since no mention of the episode appeared until 31 years after her death.

AUTHORSHIP AND BORROWING

Problems of external criticism are much less those of forgery or invention than of authorship, time, dependence of documents upon each other, and borrowing. It has already been pointed out in this chapter that annual reports of university presidents and school superintendents pose a problem of determining authorship in relation to the contribution of their assistants. A difference in style or language in the several parts of such an annual report is not so important as whether the president's or superintendent's ideas are accurately presented in the phrasing of a dean or assistant superintendent. Washington's "Farewell Address" raises the question of what contribution Madison and Hamilton made to it. A similar question of authorship is present in identifying the numbers of *The Federalist* written by Madison, Hamilton, and Jay.[27] Prominent persons in governmental positions and in other walks of public life frequently have employed "ghost" writers. It is believed that Bancroft, the historian, wrote the message that Andrew Johnson sent to Congress in December 1865, although the discovery was not made until some forty years later.

Eugene Schuyler poses a problem of circumstances of authorship, as one of three men to receive the first earned degrees of Doctor of Philosophy in the United States (from Yale in 1861), but the title of his

[27] Irving Brant, "Settling the Authorship of *The Federalist.*" *American Historical Review* 67: 71–75; October 1961.

dissertation has been unknown and his departmental field uncertain. An interesting bit of detective work reaches the following conclusion:

> To sum up this theory: Eugene Schuyler, like James M. Whiton, completed his doctorate at Yale in Philology (Classics) and received the degree at the 1861 commencement; Schuyler's major professor was Noah Porter; the dissertation was "Wedgwood on English Philology," and it appeared in the *Bibliotheca Sacra* in October, 1862; the Department of Philosophy and the Arts accepted Schuyler's lengthy review-article as fulfilling the dissertation requirements for the newly established doctorate.[28]

Borrowing has been common, especially during earlier periods when authors copied freely from a variety of sources without acknowledgment of the borrowing. For more than a century John Marshall's *Life of George Washington,* published in 1804, was considered a great original work and a classic in its defense of federalism. The work has now been pronounced a mosaic of borrowings, carelessly pieced together, with unacknowledged instances of copying found on 268 of the 488 pages in one volume.

Internal Criticism: Credibility

Internal criticism deals with the meaning and trustworthiness of statements remaining within the document after any spurious or interpolated matter has been removed from the text; in other words, it weighs the testimony of the document in relation to the truth. These questions of accuracy and value of the statements made (credibility) normally come in sequence after questions of authorship, genuineness, time, place, and actual language or text of the original document have been answered through the processes of external criticism. The shift of emphasis in internal criticism is from the document as such to statements within the document. Many authentic or genuine documents (so determined by external criticism) may not be completely accurate or truthful, and require the processes of internal criticism in the form of textual criticism, as well as investigation of such factors as the competence, good faith, position, and bias of the author of the document.

There is no sharp dividing line between the external and internal phases of historical criticism, and the two processes may progress simultaneously, with a considerable amount of overlapping. Internal criticism may use external evidence concerning authorship, or time and place of writing, in determining the truthfulness and accuracy of the statements

[28] Ralph P. Rosenberg, "Eugene Schuyler's Doctor of Philosophy Degree: A Theory Concerning the Dissertation." *Journal of Higher Education* 33: 381–86; October 1962.

made in the document. The terms *external* and *internal* refer to the purpose of the criticism and not to a specific method of dealing with sources, or whether one looks within or without the document for evidence to accomplish the particular purpose.

Before proceeding with specific illustrations, it is helpful to summarize basic principles of internal criticism:[29]

1. Do not read into earlier documents the conceptions of later times.

2. Do not judge an author ignorant of certain events, necessarily, because he fails to mention them (the argument *ex silentio*), or that they did not occur, for the same reason.

3. Underestimating a source is no less an error than overestimating it in the same degree, and there is no more virtue in placing an event too late than in dating it too early by the same number of years or centuries.

4. A single true source may establish the existence of an idea, but other direct, competent, independent witnesses are required to prove the reality of events or objective facts.

5. Identical errors prove the dependence of sources on each other, or a common source.

6. If witnesses contradict each other on a certain point, one or the other may be true, but both may be in error.

7. Direct, competent, independent witnesses who report the same central fact and also many peripheral matters in a casual way may be accepted for the points of their agreement.

8. Official testimony, oral or written, must be compared with unofficial testimony whenever possible, for neither one nor the other is alone sufficient.

9. A document may provide competent and dependable evidence on certain points, yet carry no weight in respect to others it mentions.

LITERAL MEANING AND REAL MEANING

Internal criticism is concerned with questions of the real meaning as distinguished from the literal meaning, the competence of the observer for careful and accurate reporting, and the good faith of the observer in making statements without bias or prejudice. The virtues of the historian include accuracy, love of order, logic, honesty, self-awareness, and imagination.

The attempt to discover the literal meaning and the real meaning of the document is a positive aspect of internal criticism. While the literal meaning and the real meaning are usually the same in modern documents, except for rhetorical figures of speech and ambiguities in political speeches and platforms, many of the older sources present a difficult task of determining the real meaning, because of unfamiliar or obsolete terms and reference to strange institutions or customs. The language of Cotton Mather must be interpreted, to understand what he

[29] Thomas Woody, *op. cit.,* p. 175–201.

is saying about certain events in the lives of the colonists that might seem trivial to the outside world: "If a war between us and a handful of Indians do appear no more than a Batrachomyomachie [battle of frogs and mice] to the world abroad, yet unto us at home it hath been considerable enough to make a history." Even in modern history we find rhetorical figures and literary artifices such as allegory, symbolism, irony, satire, jests, hoaxes, allusions, implications, metaphors, and hyperboles. George Bancroft's high-flown rhetoric needs tempering in determining an appropriate shade of meaning: "History has ever celebrated the heroes who have won laurels in scenes of carnage. Has it no place for the founders of states; the wise legislators, who struck the rock in the wilderness, so that the waters of liberty gushed forth in copious and perennial fountains?"[30]

COMPETENCE AND ACCURACY OF THE OBSERVER

To question either the competence and accuracy or the truthfulness and honesty of the observer is a negative aspect of internal criticism, in that every possible reason for disbelieving is sought and every statement is questioned as long as any reasonable doubt remains. An observer's competence is evaluated in relation to his status as a trained eye witness, presence of emotional stress or pressure that might affect observation, extent to which the position for observing was favorable, and extent to which memory was used after a lapse of time.

Even the secretary of a professional organization is not always an accurate observer and reporter. A history of the American Psychological Association indicates that the minutes of a recording secretary cannot always be trusted as evidence of what actually happened at a particular meeting. The published facts of the founding of the A.P.A. indicate that seven psychologists (Hall, Fullerton, James, Jastrow, Ladd, Cattell, and Baldwin) met at Clark University on July 8, 1892, to discuss the advisability and possibility of forming an association of psychologists. At the time the history was prepared Cattell and Jastrow were still living, but when asked to recall any important events concerning this founding meeting both replied that they had been unable to attend the meeting of July 8, 1892. It is true that sometimes a secretary lists in full the committee members in reporting the minutes, not noting absences, especially if the absent members have made recommendations by mail in advance of the meeting.[31]

[30] Michael Kraus, *The Writing of American History*. Norman: University of Oklahoma Press, 1953. p. 14, 115–27.

[31] Samuel W. Fernberger, "The American Psychological Association, 1892–1942." *Psychological Review* 50: 33–60; January 1943.

Wayne Dennis and Edwin G. Boring, "The Founding of the APA." *American Psychologist* 7: 95–97; March 1952.

As an example of the problem of accuracy in determining a date of birth, when institutions were celebrating in 1944 the one hundredth anniversary of the birth of G. Stanley Hall, it was found that different sources gave three birth dates for him. A biography of Hall, written by a man who had worked closely with him, included the date of February 1, 1846. Another investigator found that the vital records of Ashfield, Massachusetts, Hall's apparent birthplace, did not contain the name of G. Stanley Hall, that Hall himself did not refer to his birth date in a biographical article, that different editions of *Who's Who in America* mention different dates, and that Hall's monument in Ashfield carried the inscription, "Born, February 1, 1844," which was accepted by the second investigator. A third author communicated with all the institutions with which Hall had been affiliated, with Hall's son, and with the General Land Office, and concluded that the most probable month and day of Hall's birth appeared to be February 1, although he was not certain about the year. Despite certain evidence favoring 1844, this third investigator (a scholar and research specialist in educational history) concluded that Hall was evidently confused about his own birth date and that no final answer can be reached until some indisputably authentic record of his birth date is discovered.[32]

Verification of the date when William James established the first psychological laboratory in the United States is an interesting exercise in internal criticism. James was not sure whether it was in 1874, 1875, or 1876, but 1875 has been proved correct. The report of the Harvard treasurer for 1875 cites an appropriation of $300 to James for use in physiology. The nature of the 1875 course also shows that the equipment was for physiological psychology.[33]

When Ellwood P. Cubberley, in 1898, started to teach at Stanford University, he had never studied the history of education, as such, although his undergraduate specialization in science may have thrown some light upon the history of science. If Cubberley had had the benefit of graduate work in history, he would have read and heard much about scientific procedure, historical method, analysis of documents for evidence, and in some universities might have heard criticism of the older concepts of history, including hints concerning a new outlook. Highly desirable as this preparation for his new position might have been, Cubberley had to face the task with the equipment he had, and he developed his course in the history of education as time, energy, and insight made possible.[34] Critics of Cubberley's publications in the history of edu-

[32] William W. Brickman, *op. cit.*, p. 121–22.

[33] Robert I. Watson, *The Great Psychologists*. Philadelphia: J. B. Lippincott Co., 1963. p. 323–24.

[34] Jesse B. Sears and Adin D. Henderson, *Cubberley of Stanford: And His Contribution to American Education*. Stanford, Calif.: Stanford University Press, 1957. p. 104–5.

cation have questioned the quality of his books as historical works. The criticisms have been concerned with the method of writing history, erroneous views of history, wrong interpretations, easy generalizations, and errors in fact. Certain of these defects may have been due to Cubberley's rapid methods of work. When reading history or studying documents, he quickly perceived a major trend, and became less concerned with minor considerations, at times appearing too quick in drawing conclusions. Although Cubberley never overcame completely his lack of technical training in historical method and based much of his writing upon secondary sources, he had extensive acquaintance with a wide range of original papers, records, and documents. His contribution to the history of education has been evaluated by an enthusiastic colleague as that of depicting education as going hand in hand with politics, religion, industry, recreation, and family life, all moving forward in terms of their great common values of freedom and democracy.[35]

To cite other examples of the methods of different observers, Major William Jackson was the official secretary of the Federal Convention of 1787, but his minutes were little more than brief, disorderly notes. James Madison was an unofficial reporter, but he was an intelligent and careful eye witness. The conditions were therefore almost ideal for observation, note-taking, and transcription of his complete notes, with the result that posterity has depended on Madison's reporting of the Convention. Francis Parkman, in writing the narrative of the Anglo-French conflict for control of North America, during his vacations went on long walks through the woods to trace the battle lines and took trips to the West to gather information concerning the Indians. Because of the fallibility of memory, an entry in a careful diary or similar source by a reputable person probably is more accurate than recollection. John Quincy Adams in 1844 based on his notable diary the assertion that Andrew Jackson, a quarter of a century earlier, had approved relinquishment of the claim of the United States to Texas, whereas Jackson's denial was based only on memory.

BIAS AND PREJUDICE

A competent observer may know the truth, but for reasons of bias or prejudice may report the evidence only in part or in distorted form. The tests of truthfulness and honesty include evaluation of the observer's characteristics and statements in relation to personal or vested interest, race, nation, party, region, sect, social level, economic group, profession, conventional formulas rather than true sentiments, vanity or boasting, attempt to please some individual or group, exaggerations, and embellishments.

[35] *Ibid.*, p. 123–26.

An example of bias may be found in the writing of an author opposed to tendencies in American higher education, especially at the graduate level. Flexner criticized the theses and dissertations accepted at certain institutions, confining himself to mention of the titles, without attempting to analyze the content of a sampling of such graduate studies. Flexner made certain comparisons with the dissertations completed in Germany, and apparently was still under the impression that German universities are superior institutions where trivial subjects are never accepted as doctoral dissertations and where these graduate investigations are models of scientific writing. Available evidence has indicated that many German dissertations reveal immature thinking, a superficial grasp of the problem, amateurish methods of research, and other inadequacies. Flexner's approach discloses his bias in favor of German higher education and his lack of impartiality in analyzing American higher education.[36]

As an example of the influence of family loyalty, readers of the *Education* will recall that Henry Adams' treatment of his distinguished ancestors is both favorable and respectful. Evidence of this respect and regard for his family can be abundantly confirmed in his letters. From boyhood, Henry Adams had lived under the spell of his grandfather's and great-grandfather's writings. As a boy, he had helped his father with the proofs of an edition of the work of John Adams, and through constant use of the magnificent Adams family library became familiar with the papers of John Quincy Adams. After graduation from Harvard, he gave up the idea of editing the works of J. Q. Adams, because he thought "it is not in me to do them justice," indicating respect and reverence, as well as some insecurity and indecision at the time.

> Nevertheless, it is important to remember that Henry Adams' first significant publication in the field of American history, *Documents Relating to New England Federalism, 1800-1815,* was prepared in order to defend the reputation of his grandfather and to provide documentary evidence for the high motives of John Quincy Adams in his desertion of the Federalist party in 1807. The publication of the *Documents* in 1877 began the painstaking spadework of investigation that was to result in the publication of the nine-volume *History* more than a decade later.[37]

Other illustrations of bias or prejudice in historical writing may be summarized briefly. Thomas Carlyle was essentially a moralist, who sometimes was tempted to suppress evidence in favor of artistic effect. Francis Bacon altered both literary and documentary sources, in keeping

36 William W. Brickman, *op. cit.,* p. 177–78.

Abraham Flexner, *Universities: American, English, German.* New York: Oxford University Press, 1930. ix + 381 p.

37 Quoted from H. Stuart Hughes, *Teachers of History.* Ithaca, N.Y.: Cornell University Press, 1954. p. 50.

with his purpose, although his intentions were not deliberately to deceive but to clarify and interpret by including his own opinions. The bias of Thomas Macaulay assumed the form of a great pride in England and a theme of English superiority that appealed to national patriotism. Cotton Mather's superstition is revealed when he says, "Molestations from evil spirits have so abounded in this country, that I question whether any one town has been free from sad examples of them.[38] Brave man though he was, John Smith's vanity and boastfulness led him to write glowing accounts of his own achievements, picturing himself always a match for the Indians, except where great odds overcame him. Parson Weems glorified the name of George Washington by assigning to a great but quite human character the traits of almost superhuman nobility. The bias or prejudice of John Quincy Adams, in accusing Thomas Jefferson of loose morals, of being a free thinker (irreligious and probably atheistic), of displaying selfishness in trying to gratify ambition, of duplicity, of treachery to superiors and friends, and of deliberate falsehood, was occasioned by Adams' faulty memory at the age of sixty-three, by political differences, and by his New England attitude toward cards, horse racing, and mere amusement. George Bancroft's bias was in the form of an exaggerated patriotism; he characterized the American Revolution as a crusade of virtuous and disinterested patriots on behalf of the liberties of civilization, and described the Constitution as the product of a group of unique mental giants, never before equaled and not to be matched in the future.

Even the great German historian, Leopold von Ranke, was prejudiced in his enthusiasm for Luther, the Hohenzollerns, and Prussia, although he is customarily considered the founder of the objective school. Ranke said in his first book, when he was not yet thirty years of age, that he did not presume, as did most historians, to sit in judgment on the past, and only wished to show "what had really happened." Although Ranke is representative of the period that instituted the modern study of history, and sought to be critical, colorless, and new, we do meet the mind of Ranke, or his mind is revealed, in his works. Ranke was not successful in achieving his goal—that of repressing the poet, the patriot, the religious or political partisan—of sustaining no cause, of banishing himself from his books, and of writing nothing that would gratify his own feelings or disclose his private convictions. Among other things, there was the effect of the mystical religious faith that he drew from his Lutheran family tradition; he experienced not merely an aesthetic enjoyment of the ever-varying scene, but a view of God's government as well.[39]

[38] Michael Kraus, op. cit., p. 35.
[39] Pieter Geyl, From Ranke to Toynbee: Five Lectures on Historians and Historiographical Problems. Northampton, Mass.: Smith College Studies in History, 1952. p. 3–10.

Macaulay's style and method of conducting an argument were those of the orator who enjoys the clash and thrust of debate. Sometimes in the heat of debate, while remaining master of his argumentative powers, Macaulay was inclined to be swept along by antagonism and to lose respect for the personality of his opponent. At times certain characteristics of his mind or temperament seemed to be projected into his style in the form of straight, unhesitating phrasing, of surprising effect, and of sharp, dramatic contrasts. Macaulay "viewed with the eye of the zealot for public virtues and for progress and for the cause of liberty"; he could approve and admire, as well as detest and denounce, but seemed incapable of establishing "disinterested" contact with a human being in historic or even literary personages.[40]

A fascinating account of "detective" work to check the story concerning Amala and Kamala, supposedly nurtured by wolves in India, is given by an American sociologist and a Calcutta anthropologist, with the setting for their application of the techniques of criticism in India and with grave doubts as to the credibility of the document written by the eyewitness.[41]

In summary, the historian's values and activities may be influenced by professional standards, the institutional needs of his employer and departmental or college jurisdiction over course content for teaching purposes, availability of archives and collections of documents, attitudes and interests of the great public audience, which in one way or another pays the bills, and the culture in which the historian lives, together with the psychological and institutional purposes served by history in this social setting. Pertinent questions of objectivity need to be answered through careful study. Are personal and environmental influences almost entirely offset by rigorous professional training? On the other hand, are biases indeed inevitable and even desirable?[42]

Historical Writing: Composition

The writing of history or historical composition is the work of synthesis that follows the evaluation and criticism of sources, including the mechanical problem of documentation, the logical problem of relative importance and arrangement of topics, and the theoretical or philo-

---

[40] *Ibid.*, p. 28–30.

[41] William F. Ogburn and Nirmal K. Bose, "On the Trail of the Wolf-Children." *Genetic Psychology Monographs* 60: 117–93; August 1959.

A. L. Gesell, *Wolf-Child and Human Child.* New York: Harper & Row, Publishers, Inc., 1941. xvi + 107 p.

J. A. L. Singh and R. M. Zingg, *Wolf-Children and Feral Man.* New York: Harper & Row, Publishers, Inc., 1943. 365 + xii p.

[42] Corinne L. Gilb, "Should We Learn More About Ourselves?" *American Historical Review* 66: 987–93; July 1961.

sophical problem of interpretation. Since documentation is discussed in another chapter of this book, such details need not be repeated here, and we will turn to problems of organization and interpretation.

Although general principles of organization and presentation of materials in the technical report are outlined in another chapter, it is appropriate at this time to make specific applications to historiography. Older types of historical writing and history textbooks usually followed a chronological arrangement of materials in the form of an almanac or calendar of dates, facts, events, and names, with the chapters covering a relatively short time span, sometimes a period of several years or even a few months. A common arrangement was to mark off the chapters in terms of presidential administrations. Many historians of today regard overemphasis on facts as a major obstacle to good history and are convinced that facts must be selected for the sake of clarity and conciseness, with the needs of the present serving as an important criterion in the selection or omission of facts. Macaulay regarded facts in isolation as the dross of history (worthless matter when separated from meaning).

A topical or thematic grouping of historical materials has been recommended as a functional organization to meet the criticism that older histories of education and courses in this field were a mass of comparatively unrelated facts, with little consideration of the pertinent social forces and of the activities and problems of schools and professional workers. Good history of education observes the conditions of good storytelling, shows purpose and meaning, and provides background for better understanding of current educational problems. A history of education that adopts a functional basis of organization, in the form of major problems or areas of contemporary education, includes such chapters as: the aim, method, and curriculum of education; elementary, secondary, and higher education; and the political, psychological, and philosophical bases of education.[43]

One of the frequent mistakes, however, in organizing (in effect disorganizing) history has been to split the past into a series of "tunnels," each continuous from the remote past to the present, practically self-contained and sealed off from any other tunnel, under such historical labels as diplomatic, political, institutional, ecclesiastical, intellectual, military, economic, legal, administrative, art, colonial, social, agricultural. The artificiality of such discrete classifications is illustrated by the interrelationships of diplomatic, military, and naval histories, or by the interdependence of political, economic, social, and ideological factors.[44]

43 John S. Brubacher, *A History of the Problems of Education*. New York: McGraw-Hill Book Co., 1947. 688 p.

44 J. H. Hexter, *Reappraisals in History*. New York: Longmans, Green and Co., 1961. p. 185–214.

In recent times the historian has made more use of such illustrations as photographs, paintings, drawings, sketches, maps, and certain types of handwritten documents, although these tools should be employed only when contributing to more meaningful interpretation. Examples include: the story of a dam from construction to collapse, an expedition to explore new territory, the local history of a village, and the military governments in a state. If illustrations are used, they should be of high quality, should be organized as an integral part of the book, and should reinforce rather than detract from the text.[45]

PHILOSOPHIES AND SCHOOLS OF INTERPRETATION

Since written history has to deal with everything it can discover about man with all his complexity, there must be many varieties of historical writing, which should not be arranged in any kind of "pecking" order, such as higher and lower or legitimate and illegitimate kinds of history. This position is eclecticism in a good democratic sense.[46]

History is rewritten whenever discovery of new sources and helpful reinterpretation of old data make it possible to correct the errors and inadequacies of existing history. In applying new social theory or evidence, it is essential to give appropriate emphasis to all causal factors or forces in a synthetic or eclectic treatment of data, rather than to follow narrowly a single school of interpretation that might exclude some part of the evidence. As an example of historical reinterpretation, during the latter part of the past century social and economic conditions began to receive the attention of historians, as compared with earlier preoccupation with political and military affairs.

Historians, in terms of their major emphasis, have been classified into two groups, although every historian may be in both groups at the same or different times:

1. "Descriptive" historians, who attempt to give an account of the particular event or situation in its own unique setting
2. "Theoretical" historians, who try to find in their subject matter a basis for comparison, classification, interpretation, or generalization.

Historians frequently have borrowed ready-made generalizations, whether they know it or not, and probably would be in a stronger intellectual position if they borrow knowingly. Then they might evaluate their borrowed generalizations by the available means: "definition, qualification, reservation, comformity to known facts, logic, psychology, sta-

45 Richard D. Batman, "Illustrations and History." *Journal of the West* 3: 539–44; October 1964.

46 Crane Brinton, "Many Mansions." *American Historical Review* 69: 309–26; January 1964.

tistics, matched comparisons, genealogical endurance, or other tests." In this process at least some historians might originate and advance certain restricted, tentatively acceptable generalizations of their own.[47]

Expressed in other terms, two extreme positions in historical thought and writing have been the "present-minded" and the "history-minded," with such extreme alignments frequently obscuring important issues at stake. The "present-minded" position too often emphasizes the view that knowledge justifies itself only by a capacity to solve current problems. Many "history-minded" scholars appear distrustful of ideas and theories, and seem to believe that history is all facts. A sounder position is somewhere between the two extremes, since there is nothing intrinsic in the history-minded view that precludes ideas, theories, or generalizations, and nothing in present-mindedness that guarantees history as a panacea for current social ills or problems. This means that history will be rewritten "from day to day," in relation to what each historian does, experiences, and thinks in his own day, as he seeks new evidence and re-examines old data. The fullness and richness of history, as it is rewritten, depend largely on the varied range of experience of historians.[48]

Three new fields of historical reinterpretation have been suggested, as occasioned by certain developments:[49]

1. The end of the age of free and effective security in America
2. The end of an age of mass warfare
3. The end of the age of European hegemony or preponderant authority, sometimes referred to as the political collapse of Europe.

Illustrative general theories or philosophies of historical interpretation may be summarized briefly. These philosophies of history are broader in scope than the specific schools of interpretation, do not lend themselves readily to pragmatic tests of their workability, and have not often touched the larger or more comprehensive works in history:[50]

1. The Greek and Roman historians viewed Fate as controlling human destiny.
2. The Christian philosophy of history was based on the dominant ideas of divine concern for mankind and of changes in history as slowly tending toward the progress and universality of the true religion.
3. According to Voltaire's rationalistic theory, the events of history were attributable not to design but to chance or fortuity.

[47] Louis Gottschalk, Editor, *Generalization in the Writing of History*. Chicago: University of Chicago Press, 1963. p. 195–209.
[48] J. H. Hexter, *op. cit.*, p. 1–13.
[49] C. V. Woodward, "The Age of Reinterpretation." *American Historical Review* 66: 1–19; October 1960.
[50] Allan Nevins, *op. cit.*, p. 240–50.
    Harry E. Barnes, *A History of Historical Writing*. Norman: University of Oklahoma Press, 1937. p. 42–43, 147–206, 330–35. Revised 1962.

4. Hegel's doctrine was that every epoch in history was inspired and dominated by some specific idea.

5. The Darwinian theory of evolution, as applied to history, means that in social institutions, as well as in the animal kingdom, the rule of the survival of the fittest applies and that acquired characteristics of society are passed on to succeeding generations.

6. The Marxian philosophy applied to history is that the mode of production in economic life primarily determines the general character of the social, political, and cultural processes of life, which shift as the economic foundation changes.

7. Since the World War of 1914-18 a rhythm-philosophy explains history as a series of pulsations, the swing and counter-swing of the pendulum, a series of cycles of summer-fall-winter-spring seasons, with the present period representing a very bleak season.

Both the reader and the writer of history are interested more in the special interpretations or schools of history, as illustrated below, than in the broad philosophies of history. The more limited scope of a specific interpretation of historical evidence permits a pragmatic test of the explanatory concept, whereas it requires many centuries to test such a broad theory as the cycle or evolutionary philosophy of history. It should be recognized that the specific schools of interpretation are not mutually exclusive, but severe supplementary purposes, and that many of our best historical works are eclectic or synthetic in interpretation rather than directly related to any special interpretation or school of thought:[51]

1. The personal, biographical, or "great-man" theory is the best known and has been emphasized most by the conventional historians. It holds that the great personalities of history are the main causative factors in historical development, and that history is collective biography.

2. The spiritual or idealistic interpretation of history is found in the discovery of spiritual forces cooperating with geographic and economic factors to produce truly personal conditions, and in human activities finding expression in social relations for the more complete subjection of physical nature to human welfare.

3. The scientific and technological theory views human progress as directly correlated with the advances in natural science and technology, emphasizing that the prevailing state of scientific knowledge and its technical interpretation will determine the existing modes of economic life and activities.

4. The economic school of historical interpretation contends that the prevailing type of economic institutions and processes in society will, in a large measure, determine the nature of the resulting social institutions and culture.

51 Harry E. Barnes, *op. cit.*, p. 337–60.
Allan Nevins, *op. cit.*, p. 265–71.

5. The geographical theory holds that the actions of man cannot be fully understood or adequately described when divorced from their physical setting.

6. Sociological interpretation of history draws from sociology (the science of the life and activities of men in groups) a knowledge of both the causes and the results of group life as the basis for a generalized view of the social process and of social causation.

7. The relatively recent synthetic, eclectic, pluralistic, or "collective psychological" theory is considered the most inclusive and most important type of historical interpretation, holding that no single category of causes is sufficient to explain all phases and periods of historical development, and that only the collective psychology of any period is strong enough to dominate the attendant historical development. Therefore, the new history is necessarily eclectic in approach and interpretation in contrast to the older, conventional history which overstresses political causation or holds that historical development is entirely arbitrary.

To cite examples of how certain schools of history interpret historical development, Charles A. Beard rewrote, in terms of economic forces, the history of American colonization, American expansion, the Revolutionary and Civil Wars, and party conflicts, although later he recognized the effects of the heritage, politics, culture, economics, and international filiations of any civilization as interrelated factors in historical causation and interpretation. Ellsworth Huntington developed a geographical theory, stressing the stimulating effect of certain climates, together with rich natural resources and other factors, to explain the rise of great civilizations in such favored countries as the western part of Europe, the British Isles, and eastern North America. If an eclectic or synthetic point of view prevails in historical interpretation, the historian should be familiar with the literature and concepts in many fields of knowledge.

As an illustration of the reinterpretation of a period, British history of 1870–1914 must no longer regard the British working classes as useful, dangerous, or charitable objects, but as an integral part of their society, thus causing labor history to flourish, with proper attention to the struggles and aspirations, the way of life, and the culture of the laboring population. Therefore, in keeping with the lessons learned from social scientists, historians are less concerned with "speeches, slogans, and manifestoes, and more with changes in demographic patterns and in the structure of industries and occupations, and with the relationship of these changes to value systems, moral attitudes, and social habits."[52]

To cite an example from the field of education, many current writings

52 John Clive, "British History, 1870–1914, Reconsidered: Recent Trends in the Historiography of the Period." *American Historical Review* 68: 987–1009; July 1963.

in the history of education follow a pragmatic philosophy of history in an attempt to prove that many specific proposals of progressive education are in step with history and that the pragmatic temper is in keeping with the American pattern, even as early as colonial days. This new history of education is functional in focusing on the practical concerns of school policies and larger social issues (for example, educational opportunity, control, and policy), frequently drawing methodological models from anthropology, sociology, psychology, and political theory.[53]

HYPOTHESIS, THEME, CAUSATION, PERSPECTIVE

Examples of Hypotheses. Since an earlier chapter has dealt with the formulation and testing of hypotheses, only a few examples from history will be given at this time. Channing formulated and tested several hypotheses in seeking to determine why the Confederacy collapsed in April, 1865, with unexpected speed and completeness. He asked whether the breakdown was the result of military defeat, dearth of military supplies, starving conditions of the soldiers and people, or disintegration of southern morale and the despair of the people. Channing accepted the last hypothesis, although it is not satisfactory, since it does not tell us why morale collapsed. Multiple causation probably is the correct explanation, and Channing's interpretation would have been stronger and sounder had he assigned to each causal factor its proportionate weight. Carlyle's theory or hypothesis of historical interpretation was that great men are the major causal factors in important events, but he overlooked the effect of challenging times or crises in producing the powerful leader or hero. The hypotheses explaining the fall of the Roman Empire range from that of Gibbon on the refusal of the Roman soldiers to wear armour, to moral corruption, overtaxation, overpopulation, disintegration of the Roman army through staffing with barbarian officers, soil exhaustion, and "climatic pulsations."

Central Theme or Thesis. Once the hypothesis has been tested satisfactorily against the evidence, it may become a central thesis, unifying theme, or principle of interpretation. Such a central theme may prove helpful in gathering evidence and in interpretation, although we must be on guard against forcing the data into some particular frame of reference. Charles A. Beard advanced a thesis of economic determinism, showing in his interpretation of the United States Constitution a direct relationship between the holders of the government debt and a strong central government that would pay it off, although later he recognized the influence of other causal factors.

Frederick J. Turner's thesis concerning the effect of the frontier upon

[53] Bernard Mehl, "History of Education," in "The Philosophical and Social Framework of Education." *Review of Educational Research* 31: 7–19; February 1961.

American life and character has influenced historical interpretation, as well as literary, social, and political thought, although needed correctives later were applied to his explanatory thesis. When an author writes of the West and the frontier, the question naturally arises as to his relation to Turner. It is often said that Webb belongs to the Turner school, but Webb himself speaks otherwise, saying that he had not read the Turner essay until after completing *The Great Plains*.[54]

Toynbee cites the history of the settlement of the North American continent to support his central thesis, namely, that it is difficulties or obstacles which lead to the flowering out of a civilization. He has labeled this notion by the striking phrase, Challenge and Response.

Challenge and Response is indeed the central theme of Toynbee's philosophy of history. To him the interest of the study of humanity lies in the indomitable quality of the spirit of man. The significance, the motive forces, the causation —to him it must all be spiritual. The lot of man is cast in a material world, but Toynbee sees his relations with the material as a struggle. Man's *significant* relations at least—his emergence into civilization, his adventures and his triumphs as a civilized being, everything that distinguishes him from the animals and from the barbarians and makes him the protagonist of what we call History—all this can never be *deduced from* the material world; it can be related to the material world only in terms of opposition, and of victory.

A striking idea! And often an illuminating one. But the point that I want to make is that Toynbee has driven it to extremes, and that the system with which he has tried to bolster it up obscures the process of history as much as the idea can occasionally illumine it.[55]

Causation. The earlier historians frequently associated trivial causes or supernatural explanations with major events and important social changes. It was said that the cackling of geese and the bite of an asp enabled Rome to develop unhindered her great power and influence. The older historians believed that the cause of the Trojan War was a quarrel over a beautiful woman, Helen of Troy. It has been said that, after the Norsemen had settled somewhere near the New England coast in 1003–4, the bellowing of a bull frightened the natives, causing them to give battle. The Norsemen returned to their own country, and therefore the bellowing of a Norse bull delayed the settlement of America for 500 years.

To cite another example of causation, on the morning of June 28, 1914, Europe was still enjoying the longest reign of peace she had known in modern times, with no major war for 43 years. At noon that day, in Sarajevo, an undersized high-school student, Gavrilo Princip, assassinated Archduke Franz Ferdinand, heir to the Austrian throne, and his mor-

[54] Walter P. Webb, "History as High Adventure." *American Historical Review* 64: 265–81; January 1959.
[55] Quoted from Pieter Geyl, *op. cit.*, p. 68–69.

ganatic wife. These two shots resulted in one of history's most consequential murders and set in motion a train of events that started World War I a few weeks later, with millions of men engaged. If the two shots themselves are considered only as "sparks" that ignited the world-wide holocaust, there remains the question of the part played by a number of other factors: immediate diplomatic events, imperial rivalries of longer standing, intensification of nationalism, or development of capitalism to a culminating stage. It is argued by some scholars that important, crucial events in history are often determined by chance, by unpredictable events that may seem trivial in themselves.

Perspective. Sound historical perspective in using evidence and in interpretation enables us to evaluate events and personages, distant in time or space, in terms of the contemporaneous standards and conditions then prevailing rather than in comparison with our present-day time and culture. The cruelties of the Inquisition, for example, when compared with the practices of the Middle Ages, are believed milder than the provisions of the contemporaneous civil war, although such excesses seem inhuman in the perspective of twentieth century standards. Accurate evaluation and interpretation of the personal hygiene of a people, community, or individual of a century ago must be done in relation to the general absence of central plumbing and heating at that time. Children in the elementary school gradually gain space and time perspective through early experience with home geography and with relatively recent historical materials of the home community.

Although modern historical scholarship has undergone a technological revolution, in its possession of remarkable techniques for handling raw materials and sources, do we have and use the perspective and time to ponder at length the meaning and interpretation of the sources? Many of the ablest historians of the past have been men of action who knew life at firsthand, which they described critically and interpreted reflectively (Herodotus, Thucydides, Caesar, Macaulay, the Americans Bancroft and Adams, and more recently Churchill). The experiences of Francis Parkman and Theodore Roosevelt with the forest and frontier life enhanced the vividness and validity of their accounts of the American West. Edward Gibbon's inspiration came to him amidst the ruins of the Roman forum. Whatever technical procedures and techniques are applied in research and analysis to arrive at conclusions about the past (ideas, institutions, movements, and human experiences), the communication of these conclusions on the printed page and in the classroom is a creative act, in perspective, despite the useless debate as to whether history is an art or a science.[56]

[56] Carl Bridenbaugh, "The Great Mutation." *American Historical Review* 68: 315–31; January 1963.

To consider or use perspective, in relation to the life of Woodrow Wilson (1856–1924), he really belonged to an earlier period. He was born before the Civil War began, and grew up in the horse-and-buggy days, with tallow candles and kerosene lamps. Even when he died in 1924, there were no commercial airlines in the United States. What might Wilson have done in the League of Nations battle, if he had possessed the modern president's tool of television? How would Wilson have faced our stormy current problems accompanying a far reaching technological and social revolution?

The judgment and perspective of educational historians are often summary, sometimes contradictory, and change with time. Thomas Davidson, who knew John Dewey, did not mention him in *A History of Education* (1900), while Paul Monroe in 1905 and Ellwood P. Cubberley in 1920 emphasized the great contribution of Dewey to education.[57]

MASTERY OF MATERIALS, SYNTHESIS, STYLE

Although the writing of the technical report is treated at some length in another chapter, certain principles of presentation and literary or style aspects of historical writing may be summarized briefly at this time.

Mastery and Synthesis. Effective historical writing shows evidence of scholarship and mastery of materials. Thackeray said of Macaulay that he read twenty books to write a sentence and traveled a hundred miles to produce a line of description. Mastery of sources is always a challenge and frequently has been a burden to able historians. Livy worked with such large masses of data that he was sometimes overwhelmed and not able to synthesize or organize his materials effectively, with consequent contradictions and chronological errors. Leopold von Ranke had great respect for facts and accuracy, and found genuine history more attractive and interesting than romantic fiction, which explains in part the drive that kept him actively at work until the age of ninety-one. Failure to digest and master materials may be due to a false vanity that seeks to impress by including discarded materials and long quotations, a timidity that causes the inclusion of unnecessary data as a protection against possible attack, and lack of literary judgment, which causes some authors to believe that a patchwork of quotations and crude summaries is satisfactory history in contrast to an integrated narrative of events. With the materials carefully digested and classified in a good note system, the working outline emerges as a guide to a chronological or topical arrangement of evidence, or possibly a combination of the two.

Effective Style. Good history applies the principle of progression or moves forward with the story, frequently presenting an explanatory thesis

57 Maxine Greene, "Dewey and American Education, 1894–1920." *School and Society* 87: 381–86; October 10, 1959.

or principle of synthesis as a theory of causation, as discussed earlier in this chapter. The major elements in historical writing should stand out in bold relief, as do the main parts in other technical reports. This means that some data usually must be discarded to attain condensation and to prevent minor details from obscuring the major elements of the narrative. William Douglass, a physician, in his closing chapter on the history of Virginia included a discussion of smallpox; in writing up other colonies also, he sometimes digressed to discuss problems of medicine. In the writing and editing of biography it is a major problem to deal judiciously with sensational stories about the private life of the subject. Many of these stories are not true, and others are not major elements in the historical narrative; for example, the quite human foibles of George Washington should not be permitted to obscure his greatness of character.

There is every reason for history to possess literary excellence and effective style, although the historian will not fill in missing details through exercise of his imagination, merely for the sake of completeness and a connected story. Good history can be written simply and clearly, without emotional dramatization or exaggerated rhetoric. Modern historians interested in the practical uses of history have emphasized the desirability of effective literary style as a means of commanding the attention of the layman and general reader.

As to literary style and communication of a message to the democratic public, a president of the American Historical Association reminds us that a century ago the literary historians (romantic, unscientific, and eloquent) were widely read, including Prescott, Motley, Bancroft, Parkman, Hallam, Macaulay, Carlyle, and Froude. With the rise of "scientific" history, the subject ceased to be literature and lost much of its influence on democracy. History, however, should continue to reach the general public, since it faces no such communication difficulties as science (with its esoteric discoveries) and painting, poetry, or music (with its conflicts between innovation and conservatism). A good democratic audience expects history to be available in plentiful supply, to a considerable extent written with gusto, largely applicable to current needs, and humanized in interpretation. General readers and writers have said of the academic historian that he overemphasizes fullness of research and accuracy and undervalues insight and imagination. The academic scholar may have to teach the lay writer something about precision and depth, while the able lay author teaches the guild historian a great deal about human warmth and literary form. The professional historian has the greater obligation to facilitate this communication and cooperation, since he has the greater resources in the way of academic and professional organizations, libraries and manuscripts, grants, favorable arrangements for work and leisure, basic security, and professional and institutional prestige.[58]

In spite of limitations in the work of the earlier historians, many could express their thoughts with simplicity and power, as quoted below:

THUCYDIDES: "The whole earth is the sepulchre of famous men."

BYRON's description of Livy's writing: "Livy's pictured page."

TACITUS: "No hatred is so bitter as that of near relations." "The more corrupt the state, the more numerous the laws."

AUGUSTUS: "I found Rome of clay; I leave it to you of marble."

BANCROFT, in speaking of the failure of Raleigh to plant a colony: "If America had no English town, it soon had English graves."

On the other hand, Bancroft's rhetoric is extreme in describing the effect of the battles of Lexington and Concord: "With one impulse, the colonies sprung to arms; with one spirit, they pledged themselves to each other 'to be ready for the extreme event.' With one heart, the continent cried: 'Liberty or Death.'"

Hildreth did not often indulge himself in the flowery style in which he described Hamilton, Washington, and Jay: "We have a trio not to be matched, in fact, not to be approached in our history, if indeed, in any other. Of earth-born Titans, as terrible as great, now angels, and now toads and serpents, there are everywhere enough. Of the serene and benign sons of the celestial gods, how few at any time have walked the earth!"

Concluding Statement

Viewed as research, history is an integrated narrative of past events, written in the spirit of critical inquiry. History differs in method from the natural sciences, since it is not a discipline of direct observation or experimentation, but uses reports of observation that cannot be repeated. Good history is both science and art in that sound research is characteristic of all science and effective narration is a form of art. History has close interrelationships with other social fields, including economics, political science, sociology, psychology, comparative education, and educational history in general. Historians of the present century have emphasized that they, too, have answers to current social problems, extending far beyond the study of politics, diplomatics, constitutions, and "drum and trumpet war materials."

The earlier simple categories of sources (including documents and remains or relics) have become more complex and probably will continue

[58] Allan Nevins, "Not Capulets, Not Montagus." *American Historical Review* 65: 253–70; January 1960.

to expand in the future. Documents and remains are the most common primary sources, the first witnesses to a fact, although it has been difficult to preserve adequate collections of the physical objects known as relics or remains. Systematic oral history is a comparatively recent development.

The historian determines the authenticity and meaning of sources through the processes of external and internal criticism. External criticism (authenticity) is concerned with the genuineness of the documents as such, while internal criticism (credibility) determines the meaning and trustworthiness of statements within the document.

Historical composition or synthesis includes the mechanical problem of documentation, the logical problem of relative importance and arrangement of topics, and the theoretical or philosophical problem of interpretation. In regard to style and impartation of message, the increasing use of scientific methods has decreased the influence of history on the public, although it is important that history continue to be available and appealing to the general public, incorporating the best of the academic scholar and the lay writer. As to meaning and interpretation, since history is a reenactment of the past in the historian's mind, with a continuous process of interaction between the historian and his facts, interpretations necessarily change. As a person, the historian lives in a society that influences him, which means that to judge his history we must study both the historian and his social environment.

In summary, a definition of the "structure of history" as an intellectual discipline holds that the goals of studying the past are to:

1. Increase understanding of human behavior and of the human situation
2. Realize the past with empathy, to experience it in a fashion that makes it come alive
3. Experience the past in its own terms, rather than in terms of the present
4. Increase understanding through the methods and outlooks of both the humanities and the social and behavioral sciences
5. Develop broad understanding and mental discipline, avoiding an exclusive and narrow focus upon attempts to find solutions for specific problems of the moment.[59]

SELECTED REFERENCES

ADAMS, James T., and COLEMAN, R. V., Editors. *Dictionary of American History.* New York: Charles Scribner's Sons, 1940. 5 vols. and index.

BARNES, Harry E. *A History of Historical Writing.* Second Revised Edition. New York: Dover Publications, Inc., 1962. xv + 440 p.

BARZUN, Jacques, and GRAFF, Henry F. *The Modern Researcher.* New York: Harcourt, Brace & World, Inc., 1957. xiii + 386 p.

[59] Thomas J. Pressly, "The Structure of History." *College of Education Record* 32: 15–20; November 1965.

BOGARDUS, Emory S. *The Development of Social Thought.* Fourth Edition. New York: Longmans, Green and Co., 1960. x + 689 p.

BORING, E. G. *A History of Experimental Psychology.* Second Edition. New York: Appleton-Century-Crofts, 1950. xxi + 777 p.

BRICKMAN, William W. *Guide to Research in Educational History.* New York: New York University Bookstore, 1949. ix + 220 p.

DIAMOND, Stanley, Editor. *Culture in History: Essays in Honor of Paul Radin.* New York: Columbia University Press, 1960. xxiv + 1014 p.

EDWARDS, Newton. *The Courts and the Public Schools.* Revised Edition. Chicago: The University of Chicago Press, 1955. 622 p.

GOOD, Carter V. *Introduction to Educational Research: Methodology of Design in the Behavioral and Social Sciences.* Second Edition. New York: Appleton-Century-Crofts, 1963. Chapter 4.

GOTTSCHALK, Louis, Editor. *Generalization in the Writing of History.* Chicago: The University of Chicago Press, 1963. 255 p.

HANDLIN, Oscar, Compiler. *Harvard Guide to American History.* Cambridge: Harvard University Press, 1954. xxiv + 689 p.

HOCKETT, Homer C. *The Critical Method in Historical Research and Writing.* New York: The Macmillan Co., 1955. 368 p.

HOOK, Sidney, Editor. *Philosophy and History: A Symposium.* New York: New York University Press, 1963. x + 403 p.

HOWE, George F., and Others. *Guide to Historical Literature.* New York: The Macmillan Co., 1961. xxxv + 962 p.

International Bibliography of Historical Sciences, 1926—. New York: H. W. Wilson Co., 1930—. Published annually.

JOHNSON, Allen, and MALONE, Dumas, Editors. *Dictionary of American Biography.* New York: Charles Scribner's Sons, 1928-37. 20 vols. and index, plus supplements. Also see *Biography Index: A Cumulative Index to Biographical Material in Books and Magazines.* New York: H. W. Wilson Co., 1946—.

KAPLAN, Louis, Compiler. *A Bibliography of American Autobiographies.* Madison: University of Wisconsin Press, 1961. xii + 372 p.

KRAUS, Michael. *The Writing of American History.* Norman: University of Oklahoma Press, 1953. 387 p.

NEVINS, Allan. *The Gateway to History.* Revised Edition. Garden City, N. Y.: Doubleday & Company, Inc., 1962. 440 p.

ROBACK, A. A. *A History of American Psychology.* Revised Edition. New York: Collier Books, 1964. 575 p.

SELIGMAN, Edwin R. A., and JOHNSON, Alvin, Editors. *Encyclopedia of the Social Sciences.* New York: The Macmillan Co., 1930-34. 15 vols.

TOYNBEE, Arnold J. *A Study of History.* London: Oxford University Press, 1934-39. Abridgment by D. C. Somervell, 1947. 6 vols.

WATSON, Robert I. *The Great Psychologists: From Aristotle to Freud.* Philadelphia: J. B. Lippincott Co., 1963. 592 p.

5

Surveys

DESCRIPTION, ANALYSIS, CLASSIFICATION

This chapter presents a variety of descriptive-survey studies and techniques: investigations emphasizing general description, analysis, or classification; social, community, and school surveys; questionnaire inquiries; interview studies; observational investigations; small-group study or group-behavior analysis; critical-incident technique; action or cooperative research; content analysis of documentary materials; and such survey-appraisal procedures as rating scales, score cards, check lists, and index numbers. By delimitation of scope and purpose this book leaves to the numerous specialized volumes the various types of mental measurements and tests of achievement, intelligence, aptitude, and personality, with full recognition that many of these instruments serve data-gathering purposes in descriptive-survey investigations and in experimental, case-clinical, and developmental studies. Under each section the plan of presentation is to identify areas appropriate for descriptive-survey investigation, to characterize the research procedure or data-gathering technique, and to summarize illustrative studies. Many details must remain for treatment in the voluminous survey literature, where it is common for a book of several hundred pages to be devoted to a single data-gathering technique or procedure. In general the processes of enumeration, measurement, and evaluation are left for the textbooks on quantitative methods that deal with statistical methods, measurement, and appraisal.

Education and Status Studies

ALTHOUGH THE THEORY AND PRACTICE OF SAMPLE SURVEYS DEVELOPED IN other fields, education has come to make extensive use of this research approach. The large foundation grants frequently have required status studies to determine the present position of education in our culture and thus provide a basis for comparison and future evaluation. The major impetus for status studies, utilizing the techniques of sample surveys, has been the need for vital statistics that can be used for social research and determination of public policy; for example, the evaluation of Salk polio vaccine, the Kinsey reports, and the election straw polls. Status studies may be artificially classified into two divisions according to goals.[1]

One type is represented by the operations of the United States Government agencies in conducting status studies on many national social and economic characteristics for the purpose of collecting and publishing vital statistics, with the results made available to government, industry, labor, and educational groups as aids in policy-making. Other specific examples of application of sample-survey techniques to status studies in education include the work of the United States Bureau of the Census, school enrollment, employment of students, summary of government finances, and school districts in the United States, all representing the collection of large-scale statistics rather than single studies motivated by specific educational problems.

Examples of sample surveys to explore specific educational issues include a survey of college freshmen and sophomores to assess their perceptions of the instructor, the influence of sociocultural characteristics on educational opportunities in public-school instrumental music for eighth-graders, achievement of objectives of elementary-school science by fifth-grade teachers, impact of social stratification on occupational expectations of twelfth-grade boys, attitudes of public-school teachers in a large city toward school and living conditions, and the effect of exposure to mass media of communication on readiness for desegregation among white males eighteen years of age and older.

Another example relates to the performance of our soldiers. *The Lost Divisions* gives a sympathetic account of the difficulties involved in the sudden creation of a mass army and the near chaos that resulted from manpower policies that were considered unrealistic, vacillating, and misunderstood; and includes an analysis of the relation to performance of such background factors as age, marital status, educational level, and race.[2] *Patterns of Performance* integrates the mass statistical data and the clinical materials, and brings in some new approaches to readjustment by interpreting the follow-up data obtained through the Veterans Administration; a chapter on the management of men attempts to spell out the lessons applicable to civilian industry.[3]

[1] Rosedith Sitgreaves and Herbert Solomon, "Research Methods: Status Studies and Sample Surveys," in "Methodology of Educational Research." *Review of Educational Research* 27: 460–70; December 1957.

[2] Eli Ginzberg and Others, *The Ineffective Soldier.* Vol. 1, *The Lost Divisions.* New York: Columbia University Press, 1959. xx + 225 p.

[3] Eli Ginzberg and Others, *Patterns of Performance.* Vol. 3. New York: Columbia University Press, 1959. xix + 340 p.

Characteristics of Descriptive-Survey Studies

TERMINOLOGY

The literature and terminology of descriptive-survey investigations include such expressions as descriptive, survey, normative, status, and trend. Descriptive studies may include present facts or current conditions concerning the nature of a group of persons, a number of objects, or a class of events, and may involve the procedures of induction, analysis, classification, enumeration, or measurement. The terms *survey* and *status* suggest the gathering of evidence relating to current conditions. The expression "normative" sometimes is applied to descriptive investigations, because the purpose is to determine the normal or typical condition or practice, as in comparing local test results with a city, state, or national norm (central tendency). In certain other disciplines, such as ethics, philosophy, and religion, norm has another meaning (an ideal or desirable goal). For some studies "normative-survey" is an appropriate label, as illustrated by many investigations involving standardized tests. The expression "comparative method" is too limited for our purposes, since comparison is a part of description, in interpreting survey data as well as evidence gathered by other research techniques. For present purposes the more inclusive term *descriptive-survey studies* seems appropriate.

PURPOSES AND USES

The purpose of descriptive-survey investigations may be:

1. To secure evidence concerning an existing situation or current condition
2. To identify standards or norms with which to compare present conditions, in order to plan the next step
3. To determine how to make the next step (having determined where we are and where we wish to go).

To cite an example, the more analytical school surveys of the past two decades tell us not only where we are in a particular school system, but also recommend next steps by way of progress and suggest the methods of reaching the goal of an improved instructional program. This view is one answer to critics of the descriptive-survey method who sometimes say that it is not a forward-looking approach to the solution of educational problems. Certainly adequate survey data in the hands of an investigator of insight can be used for forward-looking purposes.

Another criticism of the descriptive-survey method is that it is superficial and not worthy of recognition as a research approach to important problems. Descriptive studies, however, do provide essential knowledge about the nature of objects, events, and persons. Furthermore, descriptive-survey specialists have devised many tools and techniques for gathering evidence, including standard tests and norms, score cards and rating scales, inventories and schedules, and public-opinion polls.

CONTRIBUTIONS TO OTHER TYPES OF RESEARCH

Descriptive-survey studies have been helpful in contributing to other types of investigation. Survey investigations of present conditions are concerned essentially with history in the making. When survey studies are repeated annually or at other intervals, such cross-section pictures of conditions at different time periods provide the data for historical studies; for example, the annual school census and the United States census make possible historical studies of school enrollment and of the growth of population in the United States. The annual reports of the school superintendent and of the university president furnish material for writing the history of the school system and higher institution.

As in many historical studies, there are occasions in descriptive-survey investigations when it is necessary to rely on verbal data or verbal statements of facts. An example of use of nonquantitative data would be a study of comparative education, involving the educational conditions and practices in another country. A survey of compulsory education in the forty-eight states would require verbal or nonquantitative data concerning the administrative machinery for enforcing the laws, the varying provisions under the state laws, and the different social and educational philosophies underlying the state legislation for compulsory education.

For some types of descriptive-survey studies, data are available in the files of state departments of education, regional accrediting organizations, and national professional associations, gathered through annual reports and in other ways. If the investigator has recourse to such sources of data, it is important for his questions and the major divisions of his inquiry to correspond with the report blanks that provide the data for state departments of education, regional groups, and national organizations. It is even more important for a program of comparable information that the records and reports of American education employ a common language or terminology in keeping with basic principles:[4]

1. Items of educational information can be comparable only when they are recorded at their sources on the basis of standard definitions.
2. Items of educational information must be arranged in classifications which are as clearly identified and defined as the items they contain.

[4] Allan R. Lichtenberger, "Principles for a Program of Comparable Information." *School Life* 45: 8–10; May 1963.
   Carter V. Good, *Dictionary of Education.* Second Edition. New York: McGraw-Hill Book Co., 1959. xxx + 676 p.

3. In each area of educational information, the categories must be so classified that information in all of the areas can be quickly and significantly related.
4. A cooperative process, nationwide in its scope, through which items of educational information are defined, is essential to an understanding and acceptance of standard definitions.
5. When items of educational information have uniform meanings, the combinations of these items are comparable.
6. State education agencies determine to a major extent the degree to which cooperatively defined items of educational information become a part of records and reports.
7. The degree of comparability of educational information depends on the extent to which standard definitions approach universal use.
8. Coordination and service at the national level are essential to the success of a national program designed to achieve comparability of educational information.

Use of documentary sources for historical purposes has been discussed in an earlier chapter. Many of the library guides to the published sources are listed in the chapters on library technique and on the historical method. The basic principles of historical criticism apply in dealing with documents for descriptive-survey purposes. Many studies in the area of comparative education are descriptive in nature.

Genetic or growth studies secure measurements of the individual or group at different stages of development and thus may be considered a series of cross sections of growth or a sequence of survey studies separated by time intervals. It is true that genetic or developmental studies usually follow an individual or a group in terms of one or only a few aspects of growth, whereas descriptive-survey investigations usually cover a larger number of traits or characteristics of the group. Many cross-cultural studies deal with status.

In group experimentation, the testing usually done at the beginning to determine current status or to provide the evidence for equating groups, as well as the end testing, may be regarded as forms of survey-testing or measurement, but so used as to serve as an important part of the total experimental procedure.

ANALYSIS AND CLASSIFICATION[5]

Many descriptive investigations are highly analytical in character and sometimes have been characterized as "analytical studies," although analysis as a process is present in all types of research. The varieties of

[5] Carter V. Good and Douglas E. Scates, *Methods of Research: Educational, Psychological, Sociological.* New York: Appleton-Century-Crofts, 1954. p. 277–547. Also see: Clare Selltiz and Others, "Analysis and Interpretation," *Research Methods in Social Relations.* Revised One-Volume Edition. New York: Henry Holt and Co., 1959. Chapter 11.

analysis in descriptive-survey studies may be illustrated by the buildings of a city school system. The investigator may be interested in a general aspect of the school buildings such as architectural style or in the component parts of the building (classrooms, laboratories, libraries, cafeterias, and other parts of the building). For purposes of an analytical study the interest may be in matters of form, pattern, or organization; for example, the grouping of the classrooms in relation to fire escapes, cafeteria, or library, or even the seating arrangement of the pupils in particular classrooms. Another type of analytical study in the descriptive-survey area concerns itself with the dynamics of the school, as illustrated by pupil-teacher relationships or teacher-principal relationships.

Classification, the recognition of similarities and differences among experiences, is a basic process in all research, including descriptive-survey studies. Grouping or the forming of categories is conducive to economy of thought. Examples of major classification plans or schemes are the Dewey decimal and Library of Congress systems for cataloguing books, the taxonomy or classification system for animals and plants in the biological sciences, and the periodic table of elements in chemistry and physics.

The primary uses of classification are as follows:

1. To provide codified data, as in dividing the data of the United States census or school census according to sex, age, place of residence, nationality, and the like
2. To form useful classes according to kind, as in classifying and reporting frequencies for the reasons high-school pupils give for leaving school before graduation
3. To afford logical order and system, as in cataloguing books in the library according to a system
4. To develop the meaning of class concepts, as in examining court decisions to determine the meaning of the category "discretionary powers of school boards"
5. To create cases through delimitation, as in studying parent-child relationships by taking different cultures (probably in different parts of the world) as representing varying categories of parental behavior
6. To standardize observations that describe, as in studying the behavior of mothers during their visits to pediatricians working in clinics
7. To select and categorize scale indicators, as in determining that the manner of a particular pediatrician is positive and reassuring (rather than negative, disturbing, and offensive) by counting the number of instances of detailed behavior classified under these different categories.

CRITERIA FOR SURVEY RESEARCH

This introductory discussion has not attempted to answer specifically whether the descriptive-survey method is a superior or an inferior ap-

proach to problem-solving. The important consideration is whether a
particular technique provides answers to significant questions, which
means that the descriptive-survey method is best for certain purposes.
Many of the illustrative survey studies in this chapter evidence ingenuity
in planning, skill in devising techniques, and insight in interpretation of
data, thus providing answers to important questions, as well as helpful
illustrations of technique and high standards for research. The challenge
is to produce survey studies of high quality, in keeping with the criteria[6]
listed below:

1. The research report usually has a distinctive form, with definite attention given to describing the methodology, the sources, the population, the
   trait being studied, and other appropriate methodological or technical
   details.
2. Presumably original observations are taken.
3. Each step in the work proceeds with meticulous care and with due consideration for the large plan and purpose of the work. The data are verified and
   evaluated.
4. The data are resolved, or organized into certain more general terms, and
   are sometimes related to a single, over-all thesis. Certainly the data will be
   summarized in some form or other, as systematic as possible. What is done
   with the data is a definite part of the contribution of the study.
5. The background, sensitivity, and general competence of the investigator,
   as well as the spirit with which he works, are vital elements. As to whether
   a study must have more or less than the qualities in this list, probably no
   definite rule can be stated. These qualities vary in degree; various types of
   research have their own criteria. One should aim, in doing his own research,
   not at the minimum requirements of research, but at a fairly full-bodied
   attack.

LIMITATIONS OF SURVEY STUDIES[7]

Although the survey method is an important tool or instrument which
has developed greatly during the past two decades and is valuable for
many purposes, it has certain limitations that restrict its use in gathering
information on such a field as consumer behavior and its underlying
causes:

1. Information that is not known to the respondents cannot be obtained in
   surveys; for example, annual increases in the value of life insurance re-
   serves (on policies owned by individual families) and amounts of deprecia-
   tion on houses or automobiles owned would be needed for the sake of an
   exact determination of amounts saved by individual families. As a general

---

[6] Quoted from Carter V. Good and Douglas E. Scates, *op. cit.*, p. 271.
[7] Lawrence R. Klein, Editor, *Contributions of Survey Methods to Economics.* New
York: Columbia University Press, 1954. p. 60–64.

rule, such information is not available to individual policy holders or owners of homes and automobiles.

2. Information that is not salient to the respondents cannot be obtained in a reliable way; for example, most people have not given much thought to the amount of money spent on food or clothing, or on most individual food and clothing items, over a year. Therefore, annual surveys are not reliable or suitable for determining such amounts of expenditures.

3. A request for information that is considered secret should be avoided, as should questioning that appears to check upon the honesty of the respondent. The success of the interview will be endangered if questions are asked about income from gambling, or about currency hidden in mattresses or locked in safety deposit boxes, or about tax returns already filed.

4. Information about activities shared by a very small proportion of the population cannot be obtained in a reliable way in cross-section surveys; for example, it has been found that over a period of years less than 3 per cent of the population purchased publicly traded common stock, while about 75 per cent of all families paid life-insurance premiums.

5. Data that can be obtained only with very great sampling error do not constitute proper topics of sample surveys; for example, it is impossible to determine through sample surveys what the highest income in a given year was. It is a matter of mere chance whether a small-sample survey finds one, two, several, or no families with an annual income of more than $100,000.

6. Information obtained from a single survey is less reliable than trend data derived from two or more consecutive surveys made by the same methods.

7. Surveys cannot be aimed at obtaining exact quantitative forecasts of things to come; for example, plans to purchase houses or automobiles during the next twelve months.

In survey studies there is real need for cooperation; for some three decades or more public-opinion agencies have developed rather reliable techniques for describing the attitudes of people concerning public affairs. Historians should welcome this method of obtaining information, which heretofore was available only indirectly, if at all, but in reality there has been little collaboration between historians and "pollsters." The difficulty or problem appears to be one of significance, in that the pollsters ask questions for the newspaper headlines rather than to gather data of lasting or permanent significance. The result is that the historian in the main disregards public-opinion surveys, and the pollsters work without the broader view of the historian that would lead to more meaningful studies. This separateness of the two fields of research suggests that the historian and the pollster should cooperate to their mutual benefit and to aid the future historian in interpreting our times.[8]

8 Paul F. Lazarsfeld, Joseph R. Strayer, and Henry David, "History and Public Opinion Research: A Debate," in *Common Frontiers of the Social Sciences*. Edited by Mirra Komarovsky. New York: Free Press of Glencoe, 1957. p. 242–78.

The Social Survey

In presenting the types and data-gathering techniques of descriptive-survey studies, we could begin with the larger and more complex investigations (such as the social, community, and school surveys) or with the simpler types of studies. We have chosen to present first the more complex types of surveys, which usually employ a variety of research procedures and instruments (such as questionnaires, interviews, observation, and other techniques).

The social survey is usually a cooperative study of a current social problem, situation, or population within definite geographical limits, ordinarily with some concern for a constructive program of social reform and amelioration.

EUROPEAN BACKGROUNDS

The background of the social-survey movement is found in the European studies of more than a century ago. Frederic Le Play, a French social reformer and economist, used social-survey methods in his monographs on family standards of living, and at the same time combined effectively case-study and statistical procedures.

It was the Revolution of 1848, once more plunging the capital into a bloodbath, that determined Le Play at last to publish the conclusions of his thought as to the true path of peaceable social reform. This initial work took the shape of a folio volume, entitled *Les Ouvriers Européens* and published at the expense of the government in 1855, comprising an introductory essay and detailed case studies of thirty-six families which Le Play had observed in the course of his travels. In the introduction, he set forth the outline of his thought. In brief, he argued that the ultimate unit in the consideration of social problems was not the individual, but the family, and that the key to human happiness was not the freedom of the individual to seek his own pleasure, but the well-being of the family, which alone could afford the individual a complete and secure happiness. The proper method of social reform, he further held, was not a speculative discussion of one or another series of principles dealing with the state and the citizen, but rather the scientific observation of particular families. Accordingly, he specified the procedure for the compilation of case studies, or family monographs, involving an examination of the background of the family, its sources of income, the conditions of its work, its habitation and diet, recreation, and moral and religious convictions and practices. As a means of rendering the observation more precise and objective, he urged a careful inventory of all its capital, including household furnishings and wardrobe, and a budget of its annual expenditures.[9]

[9] Quoted from H. Stuart Hughes, Editor, *Teachers of History: Essays in Honor of Laurence Bradford Packard*. Ithaca, N.Y.: Cornell University Press, 1954. p. 63–65.

The English statistician and reformer Charles Booth was interested primarily in the conditions of poverty in the East Side of London. He began his seventeen-volume investigation[10] in 1886, in an attempt to help social reformers find remedies for the existing evils. Among the factors affecting life and labor in London, Booth investigated income, hours and conditions of work, housing, standards of living, number of children, size of household in relation to size and type of dwelling, type and frequency of sickness, leisure activities, and club and union membership.

A later survey of London life and labor, published in 9 volumes,[11] 1930–35, was made to discover changes in the socioeconomic life of a new generation of London workers, for comparison with Booth's earlier survey. The second survey describes the habits of laboring people after the advent of the automobile, telephone, wireless, and cinema, which had greatly changed the life and work of the people of London.

TRENDS IN THE UNITED STATES

A social survey[12] in the United States was begun in 1909 by Paul Kellogg and a group of social economists and professional social workers to study the forces that affected the lives of steel workers in Pittsburgh, to discover the underlying factors in the city's growth as they affected the wage earners, to secure an inventory of an urban industrial community, and to determine how far human or social engineering had kept pace with mechanical developments in a steel district. Completion of publication of the Pittsburgh survey in 1914 stimulated many American communities to make social surveys of their own complex and changing problems. The growth of the social-survey movement was so great that by 1928 a published bibliography included a total of 2,775 titles or projects.[13]

During the 1940's and later, relatively few social surveys were undertaken by individual investigators. The increasing interest of social agencies and of the federal and state governments in social problems in local communities is evidenced by the large masses of census data and other government reports on a variety of problems, such as social security, economic conditions, employment and unemployment, wages, income, health, housing, child-welfare services, and crime and delinquency. The complexity of the social survey and the variety of research methods are

[10] Charles Booth, *Life and Labour of the People in London*. London: Macmillan and Co., Ltd., 1892–1903. 17 vols.

[11] Hubert L. Smith, *The New Survey of London Life and Labour*. London: King and Son, 1930–35. 9 vols.

[12] Paul U. Kellogg, Editor, *The Pittsburgh Survey*. New York: Russell Sage Foundation, 1909–14. 6 vols.

[13] Allen Eaton and Shelby M. Harrison, *A Bibliography of Social Surveys*. New York: Russell Sage Foundation, 1930. xlviii + 487 p.

illustrated by a social study of Pittsburgh, which included statistical analyses; ecological studies of Pittsburgh and its satellite districts as "natural" areas; case study of agencies, families, and districts as units; group and personal interviews; and schedules and questionnaires.[14]

The Community Survey

Social surveys and community studies are similar in many respects, with no sharp dividing line. The community survey, like many school surveys, is made to provide data for planning future developments, such as an adequate system of sewage disposal or new buildings for the school system, although the recommendations of the community study frequently are broader and more general than those found in the school survey.

CHARACTERISTICS AND SCOPE

In the literature of social research the term *community* sometimes refers to small and stable communities such as a peasant village, to a large and complex urban area such as a ghetto community, to large cities and small towns or villages, or to a small, temporary unit such as a trailer camp. The local community or "natural area" is characterized by sociologists as having a territorial area, common interests, common patterns of social and economic relations, a common bond of solidarity from the conditions of its abode, a constellation of social institutions, and some degree of group control.

A survey of community life in urban and rural natural areas usually deals with the historical setting, social influence of physical configuration, social isolation, social contacts, economic centers, demographic characteristics, and population mobility, with an interest in the problems of social disorganization, poverty and dependency, unemployment, child labor, health, and crime and delinquency, as well as the local government and the various social institutions and organizations (economic and industrial, labor, health, religious, social welfare, delinquency control, police and criminal, educational, and recreational).

Studies of community schools, chiefly descriptive in character, are not as broad in scope as community surveys, but do provide answers for a number of significant questions: How can schools learn the community's needs and resources so as to serve it effectively? How have schools and communities worked together to improve the school program and the community? In what ways are community-school programs effective?

[14] Philip Klein and Others, *A Social Study of Pittsburgh: Community Problems and Social Services of Allegheny County.* New York: Columbia University Press, 1938. xxvi + 958 p.

TECHNIQUES AND EXAMPLES

Examples of community surveys may be found in the chapter bibliography, in the illustrations of case studies of communities in a later chapter on case and clinical techniques, and in succeeding paragraphs. It is helpful to characterize certain manuals or guides for studying the community and to summarize illustrative community surveys drawn chiefly from the disciplines of sociology and anthropology.

Fifteen chapters of *Studying Your Community* are devoted to specific phases of community living, such as housing, education, recreation, religious activities, social insurance and public assistance, aids to family living and child welfare, health, and intergroup relations, with each chapter serving as a guide to a study or survey of that particular aspect and including provocative questions for the survey group to ask itself in order to define and sharpen the focus of the inquiry.

These fifteen chapters are supplemented by five additional ones which deal with the larger, basic issues of survey-making, and with the "how" of community studies. This portion of the book contains some valuable pointers on such questions as the choice of the geographic area to be studied, the use of census data and other reference materials, hints about interviewers and the interviewing process, the use of the survey committee or sponsoring group, designing and compiling questionnaires and schedules, and many others. This section of the book also contains some useful observations on the general background and setting of the modern community, its economic life, its governmental structure, its social and class organizations, its primary and other interrelationships, and its readiness and ability to change.[15]

In another manual or guide, Redfield views the "little community" as an ecological system, social structure, typical biography, kind of person, outlook on life, history, community within communities, combination of opposites, and a whole and its parts, with these themes constituting ways to study the small community, or methods designed to view the object of study as a whole. Redfield illustrates the various approaches with concrete cases drawn from anthropological science, including British and American works, as well as his own adventures in Mexico, in order to understand the premises on which a scientific description of a human whole (in this case the little community) can be adequately based.[16]

15 Quoted from review by C. William Chilman, *Social Service Review* 29: 432–33; December 1955, of Roland L. Warren, *Studying Your Community.* New York: Russell Sage Foundation, 1955. xii + 385 p.

16 Review by Paul Nyberg, *Harvard Educational Review* 25: 196–98; Summer 1955, of Robert Redfield, *The Little Community: Viewpoints for the Study of a Human Whole.* Chicago: University of Chicago Press, 1955. 182 p.

EXAMPLE: COMMUNITY POLITICAL SYSTEMS[17]

Janowitz brings together five case studies, from the United States, on different aspects and approaches to urban community political systems and one study of an electoral contest held in a Norwegian province. The American urban communities studies include a small trading center or town, a satellite city, a suburban community, a larger industrial city, and a giant metropolis. The methods used in these studies include historical analysis, survey techniques, statistical analysis, the ecological approach, and case study. Since these studies use different hypotheses, different methods, and different definitions, it is hard to compare them. Among the significant findings are the decline of the influence of large businessmen in community affairs, the survival of the old patronage system in an industrial satellite city, and the lack of priorities among business leaders as to their self-interests.

EXAMPLE: COMMUNITY HEALTH[18]

This book provides a good example of the type of role that the social scientist can play in the fields of health. Written by an anthropologist, it is based on a project which was designed to introduce to professional health workers the culture and society of Americans of Mexican descent. In order to gather the materials a small unincorporated community on the outskirts of San Jose, California was chosen to be the subject of the study. During the investigation Clark and her associate, Thomas McCorkle, utilized standard ethnographic techniques which included participant observation of community life and interviewing of 20 percent of the families.

On the assumption that "medical systems are integral parts of the cultures in which they occur," Clark devotes the first six chapters to a description of various aspects of life in the Mexican-American community. In chapters seven and eight a number of the Mexican-American's concepts of health and disease are introduced as well as a very illuminating discussion of what kind of role behavior he expects of the medical technician.

EXAMPLE: A MOUNTAIN COMMUNITY[19]

Tradition and change in a small segment of the southern Appalachians are expertly portrayed. Although names used are fictitious, Little Smoky Ridge, "more so than most neighborhoods . . . has suffered the abrasions of extreme

[17] Quoted from review by Harold F. Gosnell, *Science* 134: 186–87; July 21, 1961, of Morris Janowitz, Editor, *Community Political Systems.* Vol. I, International Yearbook of Political Behavior Research. New York: Free Press of Glencoe, Inc., 1961. 259 p. Reprinted from *Science* by permission.

[18] Quoted from review by Arthur J. Rubel, *Social Forces* 38: 274–75; March 1960, of Margaret Clark, *Health in the Mexican-American Culture: A Community Study.* Berkeley: University of California Press, 1959. 253 p.

[19] Quoted from review by Henry Shissler, *Rural Sociology* 24: 398–99; December 1959, of Marion Pearsall, *Little Smoky Ridge.* Tuscaloosa, Ala.: University of Alabama Press, 1959. xii + 205 p.

poverty through several generations that prohibits any foreseeable improvement of conditions."

The reader will be fascinated by the colorful descriptions of the individuals and setting of this depressed remnant of an earlier American frontier. The researcher lived for several months in this remote area observing many facets of this cultural island. The author's absorbing account is supplemented by references to similar studies.

The geographical area is discussed also. Contrary to popular belief, the Great Smoky National Park has not brought the desired benefits to this particular, isolated neighborhood. This thorough presentation of a small segment of cultural anthropology vividly reveals a contemporary illustration of a frontier type of social organization and a value system in an environment no longer helpful to either. Historical explanations add authenticity to the descriptions. Family life is reported in its physical and social dimensions. Supernatural sanctions and religious phenomena are significantly related to the life of mountain folk. Dr. Pearsall's objective account nowhere reveals any biases, and generalizations for the total area are absent.

"The final foreseeable future for Little Smoky Ridge as a neighborhood is disintegration, which has already begun, and finally death."

EXAMPLE: REGENERATION OF A CITY NEIGHBORHOOD[20]

This book tells the proud story of the regeneration, over a ten-year period, of the Hyde Park-Kenwood community on the south side of Chicago. Beneath the account of who did what, when, and how, a universal human theme is evident: the struggle between aspiration and doubt, activity and passivity, courage and despair. The conflict is resolved through the conscious rediscovery of the values of co-operative action, compassion for all persons, and the insistence that communal action respect, protect, and enhance the rights of individuals. The book tells of the exciting and, at times, terrifying confrontation of these values by the social, physical, and psychological crises of a community that is rapidly becoming a slum.

Julia Abrahamson deals with these matters objectively. She tells what the community was like and what caused its deterioration. What she says about this decline could be said about many urban communities. Then we are shown how an action group—the Hyde Park-Kenwood Community Conference —came into existence, how it formulated and tested its goals, how it set up its programs. . . .

In more mundane and practical terms, the story is the account of what people did, how it came out, and what they did next. It is a considerable story, involving just about everyone, from a Pullman porter who became a block leader, to the President of the United States. We have ministers, rabbis, housewives, businessmen, union members, teachers, scientists, policemen, legislators, high-school students, PTA members, building inspectors, aldermen, two

20 Quoted from review by Herbert A. Thelen, *School Review* 67: 469–73; Winter 1959, of Julia Abrahamson, *A Neighborhood Finds Itself*. New York: Harper & Row, Publishers, Inc., 1959. xiv + 370 p.

mayors, organization officials, grandmothers, bankers, and the whole gamut of city, state, and federal officials. Each of these has his place in the movement because he lives in the community or because his job impinges on the community. We become aware of the racial, philosophical, social, and educational differences that separate these people, and we see how they are brought together in quasi-autonomous working committees and block organizations that eventually blanket 85 per cent of the community of seventy-two thousand people. We see the first "budget" of $127.50, collected by passing the hat at a meeting, grow into an annual budget of sixty thousand dollars, two-thirds of which is raised in the community. We see the office staff grow from nobody at all to eleven full-time workers, and we are shown how literally hundreds of volunteers were helped to find intense reward and satisfaction through working in the Conference. We see the conflicts and frictions among organizations, the emergence of a powerful new organization that reaches people the Conference cannot reach, and the painful efforts of the two organizations to find a way of co-existing and complementing each other's resources, skills, and clientele. We pause to contemplate why there were two organizations—one for the grass roots and the other for the power people—and to wonder if, under other conditions, one organization could have reached both. Finally, we are astonished at the changes that are already achieved or clearly promised, involving one hundred and fifteen million dollars of private capital, thirty-eight million from federal funds, and ten million from the city of Chicago. The task is the rebuilding of 47.3 acres of blighted housing and the repair of the remaining 80 per cent of the dwelling units in the community—with all construction to follow an over-all community-approved plan for the neighborhood.

Example: A Pineapple Town in Hawaii[21]

This volume is a case study of a pineapple plantation community, village-like in its physical structure, though far more industrial than rural in a number of ways. For five years the author was employed by the mainland company which operates this plantation, lived there over a year, and has returned twice since the end of World War II. The volume describes the plantation, the community, and the three main ethnic groups—Filipinos, Japanese, and Caucasians—and then discusses community social relationships and the social changes produced largely, though not entirely, by changing technology.

While the study is largely descriptive, there are significant data on the attitudes and ways of living of the various groups and on the changing interactions among them. Kinship is decreasing in importance. Social classes are based upon both occupational status and race, with increasing emphasis on the former and attendant decline in social separation based on ethnic groups, since all groups are becoming more culturally alike.

21 Quoted from review by Edmund DeS. Brunner, *Rural Sociology* 24: 398; December 1959, of Edward Norbeck, *Pineapple Town, Hawaii*. Berkeley, California: University of California Press, 1959. xii + 159 p.

EXAMPLE: RESTUDY OF A COMMUNITY IN THE PACIFIC[22]

The tiny Pacific island of Tikopia is already well known to anthropologists, thanks to Raymond Firth, who studied this isolated Polynesian community in 1929 and whose books, *We, the Tikopia* (1936), *A Primitive Polynesian Economy* (1939), and *Work of the Gods in Tikopia* (1940), are models of the highest standards in ethnographic reporting. *Social Change in Tikopia* represents a restudy of the island undertaken in 1952 with the assistance of James Spillius. It is a record of social change in Tikopia and, at the same time, of Firth's own growth as one of the leading anthropologists of our time. His account of political organization and social control, for example, is as sophisticated for the present as was his account of economic organization for two decades ago.

The book is more than a study of social change in other respects, also. Just before Firth's arrival in 1952 a serious hurricane had swept the island and destroyed most of its food resources. Firth provides an unusual account of the society's response to sudden crisis and of its operation during a famine. Rarely do anthropologists have such an opportunity to study isolated and economically self-sufficient communities trying to cope with disaster, largely through their own efforts and cultural resources; it is especially rare when such a study can be made of a community whose operation under normal circumstances has already been recorded.

Firth reviews in detail changes in economic outlook which have resulted from increased outside contact and population growth. Of interest is his analysis of how money has come to fit into the native economy. From economic change, he proceeds to a discussion of changes in land rights and calls attention to the greater individualization of holdings; this is not a result of Western influence, as might be supposed, but a response to internal pressures on subsistence resulting from the abandonment of traditional practices of population control. Analyses of patterns of residence and marriage, the system of lineages and clans, the political structure, and the system of social control are also presented in detail with an assessment of the amount and nature of change in each. Religious changes are not included in this volume.

EXAMPLE: CHANGES IN A VILLAGE IN MEXICO[23]

The first sociological study of Tepoztlan was made by Robert Redfield and published in 1930. The second study was made in 1943 and the third in 1956-57, both by Oscar Lewis. This document devotes seven chapters to Tepoztlan,

[22] Quoted from review by Ward H. Goodenough, *Science* 131: 1434; May 13, 1960, of Raymond Firth, *Social Change in Tikopia: Re-study of a Polynesian Community after a Generation*. New York: The Macmillan Co., 1960. 360 p. Reprinted from *Science* by permission.

[23] Quoted from review by Emory S. Bogardus, *Sociology and Social Research* 44: 364; May–June 1960, of Oscar Lewis, *Tepoztlan, Village in Mexico*. New York: Holt, Rinehart and Winston, Inc., 1960. viii + 104 p.

as it appeared to the author in his earlier visits. "Chapter 8 of this book describes the village as of 1956" and notes some changes that have occurred since the earlier studies were made.

The list of changes includes: more varied and colorful clothes for the younger people, a shortage of house sites and houses, more health care including vaccinations, increase in nonagricultural occupations, a rise in the number of moneylenders, expansion of educational facilities, establishment of a movie theater, increase in number of radios, a greater child-orientedness, more permissiveness in dealing with children, a more friendly attitude of the villagers toward outsiders. The *bracero* movement, or employment of the younger men in the United States for periods of time, is noteworthy and has played a role in creating changes. This study throws light on social change in general in Mexico.

The School Survey

HISTORICAL BACKGROUND

As indicated earlier in this chapter, the social surveys of the early years of the present century studied such problems as municipal organization, housing, recreation, and sometimes education. Therefore, it is a natural sequence that the beginning of the school-survey movement dates back to approximately 1910. Before that date, investigations of school systems had been made either by the school officers as part of their regular duties or by persons interested in some particular educational problem rather than in a comprehensive survey of the school system.

During the period from 1910 to 1915 there was a tendency in school systems to invite visiting experts for a relatively short period of time, sometimes a few weeks, to make recommendations concerning such problems as buildings, teachers, curriculum, organization, educational standards and achievement, financial management, and community attitude toward the schools. The early surveys include Boise, Idaho; Montclair and East Orange, New Jersey; Baltimore; New York City; and Cleveland.

Among others, Ellwood P. Cubberley was ready to play a part as investigator and consultant in the early days of the school-survey movement by reason of his school program and interests, professional experience, and methods of work.

Thus it happened that Cubberley grew to maturity and entered university work at a time when the scientific movement was taking hold of the country, but when such study of education was very new; when the country was greatly enthusiastic about its public schools, but also when it was beginning to find fault with them; when scientific studies were beginning to cast doubts upon the foundation of the traditional programs, but when tradition was still firmly in control; when the nature of our way of life was changing rapidly and bringing to light educational needs hitherto not recognized by the school, but when few men were scholastically equipped to enter upon a scientific study of education.[24]

After 1915 there was a trend toward more specialized surveys of limited aspects or problems of education, since the large number of recommendations in comprehensive surveys sometimes had proved confusing to the school staff and to the public. It was also thought desirable to add to the administrative staff of the local school system one or more specialists trained in methods of research, measurement, and survey techniques, who could assume leadership in conducting school-survey studies, rather than to depend entirely on the leadership of visiting experts. Frequently local staff members and consulting experts cooperated in conducting school surveys. As the movement spread widely through the local and state school systems, staff members of university departments of education were not able to meet the requests for leadership in surveys, with the result that a considerable part of this leadership was carried by the United States Office of Education, the educational division of the Russell Sage Foundation, and certain bureaus of municipal and governmental research. During the second quarter of the present century and later, the research and survey divisions of certain state universities, Teachers College of Columbia University, and George Peabody College for Teachers have made a large number of school surveys.

TYPES AND SCOPE OF SCHOOL SURVEYS

In terms of purpose, modern school surveys may be divided into three types.[25] The *comprehensive survey* usually covers the following aspects of the school system:

1. Aims, outcomes, pupil achievement, curriculum, method, and instructional aids
2. Administrative problems and procedures of the schools
3. Financial policies and procedures
4. Operation and maintenance of the physical plant
5. Pupil transportation
6. Staff and personnel
7. School plant and related factors.

The *educational survey* deals with the instructional program and the related policies and procedures that affect the educational program. The

24 Quoted from Jesse B. Sears and Adin D. Henderson, *Cubberley of Stanford: And His Contribution to American Education.* Stanford, Calif.: Stanford University Press, 1957. p. 166.

25 Harold H. Church and Others, *The Local School Facilities Survey.* Bulletin of the School of Education, Indiana University, Vol. 29, Nos. 1 and 2. Bloomington: Division of Research and Field Services, Indiana University, 1953. vii + 96 p.

building survey has been the most common type during recent years, because of the pressure of the greatly increased pupil population. The educational and building surveys together constitute a comprehensive survey.

Another classification of surveys,[26] in terms of purposes or objectives, is as follows:

1. Investigative, evaluative, or status, intended primarily to appraise existing conditions
2. Deliberative, developmental, or planning, serving chiefly to make proposals for development and improvement, with a minimum of criticism of present circumstances
3. Implementation or application, going beyond developmental recommendations to create conditions in the survey procedures that will promote achievement of the survey recommendations.

It is possible to classify surveys in other ways:

1. The major aspect of the school system: school plant, educational program, comprehensive
2. Geographical area: local, state, regional, national
3. Level of instruction: elementary, secondary, higher
4. Type of preparation: junior college, teacher education, engineering, medicine, law, social work
5. Purpose or problem: to follow up youth out of school, to describe the membership of a professional organization, to describe the characteristics of a group of institutions, to poll the opinion of a group of parents, to identify trends, to engage in survey testing
6. Data-gathering technique or procedure: questionnaire, interview, observation, group-behavior analysis, content analysis, survey-appraisal. (In the interest of emphasizing research methodology, this is the classification scheme adopted for succeeding sections of the present chapter.)

For illustrative purposes, the scope and procedures of the plant survey may be summarized briefly. The school-building survey usually includes the community and the setting of the schools, an estimate of future school enrollment, school-plant planning, the pupil-transportation system, and the available financial resources to provide the school buildings. The cooperative building survey by members of the local staff and by a team of visiting specialists combines the advantages of the "expert" survey and self-survey, in that it costs less than the survey conducted entirely by experts, safeguards the objectivity of survey procedures and conclusions, and through cooperation between the local staff and visiting

[26] Dan H. Cooper, "School Surveys," *Encyclopedia of Educational Research*. Edited by Chester W. Harris. Third Edition. New York: The Macmillan Co., 1960.

experts furthers acceptance and implementation of the survey recommendations.

The visiting survey specialist has an important role in developing procedures for setting up and conducting the survey, interpreting the findings, formulating recommendations, stimulating the local staff in answering important questions, and cooperating with the local administrator in his role of leadership.

There are some disadvantages when a single survey seeks to accomplish two separate purposes, such as administrative planning for a building program and evaluation of the efficiency of the educational program and personnel. Evaluation of the educational program and personnel (and working *with* persons for their own improvement) may prove incompatible with the purposes of a survey concerned with administrative planning.

PROCEDURES AND RESULTS OF SURVEYS

The following summary[27] of the procedures and practical results of survey studies is drawn from an evaluation of the school surveys sponsored by George Peabody College for Teachers and from many surveys made by other agencies. A primary purpose of the evaluation of the Peabody school surveys was to study the activities in the local school system following a survey, by way of implementing the recommendations, with the evaluative data based on interviews, conferences, and documentary sources.

1. The formal request for a local survey usually came from the board of education, upon the recommendation of the superintendent, although frequently the initiative came from such groups as a citizens' committee, an education association, or a chamber of commerce. (School surveys have been sponsored by the United States Office of Education, regional accrediting associations, national professional organizations, state legislatures, state departments of education, and private philanthropic foundations.)

2. As a general rule the Division of Surveys and Field Services of Peabody had complete charge of plans and procedures for making the investigation.

3. Comprehensive reports and illustrated digests were prepared by the survey staff and printed, with oral reports always made to the boards of education or survey commissions and to other interested groups invited to attend the meetings.

4. As a rule the survey reports were enthusiastically received by the public and by the press, with community groups and citizens' committees actively supporting the recommendations.

[27] *A Survey of Surveys.* Nashville, Tenn.: Division of Surveys and Field Services, George Peabody College for Teachers, 1952. 56 p.

5. The superintendent of schools, more than any other individual or group, was responsible for implementing the survey recommendations, with new superintendents particularly appreciative of the guidance of the report in winning public support for school policies.

6. Members of state survey commissions played an important part in formulating survey recommendations, and assumed the responsibility for drafting bills embodying the recommendations for presentation to the legislature. It proved difficult to implement changes that depended on action by the legislative bodies of the city, county, or state, and especially when constitutional changes were necessary. Political strategy in bringing about legislative action on survey recommendations varied, with the unity of the forces supporting public education an important factor in success.

7. When survey proposals involved as a major consideration the consolidation of schools, there was always opposition in the small communities, which sometimes led to compromise or even failure in implementing the survey recommendations.

8. Almost one-half of the survey recommendations were adopted. More immediate results were brought about in city schools than in county or state systems. Differences in favor of the city over the county systems were especially significant in the areas of administration, business management, and physical plant. (In many of our school systems the survey has been the initial stage of an educational advance, through challenging the attention of the school people and the public, even though immediate results have not always followed survey investigations.)

9. The superintendents of county and city school systems reacted favorably to recommendations for reorganization of their administrative and supervisory staffs, not only adding new members but also organizing them into a few clearly defined divisions or departments under the leadership of assistant superintendents.

10. Improvement of instruction followed slowly after a survey, although the majority of the school systems reported the adoption of many significant recommendations. (The direction of survey recommendations has been toward a positive emphasis, by way of search for and encouragement of desirable educational practices, rather than a negative emphasis in the form of a search for malpractices.)

11. The quick adoption of survey recommendations for schoolhousing reflected the critical shortage of buildings following the war years; bond issues for new school buildings were generally approved in the counties and cities.

12. Recommendations for the improvement of pupil transportation were readily adopted, with state and county systems carrying out most of the concrete proposals for a complete system of school-bus operation.

13. Proposed programs for financing the schools were frequently delayed by a variety of restrictions, although state systems made some progress in financing public education.

14. Gains in revenue receipts were only moderate in county systems, whereas the compactness and well-developed channels of communication in city schools secured relatively prompt action in increasing school funds. Rec-

ommendations concerning the business affairs of the schools were well received in both cities and counties.

15. The administrative officers in four school systems thought that the survey staff should have continuing follow-up contacts by way of consultative services in the system investigated, and suggested that survey specialists should spend more time in the classroom, as background for more accurate evaluation of the quality of teaching. Many school systems now maintain a continuing survey or study, sometimes known as an evaluation or an inventory, with a cooperative planning survey at intervals of approximately ten years, and financial and personnel provisions between surveys for securing the assistance of special consultants. (The stages of implementation of survey recommendations involve the processes of group interaction or group dynamics. Certain related techniques of group-behavior analysis and action research are summarized in other sections of this chapter.)

16. It is been recognized for more than two decades that many of the recommendations of school surveys are subjective (according to one specialist, 80 per cent subjective).[28] To the extent that direct observation, score cards, check lists, and rating scales are used in school surveys, there is a considerable element of subjectivity or personal reaction on the part of the investigator. Survey conclusions depend largely on committee deliberations or interpretations, with the recommendations based largely on the opinion of committee members, or the impact of opinion on facts. To cite an example, a state school survey may recommend an expanded plan of state aid for local school districts, which is a committee recommendation rather than a factual statement, although coming from or based on facts. The recommendation involves subjectivity in the frame of reference or philosophy of the survey committee: agreement on the general goal of a good school system, acceptance of the social philosophy that a good school system is desired for all, and agreement that a particular plan of equalization of support is best for the state and the local school districts.

Indiana University, as one of the pioneers in the school-survey movement, offered instruction on the survey as early as 1915, began making surveys of Indiana schools about 1936, and between 1949 and 1958 conducted 56 school surveys. Based on an apraisal of 43 of these investigations, involving the opinions of school officers concerning the value of such surveys, the conclusions and recommendations for making school surveys are as follows:

1. That school survey staffs plan a periodic follow-up study of all school surveys within three years following the survey and make the cost of such a study a part of a continuing contract.

28 Dan H. Cooper, "Contributions of School Surveys to Educational Administration," *Educational Administration: A Survey of Progress, Problems, and Needs,* p. 46–59. Edited by William C. Reavis. Proceedings of the Fifteenth Annual Conference for Administrative Officers of Public and Private Schools, 1946. Vol. 9. Chicago: The University of Chicago Press, 1946. 216 p.

2. That, in school surveys, greater emphasis and time be given to the study of the curriculum and the improvement of learning and, further, that the survey staff be augmented by the addition of specialists in education in so far as a school corporation can afford such services.

3. That, whenever a school corporation has fewer than 400 pupils enrolled in its high school (grades 9 through 12), it should seek an opportunity to join with one or more school corporations until the new school corporation has at least 400 resident high-school pupils.

4. That a school survey be conducted whenever the local school authorities have insufficient or unreliable data upon which to project their future plan and/or whenever it is expected that strong local opposition may defeat the plans of the board because the public is uninformed.

5. That a survey be made of the administrative staff, its duties and responsibilities, following a period of reorganization or unusual growth.

6. That boards of education annually reserve for research in education an appropriation of funds which can be used periodically as needed for some form of school survey.[29]

SAFEGUARDS FOR SCHOOL SURVEYS

An excellent statement of safeguards for school surveys (applying to consultant, school system, and survey agency) is based on an evaluation of the Gary, Indiana, survey and its outcomes, by the National Commission for the Defense of Democracy through Education of the National Education Association. After pointing out that the survey has been one of the most valuable procedures for the improvement of American school systems, the Commission emphasizes that the ultimate success of a survey depends on the interest, cooperation, good will, and confidence of the staff of the school system under study, and on the dignity and sincerity with which the survey is conducted and reported.[30]

Safeguards for the school system to be surveyed are as follows:

1. Before selecting an agency to conduct the survey, the board of education and administrative staff should make a careful study of the experience and philosophy of the agencies with respect to public education.

2. An agreement should be prepared that will indicate in detail the scope of the survey, including the areas with which the recommendations will be concerned.

3. All discussion between the board of education and the survey agency should be reported in detail in official minutes of the board.

[29] Harold H. Church and Melvin S. Lewis, *An Appraisal of the School Surveys Conducted by the School of Education, Indiana University.* Bulletin of the School of Education, Indiana University, Vol. 35, No. 5. Bloomington, Indiana: Indiana University, September, 1959. x + 66 p.

[30] Virgil Rogers and Others, *Gary, Indiana: A Study of Some Aspects and Outcomes of a General School Survey.* Washington: National Commission for the Defense of Democracy Through Education, N.E.A., June 1957. 40 p.

4. The number of individuals to be employed as survey staff members and consultants should be clearly noted.
5. There should be a clear commitment that, in seeking information and in studying the school system, initial approaches should be made to persons in charge of areas under study, with free access to anyone who may have information concerning agreed-on phases of the study.
6. No factual data should be presented in the report unless they have been checked for accuracy with the person in the school system responsible for such data.
7. When the report is released, it should go simultaneously to all directly concerned (preferably, prior to its public release).
8. A plan should be developed for careful study and implementation of the survey report.

The Questionnaire

CHARACTERISTICS AND USES

By the turn of the past century many psychologists were convinced that experimental and laboratory methods did not answer many of the questions about childhood and youth. G. Stanley Hall and his students especially promoted wide use of the questionnaire, which more recently has appeared in the form of the history blank, clinical syllabus, and personality inventory or questionnaire. The terms *questionnaire* and *schedule* may be considered equivalent for present purposes, although sometimes a technical distinction is made. The questionnaire is generally regarded as a form distributed through the mail or filled out by the respondent under the supervision of the investigator or interviewer, whereas the schedule is a form filled out by the investigator or completed in his presence.

Many beginners in research turn almost automatically to the questionnaire as a device for securing answers to problems, even before the problem and technique are fully formulated, rather than to evaluate the merits of the various data-gathering methods in relation to the particular problem. A carefully devised questionnaire technique is not a simple, quick method of investigation, but requires time, patience, ingenuity, and skill. Many of these abilities and skills are important in interview studies, and in certain other descriptive-survey techniques. Therefore, cross references are appropriate in the interest of economy of space, especially between the questionnaire and interview sections of this chapter.

As to uses and applications, the questionnaire extends the investigator's powers and techniques of observation by reminding the respondent of each item, helping insure response to the same item from all respondents, and tending to standardize and objectify the observations of different enumerators (by singling out particular aspects of the situation and by specifying the units and terminology for describing the observations). While many questionnaires seek factual information, others are concerned with opinions, attitudes, and interests. National, state, and local organizations frequently have been interested in questionnaire surveys of the status of the school personnel and current practices in school systems, including school finance. In frequency of use, the questionnaire probably is outranked only by the survey test; if all the practical questionnaire and testing studies are included, the two techniques probably involve more than one-half the total studies in education.

To cite a specific example,[31] the personality questionnaire or inventory attempts to measure a variety of personality attributes: rather broad categories such as emotional adjustment, social adjustment, neurotic tendency; more specific personality traits, such as introversion, extroversion, self-sufficiency, and ascendancy or dominance; and in terms of specific theoretical conceptions of personality or different psychiatric categories. The personality questionnaire or inventory usually includes a specific number of questions or test items (approximately 100–500 in number) to be answered by the subject by checking one of three possible responses—"yes," "no," and a third category designated either as a question mark or as "cannot say." Among the better known examples are the Bernreuter Personality Inventory and the Minnesota Multiphasic Personality Inventory (MMPI).

APPROPRIATENESS AS AN INSTRUMENT

Beginners in research and many others more experienced frequently overlook the cooperative nature of the questionnaire and lack perspective concerning what may reasonably be asked of busy respondents. The questionnaire study should be important not only to the investigator and to the particular field of knowledge, but also to the respondent, whose psychology of motivation involves his attention, sympathy, interest, cooperation, and honesty in answering questions. Better motivation for respondents is likely to prevail if they can see the investigator's side of the problem and procedure, and can see the end-results in the form of a concise summary of the study and possibly in the implementation of the findings.[32]

One of the first questions the investigator should ask concerning the questionnaire is whether it is as appropriate as some other data-gathering instrument, or whether the answers may even be available in documentary

31 Sol. L. Garfield, *Introductory Clinical Psychology*. New York: The Macmillan Co., 1957. p. 115–30.

32 Douglas E. Scates and Alice Yeomans Scates, "Developing a Depth Questionnaire to Explore Motivation and Likelihood of Action." *Educational and Psychological Measurement* 12: 620–31; Winter 1952.

sources or in the literature. Would the questionnaire be as effective as the interview in investigating the job opportunities available in the printing and tailoring trades of a large city for members of certain racial and minority groups, in studying the policy of city newspapers with respect to publication of school news, in canvassing the leisure-time activities of adolescent boys in an underprivileged area of a large city, and in asking highly personal questions such as those covered in the Kinsey reports?

The question under consideration involves an important rule of evidence, to the effect that only the "best evidence," the most valid and credible, should be used. To cite an example, a particular study of certain components of the programs in Ohio high schools was based on an elaborate questionnaire, with the data reported in some 70 tables. The material in half of the tables could have been secured from the annual reports of high-school principals on file in the State Department of Education. Instead of examining these official reports, the investigator took the easy way, probably less accurate, of mailing a questionnaire. He violated the principle of using the best evidence.[33]

A sociologist's comment on a student's questionnaire is not intended to be sharp, but to emphasize the desirability and necessity of considering the appropriateness of the questionnaire in relation to other available means of gathering evidence:

> First of all, you are asking in the questionnaire certain questions you could easily answer for yourself by consulting *Who's Who in America* or the university catalogues.
>
> More serious is the objection which I have to the rest of your questions; you are asking me for my opinions on very complex questions, and you formulate your questions in a way that indicates you expect a dogmatic answer. To do real justice to these questions, which concern the objectives and methods of . . . sociology, I would have to write you an essay, or several papers. It is hard to imagine that you really expect me to do this for you; if you do not, then why ask me these questions? Furthermore, it so happens that I have expressed my ideas on these matters in several publications; I admit that my opinions are in some cases not stated explicitly but by implication. Now there is an old and well established way of getting information about other scholars' opinions and theories; that is, by reading and by critical interpretation. There is no substitute for this. My advice to you is to forget about the questionnaire and to study the literature.[34]

Does the recipient of the questionnaire have the information requested, and is he free and willing to respond? Would a state survey of

33 R. H. Eckelberry, "We Should Use the Best Evidence." *Educational Research Bulletin* 39: 44, 56; February 10, 1960.

34 Quoted from Rudolf Heberle, "On the Use of Questionnaires in Research: Open Letter to a Graduate Student." *American Sociological Review* 16: 549; August 1951.

local administrative positions early in April find that the respondents know where they will be the following September and are willing to declare their positions vacant so early in the spring? Would a local school survey of the attitudes of parents toward curriculum and method find these citizens informed about the school program and willing to comment freely when their children are still attending school? A form of questionnaire without the signature of the respondent may encourage frank and truthful answers.

STAGES AND ADMINISTRATIVE ASPECTS

A check list of certain requirements, stages, and administrative aspects of questionnaire surveys is especially appropriate for large-scale studies, and also is useful in planning smaller questionnaire studies:[35]

1. Purpose of the survey
2. Relation to other surveys or programs
3. Development of the survey plan
    a. Respondents
    b. Extent of coverage
    c. Frequency and timing
    d. Method of collection
    e. Consideration of nonsampling errors
    f. Standard definitions and classifications
    g. Processing and interpretation of the data
    h. Allowance for pretests and follow-ups
    i. Comparison with data from other sources
    j. Proposed calendar
    k. Cost estimates
4. Questionnaire and accompanying instructions
5. Pretests
6. Follow-ups
7. Development of the sampling plan for partial coverage surveys
8. Supervision of field enumeration
9. Manuals and other instructions for the conduct of the survey
10. Progress and cost reporting
11. Preparation and publication of the final report.

The graduate student also must consider certain administrative aspects in choosing his problem and procedure, including sponsorship, cost, space, time requirements, clerical aid, and tabulating or calculating machine work.

[35] *Standards for Statistical Surveys.* Exhibit A, Circular No. A-46. Washington: Executive Office of the President, Bureau of the Budget, March 28, 1952. 10 p.

SAMPLING AND SURVEY DESIGN

Sampling is a technical and statistical problem of importance in most questionnaire investigations and in many other descriptive-survey studies. The literature on application of sampling theory to practical survey problems has appeared primarily since 1940, with leadership provided in the areas of opinion-polling, market research, and census operations. Although the methodology of statistics lies outside the scope of this book, it seems appropriate to summarize the characteristics of probability samples and the limitations of "unplanned," "nonprobability," or "judgment" samples, and to refer to the literature of sample surveys in education.[36]

Probability samples have these characteristics:

1. Each individual (or primary unit) in the sample has some known probability of entering the sample.
2. The process of sampling is automatic in one or more steps of the selection of elements or units in the sample.
3. Weights appropriate to the probabilities in (1) are used in the analysis of the sample.

The limitations of unplanned, nonprobability, or judgment sampling are represented in the following items:

1. The sample of convenience (e.g., the superintendent's office is housed in the high school; the high-school teachers being convenient, he asks some of them their opinions on a matter)
2. The canvass of experts (e.g., a questionnaire to several "informed" persons for judgment on teacher shortage or school construction needs in the United States)
3. The sample based on an obsolete list or *frame* which does not adequately cover the population (e.g., using a city directory or telephone book as a basis for sampling the adult population of a community)
4. The sample with a high proportion of nonresponse (e.g., the common questionnaire study in education)
5. The pinpoint or representative-area sample (e.g., purposive selection of typical individuals, or a typical school, typical classroom, or typical community)
6. The *quota* sample, by which there is some system of selection of primary sampling units (such as communities), and assigning interviewers *quotas*

36 Francis G. Cornell, "Sample Surveys in Education," in "Statistical Methodology in Educational Research." *Review of Educational Research* 24: 359–74; December 1954.
Francis G. Cornell, "Sampling Methods," *Encyclopedia of Educational Research.* Edited by Chester W. Harris. Third Edition. New York: The Macmillan Co., 1960. p. 1181–83.

for subsampling (e.g., an interviewer is asked to select for interview 10 females who are high-school graduates between the ages of 18 and 25 living in the northeast section of a city).

To cite specific examples of design, Hyman bases much of his discussion of survey design and analysis on seven published surveys, dealing with: industrial absenteeism, public opinion and the atom bomb, American opinion on commercial radio, prejudice and personality, American sexual behavior, class consciousness, and war-bond redemption. These inquiries include certain common features, particularly with respect to the consequences of size of inquiry, organizational form, sponsorship and subsidization, and controversial subject matter. Some of these surveys present a sheer description of some phenomenon and are known as descriptive surveys, whereas other inquiries seek an explanation and are known as explanatory surveys.

Although reasonable attention has been given to problems of sampling design and theory in survey research, there has been considerable neglect of certain prior questions of the location within which the phenomenon ought to be studied, including temporal location, location in some human population, relevant units, and differentiation of the description.

Certain factors affect the quality of research findings or may lead to error in surveys:[37]

1. Variability in response
2. Differences between different kinds and degrees of canvass
   a. Mail, telephone, telegraph, direct interview
   b. Intensive vs. extensive interviews
   c. Long vs. short schedules
   d. Check block plan vs. response
   e. Correspondence panel and key reporters
3. Bias and variation arising from the interviewer
4. Bias of the auspices
5. Imperfections in the design of the questionnaire and tabulation plans
   a. Lack of clarity in definitions; ambiguity; varying meanings of same word to different groups of people; eliciting an answer liable to misinterpretation
   b. Omitting questions that would be illuminating to the interpretation of other questions
   c. Emotionally toned words; leading questions; limiting response to a pattern
   d. Failing to perceive what tabulations would be most significant
   e. Encouraging nonresponse through formidable appearance

[37] W. E. Deming, "On Errors in Surveys." *American Sociological Review* 9: 359–69; August 1944.

Herbert H. Hyman, *Survey Design and Analysis*. New York: Free Press of Glencoe, Inc., 1955. p. 143–45.

6. Changes that take place in the universe before tabulations are available
7. Bias arising from nonresponse (including omissions)
8. Bias arising from late reports
9. Bias arising from an unrepresentative selection of data for the survey, or of the period covered
10. Bias arising from an unrepresentative selection of respondents
11. Sampling errors and biases
12. Processing errors (coding, editing, calculating, tabulating, tallying, posting, and consolidating)
13. Errors in interpretation
    a. Bias arising from bad curve fitting; wrong weighting; incorrect adjusting
    b. Misunderstanding the questionnaire; failure to take account of the respondents' difficulties (often through inadequate presentation of data); misunderstanding the method of collection and the nature of the data
    c. Personal bias in interpretation.

Some estimation of residual errors that remain despite all pretesting may be secured through two general classes of methods available for treating this problem, namely, methods involving internal and external checks. The internal check is predicated on the logic that the meaning and quality of a given reply can be inferred from its relation to some other datum or reply. The most direct internal check involves the use of questions that require the respondent to elaborate an initial reply. Through another method, dependent variables may be arrayed for given factual categories.

The most obvious external check is the comparison of the datum under study with findings on the same or related problems collected by other agencies or individuals, on equivalent samples of the same population. Among the types of external checks in a German bombing survey were: interviewer ratings, criterion data from official records, use of other samples as informants, split-ballot procedures, comparison with earlier survey data, and "captured-mail" check.[38]

QUESTIONNAIRE CONSTRUCTION

In questionnaire construction important decisions relate to motivation of the respondent, significance of questions, simplicity of responses, avoidance of unnecessary specifications or details, pertinence to the situation of the respondent, clarity of purpose and questions, phrasing of items to facilitate summarization of responses, and possible precoding of the questionnaire in the interest of using tabulating machine cards for summarization. Questionnaires that go to local and state school systems, or to

[38] Herbert H. Hyman, *op. cit.*, p. 151–72.

similar educational agencies, may well formulate questions in keeping with the items of official or regular reports.

As to form, the structured questionnaire is definite, concrete, pre-ordained in terms of items, with additional questions limited to those necessary to clarify inadequate answers or to elicit more detailed responses. The form of questions may be closed (categorical) or open-end (inviting free response). The check list (usually a closed form of questionnaire) is a set of categories for the respondent to check, as in listing frequency of performance of certain duties by school officers. The completeness of the original list is especially important, since the respondent is likely to consider it all-inclusive and may depend on the list so completely that he does not write in additional items. The check responses or similar answers in the closed form of questionnaire commonly provide categorized data that greatly facilitate tabulating and summarizing processes.

The open-end or free-response questionnaire frequently goes beyond statistical data or factual material into the area of hidden motivations that lie behind attitudes, interests, preferences, and decisions. Such questions are used extensively in depth and focused questionnaires and interviews, although the work of tabulating and summarizing is time-consuming and expensive.

The choice between open and closed questions in both questionnaire and interview surveys depends on the following criteria:[39] the objective or purpose, the respondent's level of information on the particular topic, the degree of structure that characterizes respondent opinions on the topic, ease with which the material can be communicated, and the investigator's knowledge and insight into the respondent's situation. The closed question is most appropriate when the investigator's objective is to classify the respondent, when there is little question as to the adequacy of respondent information, when the respondent's opinions on the specific topic are well structured, when there are no major barriers to communication, and when the investigator is well informed about the respondent. Conversely, when the opposite of the foregoing conditions prevails, the open question is preferable.

The nonstructured questionnaire commonly serves as an interview guide, especially for focused, depth, or nondirective interviews. It includes definite subject-matter areas, but the interviewer is largely free to arrange the form and timing of the questions.

A helpful summary of criteria for constructing questionnaires includes nine items:[40]

[39] Robert L. Kahn and Charles F. Cannell, *The Dynamics of Interviewing: Theory, Technique, and Cases.* New York: John Wiley & Sons, Inc., 1957. p. 164–65.

[40] Douglas E. Scates and Alice V. Yeomans, *The Effect of Questionnaire Form on Course Requests of Employed Adults.* Washington: American Council on Education, 1950. p. 2–4.

1. It must be short enough so as not to take too much time and so that the respondent will not reject it completely.

2. It must be of sufficient interest and have enough face appeal so that the respondent will be inclined to respond to it and to complete it.

3. The questionnaire should obtain some depth to the response in order to avoid superficial replies.

4. The ideal questionnaire must not be too suggestive or too unstimulating, particularly with reference to choices.

5. The questionnaire should elicit responses that are definite but not mechanically forced.

6. Questions must be asked in such a way that the responses will not be embarrassing to the individual.

7. Questions must be asked in such a manner as to allay suspicion on the part of the respondent concerning hidden purposes in the questionnaire.

8. The questionnaire must not be too narrow, restrictive, or limited in its scope or philosophy.

9. The responses to the questionnaire must be valid, and the entire body of data taken as a whole must answer the basic question for which the questionnaire was designed.

Certain errors[41] in construction and pretesting of the questionnaire should be avoided, including questionnaires used for interview purposes:

1. Irrelevance of the research problem to respondents. If the study involves the social and psychological problems of aging, with emphasis on retirement from employment, the sample would include only respondents past sixty years of age.

2. Irrelevance or insufficiency of questionnaire items for the variable being investigated. In studying membership activity in a local union, the investigator cannot assume that what represents high activity to him will also represent high activity to his potential respondents; for example, regularity of attendance at union meetings might be an insufficient index of union activity for construction workers whose jobs frequently take them miles away from the town where the meetings are held.

3. Ambiguous or inappropriate item wording. Some people misunderstood the following question: "Which of the following groups do you think your family belongs in—upper class, middle class, working class, lower class?" Some people thought that the phrase "belongs in" meant "deserves to be in." The question was reworded to read, "If you were asked to put yourself (your family) in one of these groups—the upper class, middle class, working class, lower class—how would you answer?" Ambiguous questions result in equally confusing responses. A newspaper printed a questionnaire concerning the items read by its subscribers, without indicating for a family whether the checking should be done by one member, by the head of the family, or by each member of the family.

41 John T. Doby, Editor, *An Introduction to Social Research*. Harrisburg, Penn.: Stackpole Books, 1954. p. 207–19.

4. Inadequate categories for responses. Acceptable standard forms are: "Often —sometimes—hardly ever," "more—some—less," "very happy—fairly happy —not so happy." A dichotomous questionnaire on the administrative policy of a college, with provision for answering "for" or "against," would not represent adequately the college faculty as respondents. A third alternative for each item, such as "no definite feeling or conviction," is needed, because it is as important to know that a faculty member is neutral toward a particular policy as to know that he has a strong conviction for or against the policy.

When a question involves a number of categories for checking (sometimes a dozen or more), they should be reasonably complete and detailed, and as a rule nonoverlapping and co-ordinate. The young investigator who studied teacher turnover in a county school system included in his questionnaire a classification of eight reasons for leaving a teaching position. In summarizing the results, he found that thirty-one additional reasons had been written in by the respondents. A tryout of the questionnaire would have revealed a more complete set of classes or categories.

5. Inappropriate item sequence; overlengthiness; insensitivity to the emotional impact on the respondent of an item or series of items. These sources of difficulty can be greatly minimized by careful pretesting.

In preparing directions for answering questions, there is the challenge of keeping between one extreme of completeness and detail that seems overwhelming to the respondent and the other extreme of incompleteness and vagueness that would brand the investigator as careless and superficial. Usually the investigator must work back and forth, shuttle-like, between the questions and directions, as he constructs a questionnaire satisfactory for his purpose, with necessary adjustments as work proceeds on all parts of the questionnaire pattern.

Some questions are for purposes other than obtaining information; for example, warming up or getting the respondent's mind on the subject or area, meeting the respondent's expectation that certain questions normally will be included, and catharsis or release of possible tensions.

There is a human tendency to answer "yes" when the respondent thinks that this is the expected answer. This tendency can be partially offset by inclusion of the opposite question, so as to have a number of such pairs of questions.

In many instances the questionnaire includes two or more questions, in order to make clear the answer to a single question; for example, "the number of college courses completed" would serve as a check on an item relating to "semester hours completed."

A device in questionnaire construction for placement of detailed lists of items or subjects is to print them at the end of the questionnaire, especially when such lists do not apply to every respondent. To cite an example, a questionnaire for the field of psychology, in the interest of gathering data for the National Register of Scientific and Technical Personnel, covers two pages, with one question referring to a four-page list of specialties covering all the major fields of scholarship and research, with comprehensive coverage in the mathematical, physical and life sciences, and engineering, and less detailed coverage for social sciences and other professional areas. The item in the questionnaire proper that refers to the four-page specialties list reads as follows: "From the accompanying complete Specialties List, regardless of your current employment, please select and give below in order of decreasing competence up to six of these specialties in which you have had professional experience and/or training."

Certain decisions about questions, with respect to content, wording, and form of response, may be summarized as follows:[42]

I. *Decisions About Question Content*
    1. Is this question necessary? Just how will it be useful?
    2. Are several questions needed on the subject matter of this question?
    3. Do respondents have the information necessary to answer the question?
    4. Does the question need to be more concrete, specific, and closely related to the respondent's personal experience?
    5. Is the question content sufficiently general and free from spurious concreteness and specificity?
    6. Do the replies express general attitudes and only seem to be as specific as they sound?
    7. Is the question content biased or loaded in one direction, without accompanying questions to balance the emphasis?
    8. Will the respondents give the information that is asked for?

II. *Decisions About Question Wording*
    1. Can the question be misunderstood? Does it contain difficult or unclear phraseology?
    2. Does the question adequately express the alternatives with respect to the point?
    3. Is the wording biased? Is it emotionally loaded or slanted toward a particular kind of answer?
    4. Is the question wording likely to be objectionable to the respondent in any way?
    5. Would a more personalized or less personalized wording of the question produce better results?

III. *Decisions About Form of Response to the Question*
    1. If a check list is used, does it cover adequately all the significant alternatives without overlapping and in a defensible order? Is it of reasonable length? Is the wording of items impartial and balanced?

---

42 Claire Selltiz and Others, *Research Methods in Social Relations.* Revised One-Volume Edition. New York: Holt, Rinehart and Winston, Inc., 1959. p. 552-73.

2. Is the form of response easy, definite, uniform, and adequate for the purpose?
3. Is the answer to the question likely to be influenced by the content of preceding questions?
4. Is the question led up to in a natural way? Is it in correct psychological order?
5. Does the question come too early or too late from the point of view of arousing interest and receiving sufficient attention, avoiding resistance, etc.?

TRYOUT

Before the final form is prepared and distributed to the respondents, tryout or pretesting of the questionnaire is essential, for the purpose of validation in terms of practical use. This tryout probably will lead to revision of certain questions, deletion of useless questions, and addition of other items. Tabulation of the tryout responses in rough tables will indicate whether the answers can be tabulated satisfactorily and whether answers to the major questions are forthcoming. The manual of the United States Bureau of the Budget emphasizes that it is desirable to test the feasibility of the questionnaire survey in advance, with pretests designed and conducted to secure answers to such problems as the following:

Relative effectiveness and costs of alternative questionnaires, instructions, and operating procedures
Acceptability and intelligibility of the questions from the respondent's point of view
Possible misunderstandings of questions and procedure on the part of the interviewers
Clarity and applicability of definitions and classifications
Completeness of questions for correct coding and interpretation
Defects in the forms, maps, lists, instructions, etc.
Estimates of strata means and variances
Response rates.

VALIDITY

The validity of a questionnaire and of its parts may be judged by the following types of evidence:[43]

1. Is the question on the subject?
2. Is the question perfectly clear and unambiguous?
3. Does the question get at something stable, which is typical of the individual or of the situation?

[43] Douglas E. Scates and Alice V. Yeomans, *op. cit.*, p. 4–7.

4. Does the question pull or have extractive power? Will it be answered by a large enough proportion of respondents to have validity?
5. Do the responses show a reasonable range of variation?
6. Is the information consistent, in agreement with what is known, and in agreement with expectancy?
7. Is the item sufficiently inclusive?
8. Is there a possibility of obtaining an external criterion to evaluate the questionnaire?

FOLLOW-UP

Follow-up usually is necessary in reaching the goal of a high percentage of questionnaire returns (above 95 per cent). The following ingenious and persistent techniques of follow-up in a questionnaire analysis of a professional organization resulted in a return of 99 per cent from a membership list of 600:[44]

A card or letter calling attention to the questionnaire, one to two weeks after sending the blank.

Possibly a second reminder, probably only a post card.

Without waiting too long, a second mailing of the entire questionnaire, with a new cover page or accompanying letter; persons may have misplaced the first questionnaire, or it may have become buried on a desk.

Possibly a personal letter at this point, individually written and signed, as a special appeal for cooperation, with a return stamped envelope.

A short form of the questionnaire was mailed, asking for just a few questions or items of information (perhaps sent by airmail or special delivery), phrased so as to cover the items most essential to the study.

A second mailing of the short questionnaire was sent to a relatively small number by special delivery, with an encouraging personal letter. (It may be necessary to scratch off the list at intervals persons unduly irritated or those who have good reason for not responding; however, these names must be included in the count in calculating percentages.)

Supplementary material went to all those who had returned the abbreviated questionnaire, including a few more essential items of information, and informing them that this is the last round.

Other special means and techniques included mailing of a questionnaire to the member, partially filled out in advance with answers deemed likely for him, together with a personal letter, suggesting that the information would not be used without his approval and asking that he go the rest of the way to complete the questionnaire; forwarding of liberal postage, transportation, or communication expenses; long distance telephone; and telegraph.

44 Douglas E. Scates, "Analysis of a Professional Organization: The American Educational Research Association in 1948," *Growing Points in Educational Research.* 1949 Official Report of the A.E.R.A. Washington: The Association, 1949. p. 111–42.

PERCENTAGE OF RETURNS

Although the goal of 90 to 100 per cent returns has not been achieved generally in questionnaire surveys, definite progress in this direction is being made through improved plans for sponsorship, formulation of questions, follow-up, checking results, and studying nonresponse. The mean percentages (rounded to the nearest whole number) of questionnaire returns from a large number of survey investigations during an earlier period were as follows: 170 master's theses at Indiana State Teachers College, 72 per cent; 204 doctoral dissertations at Teachers College, Columbia University, 71 per cent; and 59 research studies reported in the *Journal of Educational Research,* 81 per cent.[45]

As an example of bias or incompleteness of returns for mail questionnaires, during World War II a selected list of farmers was canvassed for the purpose of determining the need for farm laborers. Most of the large farm operators listed their shortages, but most of the small farmers were too busy doing their own work to take time to reply, with the result that a fantastic estimate of 3 or 4 laborers was indicated to meet the needs of the average farm.[46]

EDITING, TABULATING, SUMMARIZING

The investigator may need to check the returns to determine whether different parts of the questionnaire response are consistent, to correct plain errors, and to revise the summarizing categories as indicated by the responses. One respondent checked all possible answers, revealing later in an interview that a check mark was his way of showing that he had read or checked off every item in the questionnaire. Sometimes written notes on the margins must be read and interpreted, figures rearranged or moved to the correct column, or other details checked that go beyond mechanical and routine clerical operations. After tabulation of questionnaire returns, further re-examination of the data and editing of the returns may be necessary. In a job classification of the members of a research organization, when the 600 returns had been tabulated, two general categories were relatively high: "administrators not otherwise described," 26 cases; "none of the following descriptions fits me," 18 cases. The cards for these 44 cases were re-examined and, on the basis of position, title, and institution reported, most of the 44 were reclassified into more specific and meaningful categories of jobs. In the same questionnaire survey of membership, an editorial decision was made to the effect

[45] J. R. Shannon, "Percentages of Returns of Questionnaires in Reputable Educational Research." *Journal of Educational Research* 42: 138–41; October 1948.

[46] George W. Snedecor, "On the Design of Sampling Investigations." *American Statistician* 2: 6–9, 13; December 1948.

that persons who listed "Teachers College" and "Columbia University" as having granted their degrees were referring to the same institution (Teachers College of Columbia University), with the result that the two categories were combined (accompanied by an explanatory footnote).

In dealing with questionnaire returns for purposes of tabulation, there are three choices:

1. Sometimes the questionnaire can be used directly, without copying off the material before tabulation. This is likely to be true when the questionnaire is a single page, which permits the questionnaire to be handled much like a data card.
2. In an initial list table the responses for each questionnaire (or other case) may be put on a single line, which permits a preliminary overview of the results, by way of showing (perhaps better than data cards will) what the range is likely to be.
3. Data cards have their chief advantage for purposes of cross classification or tabulation, because they can be sorted once for a trait, and then sorted again on one or more secondary traits. Data cards also can be checked readily when tabulations are made. There is the physical advantage of allowing a sub-group of cards to be removed from the main pack for use at some other place.

When tabulating machines are used to summarize questionnaire returns, the investigator probably will check back many times against original data, as in identifying the individuals at the extremes of a distribution, or listing by name in the report the individual cases at the extremes (or at the median) of a distribution. A discussion of computers and data processing is beyond the scope of this book, except as mentioned briefly under the topic of instrumentation in the chapter on experimental designs.[47]

We have already noted in this chapter the value of descriptive-survey studies in providing perspective concerning present status or current conditions, including novel or promising practices. In interpreting questionnaire results, perplexing questions concerning frequency of practice are present. Can cruciality or importance be inferred from frequency? Can the significance of an event or an activity for an individual be inferred from the frequency for the majority of the sample represented?

The Interview

In a treatment of interviewing, it is essential to consider the social and psychological meaning of the interview for the two parties involved, the cognitive and motivational processes affecting the behavior of the inter-

[47] "The Computer and Educational Research: A Symposium." *Harvard Educational Review* 31: 235–63; Summer 1961.

viewer, the reactions of the respondent, and the relation of errors in the data to the behavior of the persons in interviewing situations of various types.

INTERVIEWING AS COMMUNICATION AND MOTIVATION

The dynamics of interviewing begin with the concept that the interview is a process of communication or interaction. If the interviewer and the respondent share a common language and terminology that permit easy communication, there remains the challenge to the interviewer of motivating frank and complete answers from the respondent. The interviewer must be able to identify and, so far as possible, control the psychological forces present in the interview, which affect both the respondent and himself. The stimulus-response episodes of the interview involve the purposes, motives, attitudes, and beliefs of both the interviewer and the respondent. Social scientists have gathered evidence concerning the process of communication between people and concerning sources of bias in the interview; social psychologists have observed how people communicate with each other in small groups; and clinical psychologists have studied the interaction between the therapist and the patient in the psychotherapeutic interview.

One major form of motivation for the respondent is the psychological reward of talking to an understanding, permissive interviewer. A second type of motivation is that of accomplishing certain practical ends or purposes, as in giving information to the physician to improve one's health, to the personnel interviewer to secure a job, and to the social worker to secure advice or economic assistance. At the beginning of the interview the respondent may be motivated almost entirely by his own needs and purposes, but as the process of interaction progresses the respondent may find motivation in the psychological climate of the interview itself.

VALUES AND USES OF THE INTERVIEW[48]

Practical use of the interview in simple form is as old as face-to-face communication between two persons. In Hamlet, Polonius checked on his son by surreptitiously sending a friend to interview people in the strange town as to his son's reputation. The interviewer began by saying, in essence, "He's a gay young blade!" This opening encouraged the interviewee to comment on any escapades.

Although the interview belongs to a class of methods that yield primarily subjective data, that is, direct descriptions of the world of experience, the interests of many social scientists call for such data, how-

[48] Herbert H. Hyman and Others, *Interviewing in Social Research*. Chicago: The University of Chicago Press, 1954. p. 15–19.

ever crude the method of data-gathering may of necessity be. For example, the interview technique has certain advantages for collection of data relating to three of the most prominent emphases in social psychology, all implying subjective data: the emphasis on desires, goals, and values by students of personality; the current interest in social perception; and emphasis on the concept of attitude.

It is true that certain methods utilizing other personal documents (such as diaries, life histories, or letters) do yield an elaborate picture of the individual's world of desires and attitudes, but such techniques are relatively inflexible or inefficient for certain types of problems, in that they may not exist for the particular population of individuals to be studied, or these sources may be available only for some self-selected and possibly biased subsample of the particular population. Such life-history documents may not contain information relating to specific significant variables, since they are usually spontaneous in origin.

Many of the concepts and techniques of the questionnaire survey are useful in interviewing. The dynamics of interviewing, however, involve much more than an "oral questionnaire." Many types of information can be secured only through face-to-face contacts with people, especially data relating to personal history, family life, opinions, and attitudes. The interview has certain unique values, as compared with the questionnaire:

1. The interviewees may require the stimulus and confidential relationships of the interview in order to provide personal and confidential information which they would not ordinarily place on paper.
2. The interviewer may follow up leads and clues in a manner that is not possible by means of an instrument prepared in advance.
3. The interviewer may form some impression of the interviewee, in relation to the truth of the answers and the things that may have been left unsaid.
4. The interviewer may give information and develop attitudes on the part of the respondent, especially in a therapeutic relationship, sometimes encouraging exchange of ideas and information.

The self-administered questionnaire may provide subjective data from the respondent and has the advantages of cheapness because of the reduction of interviewer costs and the possibility of group administration, plus applicability on a systematic sampling basis, but has certain limitations not characteristic of the personal-interview technique:

1. The interview permits study of illiterates or near-illiterates for whom the written questionnaire is not applicable, which may be an important problem for investigations involving the national population, as in studies of recruits in the military forces with very limited education.
2. Since it is always possible for the respondent to read through the entire questionnaire first, or to edit earlier answers in the light of later questions,

the advantages of saliency questions become dubious, and it is difficult to control the contextual effects of other questions upon a given answer. In the interview, later questions can be hidden from the knowledge of the respondent and, therefore, can have no effect on the results of an earlier question.

3. A resourceful interviewer with insight may produce certain favorable results not possible in the self-administering situation of the questionnaire, where the mistakes of the respondent have a quality of finality. For example, the interviewer may make ratings of given characteristics of the respondent, explain or amplify a given question, probe for clarification of an ambiguous answer or elaboration of a cryptic report, or even persuade the respondent to answer a question that he would otherwise skip.

In comparison with the interview, informal observation of behavior under natural conditions usually is not a flexible method, in that the environment may not provide any avenue for the expression of the behavior relevant to the particular problem. To discover a person's thoughts may require a question, as in the case of studies concerned with the past; for example, investigations of the reactions of certain populations to strategic bombing were not undertaken until after the end of hostilities, when the natural setting of the postwar world was not appropriate to observing the reaction to the bombing of three years earlier; hence it was necessary to reconstruct the past either through the memories of the respondent as reported in the course of interviewing or through historical records.

Sometimes an observational approach to attitudes is attempted by placing the subject in a specially contrived experimental or laboratory situation in which the behavior relevant to a given inference appears. However, the behavior exhibited in this laboratory situation is as much bound by the unstated conventions of the contrived situation, and by the explicit instructions characteristic of all experiments on humans, as is the verbal report restricted or limited by the nature of the formal interview. Observation under natural conditions or in real life deals with behavior conditioned by a host of unknown momentary factors operating in environment, just as the verbal report of an individual is bound or limited by the formal interview situation. One is always playing some role in relation to some situation—laboratory, everyday life, or the interview— and the real issue is the kind of situation in which the attitudinal findings are liberated, as well as the ability to relate the findings to the particular situation. (Observational techniques are discussed at some length in a later section of this chapter.)

Many research problems merely require data that, by definition, are objective and consequently would not require interviewing. Even in many such instances, however, the interview technique has been applied extensively because of certain practical advantages; for example, the decennial census of the United States, governmental surveys of household possessions and the job record of the individual, insurance company surveys, and the political preference of the voter. The interview enables the investigator to relate the given datum to other characteristics of that same individual as measured simultaneously. For example, the records of an insurance company include a considerable amount of objective data on a health insurance policy covering a certain member of the population, but do not permit analysis of such coverage in relation to health needs and experiences, medical expenses, family income, and other significant variables. Voting records reveal the political behavior or preference of an individual, but do not indicate the social and psychological characteristics of the voter.

Often, the interview is used for practical purposes rather than to gather data for research. The following represent the variety of situations in which interviewing is appropriate, although in many instances it serves to accomplish the practical task at hand: student counseling, a variety of teacher and pupil-personnel contacts, occupational adjustment, applying for a position, employment offices, civil-service agencies, employer-employee relationships, public-opinion polls, radio and TV programs, commercial surveys and market studies, industrial surveys, advertising, censuses, social case work, psychiatric work, mental clinics, psychology, anthropology, sociology, journalism, and law. The interview is frequently employed in historical, experimental, and case-clinical studies.

OUTLINE OF TYPES OF INTERVIEWS

A working classification of interviews is as follows:

1. *According to function (diagnostic, treatment, or research)*
2. *Number of persons participating (individual or group)*
3. *Length of contact (short or prolonged)*
4. *According to the roles assumed by the interviewer and interviewee, in relation to the sociopsychological process of interaction*
   Nondirective (uncontrolled, unguided, or unstructured)
   Focused
   Depth
   Repeated, in order to trace change or development.

THE CLINICAL INTERVIEW[49]

In clinical work some form of the interview or personal contact has been used in many kinds of situations to secure information about the client and to understand his problems. The two major purposes of the interview in clinical work are diagnosis and treatment. Social workers

[49] Sol L. Garfield, *op. cit.*, p. 192–94.

employ the interview to secure information about the client's problem, his past history, family relations, and job adjustment. Other persons than the client frequently are interviewed when the client is a child, a mental defective, or a psychotic, or when there are unusual discrepancies in the client's presentation of data about himself. The psychiatric examination and even the standardized individual psychological examination are interviewing procedures.

During the clinical interview, certain nonverbal behavior on the part of the patient has useful diagnostic value, including gait, expression, posture, rate of speech, topics avoided, digressions, and word choice. In addition to the general techniques that apply to any interview situation, special procedures may be needed to deal effectively with the problems that arise in the several types of clinical interviews: the intake or admission interview, concerned chiefly with the patient's complaints; the personal and social-history interview, to gather background data with a bearing on the complaints; the screening or diagnostic interview, to arrive at a judgment concerning the patient's condition; interviews before and after psychological test administration, and as a means of introducing the patient to therapy; the interview to assist friends and relatives in their dealings with the patient; and the exit or termination interview to facilitate the patient's discharge or transition from hospital to home. (Case-study techniques are presented in another chapter.)

GROUP AND INDIVIDUAL INTERVIEWS[50]

Although there is little evidence concerning distinctive merits of group and individual interviews, certain relative advantages and disadvantages may be summarized briefly, with an introductory comment on the setting for the group interview. The size of the group should not be so large that it is unwieldy or inhibits participation by most members, and should not be so small that it lacks substantially greater coverage than in the individual interview. The optimum size is approximately 10 to 12 persons. Social, intellectual, and educational homogeneity are important for effective participation of all group members. A circular seating arrangement, with the interviewer as one of the group, is conducive to full and spontaneous reporting and participation.

The advantages of the group interview are as follows:

1. Release of inhibitions through personal comments and responses, with expressions of interest by the interviewer
2. A wider range of response as the result of a wider range of experience on the part of the group

50 Robert K. Merton, Marjorie Fiske, and Patricia L. Kendall, *The Focused Interview: A Manual of Problems and Procedures.* New York: Free Press of Glencoe, Inc., 1956. p. 136–53.

3. Recall of forgotten details of experience through the process of group interaction.

Possible disadvantages of the group interview are as follows:

1. Group interaction may result in controversies or discussions unrelated to the stimulus situation or topic. The interviewer should redirect attention to the initial problem.
2. Articulate members may be accorded the status of "leader," with the result that others may look to the leader for guidance, or one or more leaders may monopolize the discussion.
3. Continuity of group discussion sometimes is interrupted by an informant or respondent, with the result that the topic is not explored in detail.
4. The group may have an inhibiting effect of two kinds, in that interviewees may hesitate to reveal certain attitudes or experiences in the quasi-public situation of the group interview, and articulate subjects may withhold significant responses on the assumption that others in the group want to express themselves.

FOCUSED, DEPTH, AND NONDIRECTIVE INTERVIEWS

Nonstructured interviews and interview guides usually are labeled by the terminology "focused," "depth," "nondirective." Although definite subject-matter areas are involved, the interviewer is largely free to arrange the form and timing of the question. The focused interview concentrates attention on some particular event or experience rather than on general lines of inquiry about the event. The depth interview is intensive and searching, with emphasis on such psychological and social factors as attitudes, convictions, or emotions. The nondirective approach as an uncontrolled or unstructured technique permits much freedom on the part of the respondent to "talk about" the problems under study.

The focused interview is a method for collection of data developed to determine the responses of individuals to specific communication situations such as a movie or a speech. The procedural and technical aspects of focused interviewing may well be considered in terms of its relationship to other methods for collection of data, namely, observational, interview and questionnaire, and projective methods. Although focused interviewing places primary emphasis on the subject's verbal report of his definition of a specific situation and response to it, the method also possesses certain characteristics resembling closely the techniques found in projective and observational studies. During the course of the interview, the interviewer may utilize certain projective techniques to evaluate and interpret discrepancies occurring between the investigator's appraisal and the subject's report of the stimulus situation. The interviewer's objective evaluation of the particular situation to which subjects are to be exposed resembles observational procedures, in that the investigator is enabled: (1) to develop an hypothesis regarding expected and appropriate subject responses, (2) to focus the interview upon the subject's definition of and his responses to a particular situation, and (3) to appraise and interpret discrepancies occurring between his objective definition and the subject's subjective definition of the situation. An inherent disadvantage of focused interviewing is its limitation to occasions or settings where the investigator is able to secure an objective measurement of the specific social situation to which all subjects will be exposed. The limitation is relatively serious in the social sciences where there has been only limited success in objectively defining any simple or complex social situation. Focused interviewing involves an unstructured form, nondirective orientation, and artistic and empathic skills.[51]

In general the focused interview employs nondirective procedures in encouraging the respondent to structure the stimulus situation by indicating aspects of the situation most significant and by progressively exploring his responses. Nondirection in the focused interview means reliance on unstructured questions, but varying degrees of structure may be present:

1. *Unstructured question (stimulus and response-free)*
   For example, "What impressed you most in this film?" or "What stood out especially in this conference?"

2. *Semi-structured question*
   Type *A: Response-structured, stimulus-free.* For example, "What did you learn from this pamphlet that you hadn't known before?"
   Type *B: Stimulus-structured, response-free.* For example, "How did you feel about the episode of Joe's discharge from the army as a psychoneurotic?"

3. *Structured question (stimulus- and response-structured)*
   For example, "Judging from the film, do you think that the German fighting equipment was better, as good as, or poorer than the equipment used by Americans" or "As you listened to Chamberlain's speech, did you feel it was propagandistic or informative?"
   Although especially useful in opening stages, relatively unstructured questions can be profitably used throughout the interview.[52]

Depth procedures in focused interviews enable the investigator through depth responses to determine the respondent's degree of detachment or personal involvement in the experience, and the peripheral or salient

---

[51] Review by Charles G. McClintock, *Contemporary Psychology* 2: 220–21; August 1957, of Robert K. Merton, Marjorie Fiske, and Patricia L. Kendall, *op. cit.*, xx + 186 p.
[52] Quoted from Robert K. Merton, Marjorie Fiske, and Patricia L. Kendall, *op. cit.*, p. 12–17.

character of the responses. The procedures of such depth interviewing are as follows:[53]

Flexibility of Interview Situation

Flexible interviews encourage orientation to stimulus situation, rather than to interviewer, thus facilitating depth and curbing stereotyped reports.

Retrospective Focus

Focus on past experience, through reinstatement of stimulus situation, promotes elaboration of reported responses.

Focus on Feelings

Questions explicitly referring to affective aspects (e.g., "How did you feel when. . . ?" encourage reports of depth responses.

Restatement of Implied or Expressed Feelings

Occasional restatements of implied or expressed feelings prove effective by (1) inviting progressive elaboration of response, and (2) establishing common ground for mutual understanding. When interviewee indicates that he is not yet ready to admit these feelings, restatements can be extensive (in group interview) or projective (in individual interview).

Comparative Situations

Suggested comparisons between stimulus situation and significant experiences that subjects have known or can be presumed to have had often aid verbalization of effect.

GUIDING THE COURSE OF AN INTERVIEW: OVERVIEW[54]

A check list of recommendations for conducting the interview may serve as an overview for the detailed discussion that follows:

1. An interviewer generally should open an interview by asking factual nonthreatening questions.
2. The interviewer should locate the major data by unstructured "lead" questions.
3. The interviewer should make use of occasional guide questions.
4. The interviewer should make an effort to pick up leads.
5. The interviewer should cut through generalities with well-formulated probes.
6. The interviewer should stick with the fruitful areas once they open up.
7. The interviewer should reflect on the meaning of emerging data and ask questions that clarify or amplify their meaning for the research problem.
8. The interviewer should be especially alert to follow up only areas where the respondent shows emotional involvement.
9. The interviewer should try to redirect the interview to more fruitful topics when useful data are not emerging.

[53] Quoted from *ibid.*, p. 96–113.
[54] John T. Doby, Editor, *op. cit.*, p. 240–48.

10. The interviewer should be alert to "touchy" subject matters and not just blunder in.
11. The interviewer should try to turn back respondent's direct questions.
12. The interviewer should wind up the interview before the respondent becomes tired.
13. Whether an interviewer should take notes depends on the situation.

WAYS OF OPENING THE INTERVIEW

Methods of beginning the interview include the following procedures:

An indirect social approach, as when a teacher calls on the parents of one of her pupils

Spontaneous reaction to controlled stimuli, as in administering an intelligence test to a child who has not learned to read

Distribution of forms prior to the interview, especially for the purpose of collecting statistical data

A direct frank approach, usually employed for research interviews, especially when factual data are involved.

QUESTIONS AND RESPONSES

Interviewing is an art that requires appropriate training and guided experience as essential background. Careful preparation of questions for the interview is fully as important as has been emphasized in preparing the questionnaire. A well-conducted interview is not just a haphazard series of questions and answers of a pleasant conversation. The interviewer has a set of carefully prepared questions to serve as a thread of conversation, although he may vary the order of the questions to adapt to special circumstances. These characterizations apply especially to data-gathering studies; nondirective or client-centered counseling permits greater freedom by way of an unstructured interview.

Inadequate responses which call for probing or secondary questions may be partial response, nonresponse, irrelevant response, inaccurate response, or verbalized response. In addition to problems of motivation and conflict of motives, other causes of inadequate response include the following:[55]

1. The respondent may fail to understand the purpose of the question or the kind of answer needed.
2. The language or concepts may go beyond the respondent's comprehension.
3. The respondent may lack the information or background necessary to answer the question.
4. The respondent may not remember the information requested.
5. The respondent may not be able to verbalize his feelings, as in the case of intimate "depth" questions or materials.

[55] Robert L. Kahn and Charles F. Cannel, op. cit., p. 203–32.

6. The respondent may feel that the question does not fit the purpose of the interview.
7. The respondent may regard a question as going beyond the limits of what he is willing to confide in the interviewer.
8. The respondent may feel that the interviewer is unable to understand his true feelings.

SOURCES OF ERROR AND BIAS

Factors conducive to successful interviews (neglect of which may lead to failure) include the following:

An adequate number and length of interviews
Rapport and sensitivity to the interviewee
A comfortable and relaxing physical setting
A favorable reputation on the part of the interviewer, in terms of integrity and knowledge of the subject under study.

The reliability of the information obtained through the interview is affected by such factors as the following:

The desire of many interviewees to make a good impression, particularly in answering questions relating to generally accepted standards of behavior
The reluctance of many subjects to reveal highly personal information that might appear damaging to the interviewee
An attitude of confidence in and respect for the interviewer, on the part of the interviewee.

In addition to basic psychological factors or processes (intellectual, perceptual, cognitive, or motivational) affecting the interviewer and the respondent's interaction within the context of social relations with the interviewer, there are other possible sources of error or bias:[56] content and form of questions, procedures established for the interview, physical setting, mode of recording, accidental distractions, and temporary state of the parties involved. Variation and bias are likely to result when interviewers have complete freedom to interview respondents of their choice, to ask any questions desired (in any form), to make comments as they choose, and to record answers as they prefer (particularly after the close of the interview). Standardized interview procedures, however, may at times break down under the pressure of a specific situation. The history of election-forecasting reveals that the successful forecasts of a dozen years did not preclude a failure in 1948. (Interviewing and questionnaire procedures have similar problems of sampling.)

Potential sources of error and bias in the interview include firmly fixed

[56] Herbert H. Hyman and Others, *Interviewing in Social Research, op. cit.,* p. 171–72, 275.

attitudes, personality characteristics, motives, and goals that frequently are related to group memberships and loyalties (age, sex, race, religion, income, and education). Although these psychological and social characteristics or factors are potentially biasing, it is only through behavior that bias can become operative. This behavior, on the part of the interviewer, includes asking questions, probing for additional information, recording responses, and motivating the respondent to communicate. Helpful investigations of these behavioral sources of error and bias have been made, especially in social psychology and sociology. To function effectively and without bias, the interviewer needs techniques for formulation of questions, for motivation of the respondent, and for focusing communication on the content objectives of the interview; he also needs a deep understanding of the dynamics of interaction and of the psychological forces that affect the processes of the interview.[57]

RAPPORT, INTERPERSONAL RELATIONS, AND SUBJECTIVITY[58]

It is generally accepted that a friendly atmosphere of rapport and skillful probing for meaningful answers are essential to a good interview. We question the skill of an interviewer who obtains numerous "don't know" responses. In attempting to establish favorable rapport, however, the interviewer should not err in the direction of extreme chumminess with the respondent. In depth-probing, to secure meaningful responses, the investigator should not pursue the question to the extreme of distorting the situation, since some people have no hidden depths and only superficial attitudes on certain issues. At such times, repeated probing may suggest inaccurate responses and may "salt the mine."

Both interviewer and respondent contribute to the effects of interpersonal relationships. While the interviewer enters the situation with certain attitudes and beliefs that operate to affect his perception of the respondent, his judgment of the response, and other relevant aspects of his behavior, the respondent also entertains beliefs and attitudes which influence the response he makes and are at least in part a product of the personal-interview procedure. Certain respondent reactions are independent of any act or conduct on the part of the individual interviewer, and are merely a function of the interpersonal nature of the interview situation. The involvement of any respondent in an interview situation includes two major components: "task involvement" (involvement with the questions and answers) and "social involvement" (involvement with

57 Robert L. Kahn and Charles F. Cannell, *op. cit.*, p. 166–202.
58 Herbert H. Hyman and Others, *Interviewing in Social Research, op. cit.*, p. 8, 12–14, 24, 83, 138–39.

the interviewer as a personality). Validity should increase in proportion to the extent of task involvement on the part of the respondent. So far as the respondent's action derives from social or interpersonal involvement, bias will result, since the response is primarily a function of the relation between the respondent and the interviewer rather than a response to the particular task (the questions and answers).

Removal of the interviewer from the physical environment, as in the case of self-administered questionnaires, is not a complete answer to the problem of interviewer effect. Subjects filling out questionnaires may take account of the prospective readers of their replies, and thus involve an "interviewer effect," even when no interviewer is present. It is true that the social component of involvement is increased as the interviewer looms larger in the psychological field of the respondent, which means that the respondent usually will be more sensitized to the "interviewer" when the latter is physically present.

Much of the criticism of the interview technique rests on the fact that the data are derived from interpersonal situations. We should remember, however, that even in experimentation with animals in physiology and psychology, certain "interpersonal" relationships or effects may be present, as illustrated by research on conditioning in animals, although criticism of such experiments is rarely in terms of peculiar interpersonal relations between animal subject and human experimenter. (This problem is analyzed at some length in the chapter on experimentation.)

Although interviewer effect is a difficult problem in the social sciences, there are parallel errors of observation and measurement or interpretation in other sciences; for example, observer differences in reading chest x-ray films, in interpreting the results of laboratory tests, in appraising the malnutrition of children from medical examinations, or in noting the transit of stars in a telescope. We may be willing to pay the price of some crudity in the interview technique to secure the gains of essential information.

Examples of subjective or qualitative effects in the interview are numerous in the fields of clinical psychology and counseling. Differences between psychiatrists in the subtle dynamics of their interviewing behavior, differences which are possibly relevant to the variations in results reported, have been demonstrated through the application of instruments previously developed to describe social interaction processes; for example, significant differences in the degree of "activity" (ratio of talk to silence) of two psychiatrists, and similar differences in two psychiatrists with respect to an index of "tempo," another formal dimension of verbal behavior. Frequently there is interaction between the psychiatrist's previous experience and the experience of the patient under consideration. The psychiatrist, like any other human being, tends to associate unconsciously his own experiences and problems with what his patient is telling him, a reaction known as countertransference. In clinical psychology and counseling there are similar problems. In counseling, the great concern with the actual nature of the therapeutic procedure has led to a series of studies in which an accurate description of the entire content of the interview is available from electrical recordings. Comparison of the counselor's written report of interviews with an electrical transcription demonstrates that there are large and significant omissions of content in the written record, alerations in the time sequence of remarks, and lack of precision in the notes, leading to ambiguity. Presumptive evidence of differences in counseling behavior is available from studies of the attitudes of counselors toward given interviewing practices. Therefore, a basic issue is the magnitude of errors in the collection of data by interview, efficient ways of estimating the presence of such errors, and the safeguards or checks upon such errors.

Hyman found that skilled interviewers frequently have certain beliefs about their respondents and expectations as to answers, but that the existence of such role expectations, attitude-structure expectations, and probability expectations did not materially affect the behavior of interviewers so as to alter survey results. The skillful interviewer's expectatations may have a foundation in truth and consequently may enhance validity.

RECORDS AND RECORDING

Clinical interview findings, together with other related material, usually are filed in a folder or case record, including four types of information: (1) historical or background data concerning the patient's past life; (2) quantitative, or test and measurement results; (3) impressionistic or nonverbal behavior, such as gestures and posture; and (4) the treatment record, or data on medical treatment and psychiatric interview notes.

Helpful extracts from interviews and illustrative records of interviews are available in the literature under such headings as the following:

Clinical interviews under such catchy topics as the envious man, beaten man, weak feet, bad conscience, struggle within, sacrifice, overburdened mouth, and color barrier

The dynamics of interviewing, including the problems of cardiac symptoms and neurotic manifestations, experienced and inexperienced applicants for a clerical job, a production bottleneck and an office feud, and family and job adjustments of a discharged psychiatric patient

Psychiatric interview with children

Therapy through interviews.

EXAMPLE: ROLE OF THE SUPERINTENDENT[59]

. . . A report of findings from a systematic survey of role perceptions among public-school superintendents and school-board members. Since the hypotheses and findings are not unusual, the chief value of the book is its methodological orderliness and its thoroughness of exploitation of interview data in an area deserving of continued exploration.

The authors are concerned mainly with the concepts of *role consensus* and *role conflict* and their correlates. Role consensus is agreement concerning role definition. It was measured by the consistency among respondents of what they expect of a person in a given position, viz., the school superintendent's position or the school-board member's position. The respondents were incumbents of these positions. Their expectations were recorded as degrees of agreement or disagreement with lists of hypothetical obligations of superintendents or boards. The items appearing on these lists were constructed after lengthy preliminary interviews with persons similar to the respondents.

Role consensus is noted at two levels—the *macroscopic* or sociological level at which sample variance is used as the measure, and the *microscopic* or psychological level at which variance among face-to-face group members is used as the measure. *Intraposition consensus* is within the sample (or within local-board) variance; *interposition consensus* is between samples (or between superintendent and the mean of his local-board) variance.

Interviewers have made increasing use of instrumentation and forms of recording, including tape recording,[60] the telephone, radio, and television. Among the activities where tape recordings may be used effectively are the following:

1. Exploratory interviewing, as when using an unstructured or nondirective technique
2. Pretest interviewing, permitting the interviewer to subject the record to objective and intensive analysis
3. Intensive unstructured or nondirective interviewing, freeing the investigator from the mechanics of note-taking and enabling him to devote full attention to meanings
4. Interdisciplinary research, permitting the representatives of each discipline to select the data most pertinent to their own problems and interests.

Some of the questions most frequently raised about the effect of tape recording on interview data are as follows:

1. Will the use of tape recorders increase resistance to the interview and thereby raise the refusal rate? The answer to this question—based upon

[59] Quoted from review by David W. Lewit, *Contemporary Psychology* 4: 106–7; April 1959, of Neal Gross, Ward S. Mason, and Alexander W. McEachern, *Explorations in Role Analysis: Studies of the School Superintendency Role*. New York: John Wiley & Sons, Inc., 1958. xiv + 379 p.

[60] Rue Bucher, Charles E. Fritz, and E. L. Quarantelli, "Tape Recorded Interviews in Social Research." *American Sociological Review* 21: 359–64; June 1956.

our own experience and that of other investigators—would appear to be a clear "no."

2. Will the presence of the tape recorder decrease or destroy interviewer-respondent rapport? Our experience also suggests a negative answer to this question.

3. Will the presence of the tape recorder alter the responses of the respondent? No unequivocal answer to this question can be given without further systematic research. However, our impression—based upon a general evaluation and the contrast of about 300 written interviews with the approximately 700 tape recorded interviews gathered in the course of our work —is that there is no noticeable or significant effect on interview data that can be attributed to the introduction of the tape recorder.

The basic advantages of tape recording over various forms of note-taking and memory reconstruction are as follows:

1. Apart from the operational problems of obtaining proper audibility and voice fidelity, no verbal productions are lost in a tape recorded interview.

2. The tape recorded interview eliminates a major source of interviewer bias—the conscious and unconscious selection on the part of the interviewer of the material to note down.

3. The tape recorded interview not only eliminates the omissions, distortions, elaborations, condensations, and other modifications of data usually found in written interviews, but it also provides an objective basis for evaluating the adequacy of the interview data in relation to the performance of the interviewer.

4. The tape recorded interview is a liberating influence on the interviewer, because it permits him to devote full attention to the respondent.

5. Other things being equal, the interviewer who uses a tape recorder is able to obtain more interviews during a given time period than an interviewer who takes notes or attempts to reconstruct the interview from memory after the interview has been completed.

Interview transcriptions and commentaries, and records of the practice interviews of trainees, are valuable devices for training the beginner. Other techniques for acquiring the essential skills of interviewing include role-playing, with the trainee acting in turn as interviewer, respondent, and observer. Rating scales also are used in helping the interviewer evaluate the effectiveness of his techniques of probing for information.

Observational Studies

Observation, as a general rule, is concerned neither with what a respondent places on paper nor with what he says in an interview, but deals with the overt behavior of persons in appropriate situations, sometimes under conditions of normal living and at other times with some special set of factors operating. In a questionnaire or interview, the respondent may tell what he thinks he does, but human beings are not generally accurate or reliable observers of themselves. Only direct observation of overt behavior can reveal what the subject actually does. It is sometimes desirable to observe the behavior of persons when completing a questionnaire, participating in an interview, or taking a standardized test, since significant aspects of behavior or personality may be revealed under such conditions.

Direct observation as a systematic research approach in the psychological and social areas has developed during the present century, with marked progress in educational studies during the second quarter of the century. Among the factors favorable to wider use of observation as an investigational procedure were the following: establishment of centers for research in child development; the demands of the newer or progressive education; a desire to probe aspects of behavior not accessible to the conventional paper-and-pencil test, interview, or laboratory technique; a wish to obviate certain of the judgmental errors likely to enter into the customary rating procedures; and emphasis on the need for studying children in natural or social situations, and for observing the functioning child (including his social and emotional behavior), rather than relying exclusively on cross-sectional measurements of mental and physical growth.[61]

PLANNING THE DESIGN OF OBSERVATIONAL STUDIES

The following list of factors that affect reliability of observation may serve as a check list or summary of problems in planning the design of observational investigations. Poor reliability may be a function of one or more of these factors:[62]

1. Inadequate sampling
2. Lack of precision in defining behavior
3. Complexity of method of recording
4. Rapid, complex interaction
5. Difference in perspective of observers
6. Individual differences in degree of decisiveness of activities of subjects observed
7. Constant errors due to observer bias (overweighting, timing, "halo" effects, etc.)
8. Requiring high-order inferences in classifying behavior
9. Demanding the simultaneous observation of too many variables

[61] Arthur T. Jersild and Margaret F. Meigs, "Direct Observation as a Research Method." *Review of Educational Research* 9: 472–82, 597–99; December 1939.
[62] Elizabeth Gellert, "Systematic Observation: A Method in Child Study." *Harvard Educational Review* 25: 179–95; Summer 1955.

10. Excessively long periods of observation without interspersed rest periods
11. Inadequate training of observers
12. The effect of individual observers upon the behavior of the subjects
13. Degree of acquaintance with the subjects.

Another classification of factors important in planning and conducting observations was prepared originally for the field of psychology, but applies also to education and other social areas:[63]

1. Nature of the observing process
   a. Mechanisms involved in observing
   b. Active nature of observing
   c. "Mental sets" in observing
2. Scientist as observer
   a. Distinguishing facts and inference
   b. Safeguards in attitude
   c. Adequate training in observational techniques
   d. Mechanical supplements to observation
3. Temporal course of the observations
   a. Necessity for constant conditions of observation
   b. Temporal variations in subjects
   c. Temporal variations in apparatus
4. Number of observations
   a. Variability of behavior
   b. Replication of observations to achieve representativeness
   c. Statistical compared with practical significance
   d. Designing the study in order to increase the number of observations
5. Recording the observations
   a. Need for records
   b. Records to be comprehensive
   c. Accuracy of records varying with degree of conceptualization
   d. Limitations of apparatus recording
   e. Keeping a daily record.

To summarize briefly, the aspects of planning for observation include the following factors that affect the success of the investigation:

An appropriate group of subjects to observe
Selection and arrangement of any special conditions for the group
Length of each observation period, interval between periods, and number of periods
Physical position of the observer and possible effect on the subject or subjects
Definition of specific activities or units of behavior to be observed
Entry of frequencies or tallies in the record, as a total for the entire observation period or by subdivisions of time within the observation period

63 Clarence W. Brown and Edwin E. Ghiselli, *Scientific Method in Psychology*. New York: McGraw-Hill Book Co., 1955. p. 193–202.

Scope of observation, whether for an individual child or for a group
Form of recording, including consideration of mechanical techniques and such
   quantitative factors as number, time, distance, and spatial relationships
Training of the observer in terms of expertness
Interpretation of observations.

PARTICIPANT OBSERVATION

Participant observation is a dynamic process of interaction, involving registering, interpreting, and recording.

The process and the kinds of data are influenced by continuing observed-observer transactions. The role of the observer may be passive or active. In either case affective involvement with the observed develops inevitably and may range from sympathetic identification to projective distortion. The form it takes is a function primarily of the observer's experience, awareness, and personality. Anxiety and bias are sources of distortion, and their adequate handling is a major problem in refining the human instrument for gathering data.[64]

We are cautioned that participant observation needs better systematization of procedure and recording, and is something more than "having insights."

I have tried to describe the analytic field work characteristic of participant observation, first, in order to bring out the fact that the technique consists of something more than merely immersing oneself in data and "having insights." The discussion may also serve to stimulate those who work with this and similar techniques to attempt greater formalization and systematization of the various operations they use, in order that qualitative research may become more a "scientific" and less an "artistic" kind of endeavor. Finally, I have proposed that new modes of reporting results be introduced, so that the reader is given greater access to the data and procedures on which conclusions are based.[65]

The investigator may play any one of several roles in observation of social situations, with varying degrees of participation, as a visiting stranger, an attentive listener, an eager learner, or a more complete role as participant-observer. As indicated, participation or role-playing is not necessarily complete, since it is possible to take part in many of the activities of the group, as an accepted member, and at the same time act in the role of observer and interviewer. Quasi-participation is illustrated by a

[64] Quoted from Morris S. Schwartz and Charlotte G. Schwartz, "Problems in Participant Observation." *American Journal of Sociology* 60: 343–53; January 1955.
[65] Quoted from Howard S. Becker, "Problems of Inference and Proof in Participant Observation." *American Sociological Review* 23: 652–60; December 1958.

study of "corner boys" in an Italian slum.[66] The observer or investigator came in as the local historian under the auspices of a key member of a gang. In other words, the investigator may be disguised in such a manner as to be accepted as a member of the group, although he may not carry out exactly the same activities as the other members, in order to be accepted as a participant-observer. Obviously, if the group has accepted the observer as a participant, their behavior is least likely to be affected by the presence of the participant-observer.

The participant-observer commonly lives in the community or social setting under study, as he takes part in the activities and functions of the particular group or groups. In this way he gets the "feel" of what the various activities and processes mean to the regular participants. The participant-observer also plays a dual role, in that he must take an objective position after performing as a participant; otherwise his subjective reactions might distort his findings. Classic and pioneer examples[67] are *Middletown* and *Middletown in Transition*.

To cite an example in the area of school administration, a participant-observer (and investigator) served as a member of a school board and, without the knowledge of the board or community, conducted his study of the interactions and sentiments of a school district as a major source of data. For one year he kept a diary of interactions involving school board business between himself, all members of the board, citizens, and school personnel.[68]

EXAMPLE: BLACKWAYS OF KENT[69]

In research method, the book shows a happy combination of anthropological field work technique and sociological participant-observational technique. Approaching the study of the Negro subculture in the manner of an anthropologist and sociologist, Hylan Lewis, in Part One, not only places solidly the *Blackways of Kent* in their geographic, ecological, and demographic contexts but also in the broader cultural situation. In Part Two, he deals with contents

[66] William F. Whyte, *Street Corner Society: The Social Structure of an Italian Slum.* Enlarged Edition. Chicago: The University of Chicago Press, 1955. xxii + 336 p.

[67] Robert S. Lynd and Helen M. Lynd, *Middletown: A Study in Contemporary Culture.* New York: Harcourt, Brace & World, Inc., 1929. x + 550 p.

Robert S. Lynd and Helen M. Lynd, *Middletown in Transition: A Study in Cultural Conflicts.* New York: Harcourt, Brace & World, Inc., 1937. xviii + 604 p.

[68] Frank W. Lutz, "Social Systems in School Districts: A Study of the Interactions and Sentiments of a School Board." Unpublished Doctor's dissertation. St. Louis: Washington University, 1962. 200 p.

[69] Quoted from review by Jitsuichi Masuoka, *American Sociological Review* 21: 111–12; February 1956, of Hylan Lewis, *Blackways of Kent.* Chapel Hill: The University of North Carolina Press, 1955. xxiv + 337 p.

Also see John K. Morland, *Millways of Kent.* Third volume of "Field Studies in the Modern Culture of the South." Chapel Hill: The University of North Carolina Press, 1958. xxii + 291 p.

of the subculture in terms of the institutions of courtship, marriage, and the family; the economics of Negro life; religion and salvation; teaching the children; government and social control; orientations and values; and social organization. He concludes the book by touching upon the consistency and coordination of ways of life, and briefly relates the Negro subculture to the dominant or "foreign" culture of Kent.

EXAMPLE: WHEN PROPHECY FAILS[70]

At the approach of midnight one December 20, fifteen persons maintained anxious vigil in a "Lake City" living room. For all of them the occasion was momentous, but the reader of this remarkable book knows what a casual visitor to the gathering would not have guessed: for five members of the company the occasion had entirely different significance than for the other ten. Ostensibly, the entire group was awaiting spacemen who, at the appointed hour, were to rescue them in flying saucers from the world-wide cataclysm of earthquake and flood that they expected before dawn. In fact, five persons—a third of those present—were participant observers who had been following the band of believers for more than a month, awaiting opportunity to test some theoretically-based predictions about what happens in social movements "when prophecy fails." Fortunately for the reader, the prophecy did fail; less predictably, the prophecy was explicit and remained so to the crucial hour; the disconfirmation was unequivocal.

Clearly this is no routine research report. The book, an eminently readable one, represents a noteworthy venture in at least four respects, around which subsequent comments will be focused. First, it is an examplary instance in which alert social psychologists with a theory to test were able to see the relevance of a passing event, and to respond to it in time and in sufficient force to capture the pertinent data. Incidental to testing their central hypothesis, secondly, the authors provide an inside account of a miniature apocalyptic movement, an account that is fascinating quite apart from its bearing on the authors' theory. Securing the necessary information from such a socially marginal group, in the third place, tested the resourcefulness of the observers. Their account of the unusual problems they encountered and how they attempted to solve them (given in a methodological appendix) will be of special interest to investigators not intimidated by the barrier between the laboratory and "real life." Finally, the authors' temerity and success in covertly penetrating others' privacy, essential as it was to the enterprise, raises some serious problems of research ethics, problems hardly encountered when psychologists confine themselves to the accustomed laboratory or clinic. The authors have elected to present their findings without discussing the ethical ambiguities that must have troubled them and their associates. The difficulties remain, however, and the rest of us would do well to face them more explicitly.

[70] Quoted from review by M. Brewster Smith, *Contemporary Psychology* 2: 89–92; April 1957, of Leon Festinger, Henry W. Riecken, and Stanley Schachter, *When Prophecy Fails*. Minneapolis: University of Minnesota Press, 1956. vii + 256 p.

EXAMPLE: A MILITARY TRAINING PROGRAM[71]

To accomplish this purpose [of studying a military training program] it was decided that a research officer should "enlist" as a basic trainee. He would be a full-fledged member of the group under study, his identity, mission, and role as a researcher unknown to every one (except the investigators), even to his own commanding officer. This then became one of the few cases of real participant observation.

In summary, participant observation has certain advantages over such survey techniques as the questionnaire:[72]

1. The participant observer is not basically limited by prejudgment, but can reformulate the problem as he goes along.
2. Because of his closer contact with the field situation, he is better able to avoid misleading or meaningless questions.
3. The impressions of a participant field worker are often more reliable in classifying respondents than a rigid index based on one or two questions in a questionnaire.
4. The most expert and highest paid persons are in direct contact with the data in the field.
5. He can ease himself into the field situation at the appropriate pace and thus avoid rebuff by blundering into delicate situations or subject matter.
6. He can constantly remodify his categories to provide more meaningful analysis of problems under study.
7. He can generally impute motives more validly on the basis of the interlocking of aspersions and actual behavior, supplemented by occasional "feedback" reactions.
8. He can select later informants in such a way as to throw additional light on emerging hypotheses.
9. He can generally get at depth material more satisfactorily.
10. He may absorb considerable information which seems at the time irrelevant, but later proves valuable for perspective.
11. He can make use of selected informants' skills and insights by giving them free rein to report the problem situation as they see it.
12. He usually can move more easily back and forth between data-gathering in field and desk analysis.
13. Through free data-gathering he probably distorts less the difficult-to-quantify situations or aspects of a problem.
14. While ostensibly just participating, he can do covert research in delicate areas.
15. Participant observation usually involves less expense.

[71] Quoted from Mortimer A. Sullivan, Jr., Stuart A. Queen, and Ralph C. Patrick, Jr., "Participant Observation as Employed in the Study of a Military Training Program." *American Sociological Review* 23: 660–67; December 1958.
[72] John T. Doby, Editor, *op. cit.*, p. 227–29.

NONPARTICIPANT OBSERVATION

The nonparticipant observer takes a position where his presence is not disturbing to the group, such as a kindergarten or a nursery school. He may follow in detail the behavior of only one child or may describe one or two behavior characteristics of a dozen or more children. This type of observation permits use of recording instruments and gathering of large quantities of data that may be treated statistically. Also observations of different investigators may be checked against each other in terms of relative accuracy. Variations in the observations of trained and reliable observers frequently are surprisingly large.[73] Nonparticipant observation is illustrated by observing and recording conditions in such settings as a nursery school, classroom, teachers' meeting, playground, home, Sunday school, summer camp, factories, retail stores, police station, or court.

OTHER OBSERVATIONAL STUDIES

Interest in the behavior of infants and young children stimulated development of the technique of direct observation, as did a desire for improved instructional and supervisory procedure. Many of the earlier observational investigations were "omnibus" reports of everything a child did or said over long periods of minute observation, but later observational studies have been concerned with more limited characteristics of behavior, sometimes measurements of one or two traits. The older omnibus or case-history types of data were not usually suitable for statistical treatment and often reflected the particular ability or attitude of the observer himself. The later studies of limited scope are more reliable, with less personal variation between observers, and compare favorably with the reliability of paper-and-pencil instruments. Examples of the more limited observational studies are as follows: interpersonal smiling responses in the preschool years over a two-year interval, including 150 recorded observations; the spontaneous remarks of 12 nursery-school children during a period of four weeks; the behavior and changes over a period of seven weeks induced in a seven-year-old girl who moved suddenly from a small city apartment to an elegant country estate; recorded speech sounds for "only" infants and for those with older siblings; and 1001 recorded remarks overheard in conversations among the population of Manhattan.[74]

[73] Emory S. Bogardus, *The Development of Social Thought*. Fourth Edition. New York: Longmans, Green and Co., 1960. p. 654–55.
[74] Saul B. Sells and Robert W. Ellis, "Observational Procedures Used in Research." *Review of Educational Research* 21: 432–49; December 1951.

To cite an example[75] of minute observation of behavior, a record of what a seven-year-old boy did in the situations confronting him in his home, school, and neighborhood from the time he awoke one morning until he went to sleep that night represents a minute-by-minute chronology, showing him interacting with parents, teachers, adults, and other children. Eight trained observers took turns in gathering the data throughout the day. Each observational period was approximately 30 minutes in length, with brief notes made during the period and the observations dictated into a sound recorder immediately after the end of the period.

Parents with small children recognize the realism and magnitude of the problems and procedures in the observational study just described. The mother of four little boys reported that on one day her four-year-old did the following:

> Built a newspaper bonfire in the basement, using the pilot light of the hot water heater. Dribbled a quart of furniture cream from one end of the house to the other. Poured a brand new bottle of cream shampoo in the toilet. Broke a dozen eggs, a bottle of sirup, and a jar of cooking oil. Tore up his father's cigarettes and put them in the oven. His doctor tells his mother "it's normal and it'll pass," but in the meantime, his mother says, "We just can't afford him."

An observational study of the gorilla in its native habitat is fascinating in fact and style. The investigation was made over a two-year period in Africa by a behavior-oriented scientist of courage, agility, intelligence, physical stamina, and persistence, with the company and cooperation of a devoted wife. He unflinchingly observed many mountain gorillas at close range, often eye to eye. The observational difficulties involved a period of ten months when not a single day in the rain forests was clear from dawn to dusk, and rain of at least a half hour fell on two-thirds of the days.[76]

Our own curiosities and the requirements of engineers, economists, political leaders, sociologists, psychologists, and educators will not permit us to be content with a psychology of people to the neglect of a psychology of the environment of people. To cite an example, Barker and Wright have provided a sharp contrast to observation of one child's behavior in a description of 585 community settings and 10,406 episodes of child behavior. These 585 settings as a major source of data are described in 26 ways; for example, "occupancy" describes the total man-hours spent in

[75] Roger G. Barker and Herbert F. Wright, *One Boy's Day: A Specimen Record of Behavior.* New York: Harper & Row, Publishers, Inc., 1951. x + 435 p.

[76] George B. Schaller, *The Year of the Gorilla.* Chicago: The University of Chicago Press, 1964. x + 260 p.

each setting, while "penetration" indicates how important and central a person is in a setting (from leader down to spectator). If each participation in a setting in the role of a responsible functionary is taken as a performance, then the 721 midwest citizens accomplished a total of 5,659 performances, an average of about 7 performances per person per year. The second main source of data is 11 "specimen records," each describing one day's behavior of one child. Each of the 10,406 episodes in the eleven specimen records is described in terms of 29 variables, with findings presented in the form of frequency distributions; for example, the action of midwest children toward other children shows the following characteristics in decreasing frequency: domination, appeal, resistance, nurturance, aggression, submission, compliance, and avoidance.[77]

RECORDING TECHNIQUES AND INSTRUMENTS

Methods and devices for recording observations include time-sampling procedures, shorthand records of conversations and of teacher and pupil participation in classroom lessons, still and motion-picture photography for infants and young children and in sports and physical activities, a photographic dome with a one-way vision screen and tracks for movement of the camera, a clinical crib or isolation cabinet for infants, a one-way vision screen or mirror, sound-recording devices for studying language, an electric-eye ticker to count the number of autos or persons passing a given spot, a counting apparatus at the gate or door to keep a current record of attendance, an observer with a ticker device in his hand to count the number of persons passing a particular spot, mechanical recording devices attached to the radio or telephone, and an applause meter. Recording of behavior has an element of objectivity, in that the observer may look at or hear the same record as often as desired, and comparisons may be made between the judgments of different persons who use the same record. Motion pictures have the advantage of presenting the action in slow motion. With mechanical methods of recording, it is important to include enough elements of behavior to represent typical social situations rather than to be limited to characteristics so narrow and simple that they are not significant in understanding behavior in actual social settings.

Special forms or types of observation are represented by the anecdotal technique and by procedures for study of small groups or group-behavior analysis. Anecdotal records are discussed in the chapter on case and

[77] Roger G. Barker and Herbert F. Wright, *Midwest and Its Children: The Psychological Ecology of an American Town*. New York: Harper & Row, Publishers, 1955. vii + 532 p. Reviewed by Alfred L. Baldwin, *Contemporary Psychology* 1: 149–50; May 1956.

Roger G. Barker, "Explorations in Ecological Psychology." *American Psychologist* 20: 1–14; January 1965.

clinical studies, and small-group studies are presented in the next section of the present chapter. In many of these investigations of small groups, observation has provided all or part of the data.

OBSERVATION IN RELATION TO EXPERIMENTATION

The pressure of clinical problems during recent years has brought many psychologists to a realization that observation and description usually are necessary prior to experimentation. Psychology and biology are making mutual contributions to the technique of observation. Animal behaviorists with biological training have been doing the basic collecting of observational facts on animal species as a prerequisite to understanding details of behavior which can be subjected to experimentation. Intelligent planning of experiments on the effect of early experience requires a knowledge of normal behavioral events. The descriptive material throws new light on human development and suggests possibilities for research. Psychology has contributed to the technique of observation through use of duplicate observers, statistical techniques of reliability, studies of perception, and use of moving pictures in which behavioral situations may be exactly repeated and discrimination more easily taught than in most real-life situations. The training of psychology students may well include more emphasis on the technique of objective observation. Many of the important problems of human behavior lie in the area of social relationships and personality interaction where a paper-and-pencil test cannot duplicate real-life situations, which means that, as in clinical psychology, observation is the only satisfactory technique.[78]

Direct observation makes a contribution not usually present in controlled experimentation. Observational studies may deal with certain stimuli in a complex social setting to which the children react, with possible comparisons between different subjects. Such social settings are regarded as natural or normal, whereas many experimental situations and laboratory settings are considered artificial or unnatural in character. It is true that many of the conditions in carefully planned observational studies are similar to the requirements of controlled experimentation, with the exception of manipulating a variable factor, in that basic factors or conditions of observation are controlled by selection of the room, equipment, children, stimuli, and observers. Direct observation of learning in a regular classroom setting can provide us with running accounts of what happens from day to day in teaching a group of children some complex skill, generalization, or attitude, including errors and their origins, improvement and the causes, instructional difficulties and meth-

[78] J. P. Scott, "The Place of Observation in Biological and Psychological Science." *American Psychologist* 10: 61–64; February 1955.

ods of correction, plateau periods in learning and remedial techniques, and levels of pupil progress from time to time or stage to stage.[79]

OBJECTIVITY AND PREPARATION FOR OBSERVATION

Even the simplest observation in physics or in the more objective areas of psychology has in it the essence of a judgment or interpretation, and in the early days of psychology Helmholtz recognized that:

> Observation depends upon the past experience of the observer, his unconscious inferences and the resulting modification of the sensory core. . . . There is the influence of a "laboratory atmosphere" upon observational results, which means that investigators are likely to observe what they are trained to observe and there is also the contrary fact that good observers have to be trained.[80]

The uncertainties and difficulties of correct observation are illustrated by the "flying saucers" of the early 1950's, owing to indefinite concepts, exaggeration, error, imagination, and absence of essential facts.[81] Attempts at direct observation of earth satellites probably involve similar difficulties and uncertainties, although developments in space exploration during the 1960's seem almost miraculous.

The problem of objectivity in observation has perplexed survey experts and other students of administrative questions in higher education (and secondary schools as well). By the accrediting standards and procedures of earlier years, a too narrow conception of research and survey technique centered the attention of visiting committees on matters that could be enumerated or counted (students, courses, faculty members, books, average teaching loads, unit expenditures, laboratory and classroom space per student, and duties of administrative officers), to the partial neglect of careful observation and logical analysis by observers of insight. Many aspects of secondary schools and higher institutions, as appraised by accrediting teams of observers, are now reported at least in part in qualitative rather than statistical terms (including administrative organization, objectives, curriculum, instructional methods, evaluative techniques, personnel and guidance policies, and student-faculty morale).[82]

The investigator who plans to use direct observation of behavior as

[79] William A. Brownell, "A Critique of Research on Learning and on Instruction in the School," *Graduate Study in Education*. Fiftieth Yearbook of the National Society for the Study of Education, Part 1. Chicago: The University of Chicago Press, 1951. p. 62–65.

[80] Quoted from Edwin G. Boring, *A History of Experimental Psychology*. Second Edition. New York: Appleton-Century-Crofts, 1950. p. 313.

[81] Donald H. Menzel, *Flying Saucers*. Cambridge: Harvard University Press, 1953. 319 p.

[82] Norman Burns, "Higher Education." *Review of Educational Research* 22: 375–85; October 1952.

a research approach should realize that careful preparation and training are necessary. In the earlier days of the child-study movement the observational method was popular, partly because it was thought that no special preparation or apparatus was needed; one simply watched the child and reported what he saw. As an illustration of the thoroughness of training recommended for observations of the introspective type in the early days of psychology, "it is said that no observer who had performed less than 10,000 of the introspectively controlled reactions was suitable to provide data for published research from Wundt's laboratory. Some Americans, like Cattell, had the idea that the minds of untrained observers might also be of interest to psychology, and later a bitter little quarrel on this matter developed."[83]

Small-Group Study or Group Behavior Analysis

In studying small groups or in group-behavior analysis, much of the discussion of the preceding section of this chapter is pertinent, including the topics of particular aspects of behavior observed and recorded, nonparticipant and participant observation, instruments for observation, forms of recording, categories or units of behavior, time units for tallying responses, length of the observation period, scope in relation to number of subjects, training and reliability of the observer, and interpretation of observational data.

It is more time-consuming to study group-member interaction by direct observation of a group in some artificial or natural setting, as described in the preceding section. Large amounts of time are required to train judges or raters, who usually are more numerous than is true for sociometric or peer-group ratings. Direct observation is especially effective, however, in investigations that deal with such areas as communications and problem-solving. Many of the studies of group dynamics include some combination of observational and paper-and-pencil techniques.

Small-group research developed, in part, because the ideal "laboratory man" or subject for study of social behavior did not exist. Man was an interactive, dynamic force, who changed while being observed, perhaps as a result of being observed, and even seemed to influence the "objective" experimenter engaged in observing. The small group has been described as the "mediator between the inner cognitive man and the external world of objects, relations, and people," thus facilitating the exchange and flow of information which the individual needs for insight into the nature of his *self*. To cite an example, the clinical psychologist may use the small

83 Edwin G. Boring, "A History of Introspection." *Psychological Bulletin* 50: 169–89; May 1953.

group to acquire information and insight into the self of his clients and of himself as well. The psychologist and his client form a small group where the relationship may help or hinder the progress of therapy.[84]

PROCEDURES AND INSTRUMENTS

During the second half of the 1950's and the 1960's discussion and experimental activity concerned with group behavior (group processes or group dynamics) continued at a vigorous rate, with further refinement of useful observational methods and increased knowledge of variables operating to bias and distort the observations themselves. A number of investigations have been concerned with locating and studying variables affecting group-member interaction; for example, a conceptual framework for observing both the social structure and the interaction within classroom groups (problem-solving, authority-leadership, power, friendship, personal prestige, sex, and privileges). Other studies have dealt with administrative and leadership relationships within an established hierarchal organization, utilizing scales which produce sociometric data, and with peer- and self-ratings. These techniques are useful in obtaining intimate data about intragroup relations which are not easily accessible to the observer's eye or to other forms of paper-and-pencil tests.

The development and refinement of sociometric instruments are illustrated by a variety of studies: relationship between sociometric choices of preschool-age children and criteria of social behavior; a picture sociometric test for use with preschool-age children, utilizing large photographs of children in the same group and several oral sociometric-type questions; relationship between choices of friends and such variables (observed by a group of sophisticated judges in two-minute segments) as associative play, friendly approach, conversation, hostile interaction, attention, and no response; and development of social-relations instruments or scales which provide indexes of an individual's social-relations status in a group and indexes of social-group structure. Some of the activity in this area has been concerned with problems other than the development of new sociometric instruments: reliability and invalidity of the sociometric-type test in a variety of military, industrial, and educational settings; relations between sociometric choice and perceived similarity and dissimilarity; measures of prestige as revealed by a sociometric-type questionnaire and an anthropological field-worker's ratings; number of choices to be allotted the subject, in the construction of sociometric tests; ways of analyzing and charting or mapping the results of

[84] Arthur J. Bachrach, Editor, *Experimental Foundations of Clinical Psychology.* New York: Basic Books, Inc., 1962. p. 211–13.

sociometric tests; and social growth of a group over a period of time, as revealed by test-retest sociometric data.[85]

ILLUSTRATIVE STUDIES AND PROBLEM AREAS

Varied illustrations of group-behavior studies, as found in the literature, may be listed in outline form, classified according to the problem area represented:

Communications: direction of remarks between members of the group in leaderless and in trainer-dominated sessions; relationship between the type of participation in a small-group discussion and feelings of satisfaction; emotional responsiveness, as measured by a paper-and-pencil technique and by observation of the group.

Group problem-solving: effectiveness of group versus individual problem-solving, development of criteria for measuring effectiveness, and the process of group problem-solving.

Conformity behavior: amount of agreement between group participants in discussion, and effect of simulated group discussion or of a tape recording of a simulated group in producing conformity.

Social-emotional climate: use of rating instruments and scales to assess the quality of social acceptance in a classroom, consistency of teacher behavior in the area of social-emotional climate, "esprit de corps" and "group effectiveness" components of morale, and group cohesiveness.

Role behavior: structuring over a period of time of initially informal groups, role differentiation by the various members of a group, and relation between leadership, fellowship, and friendship in a group.

Assessment and selection: use of group techniques in selection and training of candidates for critical jobs, primarily through development of situational tests that yield data relevant to prediction of individual performances on a job; a functional observation room for studying small groups, including comfort and space requirements, needs of research staff, visiting spectators, and the design of the experimental room; utility of leaderless-group discussions for evaluating leadership behavior; and factors affecting the validity of the judgment of assessors, pointing to a consensus of judges' ratings for valid results.

Another classification of the literature of group processes includes: the objectives of groups; atmosphere, climate, and morale in relation to autocratic versus democratic control, dominative versus integrative control, cooperation and competition, responsibility and obligation, and morale; group structure, in terms of membership, prestige hierarchy, patterns, position and role, and cohesiveness; leadership, with respect

[85] Marvin Taylor and Harold E. Mitzel, "Research Tools: Observing and Recording Group Behavior," in "Methodology of Educational Research." *Review of Educational Research* 27: 476–86; December 1957.

to characteristics, activities, group-related behavior, and training; dynamics of groups, in terms of influence, decision-making, communication, locomotion, and conformity; and group processes in education.[86]

To cite a special application of small-group study, an attempt has been made to explore the relevance for political science of certain theories developed by sociologists and social psychologists who have been studying the behavior of small face-to-face groups. Verba shows that in the political process important decisions are made by small face-to-face groups, including courts, cabinet meetings, administrative tribunals, and legislative committees as examples of important decision-making bodies.[87]

BIBLIOGRAPHICAL AND SUMMARIZING REPORTS

The volume of literature in the area of small-group research comes from various disciplines, including sociology and psychology (with industrial, social, military, personality, child, and educational subfields), social work, industrial relations, political science, and public health. The rapid acceleration of interest in small-group study is indicated by the yearly number of publications on this subject: 21 in the 1920's, 31 in 1940–44, 152 in 1950–1953, and 200 in 1960.[88] Fortunately, the background literature on group processes and dynamics provides a theoretical frame of reference or guiding theory for investigators in this area, and helpful bibliographical and summarizing tools for the subject of group behavior are available:

A bibliography of small-group research for the period from 1900 through 1953, including 1,407 items[89]
A summary and interpretation of 169 experimental studies of small groups, covering the topics of contrasts and comparisons between the behavior of groups and individuals, manipulation of social-structure variables important to group functioning (authority relationships), effect of cultural variables (sharing of values and goals in a group), manipulation of situational conditions (such as group task, size of group, communication networks), and personality variables affecting group behavior[90]
A 94-item bibliography and summary of the research literature on group behavior for the period of the early 1950's, covering the topics of trends in

[86] William C. Trow, "Group Processes," *Encyclopedia of Educational Research*. Edited by Chester W. Harris. Third Edition. New York: The Macmillan Co., 1960. p. 602–12.

[87] Sidney Verba, *Small Groups and Political Behavior: A Study of Leadership*. Princeton, N.J.: Princeton University Press, 1961. xii + 273 p.

[88] A. Paul Hare, *Handbook of Small Group Research*. New York: Free Press of Glencoe, 1962. xiv + 512 p.

[89] F. L. Strodtbeck and A. Paul Hare, "Bibliography of Small Group Research, from 1900 through 1953." *Sociometry* 17: 107–78; May 1954.

[90] Mary E. Roseborough, "Experimental Studies of Small Groups." *Psychological Bulletin* 50: 275–303; July 1953.

small-group research, development in methodology, leader style and group atmosphere, communication in small groups, interpersonal perceptions, the decision-making process, emotional factors in group interaction, group size and the large meeting, and leadership and human-relations training[91]

A bibliography of 62 items and summary, dealing with the research tools for observing and recording group behavior, under the topics of measurement of group-membership interaction, sociometric instruments, direct observational techniques, communications, group problem-solving, conformity, social-emotional climate, role behavior, and assessment and selection.[92]

NEXT STEPS

During the 1950's and 1960's improvements and refinements in small-group study have been marked by replication of earlier investigations, development of mathematical models, interdisciplinary research, and expenditure of large amounts of money for long-range studies in natural settings, as in the military services and in industry. Further progress in group theory and methodology will depend on continuous development of more rigorous techniques of locating and measuring variables connected with group characteristics and group structure, a closer relationship between theory and data-gathering, and greater uniformity in semantics or terminology.

The Critical-Incident Technique

The critical-incident technique is a set of procedures for collecting direct observations of human behavior in such a way as to facilitate their potential usefulness in solving practical problems and in developing broad psychological principles, with emphasis on observed incidents possessing special significance and meeting systematically defined criteria. An incident is any observable human activity sufficiently complete in itself to permit inferences and predictions about the person performing the act. To be considered critical, an incident must occur in a situation where the purpose or intent of the act seems fairly clear to the observer and where its consequences are sufficiently definite to leave little doubt concerning its effects. (Some studies of critical incidents are similar to case studies, as presented in another chapter.)

EXAMPLES

The origin of the critical-incident technique may be found in time-sampling studies of recreational activities, controlled observation tests, and anecdotal records, although the method as such may be regarded

[91] Leland P. Bradford and Jack R. Gibb, "Developments in Group Behavior in Adult Education." *Review of Educational Research* 23: 233–47; June 1953.

[92] Marvin Taylor and Harold E. Mitzel, *op. cit.*

as an outgrowth of studies in the Aviation Psychology Program of the United States Army Air Forces in World War II. Illustrations of these studies include an analysis of the specific reasons for failure in learning to fly, reasons for the failures of bombing missions, critical requirements of combat leadership, disorientation while flying, and factual incidents as a basis for research on the design of instruments and controls, and the arrangement of these within the cockpit; other investigations have sought to determine critical requirements for the work of an officer in the United States Air Force, a commercial airline pilot, research personnel on a particular project, hourly wage employees in an industry, and for many other specific occupational groups or activities.

Seventeen actual incidents involve disciplinary and ethical problems arising in the relationships between teachers, administrators, pupils, and parents. Each incident is presented as an illustration of how a teacher's understanding of an interpersonal problem is affected by his philosophical and psychological frame of reference, together with comments by expert consultants.[93]

An earlier example of the critical-incident technique is found in an analysis of approximately 2,000 responses revealing attitudes of students and adults in terms of excellent and poor citizenship, in that the study is a process of analyzing free responses to critical-incidents questions on citizenship, classified under 19 categories.[94]

A study of critical incidents in psychotherapy reveals the many and great differences among schools of psychotherapy, and even among individuals within the schools, as 28 experts comment on 23 different cases. This diversity of points of view and techniques regarding the handling of specific situations is great, and raises questions regarding our basic knowledge in this field when so many experts differ so widely.[95]

> The problems or incidents are stated in a page or two with three headings: history, incident, and discussion. Discussion usually is follow-up information and the psychotherapist's own comment. After each incident is an alphabetically arranged trail of commentators' names, five to fourteen of them, with what they say. . . .
> The 23 incidents could be considered separately or as a group to evaluate

[93] Raymond J. Corsini and Daniel D. Howard, *Critical Incidents in Teaching*. Englewood Cliffs, N.J.: Prentice-Hall, Inc., 1964. xxxii + 222 p.

[94] Citizenship Education Project, *Content Analysis Manual: Classification System for Analysis of Responses to Four Questions on Citizenship*. Publication No. 9. New York: Teachers College, Columbia University, 1950. 52 p.

Citizenship Education Project, *Building Better Programs in Citizenship*. New York: Teachers College, Columbia University, 1958. 320 p. Describes the nature of the project and the techniques for planning and promoting the program at the local school level.

[95] Quoted from review by Starke R. Hathaway, *Contemporary Psychology* 5: 164–66; May 1960, of Stanley W. Standal and Raymond J. Corsini, Editors, *Critical Incidents in Psychotherapy*. Englewood Cliffs, N.J.: Prentice-Hall, Inc., 1959. xx + 396 p.

their appropriateness or representativeness among things that happen in psychotherapy, but anything said would be quite arbitrary. These incidents, or closely parallel ones, did happen to the narrators and might happen to other therapists. One could only object that the number of incidents is too small for a reliable sample. It is even less possible to review the comments. There are 166 of them! Each commentator says the kinds of things for which he can be known in his other publications. As a group, then, the collected comments by each person become a short course on his point of view.

PROCEDURES AND APPLICATIONS[96]

The five steps in the critical-incident procedure are as follows:

1. Determination of the general aim of the activity, in the form of a brief statement from the authorities in the field that expresses in simple terms those objectives to which most people would agree
2. Development of plans and specifications for collecting factual incidents regarding the activity, with the instructions to the persons reporting their observations stated as specifically as possible with respect to the standards used in evaluating and classifying the observed behavior
3. Collection of data, with the incident reported in an interview or written up by the observer himself, so as to be objective and include all relevant details
4. Analysis of data, in the form of an effective summary and description which can be used for practical purposes
5. Interpretation and reporting of the statement of the requirements of the activity, indicating both limitations and values of the results.

The two basic principles of the critical-incident technique may be summarized concisely as follows:

1. Reporting of facts regarding behavior is preferable to the collection of interpretations, ratings, and opinions based on general impressions.
2. Reporting should be limited to those behaviors which, according to competent observers, make a significant contribution to the activity.

Applications of the critical-incident procedure have been made in the following areas:

1. Measures of typical performance (criteria)
2. Measures of proficiency (standard samples)
3. Training
4. Selection and classification
5. Job design and purification
6. Operating procedures

[96] John C. Flanagan, "The Critical Incident Technique." *Psychological Bulletin* 51: 327–58; July 1954.

7. Equipment design
8. Motivation and leadership (attitudes)
9. Counseling and psychotherapy.

USE IN EDUCATION

In applying the critical-incident technique to education, it is essential to include the following aspects: observation of on-the-job behavior, evaluation of significant success or lack of success in meeting the aims of the job, reporting incidents which led to marked success or failure in meeting the aims of the job, and treatment of the data in such incidents so as to isolate and categorize the critical elements of the job. It should also be kept in mind that the technique was originally intended to study men at work on machines (including airplanes, scientific instruments, and assembly lines), whereas in the field of education men are studied as they work with men, involving human interaction and a number of variables. Therefore, certain cautions are significant.[97]

1. The use of the critical-incident technique in educational research should be restricted to studies of situations with limited complexity.
2. In designing a research project in which the critical-incident technique is to be applied, great care must be taken to insure that the problem is one in which aims and outcomes can be recognized by various competent observers with both validity and reliability.
3. Reports of critical-incident studies must stress that the technique is not designed to discriminate between several types of behavior with regard to their criticalness, except to indicate that some behaviors are critical and others are noncritical.
4. Efforts should be made to improve the method, but its use should not be discouraged because it seems to possess elements of subjectivity.
5. In reporting research using this method, great care must be taken to make clear the meaning of such terms as *critical element, critical incident,* or *noncritical elements.*
6. In view of the problems arising from the choice of observers and the interpretation of observers' reports, it is likely that the team approach can provide more fruitful results than can the individual approach.

In the area of educational evaluation, the critical-incident technique is thought to have certain values not obtainable by other techniques of measurement:[98]

1. Adequate collection of critical incidents places categories of human behavior on an empirical base, thus providing for greater validity for any subsequent measuring instrument.

97 John E. Corbally, Jr., "The Critical Incident Technique and Educational Research." *Educational Research Bulletin* 35: 57–62; March 14, 1956.
98 Lewis B. Mayhew, "The Critical Incident Technique in Educational Evaluation." *Journal of Educational Research* 49: 591–98; April 1956.

2. Collections of critical incidents provide realistic bases for any of a variety of evaluation techniques, although the incidents do not of themselves comprise a measurement instrument.
3. The critical incidents themselves can frequently serve as a source of the raw material out of which evaluation items are constructed, since incidents expressed in the words of the students may overcome the tendency either to over- or under-shoot the level of the prospective examinees.

Action or Cooperative Research

Action research (or cooperative research or cooperative-action research), as comparatively recent terminology, has appeared in the literature primarily since the midpoint of the present century, although teachers have been urged for many years to be more consistent consumers of research and to conduct appropriate studies as a means of improving instruction. The term *operational research* sometimes has appeared as a synonym for action research. Such research in the schools is an attempt to provide investigational procedures suitable for study and solution of school problems in relation to the total situation, and is a program to be conducted by teachers as part of their teaching activity, usually with the advice and cooperation of research specialists.

Long ago the basic philosophy of action research and of leadership was expressed in verse. Six hundred years before the birth of Christ (604 B.C.) the Chinese philosopher and moralist Lao-tzu spoke of leadership.[99]

> A leader is best
> When people barely know that he exists,
> Not so good when people obey and acclaim him,
> Worse when they despise him.
>
> Fail to honor people
> They fail to honor you.
>
> But of a good leader, who talks little,
> When his work is done, his aim fulfilled,
> They will say,
> "We did this ourselves."

CHARACTERISTICS AND PROCEDURES

The social psychology and group dynamics of action-research programs are based on the concept of bringing about desirable change step by step through group participation. In the early stage of a co-operative project, the role of participating observer separates study of the problem from

[99] Witter Bynner, *The Ways of Life According to Lao-tzu.* New York: John Day Co., 1944. p. 34–35.

possible fear of any change which might be required by the findings or recommendations. In later stages, participation as a member of the group identifies the individual with the project and develops attitudes favorable to support of the findings and recommendations.

Certain differences in emphasis have characterized basic or fundamental research (outlined below), as compared with action studies or programs:[100]

1. Formulation of new generalizations, explanatory principles, and scientific theories or laws that go beyond the populations and situations represented, with the expectation that some other person will bring about improvement in practice
2. High value placed on sampling procedures as a basis for generalizations
3. Careful planning in advance of the investigation and adherence to the design of the study throughout the project, with the reporting done in sufficient detail to permit repetition of the study
4. Desirability of technical training or equipment which frequently involves statistical, sampling, testing, or experimental procedures
5. Judgment of the quality of the investigation based on the possibility of generalizing the methods and findings beyond the sample and situation studied, thus adding to the body of knowledge in the particular field.

The contrasting major emphases in action research are as follows:

1. Usually stemming from an urgent practical or felt need, with a goal of application of results and improvement of practice in the particular setting where the group or investigator works, through processes of group planning, execution, and evaluation (by both research specialists and volunteer or lay participants).
2. Interest in the particular subjects investigated rather than in the total theoretical population represented by the sample under study.
3. A developmental design, with the hypothesis and method subject to modification during the course of the action program, and with due consideration of all interdependent groups concerned in any changes to be made.
4. Desirability of training in concepts of group dynamics as background for cooperative study of practical problems, with the guiding theory that of human interaction by which change is either facilitated or resisted, and with frequent difficulties of interaction with the particular community by way of choice of problem areas, specific formulation of the problem, selection of procedures, presentation of findings, and application to practices. The scientists or scholars in their role of democratic leaders stimulate and develop the talents of the group, and train and supervise the participants in the project.
5. Determination of the value of the action project in terms of the extent to which methods and findings make possible improvement in practice in a particular situation and realization of social and educational purposes.

[100] Stephen M. Corey, *Action Research to Improve School Practices*. New York: Teachers College, Columbia University, 1953. xiii + 161 p.

A TEACHING OR A RESEARCH METHOD?[101]

Questions have been raised as to whether action research is a new investigational method or a form of in-service training for school workers. Some writers contrast cooperative or action research with so-called traditional or fundamental research, as outlined above, while other persons make a distinction on the basis of the kinds of problems investigated, adaptability of the findings to real situations, motivation of the workers, kinds of generalizations sought, intrinsic value of the investigation to the practitioner, and the individual who does the research (as summarized above in part). It is doubtful that any of these distinctions, even though significant, provides the foundations for new methodology in terms of a new way of organizing or analyzing phenomena, so as to lead to the development and testing of new hypotheses (or to improved methods of testing old hypotheses). In other words, the major contribution of action or cooperative research is to in-service training and stimulation of teachers rather than as a basic research methodology paralleling the historical, descriptive-survey, experimental, case-clinical, and developmental techniques. All of these fundamental methods of investigation are available for cooperative research on the part of field workers, with the assistance of research specialists. Some types of action studies are similar in procedure to quasi-experimental design, as described in another chapter. Probably the descriptive-survey approaches are more common in action programs; to cite a specific example in a social field:

> This is an account of an unusual social-action and sociological research project conducted in a community of 13,000 in the Piedmont region in Alabama, a project made possible by a grant to University of Alabama sociologists for the purposes of studying the processes of a community self-survey in health. The major part of the volume is devoted to description and explanation of the self-survey events, presented as an application of community status-structure analysis to a relatively specific action problem and as a demonstration of the advantages of studying social process through participation in action activities, specifically through participation in the community self-survey.[102]

EXAMPLE: COLLEGE SELF STUDIES

Over a two-year period the Fund for the Advancement of Education made grants to thirty-eight colleges—seeking to analyze and reassess the aims and methods of liberal education. A committee of college presidents and deans

[101] Bernard R. Corman, "Action Research: A Teaching or a Research Method?" in "Methodology of Educational Research." *Review of Educational Research* 27: 544–47; December 1957.

[102] Quoted from review by Warren A. Peterson, *American Journal of Sociology* 61: 393–94; January 1956, of Solon T. Kimball and Marion Pearsall, *The Talladega Story: A Study in Community Process.* University, Ala.: University of Alabama Press, 1954. xxxii + 259 p.

was appointed to cooperate with the effort. Colleges themselves determined
how best to accomplish the purposes of self study. Studies were intended to go
deeper than the conventional "accreditation" survey of institutional strengths
and weaknesses, and covered aspects of concern to both faculty and administration as they looked at current operations, histories and hopes of the colleges.

An evaluative report summarizes experiences in these projects and includes
suggestions from participants as to how future programs can be strengthened.
It is written for academic and lay people who are considering "self study" as a
means of improving education. All of the participating colleges and universities prepared full reports on the studies. These documents, among others, were
examined in preparing this report. Formal visits were made to seventeen of
the colleges receiving grants, and informal visits to twelve colleges doing
similar work under independent budgets. Field interviews included discussions
with administrators, faculty members, students, trustees, alumni, and laymen.[103]

CONTRIBUTIONS AND NEXT STEPS

Many of the reports of action studies include statements to the effect
that teachers have found cherished prejudices challenged, leadership
developed, lines of communication made clearer, interest in research
engendered, curriculum change facilitated, and success in incorporating
the action approach both in the training of teachers and in the teaching
of public-school classes. These statements suggest an emphasis on problem-solving in teacher education and in instruction as an important contribution for cooperative or action research to make. The action-research
movement developed as a result of the partial failure of educational research to play a significant role in changing practice and as a means of
avoiding the separation of facts and values.

In too many instances experimenters have published data in spite
of such poor rapport with the classroom setting that their findings were
misleading. Research "imposed" upon the school by an outsider, with his
own special purposes and no objective of immediate action or change
by the school, may secure relatively rigorous results, but results not
generally applicable to the classroom. The so-called "action" investigator,
with the cooperation of teachers, may get results that are highly applicable, but probably not "true" because of extreme lack of rigor in the
research. It would seem better for the school personnel to originate the
ideas for classroom investigation, with the research designs developed
cooperatively by specialists in research methodology, who will advise in
the investigation itself, supervise the statistical analysis, and feed back
the results through a supervisor or director of research in the school
system.[104]

[103] Quoted from Robert S. Donaldson, *Fortifying Higher Education: A Story of
College Self Studies.* New York: Fund for the Advancement of Education, 1959. 64 p.
[104] Donald T. Campbell and Julian C. Stanley, "Experimental Designs for Research
on Teaching," *Handbook of Research on Teaching.* Edited by N. L. Gage. Chicago:
Rand McNally & Co., 1963. Chapter 5.

Certain problems or difficulties in conducting action or cooperative studies have included the reluctance of teachers to undertake research because of their concept of formal research, lack of time to conduct studies, difficulty of communication, and inadequate training for research activities. Suggestions for facilitating cooperative investigation have mentioned the need for a climate in the schools favorable to study and experimentation, ways to provide time for teachers to participate, and leadership and consultative help for the workers. In involving field workers more directly in programs of cooperative investigation, it will require time and effort to acquire the necessary tools and techniques of inquiry for sound research. The need for this training presents a real challenge to programs of teacher education. A second challenge relates to the amount and quality of cooperative research by teachers-college personnel themselves, which should be stimulated in several ways:[105]

1. To value and reward this type of study within the institution itself
2. To provide staff members with the research and professional literature, and with facilities for meeting together on their problems
3. To provide expert assistance in research methodology
4. To recruit staff members with an experimental attitude toward their work and a willingness to conduct research to improve it
5. To provide appropriate experience in doctoral programs in the procedures of co-operative-action research.

Quantitative or Content Analysis of Documentary Materials

Like historical research, quantitative or content analysis of documentary materials uses as sources the collections of records already in existence. The survey type of documentary analysis expresses the results in quantitative terms, and in the studies of an earlier period was concerned with counting and frequencies rather than with the meaning or message within the documents analyzed. The investigator in this area must deal with problems of locating or bringing together an appropriate collection of documents, of determining what characteristics to count or measure, and of defining the aspects selected for study.

EARLIER STUDIES

An earlier form of quantitative or content analysis used textbooks as sources, dealing with such frequencies or measures as: sentence length, word difficulty, pictures, tables, exercises for pupils, content topics and space allotment, grade placement or difficulty of material, and vocabulary

---

[105] Stepehen M. Corey, "Implications of Cooperative-Action Research for Teacher Education," *Eighth Yearbook*, A.A.C.T.E. Oneonta, N.Y.: The Association, 1955. p. 164–72.

load. Although many of these earlier analyses of textbooks were regarded as mechanical, they proved valuable in textbook-writing and in instruction, as in using standard word lists to select the vocabulary appropriate for a certain age group or grade level.

Many of the earlier content analyses of documentary materials dealt with bodies of literature larger than a collection of a dozen or two textbooks. Such studies and textbook analyses were used extensively in curriculum development, based on the hypothesis that knowledge most frequently applied (or appearing in the literature) should be included in the instructional program. In the earlier analyses of relatively large bodies of literature, illustrative topics and sources are as follows: major fields of human concern, in terms of topics covered in periodical literature; column-inches of space devoted to topics in newspapers; distribution of space to topics in the volumes of a standard encyclopedia; topics covered in a weekly news magazine; duties and traits of a good citizen, as emphasized in newspaper editorials and magazine articles on citizenship; civic and social shortcomings, identified in the editorials of newspapers and magazines; shortcomings in the written English of adults, as revealed in letters written for newspaper publication; and mathematics used in popular science, based on analysis of magazines and books.

Other earlier content analyses have been based upon specimens of child or adult usage or performance, including children's compositions and test papers, social letters, and other specimens of usage or performance. Vocabulary analysis has made possible basic word lists helpful in textbook-writing and in grade placement of curriculum materials. Error studies in such areas as reading, language usage, arithmetic, spelling, and writing have been useful in remedial and developmental aspects of instruction.

In interpreting frequency analyses of documentary materials, important questions of permanent values and social significance arise. Frequency of appearance of a topic or interest in the current literature may reflect only the passing fancy of the average reader rather than an appropriate goal or aim in improving interests and activities. In any given year the name of the leading batter in baseball or the most popular TV star probably will appear more frequently in the periodical literature than the names of George Washington or Thomas Jefferson. In interpreting error studies, as a basis for teaching the child, we need to know why he made certain mistakes and what objectives he should be able to attain, if we are to develop a sound psychology of learning. Studies of frequency of usage and errors may lead to overemphasis on very limited aspects of the child's activities and difficulties, and may fail to recognize even more important aspects of learning by way of purpose, interest, satisfaction, and emotional adjustment.

NEWER THEORY AND TECHNIQUE

The content analyses since approximately 1940 represent a more complex and subtle type of study, which should be differentiated from the rather mechanical and simple statistical studies of frequencies made during the 1920's and 1930's. As early as 1940, questions were being asked concerning a new type of content analysis; for example, analysis of propaganda in films, radio, and print in relation to responses elicited, and truth or falsity.

Especially since 1950, the complex content analyses have had little relation to the simple textbook analyses of the 1920's and 1930's, as illustrated by Berelson's survey of several hundred titles in the area of content analysis.[106] According to his findings, the content of communication includes that body of meanings through symbols (verbal, musical, pictorial, plastic, and gestural) which makes up the communication itself. Content analysis has been used to investigate such diverse topics as the following: the slogans of May Day propaganda in the U.S.S.R., dominant images in Shakespeare's plays, values in American plays as compared with German plays of the same period, treatment of minority ethnic groups in short stories published in popular magazines, comparison of newspapers and radio and their treatment of a sensational murder case, manner in which motion pictures reflect popular feelings and desires, similarities and differences in the political symbols that come to the attention of people in the major power states, and intelligence data secured from analysis of enemy propaganda.

A method for describing quantitatively and objectively any kind of verbal data (propaganda and public-opinion materials, autobiographies, clinical interviews, letters, conversational records, and other devices of personality study) includes appropriate consideration of emotional dynamics and certain psychological factors on which data can be obtained —hostility, self-approval, social perception (stereo-types), self-picture and ego-ideal, areas of frustration, and ability to take another's viewpoint.[107]

With the advent of sound recording of interviews, content-analysis studies of psychotherapy became quite common. These studies of psychotherapy may be divided into three general classes: methodological investigations, in which the aim was primarily to develop measures; descriptive studies of cases; and theoretically guided studies of therapy, that is, investigations of cause-and-effect relationships.[108]

[106] Bernard Berelson, *Content Analysis in Communication Research.* New York: Free Press of Glencoe, Inc., 1952. 220 p.

[107] Ralph K. White, *Value-Analysis: The Nature and Use of the Method.* New York: Society for the Psychological Study of Social Issues, Columbia University, 1951. 87 p.

[108] Frank Auld, Jr., and Edward J. Murray, "Content-Analysis Studies of Psychotherapy." *Psychological Bulletin* 52: 377–95; September 1955.

Newspaper reading may be analyzed in terms of five types or classes of content: public affairs (delayed reward), human interest (immediate reward), comics, illustrations, and advertising. In relation to these five classes of content, *The Continuing Study of Newspaper Reading*, a series of readership surveys made under the sponsorship of the Advertising Research Foundation, shows the following general patterns in newspaper reading.[109]

Comics, illustrations, and human interest are often read by more than half the readers.

Comics, illustrations, and human interest almost invariably have more readers for more items than public affairs or advertisements.

Most newspapers have fewer comics, illustrations, and human-interest items than public-affairs articles or advertisements. For example, many newspapers publish two to four times as many public-affairs articles as human interest items.

Few public-affairs articles and few advertisements are read by more than half the readers. About 1 public-affairs article in 10 may be read by more than 50 per cent of a sample of readers.

Some newspapers are more successful than others in attracting readers to different classes of content. Family newspapers in small cities, for example, may have more readership of articles about local public affairs but less readership for comic strips than metropolitan dailies.

In analyzing the content of radio (and TV), common classifications of programs are as follows:

Entertainment-type
Music programs—popular and dance, semiclassical and classical, old familiar and western
Drama programs—daytime serial or domestic, mystery, comedy
Variety programs—quiz, sports, miscellaneous
Information-type
News and commentators
Farm
Homemaking
Orientation-type
Religious
Talks
Forums and panels.

OTHER ILLUSTRATIVE STUDIES

To begin with TV, an analysis of television programs is classified under seventeen headings: news, weather, public issues, public events,

109 Edgar Dale and Others, *Mass Media and Education*. Fifty-third Yearbook of the National Society for the Study of Education, Part 2. Chicago: University of Chicago Press, 1954. p. 157–58, 195–204.

institutional, information, religion, drama, dance, music, fine arts, variety, personalities, quiz-stunts-contests, sports, homemaking, and children's programs.[110]

The educator in movies: The description and analysis of the educator in movies are based upon the story synopses of 81 feature motion pictures produced in the United States which portray an educator as either a major or a minor character in the film. The story synopses were selected from 2692 movie reviews in *Variety* and/or *The Green Sheet*. Any motion picture review which mentioned the characterization of an educator at a public or private school devoted to a general curriculum of study was selected for analysis. Consequently, such roles as private tutors, members of the academic staffs of such specialized institutions as military school, missionaries, corrective, fireman-, policeman-, dancing-, modelling-, sports-, and scouting-schools are excluded here. This analysis of motion pictures, therefore, must be considered in terms of the limitations set by the method.[111]

Community structure as described through newspaper analysis: A standard form permits abstracting from reports in American newspapers certain information on familial and associational roles of members of the community other than the lowest-ranking social class. From these data a picture of the kinds of interpersonal and interrole activities which constitute a local social structure can be drawn. The interfamilial participation tends toward activities centering on marriage, death, and incidents of the birth or aging processes. Newspaper reports contain much information on events involving persons in associational roles. The number of associations in a community appear to be great, and the largest amount of associational life involves shared participation about common interests of the membership rather than concerns of the larger community. Fraternal, social-recreational, and religious organizations constitute the greatest bulk of associations. Newspaper mentions also supply information on certain social characteristics such as place of nativity and locality, endogamy-exogamy which are not easily available elsewhere. Certain considerations such as newspaper policy on reporting persons of various class groups, seasonal factors in associational and familial activities, and typical forms of reporting local activities must be accounted for with respect to the validity of the picture of local social structure drawn from newspaper items. There is evidence that newspapers drawn from a range of different-sized communities will give comparable data for drawing a picture of local social structure.[112]

Behavior characteristic of a social movement: Rural community development may be viewed as a social movement. Four features or traits of a behavior collectivity which have been posited as characteristic of a social movement

---

[110] Dallas W. Smythe, "An Analysis of Television Programs." *Scientific American* 184: 15–17; June 1951.

[111] Quoted from Jack Schwartz, "The Portrayal of Educators in Motion Pictures 1950–58." *Journal of Educational Sociology* 34: 82–90; October 1960.

[112] Quoted from Robert W. Janes, "A Technique for Describing Community Structure through Newspaper Analysis." *Social Forces* 37: 102–109; December 1958.

were abstracted from existing literature. These concepts were then applied to the phenomenon of community development. Through the use of these four concepts—change, organization, geographical scope, and persistence in time— it has been possible to take the position that community development is not only a social movement in the South but that it is also a world-wide movement.[113]

Media of mass communication: Summarized, it appears that the media typically screen out such items as these: elite individuals or groups, usually business-based, gaining unfair advantage in a privileged, rather than democratic manner; shortcomings in religious behavior, such as lack of piety or respect by parishioners, discontent shown by the clergy, or "human weakness" in church relationships; doctors acting in selfish rather than professional fashion; anything calling into question national or community pride or integrity; short-comings in mother, judge, or other institutions or unpleasant role deviations. This is a knotty list, making classification difficult. The list is not exhaustive and there are exceptions in the various media, and changes over time.[114]

Problems of married working women: Articles were drawn from the three leading magazines which appeal primarily to the working woman: *Mademoi-selle, Glamour,* and *Charm.* Each monthly publication has a circulation of 550,000 or more, and all publish articles of interest to women who work. The leading articles are, in many cases, designed to help women in selection of careers, training for vocations, and solution of problems contingent upon their occupations. Over a period of a year, 1956-57, all issues of these three magazines were analyzed for articles dealing primarily with the problems of the married woman employed outside the home. Articles dealing with problems common to all working women, such as attitude toward employer, relationship to other workers, or problems of insurance and taxation were eliminated. Articles dealing with problems peculiar to the working widow or divorcee were also discarded.

Thirty-five articles were found which dealt primarily with the problem of the married working woman. The particular problem dealt with was recorded, together with the solution proposed by the author of the article. The prob-lems were then classified in three general groups: problems involving conflict among objects of striving, problems involving vagueness of goals, and problems due to failure of the objects of striving. The general attitude of the writer of the article toward the possibility of achieving a satisfactory solution was also noted.[115]

Principles of executive action: Twenty-three principles of executive action in the college and university derived from the literature of higher education in

113 Quoted from Selz C. Mayo, "An Approach to the Understanding of Rural Com-munity Development." *Social Forces* 37: 95–101; December 1958.

114 Quoted from Warren Breed, "Mass Communication and Socio-Cultural Integra-tion." *Social Forces* 37: 109–16; December 1958.

115 Quoted from Mary G. Hatch and David L. Hatch, "Problems of Married Work-ing Women as Presented by Three Popular Working Women's Magazines." *Social Forces* 37: 148–53; December 1958.

the period from 1920 to 1955 cover the writings of educators on administrative problems, as concerned with the nature of executive responsibility, selection of the chief executive, organization of the executive department, and specific responsibilities of the president of a college or university.[116]

An analysis of 4,760 cartoons contained in six popular magazines for the years 1949 and 1959 reveals considerable overlap in public image between psychologists, psychiatrists, and other psychologically oriented personnel.[117]

An analysis of journals published by state education associations, for the purpose of locating materials contributing to regional improvement, in terms of criteria relating to: a point of view of regionalism instead of traditional sectionalism; awareness of the South as a region; ample natural and human resources; deficiency of technological skill, capital wealth, and institutional services; waste of resources; a plan or program for alleviating a problem or relieving a deficiency; and progress in the direction of regional improvement.[118]

An analysis of the acts of the Indiana General Assembly relating to formal education, classified under the following subject headings: township schools, county seminaries, Indiana College (Indiana University), private educational institutions, school lands, school funds, school officials, fines and license fees, school taxes, education of special groups, and libraries.[119]

SUMMARY OF USES OF CONTENT ANALYSIS[120]

Seventeen types of uses (applications, functions) of content analysis have been identified:

CHARACTERISTICS OF CONTENT: SUBSTANCE

1. To describe trends in communication content
2. To trace the development of scholarship by way of interests and activities
3. To disclose international differences in communication content
4. To compare media or levels of communication
5. To audit communication content against objectives
6. To construct and apply communication standards
7. To aid in technical-research operations

[116] Donald Faulkner, "Principles of College Executive Action." *Journal of Higher Education* 30: 266–75; May 1959.

[117] Raymond A. Ehrle and Bob G. Johnson, "Psychologists and Cartoonists." *American Psychologist* 16: 693–95; November 1961.

[118] Nathaniel B. McMillian, *An Analysis of Regional Items in the Content of Southern State Education Association Journals*, 1935–49. Bulletin of the Bureau of School Service, Vol. 23, No. 4. Lexington: University of Kentucky, June 1951. 91 p.

[119] Velorus Martz and Stanley E. Ballinger, *A Guide to the Source Materials Relating to Education in the Laws of the State of Indiana, 1816–1851, Part I: 1816–1838.* Bulletin of the School of Education, Vol. 29, No. 4. Bloomington: Indiana University, July 1953. 96 p.

[120] Bernard Berelson, "Content Analysis," *Handbook of Social Psychology: Theory and Method.* Vol. 1. Edited by Gardner Lindzey. Cambridge, Mass.: Addison-Wesley Publishing Co., 1954. p. 488–522.

CHARACTERISTICS OF CONTENT: FORM

8. To expose propaganda techniques
9. To measure readability
10. To discover stylistic features

PRODUCERS OF CONTENT

11. To identify the intentions and other characteristics of the communicators
12. To determine the psychological state of persons and groups
13. To detect the existence of propaganda (primarily for legal purposes)
14. To secure political and military intelligence

AUDIENCE OF CONTENT

15. To reflect attitudes, interests, and values (cultural patterns) of population groups

EFFECTS OF CONTENT

16. To reveal the focus of attention
17. To describe attitudinal and behavioral responses to communications.

The units of content analysis have been the word, theme, character, item, and space-and-time measures.

The categories of content analysis have been as follows:

"What is said" categories—subject matter, direction, standard, values, traits, actor, authority, origin, target

"How it is said" categories—form or type of communication, form of statement, intensity, device.

To summarize in another way applications and trends in using content-analysis techniques:[121]

A political scientist, Alexander George, compares quantitative and qualitative techniques as applied to the analysis of political propaganda in wartime. Charles Osgood, a psychologist, is concerned with certain techniques of quantitative analysis, especially with "evaluative assertion analysis," and the methods of discovering contingencies, that is to say, the co-occurrences of symbols, in the content of a message. George E. Mahl, a psychologist, considers the inferences which may be made from speech disturbances regarding the anxiety state of the speaker. Sol Saporta and Thomas A. Sebeok, linguists, apply the methods of content analysis, especially the contingency methods, to folklore texts. A folklorist, Robert Plant Armstrong, applies quantitative methods to the folk tales of the Bush Negroes of Paramaribo, Dutch Guiana, and the Dakota Indians of the United States. John A. Garraty, an historian, discusses

[121] Quoted from review by Franklin Fearing, *Contemporary Psychology* 6: 152–53; May 1961, of Ithiel de Sola Pool, Editor, *Trends in Content Analysis.* Urbana: University of Illinois Press, 1959. 244 p.

the methods and uses of content analysis for the historian, particularly in the study of biography and autobiography. . . .

What is to be said about the future of content analysis as revealed in the *Trends*? The papers present a carefully reasoned case for certain types of approach to an exceedingly difficult problem. This reviewer has no difficulty in recognizing the important new avenues of research which are opened up, but it seems a pity that so little attention was given to nonquantitative methods. As the editor points out, quantitative and qualitative methods complement each other, but one cannot escape the impression that the writers, with the exception already noted, had so little or no interest in nonquantitative methods.

In quantitative content analysis *something* must be counted. The size of the "units of meaning"—a matter of some concern to the editor—may vary, but quantitative analysis is inevitably atomistic. Whether *atomistic* is a bad word depends, of course, on one's philosophy of science, or perhaps even on one's philosophy of life. One may wonder if all the enormously subtle and complex patterns of human discourse can be compressed into "units of meaning" regardless of size.

Survey-Appraisal Techniques[122]

The various survey-appraisal procedures, including index numbers, are beyond the scope and purpose of this book; they are treated extensively in the books on evaluation and measurement. In some of these techniques, direct judgment rather than some more objective form of evaluation is employed. The several types of direct judgment or rating are as follows:

Rating of specimens or items, as in pooling the judgments of a "jury" concerning the traits considered important for success as a teacher

Ranking of human beings, as in direct comparison of the pupils in a class with respect to some characteristic

Comparison with scaled specimens, as in a handwriting or composition scale

Check lists, with items to be marked "yes" or "no," "present" or "absent," as illustrated by check lists for school buildings, supervision of instruction, or characteristics of a successful teacher

122 William H. Angoff, "Measurement and Scaling," *Encyclopedia of Educational Research*. Edited by Chester W. Harris. Third Edition. New York: The Macmillan Co., 1960. p. 807–16.

Robert L. Ebel and Dora E. Damrin, "Tests and Examinations," *ibid.*, p. 1502–14.

Elizabeth P. Hagen and Robert L. Thorndike, "Evaluation," *ibid.*, p. 482–85.

Claire Selltiz and Others, "Placing Individuals on Scales," *Research Methods in Social Relations*. Revised One-Volume Edition. New York: Holt, Rinehart and Winston, Inc., 1959. Chapter 10.

Oscar K. Buros, Editor, *The Fifth Mental Measurements Yearbook*. Highland Park, N.J.: Gryphon Press, 1959. 1292 p. *Sixth Yearbook*, 1965.

H. H. Remmers, "Rating Methods in Research on Teaching," *Handbook of Research on Teaching*. Edited by N. L. Gage. Chicago: Rand McNally & Co., 1963. Chapter 7.

Rating scales, with a scale of values for certain aspects or characteristics, as illustrated by a series of numbers, qualitative terms (excellent—strong—average—weak—poor), named attributes, verbal descriptions (applied to buildings, playgrounds, educational institutions, teachers, administrators, supervisors)

Score cards, usually somewhat more elaborate than rating scales, as illustrated by instruments for evaluating school plants and textbooks.

An index number is an average in the sense that it combines in one figure the average of a number of different factors or variable elements. This technique has been applied to certain phases of education and to many social and economic areas. The index numbers for the purpose of rating the state school systems usually have included such factors as: "per cent of school population attending school daily," "average number of days schools were kept open," "average expenditure per child in average attendance," "expenditure per teacher employed, for salaries," and so on. Other applications or forms of index numbers have included: changes in prices of commodities, cost of school supplies, interest rate for school bonds, cost of school buildings, cost of living (food, clothing, housing, fuel and light, house furnishings, and miscellaneous), wholesale prices, retail prices, increasing costs of education, and purchasing power of teachers' salaries.

For many educational, sociometric, and psychometric areas of appraisal, tests, rating scales, score cards, and check lists have been developed and used extensively, with applications to teachers, curriculum, home environment, social distance, socioeconomic status, attitudes, opinions, morale, social and personal behavior, personality and character, temperament, interests, and selection and evaluation of personnel. An extensive literature deals with the details of appraisal techniques.

Concluding Statement

The descriptive-survey investigations are too varied in type and technique to permit more than a summary of recent trends by way of challenging theoretical concepts, improved techniques, or standards of practice. The literature and terminology of descriptive-survey investigations include such expressions as descriptive, survey, normative, status, and trend.

1. Support of foundation grants for status studies to determine the present position of education in our culture and thus provide a basis for comparison and future evaluation.
2. Increased use of the processes of analysis and classification, especially in certain complex studies. Many descriptive investigations are highly analytical in character and sometimes have been characterized as "analytical studies," although analysis as a process is present in all types of research. Classification, the recognition of similarities and differences among ex-

periences, is a basic process in all research, including descriptive-survey studies. Grouping or the forming of categories is conducive to economy of thought.

3. Increased interest of social agencies and of the federal and state governments in social problems of local communities, as illustrated by social surveys. The social survey is usually a cooperative study of a current social problem, situation, or population within definitive geographical limits, ordinarily with some concern for a constructive program of social reform and amelioration.

4. Studies of community schools to improve the school program and community. The community survey, like many school surveys, is made to provide data for planning future developments, such as an adequate system of sewage disposal or new buildings for the school system, although the recommendations of the community study frequently are broader and more general than those found in the school survey.

5. Trends in school surveys toward: the continuing survey (with a cooperative planning survey at appropriate intervals), recognition of the qualitative aspects of recommendations, and essential safeguards for consultants, school system, and survey agency. The *educational survey* deals with the instructional program and the related policies and procedures that affect the educational program. The *building survey* has been the most common type during recent years, because of the pressure of the greatly increased pupil population. The educational and building surveys together constitute a comprehensive survey.

6. New standards, depths, and uses for the questionnaire. The questionnaire is generally regarded as a form distributed through the mail or filled out by the respondent under the supervision of the investigator or interviewer, whereas the schedule is a form filled out by the investigator or completed in his presence. A carefully devised questionnaire technique is not a simple, quick method of investigation, but requires time, patience, ingenuity, and skill. Many of these abilities are important in interview studies and in certain other descriptive-survey techniques.

7. Recognition of the interview as a process of communication or interaction, and development of focused, depth, and nondirective interviewing. Although the interview belongs to a class of methods that yield primarily subjective data, that is, direct descriptions of the world of experience, the interests of many social scientists call for such data, however crude the method of data-gathering may of necessity be. For example, the interview technique has certain advantages for collection of data relating to three of the most prominent emphases in social psychology, all implying subjective data: the emphasis on desires, goals, and values by students of personality; the current interest in social perception; and emphasis on the concept of attitude.

8. Improved skills and new examples in both participant and nonparticipant observation. Observation, as a general rule, is concerned neither with what a respondent places on paper nor with what he says in an interview, but deals with the overt behavior of persons in appropriate situations, sometimes under conditions of normal living and at other times with some

special set of factors operating. The participant-observer commonly lives in the community or social setting under study, as he takes part in the activities and functions of the particular group or groups, and gets the "feel" of what the various activities and processes mean to the regular participants.

9. Further refinement of observational methods for studying group behavior and increased knowledge of variables that serve to bias and distort observations, with future progress dependent on development of more rigorous techniques of locating and measuring variables, closer relationship between theory and data-gathering, and greater uniformity of terminology.

10. Development of a critical-incident technique for collecting direct observations of human behavior, so as to facilitate their usefulness in solving practical problems and in developing broad psychological principles. In applying the critical-incident technique to education, it is essential to include the following aspects: observation of on-the-job behavior, evaluation of significant success or lack of success in meeting the aims of the job, reporting incidents which led to marked success or failure in meeting the aims of the job, and treatment of the data in such incidents so as to isolate and categorize the critical elements of the job.

11. Action or cooperative research, designed to involve field workers directly in programs of cooperative investigation, with future progress requiring time and effort on the part of teachers to acquire necessary tools and techniques of inquiry for sound research. Long ago the basic philosophy of action research and of leadership was expressed in the feeling of the participants in a task that "We did this ourselves."

12. Refined theory, technique, and use for content analysis of documentary materials. The content analyses since approximately 1940 represent a more complex and subtle type of study, which should be differentiated from the rather mechanical and simple statistical studies of frequencies made during the 1920's and 1930's.

13. Development and application of a variety of educational, psychometric, and sociometric instruments of appraisal, including tests, scales, score cards, check lists, and indexes. By delimitation of scope, this text has left to the many specialized graduate courses and books the quantitative details of testing and statistics (except as mentioned briefly from time to time for illustrative purposes): intelligence tests and measures of general mental ability, measurement and prediction of special abilities or aptitudes, personality and character tests, measures of attitudes and interests, projective methods and other devices for the study of personality, psychometric and sociometric techniques with emphasis on standardized testing and statistics, and educational or accomplishment tests in schools and elsewhere.

SELECTED REFERENCES

ABRAHAMSON, Julia. *A Neighborhood Finds Itself*. New York: Harper & Row, Publisher, Inc., 1959. xiv + 370 p.

BACKSTROM, Charles H., and HURSH, Gerald D. *Survey Research*. Evanston, Ill.: Northwestern University Press, 1963. xix + 192 p.

BANY, Mary A., and JOHNSON, Lois V. *Classroom Group Behavior: Group Dynamics in Education*. New York: The Macmillan Co., 1964. xii + 412 pp.

BEAL, George M., BOHLEN, Joe M., and RAUDABAUGH, J. Neil. *Leadership and Dynamic Group Action*. Ames, Iowa: Iowa State University Press, 1962. 365 p.

BERELSON, Bernard. *Content Analysis in Communication Research*. New York: Free Press of Glencoe, Inc., 1952. 220 p.

BERGER, Bennett M. *Working-Class Suburb: A Study of Auto Workers in Suburbia*. Berkeley: University of California Press, 1960. xiii + 143 p.

BERGER, Joseph, and Others. *Types of Formalization: In Small-Group Research*. Boston: Houghton Mifflin Company, 1962. v + 159 p.

BINGHAM, Walter V. D., MOORE, Bruce V., and GUSTAD, John W. *How to Interview*. Fourth Edition. New York: Harper & Row, Publishers, Inc., 1959. 277 p.

BUROS, Oscar K., Editor. *The Fifth Mental Measurements Yearbook*. Highland Park, N.J.: Gryphon Press, 1959. 1292 p. *Sixth Yearbook*, 1965.

CARTWRIGHT, Dorwin, and ZANDER, Alvin, Editors. *Group Dynamics: Research and Theory*. Second Edition. New York: Harper & Row, Publishers, Inc., 1960. xii + 826 p.

CHURCH, Harold H., and LEWIS, Melvin S. *An Appraisal of the School Surveys Conducted by the School of Education, Indiana University*. Bulletin of the School of Education, Indiana University, Vol. 35, No. 5. Bloomington, Ind.: Indiana University, September 1959. x + 66 p.

COHEN, Dorothy H., and STERN, Virginia. *Observing and Recording the Behavior of Young Children*. New York: Bureau of Publications, Teachers College, Columbia University, 1958. 86 p.

COLLINS, Barry F., and GUETZKOW, Harold. *A Social Psychology of Group Processes for Decision-Making*. New York: John Wiley & Sons, Inc., 1964. viii + 254 p.

COREY, Stephen M. *Action Research to Improve School Practices*. New York: Bureau of Publications, Teachers College, Columbia University, 1953. xii + 161 p.

CORSINI, R. J., and HOWARD, D. D., Editors. *Critical Incidents in Teaching*. Englewood Cliffs, N.J.: Prentice-Hall, Inc., 1964. xxxii + 222 p.

FEAR, R. A. *The Evaluation Interview: Predicting Job Performance in Business and Industry*. New York: McGraw-Hill Book Company, 1958. xii + 288 p.

FENLASON, Anne F. Revised by Grace B. FERGUSON and Arthur C. ABRAHAMSON. *Essentials in Interviewing: For the Interviewer Offering Professional Services*. Revised Edition. New York: Harper & Row, Publishers, Inc., 1962. xvi + 372 p.

GAGE, N. L., Editor. *Handbook of Research on Teaching*. Chicago: Rand McNally & Co., 1963. xiv + 1218 p.

GALLAHER, Art, Jr. *Plainville Fifteen Years Later*. New York: Columbia University Press, 1961. xvi + 301 p.

GOLEMBIEWSKI, Robert T. *The Small Group: An Analysis of Research Concepts and Operations*. Chicago: The University of Chicago Press, 1962. xii + 303 p.

GOOD, Carter V. *Introduction to Educational Research: Methodology of Design in the Behavioral and Social Sciences*. Second Edition. New York: Appleton-Century-Crofts, 1963. Chapter 5.

GUETZKOW, Harold, Editor. *Groups, Leadership and Men: Research in Human Relations*. New York: Russell & Russell, Inc., 1963. vii + 292 p.

HANDLIN, Oscar. *The Newcomers: Negroes and Puerto Ricans in a Changing Metropolis.* Garden City, N.Y.: Doubleday & Company, Inc., 1962. xvii + 177 p.

HARE, A. Paul. *Handbook of Small-Group Research.* New York: Free Press of Glencoe, Inc., 1962. xiv + 512 p.

HARE, A. Paul, BORGATTA, Edgar F., and BALES, Robert F. *Small Groups.* New York: Knopf, 1965. ix + 706 p.

HAVIGHURST, Robert J., and Others. *Growing Up in River City.* New York: John Wiley & Sons, Inc., 1962. 291 p.

HYMAN, Herbert H. *Survey Design and Analysis: Principles, Cases, and Procedures.* New York: Free Press of Glencoe, Inc., 1955. xxviii + 425 p.

HYMAN, Herbert H., and Others. *Interviewing in Social Research.* Chicago: The University of Chicago Press, 1954. xvi + 415 p.

KAHN, Robert L., and CANNELL, Charles F. *The Dynamics of Interviewing: Theory, Technique, and Cases.* New York: John Wiley & Sons, Inc., 1957. x + 368 p.

KEMP, C. Gratton. *Perspectives on the Group Process: A Foundation for Counseling with Groups.* Boston: Houghton Mifflin Company, 1964. xii + 388 pp.

KING, Charles E. *The Sociology of Small Groups: A Handbook of Theory and Experiment.* New York: Pageant Press, 1962. 111 p.

LIFTON, Walter M. *Working with Groups: Group Process and Individual Growth.* New York: John Wiley & Sons, Inc., 1961. x + 238 p.

LOPEZ, Felix M. *Personnel Interviewing: Theory and Practice.* New York: McGraw-Hill Book Company, 1965. viii + 326 p.

MAIER, N. R. F. *The Appraisal Interview: Objectives, Methods, and Skills.* New York: John Wiley & Sons, Inc., 1958. xiii + 246 p.

MERTON, Robert K., FISKE, Marjorie, and KENDALL, Patricia L. *The Focused Interview: A Manual of Problems and Procedures.* New York: Free Press of Glencoe, Inc., 1956. 186 p.

MOSER, C. A. *Survey Methods in Social Investigation.* New York: The Macmillan Co., 1958. xiii + 352 p.

MUSSEN, Paul H., Editor. *Handbook of Research Methods in Child Development.* New York: John Wiley & Sons, Inc., 1960. x + 1061 p.

NELSON, Lowry. *The Minnesota Community.* Minneapolis: University of Minnesota Press, 1960. 175 p.

NELSON, Lowry, RAMSEY, Charles E., and VERNER, Coolie. *Community Structure and Change.* New York: The Macmillan Co., 1960. xiii + 464 p.

NORTH, Robert C., and Others. *Content Analysis: A Handbook with Applications for the Study of International Crisis.* Evanston, Ill.: Northwestern University Press, 1963. xiv + 182 p.

PASCAL, G. R., and JENKINS, W. O. *Systematic Observation of Gross Human Behavior.* New York: Grune & Stratton, Inc., 1961. x + 126 p.

PITTENGER, Robert E., HOCKETT, Charles F., and DANEHY, John J. *The First Five Minutes: A Sample of Microscopic Interview Analysis.* Ithaca, N.Y.: Paul Martineau, 1960. xii + 264 p.

POOL, Ithiel De Sola, Editor. *Trends in Content Analysis.* Urbana: University of Illinois Press, 1959. 244 p.

SAUNDERS, Irwin T. *The Community: An Introduction to a Social System.* New York: The Ronald Press Company, 1958. xvi + 431 p.

SELLTIZ, Claire, and Others. "Exploratory and Descriptive Studies," *Research Methods in Social Relations.* Revised One-Volume Edition. New York: Holt, Rinehart & Winston, Inc., 1959. Chapter 3.

SHERIF, Muzafer, Editor. *Intergroup Relations and Leadership: Approaches and Research in Industrial, Ethnic, Cultural, and Political Areas.* New York: John Wiley & Sons, Inc., 1962. v + 284 p.

SHUMSKY, Abraham. *The Action Research Way of Learning.* New York: Bureau of Publications, Teachers College, Columbia University, 1958. 210 p.

SPENCER, John. *Stress and Release in an Urban Estate: A Study in Action Research.* New York: Humanities Press, 1964. xiv + 355 p.

STANDAL, S. W., and CORSINI, R. J., Editors. *Critical Incidents in Psychotherapy.* Englewood Cliffs, N.J.: Prentice-Hall, Inc., 1959. xx + 396 p.

STEIN, Maurice R. *The Eclipse of Community: An Interpretation of American Studies.* Princeton, N.J.: Princeton University Press, 1950. xi + 354 p.

STEPHAN, F. F., and McCARTHY, P. J. *Sampling Opinions: An Analysis of Survey Procedure.* New York: John Wiley & Sons, Inc., 1958. 451 p.

VIDICH, Arthur J., and BENSMAN, Joseph. *Small Town in Mass Society: Class, Power, and Religion in a Rural Community.* Garden City, N.Y.: Doubleday & Company, Inc., 1960. xviii + 337 p.

6

Developmental and Growth Sequences

STAGES OF MATURITY

This chapter discusses developmental and growth studies in terms of purposes and uses, sources for genetic research, cross-section and longitudinal techniques of investigation, longitudinal study of cultural growth, the cross-cultural method, developmental techniques in relation to other methods, principles for analysis and interpretation of growth data, stages of maturity and developmental tasks, and illustrative studies and applications in major areas of development (physical, mental, social, personality, and learning).

Purposes and Uses

THE INCREASED INTEREST OF THE TWENTIETH CENTURY IN GENETIC AND developmental psychology is related to the rapid progress of biology, which explains in part the early emphasis of genetic research on physical and anatomical development. Other early influences contributing to the genetic approach in psychology and education include: recognition of the importance of the child as an individual, formulation and development of evolutionary theories, observational and questionnaire studies of the growth of infants and young children, certain psychological movements, and the invention and use of measuring and recording instruments (especially mental tests) in growth studies. Before World War I the topic of mental growth and its measurement received little attention in the psychological and educational literature.

The concept of development is fundamentally biological and has been most commonly associated with the organization of living structures and life processes, although a developmental concept sometimes is applied to physical systems, cultures, social institutions, or systems of ideas. This concept has been applied to educational, psychological, sociological, anthropological, historical, economic, political, artistic, and aesthetic phenomena.[1]

Child psychology of the past decade, however, differs greatly from that of earlier years, in that longitudinal studies, observational methods, and a developmental orientation have largely been replaced or supplemented by short-term experimental studies of the effects of particular variables on child behavior. The "variable" approach has played an increasingly significant role in research in general psychology, and in child psychology as well.[2]

Expressed in other terms, changes over a thirty-year period in the theoretical conceptions underlying research in developmental psychology have revealed a pronounced shift away from preoccupation with purely descriptive concepts and data toward concern with more abstract psychological processes and behavior constructs:

1. Stemming almost entirely from the work of Piaget, a trend concerned primarily with cognitive function and conceptualization of the qualitative, organizational changes taking place in the growing child's mental processes.
2. Centering in the socioemotional sphere, a fusion of concepts and hypotheses from psychoanalysis, learning theory, field theory, and theoretical developments in cultural anthropology and sociology.[3]

A major purpose of genetic or developmental studies is to discover origin, direction, trend, rate, pattern, limit, and decline of growth, with a more recent interest in causes and interrelationships as factors affecting growth. For example, the relationships and pattern of development for mentality, emotional stability, and physical growth are more meaningful than separate analysis of each aspect of growth. Adequate interpretation of behavior includes consideration of direction of growth, rate, and optimal development. Direction indicates whether the child is moving forward, is stationary, or regressing. Rate indicates whether progress is slow or rapid. It is particularly important in the instruction of gifted children to know whether the level attained represents optimal development in relation to ability.

Investigations of developmental problems have been extended beyond the classroom, laboratory, nursery school, and child clinic to the church school, home, child-care agency, camp, playground, and discussion group, with interests going beyond the earlier physical and anatomical studies to phases of mental, social, and personality development. The

1 Willard C. Olson, "Developmental Psychology," *Encyclopedia of Educational Research.* Edited by Chester W. Harris. Third Edition. New York: The Macmillan Co., 1960. p. 370–75.

2 Harold W. Stevenson, "Introduction," *Child Psychology.* Sixty-second Yearbook of the National Society for the Study of Education, Part 1. Chicago: The University of Chicago Press, 1963. p. 2.

3 Urie Bronfenbrenner, "Developmental Theory in Transition," *op. cit.,* p. 538–41.

genetic approach could be applied more readily in tracing the development of the insane, criminal, and maladjusted, if suitable methods were available for identifying the several types of abnormality or maladjustment at an early age, as has been done for the gifted, so as to permit a forward movement of observation through the several stages of growth or development (the longitudinal approach). In most studies of abnormality or maladjustment, it has been necessary to work backwards to origins or causes through case and clinical methods or the life history, since these cases usually have reached some critical stage before coming to the attention of persons equipped to make appropriate studies.

Sources of Genetic Data

Among the sources for study of child development are the following:[4]

1. The present behavior of the child, including verbal output, as based on observations, measurements, and records in test or experimental situations, or on direct observation of behavior in play and social settings
2. Products of the child in the form of permanent records, including drawings, letters, and compositions
3. Records on file at home, school, and in a variety of agencies, covering school achievement, birth certificates, and health records
4. Introspections of the child
5. Memories of the child, or of the adult of his own earlier life, as based on the recording of conscious memories or of getting at more deeply buried memories by a free-association process or projective methods
6. Memories of the child's life as retained by those who have been associated with him
7. Measures of the parents, siblings, and other relatives of the child or of the environment, culture, or background in which he develops—a source that actually does not provide direct information concerning the child.

In describing the stages of maturity from 10 to 16, Gesell and associates have used the following sources of information:[5]

Developmental evaluation
Developmental examination—naturalistic observations, organization and consistency of performance of simple tasks, standardized psychometric tests, projective techniques
Visual examination—case history, visual analysis, visual skills
Physical growth evaluation—observations of response to situation, standard physical-growth measures, standardized physique photographs

4 John E. Anderson, "Methods of Child Psychology," *Manual of Child Psychology.* Second Edition. Edited by Leonard Carmichael. New York: John Wiley & Sons, Inc., 1954. p. 18–19.
5 Arnold Gesell, Frances L. Ilg, and Louise B. Ames, *Youth: The Years from Ten to Sixteen.* New York: Harper & Row, Publishers, Inc., 1956. p. 506–7.

Subject interview
Topics covering emotions, sense of self, interpersonal relationships, activities and interests, self-care and routines, action system, school, ethical sense, philosophical outlook
Teacher interview.

Cross-Section and Longitudinal Techniques

The cross-section technique requires at least a single measurement for each individual within the particular groups represented, as when height is measured for each pupil in the first six grades of a public-school system. The central tendency for each of the six grades can be calculated, the result representing "norms" of growth in height or growth trends from grade to grade or year to year, although these central tendencies are not appropriate "norms" of growth in height for an individual child. The cross-section technique has the advantage of gathering the data promptly, as in measuring at one time the height of children in the first six grades, rather than waiting for the pupils in the first grade to grow in height through a period of six years (a longitudinal technique), although cross-section studies present special problems in sampling and statistical procedure.

In following growth in height of a particular group of children or of an individual through a period of months or years by the longitudinal method, the resulting series of measurements represents growth sequences for the same group or the same individual. The longitudinal approach is considered a sounder method than the cross-section technique, although the former involves an expenditure of time and resources in waiting a period of months or years for growth to take place. While problems of sampling and statistical procedure sometimes are perplexing in cross-section studies, there are other problems related to unpredictable and uncontrollable selective elemination in longitudinal investigations, because of the casualties of death, illness, moving of families, and changes in the cooperation of children and parents. The longitudinal technique provides a significant picture of growth not present in the successive cross sections of development for different groups, since the latter do not represent the developmental stages of an individual child. For example, the cross-section approach, on an age basis, groups together at the thirteen-year level girls who are well past puberty and other girls who are some months away from puberty. Therefore, it is incorrect to say that the average increment in height for this group of thirteen-year-old girls is typical, since a preadolescent girl at this age will have a much smaller gain in height than an adolescent girl who is passing through her stage of most rapid growth. Growth curves for adolescent groups tend to "smooth" this period and to conceal the usual spurt in height during adolescence, whereas individual curves at this period reveal a rapid increment in growth.

Fairly broad problems of procedure arise in the study of child behavior and development:[6]

1. Since the subjects are children, we must know their characteristics, language, and psychology.
2. We are unable to control the environment of a child over any reasonably long period of time, which means that controls over the events in the child's life are frequently inadequate in longitudinal studies.
3. We face ethical problems, particularly if some deception of the child is necessary in the interest of research.
4. Both ethical and practical problems are present in securing subjects, and in working with the homes and with schools and institutions.

Although wider use of the longitudinal method was recommended before the middle of the century, specific precautions are necessary in dealing with certain difficulties, some of which are common to cross-section studies, as analyzed in a pioneer report:[7]

1. Difficulties in population sampling, such as the selective elimination of many of the original subjects during the course of a long-term investigation
2. Maintenance of satisfactory working relationships among subjects, parents, schools, and investigators, particularly as personnel changes take place with the passing of time
3. Motivation of children to demonstrate full rather than perfunctory performance, a real challenge in the case of repeated testing over a period of months or years
4. Systematic errors of measurement in the administration or scoring of tests, mental or physical
5. Noncomparability or uncertain psychological equivalence of tests used at different age levels, especially when the time span is from early childhood to adolescence
6. Unequal experience of groups in terms of factors affecting the results of the measurement used, but not affecting the trait itself; for example, variation in previous experience with standardized tests
7. Recording and manipulation of data; for example, work of graduate students probably not as accurate and efficient as a highly trained permanent staff or skilled punch-card operators and statistical clerks
8. Mistakes of interpretation resulting from failure to take account of the principle of regression, particularly in its effects on measurements of gain or loss.

[6] Alfred L. Baldwin, "The Study of Child Behavior and Development," *Handbook of Research Methods in Child Development.* Edited by Paul H. Mussen. New York: John Wiley & Sons, Inc., 1960. Chapter 1.

[7] W. F. Dearborn and J. W. M. Rothney, *Predicting the Child's Development.* Cambridge, Mass.: Sci-Art Publishers, 1941. p. 58–79.

Longitudinal Study of Cultural Growth[8]

The "age-unit method," adopted and modified from the longitudinal study of human development, has been suggested for describing quantitatively the growth-maturity-senescence cycles of an economic, political, or entire cultural system and for analyzing the relationships among their component parts. Tentative examples of factors that might enter into the determination of an economic age are suggested below. Some of these ages, like height age in the study of human development, appear and are measurable from the time the organism (economy, political system, or cultural group) first exists as a separately definable entity. Others, like dental age in the child, represent late emerging characteristics and cannot be measured individually or averaged into an "organismic age" until they first appear.

> *Economic age*
> Specialization of labor age
> Producing unit age
> Tool (machine) production age
> Productivity per unit-of-work age
> Food source age
> Food processing age
> Product diversification age
> Surplus goods age
> Savings age
> Investment age
> Human conservation age
> Wealth distribution age
> Commercial exchange age
> Universality of exchange system age
> Credit extension age
> Banking age
> Taxation age

Cross-Cultural Method

The cross-cultural method has been in existence since approximately the 1880's, but not until recent years has either its scope or its value been recognized fully, and there have been relatively few studies utilizing this method. Early examples of cross-cultural studies include: development of laws of marriage and descent, relationships between certain social institutions and stages of economic development, and constructs relating

[8] Thomas E. Parsons, "A Longitudinal Approach to the Study of Cultural Growth." *Social Forces* 34: 34–41; October 1955.

to kinship derived from evolutionary theory. In spite of the very limited amount of published research, however, the cross-cultural method has greatly influenced behavioral science and has proved a sensitive methodology for interdisciplinary research in this area. This approach employs statistical techniques to test theory and recently has had a major interest in matters of personality development of different cultures.

Since the late 1930's, interest has increased in an interdisciplinary approach to behavioral science, as indicated by attempts to pool the evidence and theory from the fields of anthropology, psychoanalysis, and experimental psychology. Examples of cross-cultural studies during recent years include developmental investigations of: patterns of sexual behavior, relationship between the drinking of alcoholic beverages and anxiety, kinship terminology and its relation to certain phenomena (forms of marriage, descent, and social structure), relationship between sorcery and social control, relationship between the education of the child and art forms, relationship between the content of myths and education as these both relate to aggression, relationship between certain child-training variables and need achievement, and relationship between various techniques of education and the development of superego and other manifestations of personality.

Problems of methodology in comparative or cross cultural research involve both time and space (historical and geographic) factors:[9]

1. What is the goal and why do we compare?
2. How do we compare—in terms of hypotheses, instruments, procedures?
3. What is the unit of comparative study and what do we compare?
4. What is the group or population?
5. To what extent are we concerned with replication for the sake of reliability, or comparison for the sake of validity?
6. How can we deal with such administrative and technical problems as language translation, lack of trained native personnel, and absence of basic statistical information?

One of the criticisms of cross-cultural studies relates to use of ethnographic sources written at different times by people with a variety of backgrounds and personal predilections. It is obvious that ethnographies already in existence cannot be completely rewritten, but such materials can be brought up to date in relation to a strict set of criteria. Criticisms of this method have been met by anthropologists and behavioral scientists in general through provision of appropriate training, so that a group of anthropologists may collect field data in the same way, after having the benefit of methodological training (before going into the field). Anthro-

9 Edward A. Suchman, "The Comparative Method in Social Research." *Rural Sociology* 29: 123–37; June 1964.

pology may contribute especially to the methods of studying child rearing through: (1) the concept of the culture complex, with its analysis of values, beliefs, techniques, justifications, and rationalizations; and (2) comparative study of child life in non-European societies, with identification of important variables that may have been overlooked and may prove useful in prediction of behavior, in other words, the effects of divergent cultural practices involved in rearing the young.[10]

To cite an illustration, since experimental manipulation of children's environment is not usually feasible, a number of cross-cultural investigations have depended on naturalistic study of parents' behavior, obtained by observation or report, and related to personality indices of children and adults; for example, a careful study of six widely divergent cultures— in a small New England town, in Kenya, in India, on the island of Okinawa, in Mexico, and in the Philippines. Comparisons among the six cultures are possible to an extent rarely found in the anthropological literature:[11]

1. The same information is available for each culture.
2. The work was coordinated by common theory, questions, and techniques.
3. The investigators received a common period of training and followed agreed-upon techniques of investigation in the field.

The implications of this cross-cultural method for educational research indicate that there is a broad range of methods or patterns by which a child may be brought up, that we must be aware of both the virtues and the limitations of the untrained observer, and that there are ways of training persons to look at the phenomena of behavior with a strategy of reason, logic, and objectivity. The evidence from cross-cultural research is important in socializing the child as the school faces problems involving the emotions of both the individual child and of groups of children as they come together. This approach should help education correct the mistake of remaining "culture bound."[12]

A review of the pertinent research concerning the related topic of cultural differences includes the following classification of subjects: race and culture; group differences in behavior, in terms of race mixture and cultural assimilation, group differences and age, regional differences and migration, long-range effects of cultural change, and schooling and

[10] John W. M. Whiting and Beatrice B. Whiting, "Contributions of Anthropology to the Methods of Studying Child Rearing," *Handbook of Research Methods in Child Development, op. cit.,* Chapter 21.

[11] Beatrice B. Whiting, Editor, *Six Cultures: Studies of Child Rearing.* New York: John Wiley & Sons, Inc., 1963. viii + 1017 p.

[12] Robert R. Sears, Eleanor E. Maccoby, and Harry Levin, *Patterns of Child Rearing.* New York: Harper & Row, Publishers, Inc., 1957. 549 p.

intelligence; culture and personality, including comparative surveys of national character, comprehensive studies of single cultures, and investigations of social class; levels of cultural differentials; cross-cultural testing; and group differences and the individual.[13]

In applying the results of cross-cultural research to school and instructional problems, cross-cultural education may be defined as the "changes in perception, in evaluation, and in action occurring on individuals socialized in one culture as a result of their sojourn for educational purposes in a foreign culture."[14]

The educational program in colleges and universities may well develop cross-cultural approaches in a variety of disciplines:[15]

1. Humanists and social scientists can emphasize the international aspects of their subjects, especially the processes of cultural interaction.
2. Historians may deal with the historical process of interaction between Western civilization and the civilizations of Asia and Africa.
3. Intercultural data from other civilizations may be used in philosophy, literature, art, anthropology, sociology, political science, economics, international relations, and comparative education.

(At this point a cross-reference should be made to the discussion of comparative education in the chapter on historiography and to the chapter on descriptive-survey studies.)

Developmental Techniques in Relation to Other Methods

Certain types of genetic or developmental studies use methods similar to the techniques employed in other types of research. (The importance of interdisciplinary research in the behavioral and social sciences has been emphasized in Chapter 1.) The cross-section approach, in terms of the data secured for each age group, is similar to a descriptive-survey investigation of status. Genetic studies make extensive use of the data-gathering methods described in the chapter on descriptive-survey studies.[16]

Both genetic and historical investigations are interested in the sequence

13 Anne Anastasi, "Cultural Differences," op. cit., p. 350–58.
14 Simon N. Herman and Erling Schild, "Contexts for the Study of Cross-Cultural Education." Journal of Social Psychology 52: 231–50; November 1960.
15 John W. Nason and Others, The College and World Affairs. New York: Education and World Affairs, 1964. ix + 74 p.
16 Roger G. Barker and Herbert F. Wright, Midwest and Its Children: The Psychological Ecology of an American Town. New York: Harper & Row, Publishers, Inc., 1955. vii + 532 p. Also see Herbert F. Wright, "Psychological Development in Midwest." Child Development 27: 265–86; July 1956.
Lewis M. Terman and Melita H. Oden, The Gifted Child Grows Up: Genetic Studies of Genius. Stanford, Calif.: Stanford University Press, 1947. xiv + 450 p.

or development of events, with genetic studies emphasizing growth sequences and a forward movement, while historical research involves the entire range of human events and a backward movement by means of documents and remains. The genetic and historical approaches most nearly meet in certain types of biography or autobiography with emphasis on the growth and development of the individual.

Genetic investigations that use the co-twin control technique in studying development are similar to experimentation. Some experimental factor affecting development is present for one twin, while his mate serves as the control. For example, one twin may be taught to climb the stairs, while the other proceeds to the activity of stair-climbing whenever he reaches his own stage of "readiness."

Genetic and case-clinical studies are similar in certain investigations of growth or development of an individual child, adolescent, or adult over a period of time.[17] A classic example of a type of investigation where genetic and case studies meet is a series of cases concerned chiefly with diagnosis of defects and deviations of child development in such clinical areas as amentia, endocrine disorders, convulsive disorders, neurological behavior, cerebral injury, special sensory handicaps, prematurity, precocity, and environmental retardation.[18]

During the 1950's and later, studies of the intellectual growth of children increasingly applied projective methods, especially drawing and painting, as a means of exploring the more subtle changes in the child's inner world of thoughts and feelings; for example, doll play and spontaneous drawings and paintings in studying the emotional experiences and personality development of children. Other techniques for study of personality development include observation of behavior, interviews, questionnaires, personal documents, rating scales, certain psychometric and sociometric instruments, and the projective techniques of word association, story telling, play, psychodrama, and picture methods.

The techniques of growth studies vary with the age of the subjects: for infants—experiments, direct measurements, observations, one-way vision screen, the Gesell observation dome, and motion-picture recording; preschool children—direct observation and experiments; older children and adolescents—paper-and-pencil tests, indirect measurement techniques, one-way vision screen, recording of individual behavior in a social setting, and sociometric techniques in dramatic-play situations and in diagramming social relationships.

---

[17] Robert J. Havighurst, *Human Development and Education*. New York: Longmans, Green and Co., 1953. p. 177–253. Three cases.

[18] Arnold Gesell and Catherine S. Amatruda, *Developmental Diagnosis*. New York: Harper & Row, Publishers, Inc., 1947. xvi + 496 p.

Principles for Analysis and Interpretation

PRINCIPLES OF CHILD DEVELOPMENT

Certain principles of child development, as analyzed in a pioneer report, are helpful as background for discussion of the several aspects of human growth and development:[19]

1. Developmental objectives
2. Levels of maturity
3. Differential rates of maturing
4. Variability in rate of maturing
5. Variability in differential rates of maturing
6. Differential developmental pre-eminence at various stages of growth
7. "Wholeheartedness and gradation" in emotional development
8. Indigenous motivation or spontaneous use, as a feature of growing ability
9. The principle of anticipation
10. "Laying by" or shedding as a feature of development
11. Developmental revision of habits
12. Differentiation and integration
    a. Individuation
    b. Progression from generalized to more localized response
    c. Incorporation of separately practiced operations into larger activity systems
13. Priority of "large" over "small" muscular activities in certain sections of the body
14. Interaction between various aspects of growth
15. Vicarious extension of experience
16. Early establishment of some of the basic features of personality structure
17. The play of complementary and potentially conflicting forces
    a. Dependence—independence
    b. Self-centered and "outgoing" tendencies.

INITIAL STAGE

In interpreting growth and development, certain stages and processes are significant, as reported in the classic studies of Gesell and associates. The beginning or initial stage of development is important in genetic research. The initial stages of certain types of behavior in infancy are commonly as follows: in the first quarter of the first year he gains control of the muscles that move his eyes; second quarter, reaches out for things; third quarter, sits; fourth quarter, stands upright; second year, walks

19 Arthur T. Jersild and Charlotte Fehlman, "Child Development and the Curriculum: Some General Principles." *Journal of Experimental Education* 12: 130–42; December 1943.

and runs, and articulates words and phrases; and in the third year, speaks in sentences, using words as tools of thought.[20]

QUANTITATIVE AND QUALITATIVE CHANGES

Growth or development is both quantitative and qualitative. Growth in vocabulary involves both the total number of words used (a quantitative change) and the effectiveness of usage in speaking or writing (a relatively qualitative phase of development). Qualitative changes in growth commonly are expressed in descriptive terms; for example, at different stages of development an infant commonly responds to the mirror situation as follows: at 40 weeks, smiles at his mirror image; at 52 weeks, approaches his mirror image socially and even vocalizes; and at 56 weeks, brings his face close to his image, sometimes kissing it.[21]

TRENDS AND PATTERNS

A basic continuity characterizes human psychological development, in the sense that patterns of personality and adjustment once established tend to persist over long periods of time, although environmental or constitutional factors or circumstances, under certain conditions, might alter the growth trends of particular individuals. The interrelatedness of developmental trends is noted in the positive correlation of desirable traits and in a certain unity of growth. Although in physical and social interaction, and possibly in intelligence, some alteration in direction or rate of growth is associated with pubescence, anything approaching reorganization of personality has not been demonstrated. The characteristics of any age group, such as adolescents, must be evaluated in the perspective of what has gone before and what follows.

All growth probably is substantially gradual rather than irregular or in spurts, when due consideration is given to the relatively long period of preliminary preparation, as in walking without aid. The stages of behavior that ordinarily precede walking without aid include: at 32 weeks, in sitting the infant leans forward passively, although he sits erect for a brief period, and standing he supports his entire weight, but he leans forward with considerable hip flexion; at 40 weeks, when prone he pushes with his hands and regresses, and when standing supports himself by holding the crib side-rail; at 48 weeks, when prone he creeps, and unaided pulls himself to standing, cruises sidewise holding onto the crib rail, and may even walk forward if both hands are held; and at 56

[20] Arnold Gesell and Others, *The First Five Years of Life*. New York: Harper & Row, Publishers, Inc., 1940. p. 13.

[21] Arnold Gesell and Helen Thompson, *The Psychology of Early Growth*. New York: The Macmillan Co., 1938. p. 158–63.

weeks, he stands alone at least momentarily.[22] There are exceptions to the concept or principle of gradual development, such as the familiar growth spurt at adolescence, and even on occasional reversal, as illustrated by a decrease in the neck girth during the infant's first year.

STAGES OF GROWTH AND INTEGRATION

Reasonable unity or integration in development prevails at a particular stage of growth, although there are many exceptions. The normal boy of 10 has reached similar stages of development, intellectually, educationally, socially, and physically. On the other hand, an exceptional boy of 10 may be small in physical size but will answer questions on a quiz show at the college level in science and mathematics. Another exception to the concept of integrated growth at a particular stage is the adolescent boy who may be 6 feet in height but quite immature socially and emotionally. The vestibule of the ear is of adult size at birth, but the heart has not fully completed its growth at the age of 20. As a general rule, the several aspects of development tend to cluster around a "center of gravity of growth" for the individual.

INDIVIDUALITY OF GROWTH

Although there are stages of maturation and behavior that reveal basic or common trends in development, not even identical twins grow up in exactly the same way. Individuality of behavior in motor activity relates to such items as output of energy, bodily activity and fatigability, and postural demeanor, with the latter noted to determine whether it is tense, relaxed, poised, steady, or variable. Adaptive behavior varies in terms of insight, inquisitiveness, originality, decisiveness, and initiative. Language is characterized by individual differences in articulation, flow of speech, inflections, inhibitions, conversational rapport, and expressiveness. Personal-social behavior reflects variations in emotional vitality; motivation; reaction to success, failure, and fatigue; reaction to novelty and surprise; and sense of humor.[23]

To cite a specific example of very early development, Francis Galton was a genius in psychology and statistics whose IQ was estimated by Terman as approximately 200. Francis was the last of nine children, and the next child was seven years older, so that Francis had no playmates of his own age within the family and was something of a "pet." His sister, to some extent an invalid, devoted her time to his early studies. She made Francis learn his letters in play and he was able to point to each before he could speak. By the time the boy was two and a half he could

22 Arnold Gesell and Helen Thompson, *op. cit.*, p. 156–62.
23 Arnold Gesell and Others, *op. cit.*, p. 296–308.

read simple fairy tales, and could sign his name before he was three. One of his first letters, written to his sister, reads as follows:

> My dear Adèle, I am four years old, and I can read any English book. I can say all the Latin substantives, adjectives and active verbs, besides fifty-two lines of Latin poetry. I can cast up any sum in addition and multiply by 2, 3, 4, 5, 6, 7, 8, (9), 10, (11). I read French a little and I know the clock. Francis Galton. Feb(r)uary 15, 1827. [The "9" has been erased and the "11" has a slip of paper gummed over it; it is not clear who corrected the spelling of the month.][24]

LIMITS OF GROWTH AND OLD AGE

There are limits beyond which a man may not run or swim, may not build a tower or dig a mine, but there is no limit to wisdom. The way is open to better poets than Homer, more efficient rulers than Caesar, and more creative inventors than Edison.

This means that the upper limits of physical growth or performance can be determined with considerable precision, as in height or speed of running, but little is known concerning maximum mental development or performance. It may be that "quantitative" growth of intelligence continues until 18 or 19 years or even later, although qualitative and functional development of intelligence in terms of vocabulary, information, and insight or power in contrast to speed of reaction probably continues well beyond the age of 20.

Lehman's studies of the relationship between creativity or production of "masterpieces" and age indicate that most creative work of talented individuals is done at a relatively early age. To many persons this is a disturbing fact, because psychologically it would mean that a scientist, scholar, or artist does not develop creatively in the sense of producing "masterpieces" after thirty-nine or forty and that there is a very limited relationship between science (or creativity) and experience. In other words, it would seem that more experience does not help the scientist in contributing creatively to science. A possible explanation is found in the biographies of individual great chemists and other scientists, indicating that, as these able men grew older, administrative and public duties absorbed an increasing amount of the time and energy that previously had been applied to scientific work. This explanation would indicate that age in itself is not necessarily a cause for creative decline. In his book, Age and Achievement, Lehman lists sixteen general causative factors that helped to account for his statistical findings.[25]

[24] Cyril Burt, "Francis Galton and His Contributions to Psychology." British Journal of Statistical Psychology 15: 1–49; May 1962.

[25] Harvey C. Lehman, Age and Achievement. Princeton: Princeton University Press, 1953. xiv + 358 p.

Harvey C. Lehman, "The Age Decrement in Outstanding Scientific Creativity." American Psychologist 15: 128–34; February 1960.

Stated more specifically, the typical young scientist's mind is not filled with a variety of facts or responsibilities, and he is just "ignorant" enough to undertake the seemingly unreasonable or unlikely, and yet come up with a solution, sometimes a significant discovery that overthrows entrenched ideas. Once an original discovery has been made, the young scientist or scholar finds it increasingly difficult to make another, because of the distractions of providing information for other workers, committee service and meetings, administrative duties, and sometimes even jockeying for position.

The significance of all this is that, once he has been creative, the young scientist finds it very difficult to become creative again. Committees, review articles, symposia, and society meetings consume him. He has no time or spirit left for creativity. He loses his willingness to strike out into the wilderness. He begins to follow the safe and well-worn paths. He does not know that he has but a few years to go after the big discoveries, and that, with age, so many things will crowd out his chance to try again.

To discover the really new requires not only an attitude of mind but the ability to keep the roads to the solution of problems clear and, finally, to drive full speed down them. The timorous, insulated mind will not make the grade. Roads will be blocked by too much equipment, too much money, and too much seeking after status and security. The power to drive down the roads must be self-generated—a restless urge satisfied only by movement culminating in achievement. The price is high, the material rewards are minor, and the satisfactions must come chiefly from within. If you willingly pay this price, you have a ticket of admission to the ranks of the creative. However, the society of man is a great leveler; not to be leveled requires singular force of character. From such stuff creativity arises. To keep it alive in the face of the social forces that accompany maturity requires even greater strength. It is more than worth a try.[26]

In an effort to increase the nation's scientific competence, much attention has been concentrated on primary and secondary education, with the hope of persuading many students to elect a science major in college. Many scholarships, fellowships, and assistantships are available in college, graduate school, and even in the early postdoctoral years. A major challenge, however, is to find appropriate measures for extending the creative period of the mature scientist, who really has demonstrated his potential ability and does not represent the gamble always present in predicting the future contribution of the embryonic scientist. Diminished creativity following early flowering of many scientists is not usually a lessening of potential mental ability, as indicated in preceding paragraphs, but commonly is associated with decreased motivation, obsolescence of his personal store of knowledge, failure to develop new interests, administration of research grants, supervision of staff and students, and family responsi-

26 Irving H. Page, "Age and Creativity." *Science* 138: 947; November 30, 1962.

bilities. Industry, government, and the academic world should recognize these distracting conditions and take appropriate steps to extend the creative life of the mature scientist.[27]

It has also been suggested that as the total output of science has increased, the percentage of research or scholarly literature cited by historians has declined. (Frequency of citation in the literature is used as one method of determining creativity.) This may be due to the limitations of the historians and of book size rather than to age changes in the creativity of scientists. The honor of having one's work mentioned in histories or included in historical anthologies may have been bestowed to a diminishing proportion of the publications of successive decades, which would mean that citation in histories of science has become more difficult to attain for young and old alike. In other words, a scientist's quantity and quality of output may have remained approximately constant through the decades of his life, but the increasing difficulty of securing citation during the later decades of his life (the recent decades of the twentieth century) may give the false impression of a decline in creativity or productivity.[28]

A good example of problems in discovery and development of talent and creativity is available in the field of psychology. In view of the fact that for a sample of significant contributors to psychology, only 4 per cent had thought of psychology as a career when in high school and only 23 per cent when in the first two years of college, it has been urged that we find ways for earlier discovery and development of talent in psychology. Among older psychologists, one reason for relatively late development of interest in the field was the fact that psychology was not usually offered in their time before the junior year of college. E. L. Thorndike declared that he had no "memory of having heard or seen the word psychology until my junior year at Wesleyan University when I took a required course in it." A few budding psychologists had earlier interests, but no courses were available; for example, Hunter at the age of 15 had purchased and read Darwin's *Origin of Species* and at 17 became interested in psychology after a preparatory school roommate lent him a text in the field. Pillsbury wrote that when 14 and in the second year of high school he had chanced upon a copy of Carpenter's *Mental Physiology* in his father's library, read it with great interest, and declared that he would like to specialize in psychology; however, not until upper class work with Wolfe at Nebraska did that interest really get underway. At the age of 14 or 15 Cyril Burt was reading Ward's article on psychology in the *Encyclopaedia Britannica* and starting manuscript notes "which

[27] Philip H. Abelson, "Revitalizing the Mature Scientist." *Science* 141: 597; August 16, 1963.

[28] Wayne Dennis, "The Age Decrement in Outstanding Scientific Contributions: Fact or Artifact?" *American Psychologist* 3: 457–60; August 1958.

proposed to cover the whole range of human character-qualities." Terman described observations he had made, while still a boy, regarding memory and afterimages. Jastrow, Judd, Hunter, and E. L. Thorndike obtained the doctorate when 23 and Washburne when only 22. In spite of late choice of field, notable early American psychologists tended to get into their career at a young age: four obtained the undergraduate degree at 19, and the doctorate often took only three years, Judd using only two.[29]

To cite another example of early development, Norbert Wiener (1894–1964) received his A. B. degree from Tufts College at the age of fourteen and Ph. D. from Harvard at the age of nineteen. He was affectionately called "America's oldest child prodigy," and was a genius of many and varied talents, including a great interest in the socioeconomic aspects of automation of industry.

As to deterioration with age, in terms of physical and physiological development, adulthood is reached soon after the age of 20, followed by a few years at the peak of physical efficiency, and then some physical deterioration actually beginning as early as the late 20's, as is well known in the athletic sports. The peak of physical maturity and physiological equilibrium are lost in part only a few years after attainment. Fortunately, the relatively early deterioration of the anatomical and physiological functions may be offset by creative imagination, enriched experience, and good judgment, thus permitting the intellect to operate in a socially effective manner. Changes in test performances of a quantitative sort during maturity and old age may be offset by qualitative aspects of intellectual performance. It is well known that senescence or disease may produce marked changes in behavior and even disintegration of personality.

There is the remarkable story of a man who graduated from medical school at the age of 64, after earning seven other degrees: chiropody, bachelor of law, bachelor of science, two master's diplomas, doctor of philosophy, and doctor of judicial science. To cite another example of further growth and development at an advanced age, an eminent state commissioner of education after retiring went through law school and practiced law in his 70's. It would be interesting and profitable to follow the growth, development, and experience for a month or a year of a first-year teacher, a new supervisor, or a beginner in school administration.

During the 1950's and later there was increased study of the psychological and social adjustment of people as they grow older, but the concept of adjustment as applied to adults in a modern society is so complex that these studies have merely served to outline the problem and to sug-

[29] S. L. Pressey, "Toward Earlier Creativity in Psychology." *American Psychologist* 15: 124–27; February 1960.

gest some useful approaches to it, leaving a thorough exploration to the future. An important characteristic of current research in gerontology is the amount of study being devoted to middle age rather than to old age. This signifies an interest in the process of aging and in knowledge which will provide a basis for a preventive mental hygiene that will help people make a better adjustment in their later years. The studies of aging in relation to social and psychological adjustment during the 1950's and later may be classified under the following broad headings: meaning and scope of adjustment in the later years, measurement of psychological adjustment in later maturity, adjustment and social relations, increased social isolation, income and standard of living, living conditions and personal adjustment, retirement, public attitudes about aging, health and adjustment, changes in intellectual and physical capacities, motivation and learning, and education for aging. We have done better in studying problems of disease, housing, and economics than in providing a developmental psychology of the later years in terms of learning, perception, and personality.[30]

Another review of research in the field of geriatrics considers aging in relation to: psychobiology; the individual organism; antomation; problem solving; motivation; social interests and needs, and emotional reactions; confidence and caution; and expectations, set, and attitude toward change.[31]

Scientists study psychological adjustment for two general purposes: the purely scientific purpose of getting an accurate description of the behavior of people, and to discover how to help people become happier, more successful in their pursuit of the goals of life, or better adjusted.

Probably the all-pervading question in aging and in geriatrics is whether one can hope to approximate Browning's wishful insight.

> Grow old along with me.
> The best is yet to be:
> The last of life for which the first
> was made.

DIAGNOSIS AND PROGNOSIS

Interest in developmental diagnosis and causation came later than the investigations limited to determination of growth norms or sequences. A common error in identifying causation is failure to recognize the combined effects of two or more causal factors that are interrelated func-

[30] Sidney L. Pressey, "Adulthood and Old Age," *Encyclopedia of Educational Research, op. cit.,* p. 42–47.

[31] David P. Ausubel and Others, "Aging and Psychological Adjustment: Problem Solving and Motivation," in "Growth, Development, and Learning." *Review of Educational Research* 31: 487–99; December 1961.

tionally, as illustrated by the difficulty of separating the influence of nature from nurture on achievement. The causal factors that affect growth and development include: race; age; sex; familial heredity; prenatal conditions; birth trauma; birth order; maternal age at pregnancy; endocrine factors; nutritional factors; health factors; disease and infections; seasonal conditions; atmospheric conditions (temperature, humidity, and pressure); national-racial culture; socioeconomic status; educational agencies; social pressure; family and neighborhood; acquaintances and friends; intelligence; knowledge; experience, exercise, and training; interests and motivation; and emotional adjustments.

Interest and progress in the area of developmental diagnosis are illustrated by a full-length treatise which presents in some detail a wide range of diagnostic problems: techniques for the developmental examination of behavior and norms of development; diagnosis of the defects and deviations of development (amentia, endocrine disorders, convulsive disorders, neurological diagnosis of infant behavior, cerebral injury, special sensory handicaps, prematurity, precocity, environmental retardation, and clinical aspects of child adoption); and protection of early child development, as related to diagnosis, guidance, and developmental supervision.[32]

The discussion in this chapter relating to causal factors affecting physical and mental growth suggests the difficulties of developmental prognosis and prediction. Prediction in such areas as constancy of the I.Q., height, time of maturity, and age at which growth will cease is possible only to the extent that valid techniques or instruments of measurement are available, that early development provides a stable base from which subsequent growth proceeds, and that later development is affected by the same causal factors as operated in the earlier stages of growth. As indicated earlier in this chapter, it is much simpler to predict in the area of physical growth and performance than in the fields of mentality and personality development.

To cite a life-history example, prediction of success in science and research by university administrative officers and others has often been short sighted. David Starr Jordan pointed out in his autobiography that during an early period of his life, 1875–78, he failed to get an appointment at any of the institutions to which he had applied. These included Purdue, the University of Wisconsin, Princeton, Vassar, Williams, the University of Michigan, the University of Cincinnati, Cornell, and the Imperial University of Tokyo. At the time, he was teaching in the Indianapolis High School and in Northwestern Christian University, which later became known as Butler University. In reference to his application at Cincinnati, he wrote, "I was selected for the professorship of natural

32 Arnold Gesell and Catherine S. Amatruda, *op. cit.*

history in the University of Cincinnati by the acting president, Dr. Henry Turner Eddy, my excellent teacher in applied mathematics at Cornell. But the then Board of Trustees failed to ratify, giving as the more or less legitimate reason that they already had among their dozen or so professors three from Cornell." In time Jordan became the leading ichthyologist of his day, a nationally known educator as president of Stanford University, and in 1909 president of the American Association for the Advancement of Science.[33]

Related problems and examples of diagnosis and prognosis are presented in the chapter dealing with case and clinical studies.

Developmental Tasks and Stages of Maturity

During the 1950's the developmental-task concept was applied to the field of education. This concept evolved from the research on child and adolescent development during the 1930's and resulted in a science of human development cutting across disciplines in the biological and the social sciences. More recently this concept has been explored on the basis of psychological and sociological research on attitudes and social roles, and also has been applied to adulthood and old age.

A developmental task is one which "arises at or about a certain period in the life of the individual, successful achievement of which leads to his happiness and to success with later tasks, while failure leads to unhappiness in the individual, disapproval by society, and difficulty with later tasks." Such tasks arise from three sources: physical maturation, cultural pressure (the expectations of society), and individual aspirations or values.[34]

To cite an example, the central task of adolescence, "achieving identity," includes the following developmental tasks: learning a masculine or feminine social role, accepting one's body, achieving emotional independence of parents and other adults, selecting and preparing for an occupation, and achieving a scale of values and an ethical system to live by.

By way of illustration, the developmental tasks of middle childhood include:[35]

1. Learning physical skills necessary for ordinary games
2. Building wholesome attitudes toward oneself as a growing organism
3. Learning to get along with age-mates

[33] Ralph W. Dexter, "Can One Predict Success in Science?" *Science* 139: 670; February 15, 1963.
[34] Robert J. Havighurst, "Research on the Developmental-Task Concept." *School Review* 64: 215–23; May 1956.
[35] Robert J. Havighurst, *op. cit.*, p. 25–41.

4. Learning an appropriate masculine or feminine social role
5. Developing fundamental skills in reading, writing, and calculating
6. Developing concepts necessary for everyday living
7. Developing conscience, morality, and a scale of values
8. Achieving personal independence
9. Developing attitudes toward social groups and institutions.

Gesell and associates have outlined maturity traits and gradients of growth:[36]

1. *Total action system:* physical growth, sex interest, health, tensional outlets, response to the examination and interview
2. *Self-care and routines:* eating, sleep, bath, clothes, care of room, money, and work
3. *Emotions:* in general, anger, worries and fears, humor, affectivity, self-assertion, expressing feelings
4. *The growing self:* in general, self-evaluation, wishes and inclinations, the future
5. *Interpersonal relationships:* mother-child, father-child, siblings, family, same-sex friends, opposite-sex friends, crushes, parties
6. *Activities and interests:* outdoor activities, indoor activities, clubs and camps, reading, radio, television, phonograph, movies
7. *School life:* in general, school subjects and work, teacher-child relationship
8. *Ethical sense:* right and wrong, sense of fairness, response to reason, honesty, swearing, drinking, smoking
9. *Philosophical outlook:* time and space, death and deity.

Examples and Applications

In a large measure, developmental and growth studies have been centralized and co-ordinated through such university centers as California at Berkeley, Columbia, Chicago, Harvard, Iowa, Michigan, Minnesota, Stanford, and Yale, as illustrated in the references of this chapter.

EXAMPLE: GENETIC STUDIES OF GENIUS[37]

At the time of the follow-up reported in this volume, most of the subjects of the [pioneer] Gifted Child Study had reached their mid-forties. Like the preceding volume, this book is complete in itself, providing a summary of the earlier stages of the project in the first two chapters. The remaining chapters are devoted to the results of the third major follow-up, including test, questionnaire, and interview data on the gifted subjects, their spouses, and their offspring. Field data were gathered in 1950-52, thirty years after the initiation

36 Arnold Gesell, Frances L. Ilg, and Louise B. Ames, *op. cit.,* p. 35.

37 Quoted from review by Anne Anastasi, *Contemporary Psychology* 5: 46–47; February 1960, of Lewis M. Terman and Melita H. Oden, *The Gifted Group at Mid-Life: Thirty-Five Years' Follow-Up of the Superior Child.* Genetic Studies of Genius, Vol. 5. Stanford, Calif.: Stanford University Press, 1959. xvi + 187 p.

of the study, and were supplemented in 1955 through a mail questionnaire. The unparalleled amount of cooperation obtained in this project is indicated by the fact that 95% of the 1437 living subjects participated actively in the field study. . . .

Terman's own participation in the project which he started in 1921 and with which he was so closely identified ended with his death in 1956. The present volume was completed by Mrs. Oden, who served as research associate on the project since 1927. Through Terman's foresight, however, arrangements for the continuation of the study had been made before his death. This unique aspect of the project has been aptly characterized by Robert R. Sears, its present research director, in the following words: "We can be grateful for the courage and vision of the man who finally broke the barrier of the limited lifetime allotted to any one researcher, and got under way a study of man that will encompass the span of the *subjects'* lives, not just those of the researchers."

EXAMPLE: A SPECIAL EDUCATIONAL PROGRAM[38]

A unique follow-up of a special educational program organized in the University School at Ohio State University in the 1930's was based on data from the graduating class (55 persons) of 1938, including biographical questionnaires and extended personal interviews. The purpose of this longitudinal study of students participating in a special program was to determine the effects of the high-school curriculum on adult life or to discover the relation between the high-school experience and the adult living of the "guinea pigs." This type of investigation aids substantially in evaluating the long-term goals of educational programs.

EXAMPLE: GROWING UP IN A SMALL CITY[39]

In a longitudinal view of youth in a small midwestern city the subjects, 247 boys and 240 girls, were studied from 1951, when they were eleven years old and in the sixth grade, until 1960 when they were attending college, working, or, in the case of more than half the girls, married and starting families. Social class data were collected, subjects and their parents were interviewed, and batteries of various kinds of tests (intelligence, personality, sociometric, and rating scales) were administered.

PHYSICAL GROWTH[40]

Physical growth is a biological process that involves rates, directions, and patterns of change and development affected by a variety of diverse and complex external and internal factors and causes. It encompasses a

[38] Margaret Willis, *The Guinea Pigs after Twenty Years*. Columbus: The Ohio State University Press, 1961. xv + 340 p.

[39] Robert J. H. Havighurst and Others, *Growing Up in River City*. New York: John Wiley & Sons, Inc., 1962. vii + 189 p.

[40] Kai Jensen, *op. cit.*, p. 964–71.

diversity of detectable and measurable changes in size, shape, or function occurring in living organisms with the passage of time. Many scientific disciplines study physical growth from a variety of angles at different levels with increasingly refined and ingenious methods and techniques. Challenging and rewarding fields for study have included: genetic origins and backgrounds; reproduction; cell multiplication; protein synthesis; the role of chemical excitors and inhibitors; cell migration; prenatal development; birth phenomena; developmental history of special tissues, organs, and intact organisms; increases in body measurements and changes in shape; comparative growth of groups, interindividual and intraindividual growth; and environmental conditioners and impacts.

MENTAL DEVELOPMENT

Before the middle of the present century, investigations of mental development dealt primarily with the period of childhood and adolescence. Longitudinal studies now have begun to provide information on age changes later in the life span of individuals first tested in childhood or adolescence. During the 1950's and later research workers showed an active interest in the consistency of test performance at different ages and in factors related to change in test performance; effect of environmental variables on mental development; role of emotional and motivational factors; extent to which I.Q. changes represent true changes in relative standing or are attributable instead to test construction, test standardization, or other psychometric factors; group and individual differences; test performance of institutional and defective children; studies of various socioeconomic and ethnic groups; differential responses of groups with different physical and mental disorders; and mental development of the infant in relation to predictive value of tests given in infancy. The topics under which the studies of mental development during the 1950's and later were reviewed include the following: abilities at different developmental levels, adult mental abilities, constancy of the I.Q., intelligence and achievement, sex differences in intelligence, inteligence and socioeconomic status, differences among ethnic groups, bilingualism, genetic influences on intelligence, institutionalized and defective children, mental abilities in psychiatric groups, intelligence and personal and social adjustment, and mental, physical, and physiological relationships.

LEARNING

A review of investigations on growth and development takes the position that such research can be interpreted most meaningfully to the educational specialist if considered in relation to classroom learning.[41]

41 Quoted from David P. Ausubel and Others, "Growth, Development, and Learning." *Review of Educational Research* 31: 449–50; December 1961.

Developmental trends during the life span—particularly those of a cognitive nature, but not excluding trends in social, emotional, and personality development—are obviously relevant. Since these trends influence the cognitive, motivational, interpersonal, and social determinants of classroom learning at every age, they must be taken into account by all persons concerned with teaching and curriculum development.

Perceptual and cognitive development . . . have greater relevance for cognitive aspects of classroom learning than do social, emotional, and personality development. After a quarter-century of virtual neglect, during which educational and developmental psychologists have emphasized personality and social development in teaching and research, cognitive development has emerged as an important focus of research and general interest for the educator.

The development of a universally accepted definition of learning is greatly needed and would not necessarily limit either the number or variety of studies or the differences in perceptual or theoretical framework of the investigators. An acceptance of such a definition, however, not only would provide a more effective opportunity to synthesize for the use of research but would also enable the investigator to make contributions more in harmony with the total field than at present. Although the name used to identify a particular phenomenon is not of significance in itself, the assumptions upon which experimentation is based are highly significant. It is often easier to make an assumption from the name given than from the reality itself.

Apparatus and procedures are now available for careful study of children's learning, with considerable work already completed on conditioning, discrimination learning, rote verbal and motor learning, and concept formation. However, systematic study of a particular area of children's learning is still rare, with most experiments in the form of single-shot investigations rather than a series or patterns of careful, planned studies; for example, we need to analyze the learning performance of children in the relatively complex rote-learning and concept-formation situations. To cite a promising development, laboratory methods and apparatus in the form of teaching machines have been applied to the teaching of academic content, with provision for control and manipulation of the psychologically potent factors of amount of practice, immediacy of reinforcement, stimulus-presentation methods, and problem sequence.[42]

A number of trends in the literature on learning indicate that a new frame of reference is being accepted: a change from concern for facts to a concern for generalizations and laws; a change of focus from the experimenter to the learner, from emphasis on outcomes to emphasis on process, from judgment based on magnitude to that based on rate,

42 Charles C. Spiker, *op. cit.*, Chapter 9.

from the cross-section to the longitudinal basis, from specifics to patterns or configurations, and from independent findings to findings related to each other. Much of the recent literature has been concerned with the learner's perception of the self-concept; understanding, transfer, and retention; problem-solving; and attitudes and values.

By way of summary of trends and a look ahead, certain lines of psychological research into children's learning probably will include the following: [43]

1. For the long run, biological accounts of maturation, sensory development, brain function, emotion, and attention; and study of animal learning and development for the kinds of generalizations child psychologists are seeking to establish and for meaningful connections with physiology and biochemistry

2. For the short run, several developments of importance:
    a. More standardization of today's somewhat arbitrary variations in equipment and procedures
    b. More use of automated procedures, recording, and data analysis to increase the yield of information per child and to help reduce experimenter influence
    c. More research on sensory, attentional, and individual-difference processes in children, to further the tying-in of these processes with learning
    d. More efforts toward a task taxonomy, a scheme which might help relate the results found in one procedure to those found in others

3. The basic and continuing need for speculation, integration, and theory, resulting in larger conceptual schemes (imaginative, intelligent, disciplined).

PERSONALITY AND SOCIAL DEVELOPMENT

Modern personality theories assign a leading role in personality formation to the events of the preschool years. Although the need for knowledge and understanding of the important early processes has long been acutely experienced, the relative dearth of sound studies of early personality development indicates a hiatus between theory and observation. The scarcity of relevant studies probably is the result of several factors: a lack of technical devices for assessment of the behavior of young children comparable to the procedures currently utilized in studies of adults, and the cultural lag that permits less recognition of efforts in this area than of work in the more adequately financed and currently fashionable fields. The use of conventional psychometric devices has not proved adequate, with interest focused on projective and play techniques. The Rorschach Test has been a common projective device selected for young children, with recent studies concentrated on the normative aspects of

43 Sheldon H. White, "Learning," *Child Psychology.* Sixty-second Yearbook of the National Society for the Study of Education, p. 223-24.

performance. The studies of personality development in infancy and the preschool years during the 1950's and later may be classified under the headings of child-rearing practices (demographic differences and relation to development), family relationships and attitudes (mother-child relationships, early separation, father-child relationships, and sibling relationships), frustration and aggression, adjustment, behavior disorders, prematurity, hospitalization, measuring instruments, and play therapy. Studies of personality and social development in childhood and adolescence have been classified under the broad headings of family structure and intra-familial dynamics, aggressive behavior and delinquency, socio-sexual adjustment, adolescence, exceptional children, counseling, appraisal instruments and procedures, and personality traits, interests, and attitudes.[44]

Personality and social development during the 1950's and later received considerable attention from psychologists, psychiatrists, sociologists, and anthropologists, which suggests an interdisciplinary approach. The individual is being viewed increasingly as a unique, unified, and whole personality with the ability to act according to his own self-determination and not just in response to present and past occurrences, which places major emphasis on striving and goal-directed behavior.

Encouraging evidence of methodological ingenuity in studying personality development is present in the literature.[45]

1. A trend away from traditional mechanistic methods of test construction, with their single-measure indices of reliability and validity, toward multiple approaches for establishing the construct validity of the theory underlying the measuring instrument

2. Investigation of a particular variable simultaneously through fantasy and overt behavior with the aim not merely of demonstrating a positive correlation between the two but of exploring the situational conditions and processes that appear to account both for the continuities and discontinuities in the two spheres of expression.

3. The effort to supplement traditional objective and projective instruments with systematic behavioral observations and experimental procedures that are sufficiently simple and attractive to be applicable to children but permit controlled manipulation of situational factors

4. The articulation of social and cultural variables into the procedures employed for the appraisal of personality characteristics.

[44] Robert J. Havighurst, "Social Development," *Encyclopedia of Educational Research*, p. 1287–90.

David P. Ausubel, "Emotional Development," *Encyclopedia of Educational Research*, p. 448–53.

[45] Urie Bronfenbrenner and Henry N. Ricciuti, "The Appraisal of Personality Characteristics in Children," *Handbook of Research Methods in Child Development*. Edited by Paul H. Musson. New York: John Wiley & Sons, Inc., 1960. Chapter 18.

As a goal for the future, incorporation of the attitudes and values of children into more general developmental theory would be valuable to both developmental and social psychology. Concepts of attitudes and values have proved useful in investigating the social contexts of children, and should be explored further in intrafamilial contexts—the effects of parental handling upon children's attitudes and value systems, and the interactive effects of children's attitudes and values and parental handling upon other consequents in child development.[46]

Continuing recent emphases of the 1960's in a variety of developmental problems indicate a marked contrast to earlier interests in growth and development:[47]

1. Intellectual development
   a. Relationship between innate and acquired factors in perception
   b. Articulation of perception and cognition
   c. Continuity versus discontinuity in cognitive development
   d. Stability and plasticity of mental functioning
2. Personality and social development
   a. Family influences
   b. Peer and school influences
   c. Cultural influences.

Concluding Statement

Thousands of references are listed in the issues of the *Review of Educational Research* devoted to growth and development, with much of this research sponsored in child-study divisions of higher institutions and with helpful support from the foundations. These resources, however, are not adequate for the expensive and time-consuming longitudinal and experimental investigations, which suggests the need for public interest and support, including the cooperation of teachers, administrators, parents, and children. The concepts, procedures, and applications of developmental or growth investigations may be summarized briefly as follows:

1. An interest in origin, direction, trend, rate, pattern, limit, and decline of growth. The concept of development is fundamentally biological and has been most commonly associated with the organization of living structures and life processes, although a developmental concept sometimes is applied to physical systems, cultures, social institutions, or systems of ideas, and has been applied to educational, psychological, sociological, anthropological, historical, economic, political, artistic, and aesthetic phenomena.

[46] Marian R. Yarrow, "The Measurement of Children's Attitudes and Values," *Handbook of Research Methods in Child Development*, Chapter 16.

[47] Arthur P. Coladarci and Others, "Growth, Development, and Learning." *Review of Educational Research* 34: 945–618; December 1964.

2. Encouragement of carefully planned longitudinal and experimental investigations, and improved sampling procedures in cross-section studies. A shift away from purely descriptive concepts and data toward more abstract psychological processes and behavior constructs.

3. Application of the longitudinal approach to study of the growth-maturity-senescence cycles of an economic, political, or entire cultural system. Some of these ages, like height age in the study of human development, appear and are measurable from the time the organism (economy, political system, or cultural group) first exists as a separately definable entity. Others, like dental age in the child, represent late emerging characteristics and cannot be measured individually or averaged into an "organismic age" until they first appear.

4. Use of the cross-cultural method in the behavioral sciences, with statistical techniques employed to test theory, and recently with a major interest in matters of personality development in different cultures. Anthropology may contribute especially to the methods of studying child rearing through: (a) the concept of the culture complex, with its analysis of values, beliefs, techniques, justifications, and rationalizations; and (b) comparative study of child life in non-European societies, with identification of important variables that may have been overlooked and may prove useful in prediction of behavior.

5. Formulation of basic principles for analysis and interpretation of genetic data. A basic continuity characterizes human psychological development, in the sense that patterns of personality and adjustment once established tend to persist over long periods of time, although environmental or constitutional factors or circumstances, under certain conditions, might alter the growth trends of particular individuals. The interrelatedness of developmental trends is noted in the positive correlation of desirable traits and in a certain unity of growth.

6. Further progress in identification of maturity traits and gradients of growth, stages of development or maturity, and developmental tasks. A developmental task is one which "arises at or about a certain period in the life of the individual, successful achievement of which leads to his happiness and to success with later tasks, while failure leads to unhappiness in the individual, disapproval by society, and difficulty with later tasks."[48]

7. Increased interest and recently devised procedures in certain major areas of development (physical, mental, social, personality, learning, and old age). Apparatus and procedures are now available for careful study of children's learning, with considerable work already completed on conditioning, discrimination learning, rote verbal and motor learning, and concept formation. As a goal for the future, incorporation of the attitudes and values of children into more general developmental theory would be valuable to both developmental and social psychology.

8. To cite an example involving the maturation of scientists, interviews with eminent research scientists in the biological sciences, physical sciences, and

[48] Robert J. Havighurst, "Research on the Developmental-Task Concept." *School Review* 64: 215–23; May 1956.

social sciences in 1947-49 and with the same men in 1962-63 revealed that the life of an established scientist changes little over the years, unless he goes into administration. These men continued their contributions at a high level in their chosen fields, and remained happy in their work.[49]

SELECTED REFERENCES

AMES, Louise Bates, and ILG, Frances L. *Mosaic Patterns of American Children*. New York: Harper & Row, Publishers, Inc., 1962. v + 297 p.

AUSUBEL, David P., and Others. "Growth, Development, and Learning." *Review of Educational Research* 31: 445–572; December 1961.

BIRREN, James E. *Relations of Development and Aging*. Springfield, Ill.: Charles C Thomas, 1964. x + 296 p.

COLADARCI, Arthur P., and Others. "Growth, Development, and Learning." *Review of Educational Research* 34: 495–618; December 1964.

GOOD, Carter V. *Introduction to Educational Research: Methodology of Design in the Behavioral and Social Sciences*. Second Edition. New York: Appleton-Century-Crofts, 1963. Chapter 6.

HARRIS, D. B., Editor. *The Concept of Development: An Issue in the Study of Human Behavior*. Minneapolis: University of Minnesota Press, 1957. x + 287 p.

HOFFMAN, Martin L., and HOFFMAN, Lois W., Editors. *Review of Child Development Research*. Vol. 1. New York: Russell Sage Foundation, 1964. ix + 547 p.

KAPLAN, Bert, Editor. *Studying Personality Cross-culturally*. New York: Harper & Row, Publishers, Inc., 1961. x + 687 p.

LEVIN, Harry, MELTZER, Nancy S., and Others. "Educational Programs: Early and Middle Childhood." *Review of Educational Research* 35: 103–64; April 1965.

LINDZEY, Gardner. *Projective Techniques and Cross-Cultural Research*. New York: Appleton-Century-Crofts, 1962. ix + 339 p.

LIPSITT, Lewis P., and SPIKER, Charles C., Editors. *Advances in Child Development and Behavior*. Vol. 1. New York: Academic Press, Inc., 1964. xiii + 387 p.

MUSSEN, Paul H., Editor. *Handbook of Research Methods in Child Development*. New York: John Wiley & Sons, Inc., 1960. x + 1061 p.

NORTHROP, F. S. C., and LIVINGSTON, Helen H., Editors. *Cross-Cultural Understanding: Epistemology in Anthropology*. New York: Harper and Row, Publishers, Inc., 1964. xvi + 396 p.

RITCHIE, Oscar W., and KOLLER, Marvin R. *Sociology of Childhood*. New York: Appleton-Century-Crofts, 1964. x + 333 p.

WHITING, Beatrice B., Editor. *Six Cultures: Studies of Child Rearing*. New York: John Wiley & Sons, Inc., 1963. viii + 1017 p.

[49] Anne Roe, "Changes in Scientific Activities with Age." *Science* 150: 313–18; October 15, 1965.

7

The Individual and Case Study

DIAGNOSIS AND THERAPY

This chapter presents the several types of case study, applications and uses of clinical and case techniques, sequence or stages
in case study and case work (symptoms, examination and history, diagnosis, therapy, and follow-up), clinical and case records, ethical standards, relationship between case-clinical and
statistical methods, and illustrative case histories.

Types of Case Study: Individuals, Institutions, Communities

THE BASIC APPROACH OF THE CASE STUDY IS TO DEAL WITH ALL PERTINENT
aspects of one thing or situation, with the unit for study an individual,
a social institution or agency such as a family or a hospital, or a community or cultural group such as a rural village, a steel town, or a trailer
camp, as illustrated by numerous titles in the literature. The case is some
phase of the life history of the unit of attention, or it may represent the
entire life process.

Case studies of individuals may be an autobiography of a mental patient or of a criminal, a personal account of a psychoanalysis, a biography
of child development, an autobiography of an evolving philosophy and
psychology of teaching, or the childhood and youth of a prodigy.

Case studies have been made of such social institutions or agencies as
the family, marriage, a higher institution of learning, a hospital clinic,
and a movie.

Case studies of communities or cultural groups have included such
units as a rural village, an industrial community, a war-boom community,
a factory setting, a ghetto, and a trailer camp. Certain community studies
mentioned in the chapter on descriptive-survey research may also serve
as examples of the case approach.

A distinction sometimes is made between case study, case work, and
case method. From the point of view of research, case study means intensive investigation of the case unit, especially with respect to initial status
or symptoms, collection of explanatory data, and diagnosis or identifica-

tion of causal factors, looking toward remedial or developmental treatment. Case work frequently is interpreted as the process of therapy and follow-up in relation to developmental, adjustment, or remedial procedures. Although case study and case work frequently are done by different persons or agencies, they are complementary. The case method of instruction is a plan of organizing and presenting materials in such fields as law, medicine, social work, psychology, and education, based on case materials produced through case-study investigation.

Applications and Uses[1]

Case-study procedures have been extensively followed in such fields as law and juvenile delinquency, medicine, psychiatry, psychology, education, counseling and guidance, anthropology, sociology, social work, economics, business administration, political science, and journalism. Although case study was once limited primarily to problems of maladjustment, such as truancy or failure in school, a broken or poverty-stricken home, or an underprivileged or malfunctioning community, this approach more recently has been extended to investigation of normal or bright children, successful institutions and agencies, and well-organized communities or effectively functioning cultural groups. Case study has been helpful in providing classifications or categories of individuals referred to such agencies as a bureau of juvenile research or a juvenile court; information on social and institutional group patterns in families, schools, and communities; case materials for teaching purposes; supplementary interpretations and illustrations for statistical findings; and generalizations through the accumulation of careful case reports, especially in the field of medicine.

The usefulness of the clinical and case approach may be illustrated by the field of clinical psychology in general, and more specifically by personality study and counseling psychology. Clinical psychologists perform a variety of services in many settings, dealing with a wide range of human problems. However, within this apparent diversity of clinical psychology there is considerable unity. Psychologists first try to achieve an understanding, based on the hypotheses and techniques of their professional field of knowledge. Then they apply their understanding, so as to help the people help themselves, with such activities frequently labeled "diagnosis" and "therapy." Clinical psychology has grown not so much by the invention of new basic functions as by the extension and develop-

[1] Eli A. Rubinstein and Maurice Lorr, Editors, *Survey of Clinical Practice in Psychology.* New York: International Universities Press, 1954. xvii + 363 p.

Arthur Burton and Robert E. Harris, Editors, *Clinical Studies of Personality.* Vol. 2 of Case Histories in Clinical and Abnormal Psychology. New York: Harper & Row, Publishers, Inc., 1955. xiii + 836 p.

ment of fundamental procedures; for example, in the diagnostic area, methods for assessing and describing broader aspects of personality are supplementing the older techniques for testing intelligence and school achievement.

Clinical psychology has been of service in a variety of centers and settings, as represented by especially long-standing service in the psychological clinic at the University of Pennsylvania, the Institute for Juvenile Research for the State of Illinois, the Training School at Vineland in New Jersey, Worcester State Hospital, the Menninger Foundation, and the Wichita Guidance Center. Government agencies with large-scale programs of clinical psychology include the Veterans Administration, United States Army, United States Navy, United States Air Force, and the Public Health Service. Clinical centers concerned primarily with mental-health problems are represented by the medical school psychiatric clinic, the psychological-service center, private clinical practice, the old-age counseling center, the clinic for alcoholics, the student-counseling bureau, and industrial-employee counseling. Clinical centers dealing chiefly with antisocial behavior include the municipal court, the juvenile court and youth authority program, the training school for delinquents, and prison. Clinical centers concerned primarily with educative, remedial, and rehabilitative problems include the rehabilitation center, school system, reading clinic, hearing clinic, and speech clinic.

Several factors have aided the development of case studies of personality:

1. Increased awareness of the incidence of mental illness
2. Increased construction of hospitals and clinics with facilities for psychiatric research
3. Further development of intelligence, word-association, and projective tests
4. Positions in hospitals and clinics for clinical psychologists
5. Use by psychologists of certain concepts and practices developed in medicine, particularly the case method.

Counseling psychology is a specialty within the area broadly designated as applied psychology, and utilizes concepts, tools, and techniques also used by several other specialty groups, notably social, personnel, and clinical psychology. Historically, counseling psychology has drawn upon three distinct movements: vocational guidance, psychological measurement, and personality development.

In many instances case study is supplementary to or related to other investigational procedures. The life history of an individual, of an institution, or of a community resembles historical research in sources and techniques. Case investigation uses many of the data-gathering instruments described in the chapter on descriptive-survey studies. Case and genetic investigations of an individual have common interests in growth and development, although ordinarily the direction of movement in case study is backward, whereas in genetic research the movement is forward as growth takes place.

Sequence or Stages in Case Study and Case Work[2]

The goals of case study and case work include the following characteristics:

1. Continuity of data and procedure, although a logical sequence is not always possible in life situations where the movement of examination, diagnosis, and therapy may be shuttle-like.
2. Completeness and validity of data, covering initial status, examination results, and history.
3. Synthesis in the form of adequate diagnosis and prognosis, although it is recognized that the concepts of nondirective or client-centered therapy tend to minimize the process of diagnosis as a basis for therapy.
4. Relationships with the client and case recording maintained on a confidential basis.

The cycle of complementary steps in case study and case work is as follows:

1. Recognition and determination of the status of the phenomenon to be investigated; for example, reading disability.
2. Collection of data relating to the factors or circumstances associated with the given phenomenon; factors associated with learning difficulty or reading disability may be physical, intellectual, pedagogical, emotional, social, or environmental.
3. Diagnosis or identification of causal factors as a basis for remedial or developmental treatment; defective vision may be the cause of difficulty in reading.
4. Application of remedial or adjustment measures; correctly fitted glasses may remove the cause of the poor performance in reading.
5. Subsequent follow-up to determine the effectiveness of the corrective or developmental measures applied.

Initial Status or Symptoms of the Case

The first step in case study is to identify the unit for investigation in the form of some aspect of behavior, or phase of the life process, or need-situation, as in truancy, delinquency, exceptional talent, or a broken home. Whereas the case has commonly centered on the need-situation

[2] Gordon Hamilton, *Theory and Practice of Social Case Work*. Second Edition. New York: Columbia University Press, 1951. vii + 328 p.

as the unit of attention, client-centered or nondirective therapy has focused attention on the individual or subject. With increased knowledge and improved techniques, cases in new areas have been identified for corrective or developmental treatment; for example, in the field of special education recognizing in turn the need for therapy of the physically handicapped, then cases of low mentality, special talents, and deficiencies in the school subjects, and later the various types of social maladjustment or culturally disadvantaged involving personality difficulties and behavior disorders. With increased knowledge, cases of child delinquency have become subdivided to represent such problems as parental rejection, parental overprotection, poverty and low social status, emotional immaturity, and rebellion against authority. It is not possible even to count the several types of cases for remedial or developmental attention until the scope of the various categories is defined as a basis for labeling a child as exceptional: the extent of deficiency necessary in vision or hearing to be labeled subnormal, the level of general intelligence or of special talent to be considered superior, and the line between normality and social, emotional, personality, or behavior disorders. Many of the data-gathering instruments and procedures discussed in the chapter on descriptive-survey research are available for the first step of case study and also for later steps, especially in collection of data through the examination and case history.

Examination and History as Sources of Data

Determination or identification of the status of the situation or unit of attention leads into the collection of data through the examination and life history, which suggests that the first and second steps of case study are supplementary. The emphasis in the second stage, however, is on evidence that may serve as a basis for diagnosis through identification of the explanatory or causal factors. This step in case study has available for use the several descriptive-survey instruments and procedures, as well as the life history, biography, autobiography, letters, and diaries. The case study usually includes an examination of psychophysical, health, educational, and mentality factors, as well as a health, school, family, and social history. Certain of the common testing instruments may be characterized briefly.

TESTING INSTRUMENTS[3]

Intelligence-testing in modern clinical psychology is far more than the automatic administration of routine test procedures. It involves a

[3] L. A. Pennington and Irwin A. Berg, Editors, *An Introduction to Clinical Psychology*. Second Edition. New York: The Ronald Press Company, 1954. p. 154–55, 181, 215.

judicious choice of instruments, precise knowledge of the characteristics of intelligence scales, skill in interpreting test results, ability to evaluate the results of highly controversial research, and formulation of insightful hypotheses to account for a patient's behavior. In short, the clinician is both a proficient laboratory experimenter and an impartial, understanding observer of human behavior.

From personality, interest, and achievement tests the clinician secures information which often can be gathered from no other source. Scores from these inventories may suggest hypotheses to the clinical psychologist, who must then verify them and integrate his data into an adequate descriptive picture of his patient for the purposes of diagnostic, prognostic, and treatment problems.

Projective methods utilize ambiguous stimuli to which subjects are encouraged to respond freely in their own way, as illustrated by ink blots, pictures, art and drama media, and paper-and-pencil techniques. It is assumed that attention is selective and that perception is motivated by the wishes and attitudes of the responding person, with the result that the content perceived and the manner of organizing the material reveal significant dynamic aspects of personality (useful for diagnosis, prognosis, and research).

LIFE HISTORY

As sources of data for case study, from an analytical rather than an historical approach, more frequent and better use may well be made of such personal documents as the life history, biography, autobiography, diaries and journals, letters, records of dreams, and expressive interviews. Such personal materials include retrospective autobiographies, contemporaneous life histories, and episodic and topical documents. Data obtained from personal documents may make a contribution by way of supplementing ecological and statistical information, so as to provide a more inclusive interpretation of the problem, and may serve as a basis for prediction of human behavior.

As a longitudinal observation of culture, the life history emphasizes the natural history of the individual, his reactions to early social stimuli which have led to development of attitudes and values, evolution of a philosophy of life, personal experiences, anecdotes, mental and social conflicts, crises, adjustments, accommodations, and release of tensions. As an intimate personal document or confession which records through introspection inward stresses and attitudes rather than external events, the life history differs from the usual autobiography secured from famous persons (with one eye on publication). The life history, dealing with individuals who have encountered mental and social crises or conflict situations, does not stress judgments of merit. The subject may tell his own story or an interviewer may record the life history, as "a deliberate attempt to define the growth of a person in a cultural milieu and to make theoretical sense of it." Basic criteria for evaluating the life-history approach have been stated in a pioneer study:[4]

1. The subject must be viewed as a specimen in a cultural series.
2. The organic motors of action ascribed must be socially relevant.
3. The peculiar role of the family group in transmitting the culture must be recognized.
4. The specific method of elaboration of organic materials into social behavior must be shown.
5. The continuous related character of experience from childhood through adulthood must be stressed.
6. The social situation must be carefully and continuously specified as a factor.
7. The life-history material itself must be organized and conceptualized.

The purposes and procedures of a classic life history or autobiography may be helpful as background for understanding this approach:[5]

1. To prepare a relatively full and reliable account of an individual's experience and development from birth on, or a comprehensive life history emphasizing personality problems
2. To accumulate and arrange in natural order a socially and culturally oriented record of an individual in a "primitive society" for the purpose of developing and checking certain hypotheses in the field of culture.
3. To attempt at least a partial interpretation of the individual's development and behavior
4. To utilize the investigation for the formulation of generalizations and the testing of theories in the field of individual behavior with respect to society and culture (reserved for further study).

AUTOBIOGRAPHY, BIOGRAPHY, AND DIARIES

Autobiography, biography, and diaries have been resorted to frequently as sources in historical studies. Autobiography as historical narration and the diaries of distinguished persons who have anticipated publication usually have been relatively formal documents. The movement in autobiography and biography is backward (written in retrospect), whereas the movement in a diary is forward, with entries recorded as events take place. Autobiography contributes to case study through providing the life history of an individual, a tribe, race, or community; is helpful in studying reticent or resistant persons; is economical for use in

---

[4] John Dollard, *Criteria for the Life History*. New Haven: Yale University Press, 1935. p. 3. Reprinted in 1949 by Peter Smith.

[5] Leo W. Simmons, Editor, *Sun Chief: The Autobiography of a Hopi Indian*. New Haven: Yale University Press, for the Institute of Human Relations, 1942. xii + 460 p.

groups; and may serve therapeutic purposes for the subject by release of tensions and insight into his own life. Diaries kept without undue concern for publication may reveal interests, desires, tensions, and conflicts not apparent in the more formal autobiography (usually written for publication), although the persons who keep diaries and permit their use are a rather select group of individuals. The general principles of historical research apply in dealing with personal documents.

To cite as an example the autobiography of an educator, Spaulding has written in two volumes what is substantially his life history to the end of his administrative work in the public schools. The first volume[6] carries the story to the completion of his graduate study in Europe and at Clark University, including early life on a farm in New Hampshire, schooling in the district and college-preparatory schools in New England, four years at Amherst College, a doctoral program at the University of Leipzig, and postdoctoral year at Clark University. The second volume[7] is substantially an anecdotal history or case study of the development of the city superintendency during the first quarter of the twentieth century. It is the story of the evolution and application of a philosophy of education to the organization and administration of the public schools. The individual probably is not fully aware of the pattern and sources of his own philosophy until he attempts what Spaulding has done in his autobiography or life history.

Another autobiography is the story of an 81-year-old man who began to teach at the age of seventeen in a one-teacher school in Pennsylvania in 1891. His long years of service were as teacher, principal, superintendent, and teacher or executive in 17 American colleges in 10 states, as author, organizer of professional groups, editor, and lecturer before many thousands of educational and professional groups. The autobiography is to a considerable extent an anecdotal history of education and of the education of teachers, covering almost the entire modern period of educational history and teacher education during the twentieth century. Here are the beginnings of teaching as a profession, the development of small local school systems, the struggles of boards of education on professional problems, the efforts of school administrators to professionalize their staffs in larger cities, and the organization of a program to prepare the professors who staff the teachers colleges.[8]

An especially interesting group of personal documents is an approach

---

[6] Frank E. Spaulding, *One School Administrator's Philosophy: Its Development.* New York: Exposition Press, 1952. 352 p.

[7] Frank E. Spaulding, *School Superintendent in Action in Five Cities.* Rindge, N.H.: Richard R. Smith, 1955. xx + 699 p.

[8] Ambrose L. Suhrie, *Teacher of Teachers.* Rindge, N.H.: Richard R. Smith, 1955. 418 p.

to the history of psychology through the autobiographies of eminent psychologists.[9]

The "autobiography of a schizophrenic" as a descriptive title may be inaccurate, since the author set out to prove that he was never "insane" and perhaps not even mentally ill; yet he does demonstrate that mental illness has been misunderstood and badly mistreated even in some of our better hospitals.[10]

A book of nine word portraits or type-persons or case histories may offer suggestions for similar studies of the teacher, supervisor, administrator, or professor. Bauer and his colleague have created type-persons as they live, think, and act in the Soviet milieu. The data are true, based on interviews with escaped refugees from the Soviet Union who have reported their own experiences and have revealed their knowledge of conditions within their motherland. The portraits are fiction, composites of the data collected, with the smallest amount of fabrication necessary to make them into stories. The nine synthesized types of persons are: the student (three of them), the woman collective farmer, the woman doctor, the Party secretary, the housewife, the writer, the factory director, the tractor driver, and the secret police agent. These portraits are not actual case histories, nor are they even exactly fiction, since the characteristics of the people and the events of their stories are always subordinated to the facts of the records; the persons themselves are synthesized types.[11]

An application of psychoanalytic psychology to the biographical data of famous creative individuals has the two purposes of comprehending the subject of the biography in terms of the dynamic forces of his developmental experience, and of understanding the nature of the creative man and the creative process. For these purposes, the main value of psychoanalytic psychology lies in its ability to analyze and to structure meaningfully highly complex and diverse biographical information, by way of establishing cause-and-effect relationships between the data of infancy, childhood, and adult life.[12]

The biography of an imposing impostor deals with a man, Ferdinand W. Demara, who attained unusual publicity and notoriety. The story leaves many aspects of Demara's behavior only partly explained, but the author had to depend largely on what the subject chose to tell, and

[9] Herbert S. Langfeld and Others, Editors, *A History of Psychology in Autobiography*, Vol. 4. Worcester, Mass.: Clark University Press, 1952. xii + 356 p.

Edwin G. Boring, *Psychologist at Large*. New York: Basic Books, Inc., 1961. 371 p.

[10] William L. Moore, *The Mind in Chains: The Autobiography of a Schizophrenic*. New York: Exposition Press, 1955. 315 p.

[11] Review by Edwin G. Boring, *Contemporary Psychology* 1: 149; May 1956, of Raymond A. Bauer and Edward Wasiolek, *Nine Soviet Portraits*. New York: John Wiley & Sons, Inc., 1955. ix + 190 p.

[12] Edward Hitschmann, *Great Men: Psychoanalytic Studies*. New York: International Universities Press, 1956. xiii + 278 p.

Demara was at one time or another in the interviews temperamental, recalcitrant, grandiose, or unpredictable. The early part of the subject's life, from birth through adolescence, is too briefly told to provide adequate clues to the powerful inner forces and to the family relationships that underlie his later behavior and difficulties. Damara later appeared in Hollywood, the true land of make-believe, where he played eight roles in a film, supervising the filming of his own biography. Subsequently he said that the "Great Impostor is dead," when he was running a house for wayward boys in California known as the "New Life Youth Ranch," with the California State Department of Welfare interested in having a look at its management.[13] In 1966 he was leading a religious life.

Causation and Diagnosis[14]

Diagnosis seeks to formulate a theory or hypothesis of causation, pointed toward the adjustment or development of the individual, institution, or community. Diagnosis and treatment may at times be parallel or even move shuttle-like. Diagnosis is prognostic in recommending therapy, and when adjustment procedures fail, further search for causal factors and a second diagnosis may be necessary. If adjustment proves only temporary, as revealed in the last step of follow-up, further diagnosis and therapy are indicated. For evidence, diagnosis depends on the data gathered in the earlier phases of case study. It has already been indicated in this chapter that nondirective or client-centered therapy minimizes the diagnostic process in advance of psychotherapy, although recognizing the basic necessity for physical diagnosis in dealing with organic disease.

Adequate diagnosis of difficulties must meet certain basic requirements relating to significant objectives, valid evidence of strengths and weaknesses, objectivity, reliability, specificity, comparable and exact data, practicability, and expertness. Most of the data-gathering instruments and procedures described in the chapter on descriptive-survey research can be adapted to provide evidence on which successful diagnosis rests. Diagnosis as an aspect of case study, like other research approaches, finds the problem of causation complex and perplexing. To cite examples, factors that may be associated with learning difficulty are physical, intellectual, pedagogical, emotional, social, and environmental. Causes of poor performance in reading may be perceptual (visual and auditory),

13 Robert Crichton, *The Great Impostor*. New York: Random House, 1959. 218 p.
14 Max L. Hutt, "Diagnosis," *Encyclopedia of Educational Research*. Edited by Chester W. Harris. Third Edition. New York: The Macmillan Co., 1960. p. 376–80.
   Goldine C. Gleser, "Prediction," *Encyclopedia of Educational Research*, p. 1038–46.
   Robert I. Watson, *The Clinical Method in Psychology*. New York: Harper & Row, Publishers, Inc., 1951. p. 21–153, 527–761.
   Robert I. Watson, Editor, "Diagnostic Methods," *Readings in the Clinical Method in Psychology*. New York: Harper & Row, Publishers, Inc., 1949. p. 183–443.

motor, intellectual, linguistic, emotional, and methodological. Factors affecting the behavior of the problem child may be hereditary, physical, mental, familial, economic, cultural, social, and educational. Defects and deviations of development may be in the form of amentia, endocrine disorders, convulsive disorders, neurological defects, cerebral injury, special sensory handicaps, prematurity, precocity, and environmental retardation.[15] It usually is necessary to look beneath the surface to find the basic or primary cause of maladjustment; on the surface we may see only a secondary, tertiary, or contributory cause or condition. For example, difficulty in reading as a primary cause of maladjustment may lead to failure in the school subjects, truancy, and misbehavior (probably only secondary or tertiary factors in this instance).

To cite an example in the area of counseling, school psychologists, guidance specialists, and school social workers need a common knowledge of psychological principles and of educational aims and practices. It is highly desirable that school psychologists be equipped, like competent high-school counselors, to do diagnostic and counseling work. It is equally desirable that counselors, deans, and visiting teachers be better trained in the psychological principles and techniques that are appropriate. The school psychologist may well be an educationally oriented clinical psychologist (in contrast to the medically oriented clinical psychologist), who serves as a diagnostician, therapist, and consultant in the preventive and alleviative work of adjustment.[16]

Therapy and Developmental Adjustment

PURPOSES

The purpose of diagnosis is realized in some form of effective therapy or developmental adjustment. Therapy and follow-up sometimes are labeled as case work, as distinguished from case study or case investigation, and in many instances these later steps are the work of other specialists (as in medicine). It has been indicated earlier that there is no sharp division between the earlier steps of case investigation and diagnosis, and the later phases of therapy and follow-up. In gathering information through the examination and case history, certain treatment or therapy may be possible, and in the stage of treatment additional evidence may appear. The supplementary and cooperative relationships

15 Arnold Gesell and Catherine S. Amatruda, *Developmental Diagnosis: Normal and Abnormal Child Development, Clinical Methods and Practical Applications*. Revised Edition. New York: Harper & Row, Publishers, Inc., 1947. xvi + 496 p.

16 Review by Donald E. Super, *Contemporary Psychology* 2: 35–37; February 1957, of Stanley S. Marzolf, *Psychological Diagnosis and Counseling in the Schools*. New York: Holt, Rinehart and Winston, Inc., 1956. xiv + 401 p.

of the specialists engaged in the several steps of case study and case work may be illustrated by the type of conference frequently arranged for planning the therapy of the problem child, with participation by such workers and agencies as the clinic staff, school, visiting teacher, court, probation officer, child-placing agency, family agency, and children's institution.

Frequently, complex or multiple causation of maladjustment may lead to a diagnosis and to therapy requiring the cooperation of a number of specialists. Child-guidance clinics and mental-hygiene programs, working with problem and delinquent children, have combined the resources of psychiatrists, physicians, psychologists, social workers, sociologists, and sometimes teachers and specialists in the field of education. Adequate treatment in child guidance requires the cooperation of clinic, community, home, school, case-working organization, recreational program, and child-placement agency.

The primary purpose of therapy is development of the potentialities of the individual for growth and improvement. In a learning situation this means focusing of attention on the pupil in relation to a specific difficulty or opportunity for growth rather than on the formal organization of a subject of instruction as such. To cite another illustration, the purposes of social treatment or therapy are concerned with preventing social breakdown, conserving strength, restoring social function, making life more comfortable or compensating, creating opportunities for growth and development, and increasing the capacity for self-direction and social contribution. More specific examples of assistance given to a client by a case worker would include financial aid, help in seeking employment, facilitating health plans, entrance into an appropriate group activity, and modifying the attitudes of associates.

PREVENTIVE MEASURES AND SELF-HELP

Adjustment procedures are outlined in this chapter with recognition of the desirability of preventive measures, as illustrated by current emphases in medicine, dentistry, and the field of health in general. Regular physical and health examinations, including the testing of sight and hearing, may indicate corrective measures which will prevent later maladjustments. Effective programs of education, work, recreation, and guidance in school, home, community, church, and other social institutions and agencies will do much to prevent the maladjustment known as the "youth problem," including juvenile delinquency.

In all forms of therapy, the importance of self-help is recognized, as illustrated by the patient's will or desire to recover from an illness. This basic principle of therapy or treatment is recognized in such concepts as encouraging the subject in his own efforts, thinking things through together, and increasing the capacity for self-understanding and self-direction.

Favorable mental attitudes on the part of specialists, parents, and child contribute materially to the process of therapy. Effective remedial or developmental treatment is based on genuine concern for the well-being of the child or client, cordial relationships of mutual confidence, and understanding and control of prejudices and emotional reactions. Favorable initial attitudes are especially significant in short contacts, as in large school systems and social transient work, where critical decisions may be made in one or two brief interviews; for example, employment of a teacher or arrangements to return a young traveler to her distant home.

The principle of self-help in the process of therapy is illustrated by nondirective or client-centered procedures, which have revealed certain improvements in the subject:[17]

1. Change or movement in therapy, as revealed in the type of verbal comment presented by the client; for example, from talk about his problems and symptoms, to insightful statements showing some self-understanding of relationship between his past and current behavior, to discussion of new actions in accord with his new understanding of the situation.

2. Change in the client's perception of and attitude toward self: (a) sees himself as a more adequate person, with increased worth and greater possibility of meeting life; (b) draws on more experiential data, thus achieving a more realistic appraisal of himself, his relationships, and environment; (c) tends to place the basis of standards or values within himself rather than in the experience or perceptual object.

TREATMENT OF LEARNING DIFFICULTIES

Basic principles underlying therapy or treatment of learning difficulties are as follows:[18]

1. *Treatment must be based on a diagnosis.*
   a. Locate weaknesses that require correction.
   b. Establish the type of treatment needed.
   c. Clearly formulate the remedial program.
   d. Modify the program as may be advisable.
   e. Use a variety of remedial techniques.
   f. The child should help formulate the program of treatment.

[17] Carl R. Rogers, *Client-Centered Therapy: Its Current Practice, Implications, and Theory.* Boston: Houghton Mifflin Company, 1951. p. 131–96.
   Robert I. Watson, *The Clinical Method in Psychology,* p. 21–153, 527–761.
[18] Leo J. Brueckner and Guy L. Bond, *The Diagnosis and Treatment of Learning Difficulties.* New York: Appleton-Century-Crofts, 1955. p. 77–100.

2. *The child's personal worth must be considered.*
    a. Avoid stigmatizing pupils in classification and grouping.
    b. Consider the child's emotional state.
    c. Correct faulty attitudes.
    d. Recognize the importance of group as well as individual work.
3. *Corrective treatment must be individualized.*
    a. Outcomes and methods should be commensurate with the child's ability.
    b. Treatment should be specific and not general.
    c. Fatigue should be noted and practice spaced.
4. *The program must be well motivated and encouraging to the child.*
    a. The teacher must be optimistic.
    b. Success of the student must be emphasized.
    c. Errors should be pointed out in a positive way.
    d. Growth should be made apparent to the child.
    e. Treatment should not conflict with other enjoyable activities.
    f. Purpose should always be established.
    g. The results of the learning experience should be utilized and evaluated.
5. *Materials and exercises must be carefully selected.*
    a. Materials must be suitable in level of difficulty and type.
    b. Materials must be suitable in interest and format.
    c. Materials must be abundant and not artificial.
6. *The entire environment of the child must be considered.*
    a. Adjustments must be made in the child's school program.
    b. The home environment must be favorable.
7. *Continuous evaluations must be made.*
    a. A cumulative record must be kept.
    b. A follow-up is necessary.
8. *Sound teaching procedures must be utilized in the treatment of learning difficulties.*

PRINCIPLES AND TECHNIQUES OF PSYCHOTHERAPY

All systems of psychotherapy involve in varying measures certain kinds of experiences, and the effectiveness of a particular form of therapy depends on the extent to which it provides opportunities for the client "to experience closeness to another human being without getting hurt, to divest symbols associated with traumatic experiences of their anxiety producing potential, to use the transference situation to learn not to need neurotic distortions, to practice being responsible for himself, and to clarify an old or learn a new cognitive system for ordering his world."[19]

Psychotherapy involves difficulties, in that our diagnostic instruments fall short of desirable standards of validity and reliability. We are uncomfortably aware of elements of truth behind the facetious characterization of psychotherapy as "the art of applying a science which does

[19] Nicholas Hobbs, "Sources of Gain in Psychotherapy." *American Psychologist* 17: 741–47; November 1962.

not yet exist," although our therapeutic anxiety is relieved somewhat by dependence on the best available techniques and procedures of psycho-diagnosis.[20]

Psychotherapy is limited or handicapped by the tendency of some clinicians, teachers, and students to overemphasize certain approaches at the expense of others, thus failing to recognize at least three major sources of error in therapy:[21]

1. No single approach to psychotherapy has been found that can explain the behavior of all individuals or is pertinent to all persons.
2. An individual with a specific problem may fail to respond to a single type of therapy; as the individual's needs change the therapeutic techniques must be changed, if the patient is to derive maximum benefit.
3. Since therapists differ in personality structure, need systems, and value systems, the therapeutic techniques must be suited to the needs of the therapist.

Psychological research has identified the wide range of individual differences in physical, intellectual, pedagogical, emotional, social, and environmental factors that must be considered in diagnosis and therapy. To illustrate by a specific example, variations in the treatment of children with individual problems of adjustment include: (1) change of environment through the foster home or institutional placement; (2) modification of environment through adjustments in the parents' attitudes, family relationships, school and instructional program, clubs, groups, and camps; and (3) treatment of the individual through a variety of therapeutic approaches, including psychoanalysis, nondirective interviewing and therapy, group psychotherapy, projective techniques, play therapy, physical treatment, occupational therapy, psychodrama, sociodrama, and hypnodrama.

The variety and complexity of the problems of clinical and case study may be illustrated in further detail from the field of psychotherapy. The varieties of psychotherapy include supportive therapy, insight therapy with re-educative goals, and insight therapy with reconstructive goals.[22]

Among the techniques and procedures utilized in supportive therapy are guidance, environmental manipulation, externalization of interests, reassurance, prestige suggestion, pressure and coercion, persuasion, emotional catharsis and desensitization, muscular relaxation, hydrotherapy,

[20] Paul E. Meehl, "The Cognitive Activity of the Clinician." *American Psychologist* 15: 19–27; January 1960.

[21] James L. McCary and Daniel E. Sheer, Editors, *Six Approaches to Psychotherapy.* New York: Holt, Rinehart and Winston, Inc., 1955. p. 4–5.

[22] Lewis R. Wolberg, *The Technique of Psychotherapy.* New York: Grune and Stratton, 1954. xiv + 869 p.

drug therapy, shock and convulsive therapy, and inspirational group therapy.

Insight therapy with re-educative therapeutic approaches includes "relationship therapy," "attitude therapy," distributive analysis and synthesis, interview psychotherapy, therapeutic counseling, therapeutic casework, reconditioning, re-educative group therapy, semantic therapy, and bibliotherapy.

Insight therapy with reconstructive goals includes the three main "types": "Freudian psychoanalysis," "non-Freudian psychoanalysis," and "psychoanalytically oriented psychotherapy."

Supportive, re-educative, and reconstructive therapies have certain similarities and differences with respect to the duration of therapy, frequency of visits, taking of detailed histories, routine psychologic examinations, kinds of communications obtained from the patient, general activity of the therapist, frequency of advice-giving to the patient, handling of transference, general relationship of the patient to the therapist, physical position of the patient during therapy, handling of dream material, and adjuncts utilized during treatment.

The beginning phase of treatment in psychotherapy includes a number of problems relating to the initial interview: the first contact with the patient, collating essential data, making a diagnosis, formulating the tentative dynamics, estimating the prognosis, estimating the patient's general condition, making practical arrangements for psychotherapy, securing essential consultations, and dealing with inadequate motivation.

The principal techniques by which the therapist helps the patient in the acquisition of insight include interview procedures, free association, dream analysis, and the examination of attitudes toward the therapist (including transference).

In the terminal phase of psychotherapy, success is judged from the standpoint of the patient, of society, and of the therapist, and in terms of the "ideal" objectives of mental health.

Adjunctive aids in psychotherapy include group therapy, hypnotherapy, narcotherapy, and bibliotherapy.

Among the emergencies that sometimes develop during psychotherapy which require prompt and cautious handling are: suicidal attempts; psychotic attacks; excitement, overactivity, and antisocial behavior; panic states; acute alcoholic intoxication; acute barbiturate poisoning; severe psychosomatic symptoms; and intercurrent incurable somatic illness.

Certain kinds of conditions make extensive therapeutic objectives difficult to achieve, and require specific techniques or combinations of methods, especially in dealing with problems often encountered in the treatment of the different neurotic, psychophysiologic, personality, and psychotic disorders.

Group psychotherapy has been used to good effect with patients suffering from a variety of psychosomatic disorders and with addicts, alcoholics, stutterers, unmarried mothers, mothers of emotionally disturbed children, delinquents, and the aged. It has been of value in mental hospitals, child guidance, family service, marital counseling agencies, community mental-health programs, and industry. As a rule, group psychotherapists have been more willing than individual therapists to record their sessions by mechanical and observational methods, which augurs well for improvement of the therapeutic process and for future development of group psychotherapy.[23]

The literature includes many full-length treatments of therapy, some of which are listed in the chapter bibliography.

Follow-up

The final stage in case and clinical work is follow-up to determine whether the treatment is successful, as illustrated by the physician's attention to the patient during the stage of convalescence. Failure to make satisfactory progress following treatment may require a new diagnosis and another form of therapy. It is common to utilize the techniques of experimentation in evaluating the success of treatment, especially in the field of medicine. By way of a pioneer example of follow-up, case study has been used as one approach in following a group of bright children over a period of years through school into maturity.[24] The school, home, and other environmental conditions may be thought of as the therapy or treatment for the bright children, with a follow-up to determine the adjustment of the subjects after reaching maturity.

Clinical and Case Records[25]

DESIRABLE CHARACTERISTICS

Adequate case records serve useful purposes in treatment, especially when the regular worker or client moves to another locality, or when a case is reopened; as a medium for study of social problems; and for instructional materials in training students. Adequate records possess the

23 Review by Norman A. Polansky, *Social Service Review* 30: 372–73; September 1956, of S. R. Slavson, Editor, *The Fields of Group Psychotherapy.* New York: International Universities Press, 1956. xiii + 338 p.

24 Lewis M. Terman and Melita H. Oden, *The Gifted Child Grows Up: Genetic Studies of Genius.* Stanford, Calif.: Stanford University Press, 1947. xiv + 450 p.

25 Gordon Hamilton, *Principles of Social Case Recording.* New York: Columbia University Press, 1946. vii + 142 p.

Kenneth R. Hammond and Jeremiah M. Allen, *Writing Clinical Reports.* Englewood Cliffs, N.J.: Prentice-Hall, Inc., 1953. p. 169–231.

attributes of accuracy and objectivity, conciseness and clarity, ease of reference and visibility, and uniformity and "up-to-dateness," with suitable provision for cumulative recording of interviews, the narrative, letters, anecdotal information, summaries, and interpretation and treatment.

Accuracy goes beyond the recording of information as received, in order to insure the correctness of the data in relation to the truth, as discussed in the chapter on the historical method (with respect to the reliability of witnesses and the criticism of documents).

Effective recording in case study, like adequate reporting in any area of investigation, must be an active process of attention and discriminating selection from a considerable mass of materials, with a balance to strike somewhere between the completeness necessary for objectivity and the brevity essential for clarity. Many of the comments of the chapter on technical reporting and of the section on note-taking in the chapter on library usage are appropriate and suggestive in case-recording and in the preparation of case reports. Uniformity of records within the agency, institution, or school system, and between similar social or educational services in different territories, facilitates research, interchange of information, and ready use.

With respect to the recording of interviews in case study, the discussions of interviewing and of mechanical techniques of observation and recording in the descriptive-survey chapter are pertinent. In social case-recording, the narrative usually begins with the first interview. When conditions are favorable, the first interview should be reasonably complete. It is relatively simple to record information concerning identity, address, legal residence, financial status, and units of food, shelter, or education, but both interviewing and recording become more complex in dealing with human relationships and with the related process and movement within the interview.

The narrative or running record in case study may be entered either chronologically or topically, or by some appropriate combination, as discussed in the chapter on historical writing. In chronological recording, the contacts and interviews are entered in diary fashion as they occur, although some marginal headings may give a superficial appearance of topical organization. The chronological narrative may have large subdivisions corresponding approximately with the case-study stages of initial status, examination, diagnosis, therapy, and follow-up. These large headings also are suitable for topical or thematic organization of materials. Topical recording combines and condenses information from a number of contacts or interviews under such large themes as family and home setting, neighborhood and group life, cultural background, education, recreational activities and interests, health, mental attitude, occupation, and income and resources. Topical recording presents original data or subject matter, whereas the several types of "summaries" condense and point up material which has previously appeared in the record.

Since letters and written reports frequently serve as substitutes for direct contacts in the form of personal visits and interviews, they are an important part of case records, especially as a medium of communication between social-work, medical, clinical, legal, and educational agencies. Letters and reports today stress the immediate situation and the therapy or adjustment rather than present a complete summary of the case. Certain forms or blanks have been developed for routine types of communication between agencies, especially between the public schools and other social agencies.

CUMULATIVE AND ANECDOTAL RECORDS[26]

Clinical work and case study, as well as counseling in the schools, depend to a large extent on the data in cumulative records, including anecdotal records. The cumulative record is maintained for a client or pupil over a considerable period of time, usually a number of years, with additions to the record at relatively frequent intervals; for example, marks in the school subjects, educational and aptitude test scores, social and character ratings, school attendance, health, home conditions and family history, participation in the activities program, interests, and attitudes. Cumulative records are useful in meeting instructional needs, for discovery of causes of behavior difficulties and failures, identification of talents and special abilities, placement, and counseling on a variety of problems.

To summarize, important items to be included as a part of cumulative records are as follows:

1. Autobiography, including family background, home and neighborhood environment

[26] Wendell C. Allen, *Cumulative Pupil Records: A Plan for Staff Study and Improvement of Cumulative Pupil Records in Secondary Schools.* New York: Teachers College, Columbia University, 1943. 69 p.

Joan Bollenbacher, "Student Records and Reports—Elementary and Secondary," *Encyclopedia of Educational Research,* p. 1437–41.

Royce E. Brewster, "The Cumulative Record." *School Life* 42: 16–17; September 1959.

Melvene D. Hardee, "Student Records and Reports—College and University," *Encyclopedia of Educational Research,* p. 1433–36.

A. E. Hamalainen, *An Appraisal of Anecdotal Records.* Contributions to Education, No. 891. New York: Teachers College, Columbia University, 1943. 88 p.

Gordon Hamilton, *op. cit.*

Kenneth R. Hammond and Jeremiah M. Allen, *op. cit.*

Judith I. Krugman and J. Wayne Wrightstone, *A Guide to the Use of Anecdotal Records.* Educational Research Bulletin of the Bureau of Reference, Research and Statistics, No. 11. New York: Board of Education, May 1949. 33 p.

A. E. Traxler, *The Nature and Use of Anecdotal Records.* Revised Edition. Educational Records Supplementary Bulletin D. New York: Educational Record Bureau, 1949. p. 4–8.

2. Health history, including physical and medical examination data
3. Standardized test records
4. School marks
5. Anecdotal items
6. Participation in cocurricular activities
7. Work experience.

In filing all pertinent information concerning the individual in one place as a unit, a folder is essential for samples of school work, test forms, behavior deviations, and adjustment or treatment procedures. Child-guidance clinics for example, have sought especially to integrate into a unit record the medical, psychological, psychiatric, social, and also the school evidence.

Anecdotal materials have come to be a significant part of the cumulative record. A type of cumulative individual record which emphasizes episodes of behavior important in the development of character or personality is known as the anecdotal-behavior journal. These anecdotes include not only maladjustment, but also positive and constructive episodes, the admirable behavior of well-adjusted pupils, and the outstanding accomplishments of the superior or talented. The anecdote as a revealing episode of conduct is in the form of a word picture or verbal snapshot. To be most helpful, anecdotes should possess the characteristics of objectivity, factual emphasis, clarity, and subjectivity (in the sense that an artistically composed photograph is subjective, with a center of attention and with subordination of inconsequential details). Anecdotal records serve useful purposes by way of mutual understanding between faculty and pupils, counseling relationships, curriculum development, appraisal of outcomes, and case instruction in professional programs for preparation of teachers and others.

Although highly standardized or formalized procedures are incompatible with the nature of anecdotal recording, certain steps or sequential stages are desirable in introducing the plan into a school:[27]

1. Enlisting the cooperation of the faculty, including counselors, and development of an understanding and acceptance of the ideal of individualized education.
2. Deciding how much should be expected of observers who write anecdotes, possibly a reasonable minimum number per week.
3. Preparing forms, which are usually very simple, as illustrated by forms in current use; an outline adapted to most situations provides blank spaces for identifying the pupil, class, and observer, with separate columns for date, incident, and comment.

[27] Judith I. Krugman and J. Wayne Wrightstone, *op. cit.,* p. 8–14, 23–24.
Arthur E. Traxler, *op. cit.,* p. 9–22.

4. Obtaining the original records, including a plan for jotting down the name of the pupil and an appropriate catch word at the time of the incident, with a period set aside toward the end of the day for recording the anecdotes concerning significant behavior episodes observed during the day; a reasonable, although not equal, distribution of anecdotes among the pupils is desirable.

5. Central filing, as emphasized in the earlier discussions of cumulative records, in order that incidents described by different observers over a period of time may be assembled and compared to note trends.

6. Periodic summarizing, preferably under topical headings, as recommended earlier in the discussion of case-recording.

Certain precautions and procedures are essential in dealing with problems which frequently arise in the preparation of anecdotes:[28]

1. Accuracy and objectivity in observation and in recording are imperative, as emphasized in the discussion of case-recording; statements of opinion must be separated from the report of the incident itself.

2. Anecdotal records should not be used as a defense mechanism by the teacher to justify some action on his part, such as loss of temper or harsh discipline.

3. In many instances, a brief description of the background against which a behavior incident occurred is necessary, since there is a grave danger of misinterpretation in isolating an episode from its social setting.

4. In summarizing and interpreting anecdotal records, one must be on guard against acceptance of a relatively small number of anecdotes as a valid picture of the total behavior pattern of the pupil; an understandable picture is based on some degree of repetition of similar behavior reported from a number of situations in different areas of conduct.

5. As in case study in general, anecdotal records must have professional and confidential treatment, in order that unfortunate behavior incidents may not prejudice the future adjustment and success of the pupils represented.

6. A workable plan for handling the load of clerical work and for summarizing anecdotes is necessary before a school commits itself to the writing of anecdotes.

7. Urgent needs for adjustment, as revealed through anecdotes, should not encourage hasty generalizations and should not be used as excuses for short cuts in personality adaptation, which is usually a long-term process.

8. Observers should strive to record evidence of growth and favorable adjustment even more diligently than examples of undesirable behavior.

9. Teachers must be on guard against overemphasizing inconsistencies in behavior or incidents that are not at all typical of the behavior of the particular pupil; sometimes behavior at the beginning of the school year is atypical, although anecdotes recorded during the first few weeks may possess some significance as single incidents for understanding the pupil;

[28] Judith I. Krugman and J. Wayne Wrightstone, *op. cit.*, p. 3–5, 15–20.
Arthur E. Traxler, *op. cit.*, p. 22–26.

however, without repetition episodes give little insight for determining developmental patterns of behavior, and deviations cannot be recognized until the usual patterns have been established through a repetition of incidents in different situations.

Ethical Standards

Since the primary function of records is to render treatment of the case more effective in terms of adjustment of the client, and to serve community interests in dealing with social problems, the ethical implications of case-recording are important. It may be wise to omit personal or nonessential information of a confidential nature that throws little light on diagnosis and therapy, although other possibilities or alternatives are to inform the client in advance of the nature and use of case records, to label such personal material "confidential," or to assume that all case records are confidential and will be so treated. Problems arise in deciding what use to make of evidence concerning the efficiency of staff members, the mistakes of fellow workers, and the policies of the agency or institution. Accuracy and objectivity require that the facts be entered in the record, where they usually speak for themselves, and may prove useful in improvement of both staff and program. Workers must keep within their own bounds of training and experience in making diagnoses and interpretations; for example, a teacher may communicate certain objective facts concerning a pupil's health or mental level, but diagnosis and treatment usually must be left to the physician or psychologist. Safeguarding of confidential records is a heavy responsibility, and ordinarily professional workers will not risk using case records outside the office where they are filed.

The ethical standards of psychologists involve nineteen specific principles relating to responsibility, competence, moral and legal standards, misrepresentation, public statements, confidentiality, client welfare, client relationship, impersonal services, announcement of services, interprofessional relations, remuneration, test security, test interpretation, test publication, research precautions, publication credit, responsibility toward organization, and promotional activities.[29]

As to diagnosis and therapy, a serious quandary may confront clinical psychologists both in the operation of a clinic and in the administration of a training program for graduate students. To what extent may one clinical installation or another be unintentionally sacrificing the treatment of patients to their use as data in experiments or to their manipulation through recordings and observations for the training of the students,

29 "Ethical Standards of Psychologists." *American Psychologist* 18: 56–60; January 1963.

with only marginal thought given to the welfare of the patient?[30] It is agreed that clinical psychologists must have opportunities to conduct experimental and case studies and to verify psychotherapeutic hypotheses. They also must develop criteria or guide lines to determine whether a patient's ethical rights are being observed and whether sound therapy is occurring in situations providing research evidence and training for therapists.

Relation Between Case-Clinical and Statistical Methods

A major problem of methodology in clinical psychology is to determine the relation between the clinical and the statistical or actuarial methods of prediction. In the actuarial or statistical type of prediction, we may classify the subject on the basis of objective facts from his life history, his scores on psychometric tests, behavior ratings or check lists, or possibly subjective judgments secured from interviews. We check this classification against a statistical or actuarial table which gives the statistical frequencies of behavior of various sorts for persons belonging to the particular class.

In the clinical or case-study method of prediction, we may arrive at some psychological hypothesis regarding the structure and dynamics of a particular individual, on the basis of interview impressions, other data from the life history, and possibly certain psychometric information, as in a psychiatric staff conference.

Various terms are applied to the method or approach preferred; for example, those who favor the statistical method have referred to it as "operational, communicable, verifiable, public, objective, reliable, behavioral, testable, rigorous, scientific, precise, careful, trustworthy, experimental, quantitative, down-to-earth, hardheaded, empirical, mathematical, and sound." Those who dislike the statistical method have labeled it as "mechanical, atomistic, additive, cut-and-dried, artificial, unreal, arbitrary, incomplete, dead, pedantic, fractionated, trivial, forced, static, superficial, rigid, sterile, academic, oversimplified, pseudoscientific, and blind."

The clinical method, on the other hand, is labeled by its proponents as "dynamic, global, meaningful, holistic, subtle, sympathetic, configural, patterned, organized, rich, deep, genuine, sensitive, sophisticated, real, living, concrete, natural, true to life, and understanding." The critics of the clinical method are likely to view it as "mystical, transcendent, metaphysical, supermundane, vague, hazy, subjective, unscientific, unreliable, crude, private, unverifiable, qualitative, primitive, prescientific,

[30] Harriet E. O'Shea, "Research and Training: Are They Sometimes Sirens Leading Therapy Astray?" *Journal of Psychology* 48: 103–5; July 1959.

sloppy, uncontrolled, careless, verbalistic, intuitive, and muddleheaded."[31]

It is a common error to group together the terms *quantitative, statistical,* and *experimental,* setting them in opposition to *qualitative, clinical,* and *nonexperimental.* Some phenomena of behavior cannot be studied satisfactorily in the laboratory, and some quantification of clinical evidence is desirable. What we need is a balanced approach in selecting techniques appropriate for the problem at hand.

Can a clinician, as an applied member of the field of psychology, call himself a scientist? Students find themselves caught in this dilemma, generally about the beginning of their second graduate year, and prove to be an irritating source of questions like: "How can I be a scientist when the obvious fact is that in the clinic I have very little control over all of the variables in operation?"[32] One answer is that we have learned much by continually accepting therapeutic change as validating theoretical hypotheses. From this view, clinicians are scientists, must subject their hypotheses to careful trial, and must keep in touch with the pertinent scientific knowledge.

Illustrations of Case Histories and Studies

Students of psychology and education have not been fully trained to construct adequate case histories, to gather the relevant information, and to organize and interpret the findings. Other factors have interfered with the development of a library of case histories (normal and abnormal), including the conditions that make it difficult to obtain the data necessary for an understanding of any personality:[33]

1. Every life is long and complicated to the psychologist, and many hours are required for the exploration of even a few segments of it.
2. Man's power to recall his past is limited.
3. Man tends to guard his reputation when scientific scrutiny seeks to look at some crucial area of his secret life.
4. The psychologist's conscience, acknowledging that every man is entitled to his privacy, forbids unscrupulous intrusions.

Additional factors which have interfered with building a body of case histories are the difficulties in making dependable observations under clinical or experimental conditions, in formulating correct interpretations, in publication of a revealing, recognizable portrait of a still living

---

[31] Paul E. Meehl, *Clinical Versus Statistical Prediction: A Theoretical Analysis and a Review of the Evidence.* Minneapolis: University of Minnesota Press, 1954. p. 3–9, 136–38.

[32] Joseph F. Rychlak, "Clinical Psychology and the Nature of Evidence." *American Psychologist* 14: 642–48; October 1959.

[33] Arthur Burton and Robert E. Harris, *op. cit.,* p. 15–16.

person, and in finding a publisher and an audience. In spite of the difficulties in producing adequate case histories, the book-length treatments in the chapter bibliography and in the literature contain many illustrative case and clinical studies in such fields as education, psychology, psychiatry, mental hygiene, guidance and counseling, therapy, behavior problems and delinquency, child development, social work, and sociology. A number of the earlier examples of community or village surveys may also be classified as case studies (Chapter 5). The following case reports are examples of individuals, institutions, and communities.

To cite an example of a case history and verbatim account of treatment sessions, a little boy of five years, Dibs, was withdrawn and emotionally deprived, but gifted and with an extraordinary vocabulary and reading skills. The therapy was unusually successful, as determined by a follow up some years later, and at the age of fifteen Dibs was a brilliant, sensitive boy concerned about people and a real leader.[34]

As an example of an unusual case report, a man suffered a devastating and debilitating "stroke," and for a time was completely non-ambulatory and speechless, but he learned to walk again, to adapt to traumatic psychological forces, to attain a high degree of stability, and to write again. In the case report he tells chronologically of his experiences in recovering from the "accident inside his skull," including the role of physicians, nurses, speech therapists, psychologists, physiotherapists, and friends.[35]

EXAMPLE: CHILDHOOD EMOTIONAL DISABILITIES[36]

The cases presented in this volume include a wide range of disorders, although they are not necessarily a representative sample of the range of child disabilities that one commonly encounters in a child-guidance clinic. Each case opens with a developmental history and a brief description of the emotional interrelationships within the family, which is followed by a detailed account of the collaborative treatment that includes the child and the simultaneous treatment of one or both parents. Considerable case material, interspersed with interpretative comment, is presented to illustrate therapeutic methods and patterns of family dynamics. Although little direct verbatim material is included, the abstracts of the therapeutic sessions seem to convey adequately the flavor of the therapeutic interaction. Reading through these cases one is impressed with the therapists' sensitivity to the patients' needs and the consider-

34 Virginia M. Axline, *Dibs: In Search of Self.* Boston: Houghton Mifflin Co., 1964. xiii + 186 p.

35 Eric Hodgins, *Episode: Report on the Accident Inside My Skull.* New York: Atheneum Publishers, 1964. xi + 272 p.

36 Quoted from review by Albert Bandura, *Contemporary Psychology* 2: 14–15; January 1957, of George E. Gardner, Editor, *Case Studies in Childhood Emotional Disabilities.* Vol. 2. New York: American Orthopsychiatric Association, 1956. vii + 368 p.

able flexibility in treatment. At a time wehn therapeutic rituals and rule-of-thumb methods are prevalent, these papers make for refreshing and instructive reading. Unfortunately, apart from the therapists' general impressions, little attempt is made to evaluate the procedures and outcomes through the use of data external to the therapeutic process.

Most of our clinical methods and classification systems have been designed primarily for the purpose of individual diagnosis and few adequate procedures have been developed for yielding a family diagnosis. The articles in the volume demonstrate how the case method can be used successfully to give a comprehensive picture of the constellation of intrafamily relationships and the changes in the family pattern during treatment. The limitations of the case method, nevertheless, tend to make these papers better as a source of hypotheses for more definitive studies than as a source of systematic knowledge about family disturbances.

The types of disorders and problems represented in these cases are as follows:

Collaborative treatment of mother and boy with fecal retention, soiling and a school phobia
The planned return of a placed child to own family
The defense mechanisms of a six-year-old
The use of a therapeutic nursery school in cooperation with clinical treatment of an acute separation problem
Pupils psychologically absent from school
The dynamics of encopresis
On the significance of the anal phase in pediatrics and child psychiatry
Brother identification in an adolescent girl
The dynamic significance of the mother-child relationship in the case of a young delinquent with psychotic mechanisms
Ego treatment causing structural change in personality
Is trying enough? A report of treatment during the latency period of a girl with atypical development
The psychological problems of the congenitally blind child
Two phases in the treatment of a hyperactive, destructive boy
Treatment of the adolescent delinquent
A technical problem in the beginning phase of psychotherapy with a borderline psychotic child.

EXAMPLE: THREE PATIENTS IN ONE[37]

A bewildered young woman sought treatment for severe headaches. She turned out to be three patients in one. Her two psychiatrists studied their patient

[37] Quoted from review by William S. Taylor, *Contemporary Psychology* 2: 289–90; November 1957, of Corbett H. Thigpen and Hervey M. Cleckley, *The Three Faces of Eve*. New York: McGraw-Hill Book Company, 1957. ix + 308 p.
Evelyn Lancaster with James Poling, *The Final Face of Eve*. New York: McGraw-Hill Book Company, 1958. x + 290 p.

with the best traditional care together with special checks and modern methods. Evidently these authors, like a number of their predecessors in the field, were completely surprised to find that their patient was a multiple personality. They tested every possibility of play-acting, escape, fraud, and fun. They avoided reading accounts of other cases while working with this one. They scrutinized their own interests and asked themselves, after Bernheim, "Who is hypnotizing whom?" They checked the patient's statements with statements from the same personality, other personalities, relatives, friends, other observers, and records. They observed naive persons' reactions to the several personalities; they exhibited the several personalities to professional colleagues for interpretation; and, from experts who knew as little as possible about the patient, for each personality they obtained interpretations of the handwriting, the results of intelligence tests, projective tests, and Osgood and Luria's semantic differential test. They obtained electroencephalograms, sound recordings and sound films.

The recordings and sound films the authors used as part of the therapy. The case, like a number of the earlier ones in the literature, was worked through to an excellent synthesis; one which, though the authors say they cannot be sure about this, seems durable.

The entire study supports the observations of prior authors about multiple personality: the build-up of meanings that can make for stress; conflicts in childhood and maturity; lapses, relevant sleepwalking; neurotic symptoms; hallucinations engendered by a co-conscious personality; transitional syncopes; various amnesias; the several personalities' differences in facial expression, manner, voice, speech, handwriting, interests, thought, character, and maturity; between personalities, barriers neither perfect nor wholly unchanging; one-way amnesia between certain personalities, and mutual amnesia, for a time, between others; each personality's striving to function as fully as possible; use of hypnosis to recover dreams, other memories, and larger organizations; light on psychotherapy; the changing, growing self; the integrative role of an inclusive interest; and the throes of coalescence or synthesis.

The findings are thought new, to the effect that one of the personalities, Eve Black, could not be hypnotized; one, Jane, emerged with mature powers, general orientation, and language, but with no specific memories; each of the most disparate personalities, Eve White and Eve Black, was sad at having to "die," and the most inclusive of the three personalities, Jane, was sad to "lose" her erstwhile "sisters." New too, and significant, are the special methods of study as applied to multiple personality, and the whole picture of a contemporary young woman, with her playfulness, selfishness, affection, humanity, idealism, and practical judgment most revealingly tried, segregated, and finally synthesized in a normal urge to live as a mature person.

Example: Personality

The "study of lives" has been analyzed in terms of the following "themes," with "a stout affection for human beings coupled with a consuming interest in their emotions and evaluations, their imaginations and beliefs, their purpose and plans, their endeavors, failures and achievements."[38]

1. Personality is a dynamic, lifelong process, and the study of the individual in full complexity and extension is a proper concern of the psychologist.
2. Not only real and present people, but literary, historical, and mythological figures teach about human nature.
3. Personality is proactive rather than reactive, and creativity is an essential quality of man.
4. The study of personality requires techniques for investigating "live feelings, fantasies, and adaptations."
5. Scientific advance depends on distinguishing and describing the important units and variables of personality.
6. Human values, often ignored or excluded, are the proper concern of a science of personality.

EXAMPLE: THE INEFFECTIVE SOLDIER[39]

Volume II, *Breakdown and Recovery,* is a collection of 79 dramatically told case histories, chosen to illustrate how factors in the life of the soldier bear on whether he breaks down and, if he does, whether he recovers. It has a good list of the resources within the individual that help mental health: stamina, good intelligence, a desire to get ahead, generous and understanding parents, a self-reliant and capable wife, and good stabilizing work. Beyond these—for military life—the support or lack of support a man received from his peer group and from the military organization itself and the severity and duration of the stress he was exposed to are of importance.

Because the stories are brief, they are oversimplified. Some of the points illustrated through the thumb-nail case histories will seem self-evident to the psychologists who were there. But the lessons learned in one military generation, like those in one academic generation, often have to be learned again later through hard experience, and spelling out the obvious may then help. This volume should be full of lessons for currently active military psychologists and psychiatrists and those working in the Veterans Administration.

EXAMPLES: THE COLLEGE

This is a case study of the first four years of San Jose Junior College, in the process of assuming its initial structure and of meeting the needs of a new type of student body, including the characteristics of the college, job requirements of the teacher, orientation of the administrative staff, and aptitude of the students. More specifically, the study deals with the pressures of modern society affecting students and curriculum programs, essential elements shaping the "personality" of the college, administrative setting in a local public school

[38] Robert W. White, Editor, *The Study of Lives: Essays on Personality in Honor of Henry A. Murray.* New York: Atherton Press, 1963. xi + 442 p.

[39] Eli Ginzberg and Others, *The Ineffective Soldier. Breakdown and Recovery,* Vol. 2. New York: Columbia University Press, 1959. xx + 284 p.

district, aims and ambitions of the students, formal organization of the college, composition of administrative and instructional staff, and the role of the junior college in a system of higher education. The data were collected through informal interviews, observation, analysis of documents, and questionnaires.[40]

[Many reports under the caption of "case" studies are descriptions of status rather than diagnostic and therapeutic treatments; for example, the academic administration of nine liberal arts colleges, describing faculty personnel, curriculum, instruction, student services, budget, and the dean's office.][41]

EXAMPLE: METHODS OF OPERATIONS RESEARCH[42]

[Operational research may be simply defined as "the application of scientific methods of investigation to the kind of problems that face executive and administrative authorities."][43]

Although not explicitly advertised as such, this book is a collection of articles on the methods of operations research, written at an elementary level that is suitable for engineers and management personnel. There are introductory articles on the general philosophy and methodology of operations research and specific articles on such techniques as linear programming, queueing theory, theory of games, simulation studies, information theory, and other systems methods. Finally there is a collection of case studies. The chief defect in these articles is a tendency to verbosity on the part of some of the contributors.

By far the most fascinating and persuasive section is that on case studies. Of particular interest is an article by Zimmerman on the simulation of tactical war games; the discussion follows the course of a particular game step by step. Other articles detail studies on the operation of a hospital and a newspaper and analyze the cost and value of reports in a telephone company.

An article by Ellis Johnson (reprinted from the *Journal of Operations Research*) on operations research in the world crisis in science and technology goes far to illustrate the limitations of overenthusiastic applications of operations research considerations.

EXAMPLES: FIVE PRIMITIVE AND PEASANT SOCIETIES[44]

The publication of the books under review now makes it possible for students and laymen to own first-hand accounts of five primitive and peasant societies, whereas earlier such source materials were either expensive or (mostly) un-

[40] Burton R. Clark, *The Open Door College: A Case Study*. New York: McGraw-Hill Book Company, 1960. xvi + 208 p.

[41] John S. Russel and Archie R. Ayers, *Case Studies in the Liberal Arts College: Academic Administration*. U.S. Office of Education Bulletin 1964, No. 12. Washington: Government Printing Office, 1964. v + 184 p.

[42] Quoted from review by George Weiss, *Science* 132: 543; August 26, 1960, of Charles D. Flagle, Jr., William H. Huggins, and Robert H. Roy, *Operations Research and Systems Engineering*. Baltimore: The Johns Hopkins Press, 1960. x + 889 p. Reprinted from *Science* by permission.

[43] Norman T. J. Bailey, "Operational Research," *Society: Problems and Methods of Study*. London: Routledge & Kegan Paul, 1962. p. 111–25.

[44] H. G. Barnett, *Being a Palauan*. New York: Holt, Rinehart and Winston, Inc., 1960. vii + 87 p.

available except in major libraries. These "case studies" are useful, too, not only because they are much cheaper than the usual ethnological monograph, but also because they have been written especially for this series, which envisages a readership composed of non-professionals. Hence, they are all much more readable than the monographs which ordinarily are laden with esoteric detail.

Each book stands alone, of interest in its own right, and can be purchased separately. It is apparent, however, that the series has aims of its own. The five books together provide an ethnological "scatter"; that is, the student benefits by studying cultures which are distinct from one another as types and are also widely separated geographically.

Despite the diversity represented, however, the series does not lend itself well to cross-culture comparisons nor does it elicit generalizations. The aim of the series is not to provide comparative materials, but instead each work is written around its own independent theme or focus—each is a distinctive "case." There is space here to mention briefly the themes, but not to evaluate. Fortunately, each author is a foremost authority on the peoples discussed.

Barnett's contribution, as suggested by its title, presents Palauan culture in behavioral episodes and in terms of the experiences and feelings of particular persons. It therefore gives the reader a feeling for the functioning culture so that it seems more "real" as well as more interesting than in the usual monographic writing. Beattie's account of Bunyoro is focused on the past history of this African kingdom as this is related to its present (and rapidly changing) condition. Hart and Pilling are able to contrast the Tiwi at two stages of modern acculturative change. Hart studied them in 1928–1929 and Pilling in 1953–1954, making for an unusual collaborative account of Australian aborigines who are, in any case, always of interest. Hoebel presents the Cheyenne in a more standardized set of ethnographic descriptive categories than those employed by the other authors, and as a consequence the reader feels that it is a rather fuller account of the total culture, however boiled down; it is not focused on some particular problem or interest. Lewis' book, on the other hand, puts the peasants of Tepoztlan in a much broader and deeper context than do any of the others. He sees them as part of Mexico, the New World, and Spain; he also gives historical perspective from pre-Columbian to modern times, with particular consideration for the effects of the striking technological changes of recent years. I should remark, finally, that however distinct from one another in organization and focus, all the books succeed in various ways in including the more essential descriptive data.

John Beattie, *Bunyoro: An African Kingdom.* New York: Holt, Rinehart and Winston, Inc., 1960. ix + 86 p.

C. W. M. Hart and Arnold R. Pilling, *The Tiwi of North Australia.* New York: Holt, Rinehart and Winston, Inc., 1960. ix + 118 p.

E. Adamson Hoebel, *The Cheyennes: Indians of the Great Plains.* New York: Holt, Rinehart and Winston, Inc., 1960. vii + 103 p.

Oscar Lewis, *Tepoztlan: Village in Mexico.* New York: Holt, Rinehart and Winston, Inc., 1960. viii + 104 p.

Quoted from review by Elman R. Service, *American Sociological Review* 25: 777–78; October 1960.

Concluding Statement

Significant trends and emphases in clinical and case study may be summarized briefly as follows:

1. Extension of the case approach to include study of social institutions or agencies and communities or cultural groups: a college, a hospital clinic, a rural village, or an industrial community.

2. Application and use in a number of professional fields and to a wide range of human problems: law and juvenile delinquency, medicine, psychiatry, psychology, education, counseling and guidance, anthropology, sociology, social work, economics, business administration, political science, and journalism.

3. Recognition of the complementary functions of the several stages in case study and case work: initial status and symptoms, examination and history, diagnosis, therapy, and follow-up.

4. Fuller and better use of such personal documents as the life history, autobiography, biography, diaries and journals, letters, records of dreams, and expressive interviews. Data obtained from personal documents may make a contribution by way of supplementing ecological and statistical information, so as to provide a more inclusive interpretation of the problem, and may serve as a basis for prediction of human behavior.

5. Recognition of the significance of multiple causation in diagnosis and of the corresponding need for a variety of therapeutic techniques. It usually is necessary to look beneath the surface to find the basic or primary cause of maladjustment; on the surface we may see only a secondary, tertiary, or contributory cause or condition. Frequently, complex or multiple causation of maladjustment may lead to a diagnosis and to therapy requiring the cooperation of a number of specialists.

6. A concept of therapy as development of the potentialities of the individual for growth and improvement, including adjustment procedures in the form of preventive measures, self-help, and client-centered techniques. In all forms of therapy, the importance of self-help is recognized, as illustrated by the patient's will or desire to recover from an illness.

7. Development and application of a variety of methods of psychotherapy, including group therapy. Psychotherapy involves difficulties in that our diagnostic instruments fall short of desirable standards of validity and reliability. We are uncomfortably aware of elements of truth behind the facetious characterization of psychotherapy as "the art of applying a science which does not yet exist," although our therapeutic anxiety is relieved somewhat by dependence on the best available techniques and procedures of psychodiagnosis.

8. Further improvement in case records, as well as wider use of cumulative and anecdotal records, with a place for autobiography, health history, test scores, school marks, cocurricular activities, and work experience.

9. Formulation of ethical principles or standards, particularly in the field of psychology, but with applications to other clinical and case areas (espe-

cially in diagnosis and treatment). Since the primary function of records is to render treatment of the case more effective in terms of adjustment of the client, and to serve community interests in dealing with social problems, the ethical implications of case-recording are important.

Expressed in broader terms, the social and ethical responsibilities of scientists grow out of their obligations "to cherish complete truthfulness; to avoid self-aggrandizement at the expense of one's fellow-scientist; fearlessly to defend the freedom of scientific inquiry and opinion; and fully to communicate one's findings through primary publication, synthesis, and instruction." These social obligations of scientists and corresponding systems of values involve the advertisement of the benefits of science, warning of risks, and consideration of the nebulous realm of quandaries; for example, in dealing with the threat of nuclear war and the population explosion. While the scientist cannot make the choice of goals and values for his people, he has a social duty and function to inform society and its leaders concerning alternatives, and to insist on full consideration of the complex problems that grow out of scientific discovery.[45]

10. Recognition of the supplementary functions of case-clinical and statistical methods. It is a common error to group together the terms *quantitative, statistical,* and *experimental,* setting them in opposition to *qualitative, clinical,* and *nonexperimental.* Some phenomena of behavior cannot be studied satisfactorily in the laboratory, and some quantification of clinical evidence is desirable. What we need is a balanced approach in selecting techniques appropriate for the problem at hand.

11. Appearance of a considerable body of case-history material, in spite of certain difficulties in producing and publishing adequate case histories, in such fields as education, psychology, psychiatry, mental hygiene, guidance and counseling, therapy, behavior problems and delinquency, child development, social work, and sociology.

SELECTED REFERENCES

ALEXANDER, Theron. *Psychotherapy in Our Society.* Englewood Cliffs, N.J.: Prentice-Hall, Inc., 1963. ix + 181 p.

ANDERSON, Robert T., and ANDERSON, Barbara G. *The Vanishing Village: A Danish Maritime Community.* Seattle: University of Washington Press, 1964. xi + 148 p.

BELLER, E. Kuno. *Clinical Process.* New York: Free Press of Glencoe, Inc., 1962. xx + 394 p.

BENNETT, Ivy. *Delinquent and Neurotic Children: A Study with One Hundred Case Histories.* New York: Basic Books, Inc., Publishers, 1961. xii + 532 p.

BETTELHEIM, Bruno. *Paul and Mary: Two Case Histories From "Truants From Life."* Garden City, N.Y.: Doubleday & Company, Inc., 1961. xxx + 435 p.

---

45 Bentley Glass, "The Ethical Basis of Science." *Science* 150: 1254–61; December 3, 1965.

BRAMMER, Lawrence M., and SHOSTROM, Everett L. *Therapeutic Psychology: Fundamentals of Counseling and Psychotherapy.* Englewood Cliffs, N.J.: Prentice-Hall, Inc., 1960. xvii + 447 p.

BUCHHEIMER, Arnold, and BALOGH, Sara C. *The Counseling Relationship: A Casebook.* Chicago: Science Research Associates, 1962. vii + 234 p.

BURTON, Arthur, Editor. *Psychotherapy of the Psychoses.* New York: Basic Books, Inc., Publishers, 1961. x + 386 p.

CASAGRANDE, Joseph B., Editor. *In the Company of Man: Twenty Portraits by Anthropologists.* New York: Harper & Row, Publishers, Inc., 1960. xvi + 540 p.

COHEN, Y. A. *Social Structure and Personality: A Casebook.* New York: Holt, Rinehart and Winston, Inc., 1961. xiv + 528 p.

CURTI, Merle. *The Making of an American Community: A Case History of Democracy in a Frontier County.* Stanford, Calif.: Stanford University Press, 1959. vii + 483 p.

DEWALD, Paul A. *Psychotherapy: A Dynamic Approach.* New York: Basic Books, Inc., Publishers, 1964. xvii + 307 p.

EVANS, Jean. *Three Men: An Experiment in the Biography of Emotion.* New York: Alfred A. Knopf, Inc., 1954. xviii + 298 p. (Case reports.)

FORD, Donald H., and URBAN, Hugh B. *Systems of Psychotherapy: A Comparative Study.* New York: John Wiley & Sons, Inc., 1963. xii + 712 p.

FOULKES, S. H. *Therapeutic Group Analysis.* New York: International Universities Press, Inc., 1964. 320 p.

GARTON, Nina R., and OTTO, Herbert A. *The Development of Theory and Practice in Social Casework.* Springfield, Ill.: Charles C Thomas, 1964. xvii + 181 p.

GINOTT, Haim G. *Group Psychotherapy with Children: The Theory and Practice of Play Therapy.* New York: McGraw-Hill Book Co., 1961. xvi + 208 p.

GOOD, Carter V. *Introduction to Educational Research: Methodology of Design in the Behavioral and Social Sciences.* Second Edition. New York: Appleton-Century-Crofts, 1963. Chapter 7.

HARTLEY, E. L., and WIEBE, G. D. *Casebook in Social Processes.* New York: Thomas Y. Crowell Company, 1960. x + 534 p.

HAWORTH, Mary R., Editor. *Child Psychotherapy: Practice and Theory.* New York: Basic Books, Inc., Publishers, 1964. xv + 459 p.

HOLLAND, Glen A. *Fundamentals of Psychotherapy.* New York: Holt, Rinehart and Winston, Inc., 1965. xi + 308 p.

HOLLIS, Florence. *Casework: A Psychosocial Therapy.* New York: Random House, Inc., 1964. xx + 330 p.

HOLMES, Donald J. *The Adolescent in Psychotherapy.* Boston: Little, Brown and Company, 1964. xviii + 337 p.

HUGHES, Helen M., Editor. *The Fantastic Lodge: The Autobiography of a Girl Drug Addict.* Boston: Houghton Mifflin Company, 1961. x + 267 p.

KLEIN, Melanie. *Narrative of a Child Analysis: The Conduct of the Psychoanalysis of Children as Seen in the Treatment of a Ten Year Old Boy.* New York: Basic Books, Inc., Publishers, 1961. 496 p.

KVARACEUS, William C. "Behavior Problems," *Encyclopedia of Educational Research.* Chester W. Harris, Editor. Third Edition. New York: The Macmillan Co., 1960. p. 137–42.

KVARACEUS, William. "Delinquency," *Encyclopedia of Educational Research*. p. 365–69.

LEWIS, Oscar. *The Children of Sanchez: Autobiography of a Mexican Family*. New York: Random House, Inc., 1961. xxxi + 499 p.

LONDON, Perry. *The Modes and Morals of Psychotherapy*. New York: Holt, Rinehart and Winston, Inc., 1964. x + 278 p.

LURIE, Nancy O., Editor. *Mountain Wolf Woman, Sister of Crashing Thunder: The Autobiography of a Winnebago Indian*. Ann Arbor: The University of Michigan Press, 1961. xx + 142 p.

MCKINNEY, Fred. *Understanding Personality: Cases in Counseling*. Boston: Houghton Mifflin Company, 1965. xiv + 338 p.

MEEHL, Paul E. *Clinical Versus Statistical Prediction: A Theoretical Analysis and a Review of the Evidence*. Minneapolis: University of Minnesota Press, 1954. x + 149 p.

MINTZ, S. W. *Worker in the Cane: A Puerto Rican Life History*. New Haven: Yale University Press, 1960. xiv + 288 p.

MOWRER, O. Hobart. *The New Group Therapy*. Princeton, N.J.: D. Van Nostrand Co., Inc., 1964. ix + 262 p.

MULLAN, Hugh, and ROSENBAUM, Max. *Group Psychotherapy: Theory and Practice*. New York: Free Press of Glencoe, Inc., 1962. xvi + 360 p.

MULLAN, Hugh, and SANGIULIANO, Iris. *The Therapist's Contribution to the Treatment Process: His Person, Transactions, and Treatment Methods*. Springfield, Ill.: Charles C Thomas, 1964. xvii + 280 p.

PATTERSON, T. T. *Glasgow Limited: A Case-Study in Industrial War and Peace*. Social and Economic Studies No. 7 of the Department of Social and Economic Research, University of Glasgow. London: Cambridge University Press, 1960. x + 243 p.

RAPOPORT, R. N., and Others. *Community as a Doctor: New Perspectives on a Therapeutic Community*. Springfield, Ill.: Charles C Thomas, 1961. x + 325 p.

RITCHIE, James E. *The Making of a Maori: A Case Study of a Changing Community*. Wellington, New Zealand: A. H. & A. W. Reed, 1963. xi + 203 p.

ROGERS, Carl R. *On Becoming a Person: A Therapist's View of Psychotherapy*. Boston: Houghton Mifflin Company, 1961. xii + 420 p.

ROGERS, Carl R. *Client-Centered Therapy*. Boston: Houghton-Mifflin, 1965. xii + 560 p.

ROKEACH, Milton. *The Three Christs of Ypsilanti: A Narrative Study of Three Lost Men*. New York: Alfred A. Knopf, Inc., 1964. ix + 336 p.

ROSENBAUM, Max, and BERGER, Milton, Editors. *Group Psychotherapy and Group Function*. New York: Basic Books, Inc., Publishers, 1963. xi + 690 p.

SCHOFIELD, William. *Psychotherapy: The Purchase of Friendship*. Englewood Cliffs, N.J.: Prentice-Hall, Inc., 1964. vi + 186 p.

SCHULMAN, Jerome L., and Others. *The Therapeutic Dialogue: A Method for Analysis of Verbal Interaction*. Springfield, Ill.: Charles C Thomas, 1964. 163 p.

SLAVSON, S. R. *A Textbook in Analytic Group Psychotherapy*. New York: International Universities Press, Inc., 1964. ix + 563 p.

SNYDER, William U. *Dependency in Psychotherapy: A Casebook*. New York: The Macmillan Company, 1963. iii + 424 p.

SNYDER, William U. *The Psychotherapy Relationship*. New York: The Macmillan Co., 1961. xiv + 418 p.

STRUPP, Hans H., and LUBORSKY, Lester, Editors. *Research in Psychotherapy*. Vol. 2. Washington: American Psychological Association, 1962. iii + 342 p.

TAFT, Jessie. *The Dynamics of Therapy in a Controlled Relationship*. New York: Dover Publications, Inc., 1964. xvii + 296 p.

TARACHOW, Sidney. *An Introduction to Psychotherapy*. New York: International Universities Press, Inc., 1963. vii + 376 p.

VAN DEN BERGHE, Pierre. *Caneville: The Social Structure of a South African Town*. Middletown, Conn.: Wesleyan University Press, 1964. x + 276 p.

VOILAND, Alice L., and Associates. *Family Casework Diagnosis*. New York: Columbia University Press, 1962. xii + 369 p.

WHITAKER, Dorothy S., and LIEBERMAN, Morton A. *Psychotherapy Through the Group Process*. New York: Atherton Press, 1964. x + 305 p.

WILSON, William E. *The Angel and the Serpent: The Story of New Harmony*. Bloomington, Ind.: Indiana University Press, 1964. xiv + 242 p.

WOLPE, Joseph, and Others, Editors. *The Conditioning Therapies: The Challenge in Psychotherapy*. New York: Holt, Rinehart and Winston, Inc., 1964. viii + 192 p.

ZALEZNIK, Abraham, and MOMENT, David. *Casebook on Interpersonal Behavior in Organizations*. New York: John Wiley & Sons, Inc., 1964. xvi + 587 p.

8

Experimental Design

CONTROL OF VARIABLES

This chapter on experimentation includes the topics of independent and dependent variables, control of variables, validity of experimental designs, pre-experimental designs, true experimental designs, quasi-experimental designs, other special classifications of experimental designs, inference and generalization, training for experimentation, appropriate standards and problems for experimental investigation, role of the teacher in classroom experimentation, ethics, relations of experimentation to other research techniques, and instrumentation.

Since the typical reader of this book is a graduate student in his first year or two of study following the bachelor's degree, with only limited training in statistics, measurement, and quantitative methods, this chapter is a descriptive account of controlled experimentation. The statistical and mathematical details of experimental design are treated fully in the references listed in the chapter bibliography. Such concepts are commonly presented in a second-level statistics course. In presenting the several types of experimental design, the limitations of older methods of experimentation (one group, parallel group, and rotation group) and of exhaustive person-to-person matching or pairing have been recognized, these techniques having given way to the more recent methods of statistics and experimental design.

Variables in Controlled Experimentation

INDEPENDENT AND DEPENDENT VARIABLES: EXAMPLES

EXPERIMENTATION DIFFERS FROM DESCRIPTIVE-SURVEY METHODS AND FROM other techniques of investigation, in that the experimenter has some degree of control over the variables involved and the conditions under which the variables are observed. The relationship between socioeconomic status and opinion on some issue can be determined by a survey investigation through appropriate observation (questionnaire, interview, or some other appropriate data-gathering instrument). In this instance the two variables, socioeconomic status and opinion, are fixed, and the investigator has no control over the variables; he does not manipulate or change either socioeconomic status or opinion.[1]

In experimentation the investigator controls (manipulates or changes) certain independent variables and observes the changes that take place in the form of dependent variables. The investigator may wish to note the effect of a film strip or a lecture (an independent variable) on the performance of the subjects, as measured by an appropriate test (a dependent variable). To cite other examples of the simplest form of experimentation, involving an independent variable and at least one dependent variable, a blow (independent or experimental variable) delivered to the patellar tendon of the bended knee causes the leg to straighten (dependent variable or result). An independent or experimental variable (a loud noise producing the condition of being startled) may result in an increase in arterial pulse rate, perspiration, and an increased diameter of the pupils of the subject's eyes (dependent variables or results).[2]

In a well-known experiment, Dr. Jonas Salk tested polio vaccine in 1954, first on animals and then on human beings. It was a large-scale experiment, including children from every part of the United States, especially from areas where there was a high incidence of polio. Three injections of vaccine were given to 440,000 school children, placebo or "dummy" shots were given to 210,000 youngsters as a control group, and no injections at all to approximately 1,180,000 children as a second control group. To achieve maximum similarity of conditions for the experimental and control groups, each bottle of injection material was made to appear exactly alike, with identification by a code number which was known only to the scientists who planned the experiment but not to the doctors who injected the vaccine. Many experts in statistics and experimental design aided in planning the experiment and analyzing the results, including information on age, sex, the area in which the child lived, the kind of health and educational facilities available, and other related data.[3]

Experimental design frequently has been relatively simple and at the same time effective (even as early as 1900). Major Walter Reed in Cuba

[1] Allen L. Edwards, "Experiments: Their Planning and Execution," *Handbook of Social Psychology: Theory and Method.* Vol. 1. Edited by Gardner Lindzey. Reading, Mass.: Addison-Wesley Publishing Company, Inc., 1954. p. 260–61.

[2] John C. Townsend, *Introduction to Experimental Method: For Psychology and the Social Sciences.* New York: McGraw-Hill Book Co., 1953. p. 52–57.

[3] Philip Goldstein, *How to Do an Experiment.* New York: Harcourt, Brace & World, Inc., 1957. p. 44–46.

sought the cause and prevention of yellow fever with the following experimental conditions:[4]

> In House No. 1 men lived with soiled bed clothing used by men who died from yellow fever, but the house was barred to mosquitoes—no yellow fever developed. To test any possible natural immunity, one of these men later received a shot of virulent yellow-fever blood and another was bitten by the mosquitoes—both came down with almost fatal yellow fever.
>
> House No. 2 was sanitary and clean, divided into two parts by a fine-meshed screen. In one part a man was bitten repeatedly by the infected mosquitoes and contracted a nasty case of yellow fever. In the other half of the house, with no mosquitoes, two men slept safely for eighteen nights. A dirty pesthole of a house (with no mosquitoes) was safe; a clean house (but with mosquitoes) was dangerous.

In an experiment to test the effects of isolation, monkey infants were removed from their mothers and raised in separate wire cages with heating pads covered with soft gauze diapers. Nurses fed them a standard baby formula. A critical factor in control was to keep the little ones completely apart not only from their mothers, but from one another, and this was not so easy. Evening care was assigned to Kathy, who was studying to become an elementary teacher. One of the experimenters, when checking his wards one night, found Kathy sitting on the floor, surrounded by seven baby monkeys, all eight of the primates playing happily together. Before the horrified scientist could express his outrage, Kathy shook her finger in his face and said: "It is improper and immoral to blight the social development of little children. I am right and you are wrong!" While a year's time and an investment of $5,000 were lost, the psychologist had to admit that Kathy had the right maternal instincts. Later developments in the psychologist's experiment with isolation proved that Kathy was completely right concerning the blighting effects of isolation on the social-sexual life of monkeys.[5]

The reader may draw his own conclusions concerning the experimental procedures used by a young woman enrolled in an undergraduate psychology course, particularly her method of "calming down" experimental subjects. The following verbatim copy of the report submitted by the student was to meet the course requirement of training an animal during the semester, in order to make more meaningful the laws of learning and the principles of research:

> I began training the cricket about a month and a half ago to walk a T maze for a reward of food and water. Water was given at other times when the

4 Paul de Kruif, *Microbe Hunters*. New York: Harcourt, Brace & World, Inc., 1954.
5 Harry F. Harlow, "The Heterosexual Affectional System in Monkeys." *American Psychologist* 17: 1–9; January 1962.

cricket seemed to be weak from thirst. At first he was highly active and would not walk at all, but hopped around frantically. After I accidentally pulled one hind leg off and caught his head with the lid of the cage he calmed down. This was either due to damage, but since it was a sufficient time since I had started the experiment, I prefer to think he was learning. Anyway, he would then walk and explore the maze and he definitely preferred the left side. Therefore I would only reward him on the right side when he went there and after awhile he would go to the right side at least 3 out of 4 times. Four trials were about all he would do without becoming frightened and active to the point of running around and around. When the maze was first presented he would walk slowly down it and then go right and I believe he did learn this as the paper on the bottom was changed each trial and he could not have smelled any food or water that was there from previous trials.

On the day I was to bring the cricket to class for demonstration I put him in a small plastic container with holes punched in it. This was to keep him from getting to the maze and food which I was carrying in his regular large plastic cage. This was done about four hours before class and either from suffocation or his weakened condition (he had not been fed over the weekend but did have water) he was dead when I was ready for the demonstration. However, he had learned the response I had experimented with him. Before him I tried roaches and a female cricket. The roaches died and the female cricket wouldn't respond at all and I would have to give her food and water to keep her alive, and I realized she never would learn to walk a maze under those conditions, so I taught the male cricket.[6]

Many hundreds and even thousands of other examples of experiments may be found in the references of the chapter bibliography, the *Encyclopedia of Educational Research, Review of Educational Research, Psychological Abstracts,* and *Annual Review of Psychology.*

CONTROL OF VARIABLES

In experimentation the investigator seeks to control variables for three purposes: to isolate the determiners of activity or behavior individually and in combinations; to carry them as magnitudes either singly or in combinations; and to describe quantitatively the extent of their expression and their interacting effects, again, either as single determiners or as combinations of determiners.[7]

Single-Variable Experimentation. The simple and narrow concept of the "rule of the single variable" was formulated at a time in the earlier period of experimentation when it was believed that all variables (independent) must be held constant except one, with a "one-to-one" corres-

[6] Edwin O. Timmons, "Methodology." *American Psychologist* 18: 717–18; November 1963.

[7] Clarence W. Brown and Edwin E. Ghiselli, *Scientific Method in Psychology.* New York: McGraw-Hill Book Company, 1955. p. 76.

pondence between a particular cause and a specific effect, as when one end of a lever is pushed down, the other end goes up (a predictable amount). Today many specialists in statistics and experimental design regard such a theory of causation as narrow and mechanical, and as characteristic of past investigations in physical science, since the efficient statistical methods and experimental designs now available make it possible to handle several independent variables in the same design and to have as many dependent variables as may seem necessary.

> . . . The seventeenth, eighteenth, and nineteenth centuries formed the period in which physical science learned how to analyze two-variable problems. Thus during that three hundred years, science developed the experimental and analytical techniques for handling problems in which one quantity say, a gas pressure—depends primarily upon a second quantity—say, the volume of the gas. . . . These two-variable problems are essentially simple in structure, and precisely for the reason that the theories or the experiments related to them need deal with only two quantities, changes in one of which cause changes in the other.[8]

Multivariate Experimentation. While this simple type of experimental design contributed to progress in the earlier stages of physical science, scientists more recently have gone beyond the simple two-variable problems to attack problems involving a large number of factors, resulting in statements of probability. Certain complex problems of the human and behavioral sciences do not lend themselves to either the ordinary experiment or the probability approach, however, and await solution through some appropriate combination of statistical and experimental methods. To cite an illustration, experiments may be multivariate in either or both of two senses:[9]

> More than one "independent" variable (sex, school grade, method of teaching arithmetic, style of printing type, size of printing type, etc.) may be incorporated into the design and/or more than one "dependent" variable (number of errors, speed, number right, various tests, etc.) may be employed.

Control in the Social and Behavioral Sciences. The characteristics of the social object and the social context of the experimenter are sufficiently different from experimentation in the physical sciences to warrant special consideration. There are differences between physical data and social

---

8 Quoted from Warren Weaver, Editor, *The Scientists Speak.* New York: Boni and Gaer, 1947. p. 1, 2.

Warren Weaver, "A Quarter Century in the Natural Sciences," in *The President's Review, Rockefeller Foundation Annual Report, 1958.* New York: The Foundation, 1958. p. 7–122.

9 Quoted from Donald T. Campbell and Julian C. Stanley, "Experimental and Quasi-Experimental Designs for Research on Teaching," *Handbook of Research on Teaching.* Edited by N. L. Gage. Chicago: Rand McNally & Co., 1963. Chapter 5.

data which must be considered before the experimental method is carried over bodily from physical science to social science. The social scientist encounters difficulties in holding extraneous influences constant, and is seldom in a position to remove these influences physically, although society sometimes creates situations in which such extraneous influences are physically held constant. In taking over the experimental method from the older sciences, the social scientist is compelled to examine it in terms of problems and assumptions in relation to the specific social problem for investigation.[10]

The influence of social and psychological forces or factors other than the independent variable in experimentation has come to be known as the "Hawthorne effect"; for example, the higher motivation of teachers and pupils in an experimental situation, the personality or enthusiasm of the teacher, or the very novelty and attractiveness (maybe only temporary) of a new system of instruction.

> The Hawthorne effect is a phenomenon characterized by an awareness on the part of the subjects of special treatment created by artificial experimental conditions. This awareness becomes confounded with the independent variable under study, with a subsequent facilitating effect on the dependent variable, thus leading to ambiguous results.[11]

This active participation and response of the subject have been viewed as a very special form of social interaction sometimes discussed in the literature under such headings as the "social psychology of the experiment" and the "demand characteristics of the experimental situation."[12] Since it is known that an experimenter can easily influence his subjects to give him the response he wants, this presents the problem of how to cope with unconscious influence. Contradictory and unexpected findings may be due to the fact that the experimenter unknowingly has communicated his desires or expectations to his subjects. In handling rats, for example, an extra pat or two for a good performance in running the maze or a none-too-gentle toss into the cage for a poor performance probably would communicate the experimenter's attitude or desire (as a form of experimenter bias), although it is granted that no "good" investigator would do these things.[13]

It is even possible that an experimenter may influence his assistants

10 Arnold M. Rose, "Conditions of the Social Science Experiment," *Theory and Method in the Social Sciences.* Minneapolis: University of Minnesota Press, 1954. p. 273–81.

11 Desmond L. Cook, "The Hawthorne Effect in Educational Research." *Phi Delta Kappan* 44: 116–22; December 1962.

12 Martin T. Orne, "On the Social Psychology of the Psychological Experiment: With Particular Reference to Demand Characteristics and Their Implications." *American Psychologist* 17: 776–83; November 1962.

13 Robert Rosenthal and Kermit L. Fode, "The Effect of Experimenter Bias on the Performance of the Albino Rat." *Behavioral Science* 8: 183–89; July 1963.

so as to result in bias in dealing with the subjects, in other words, interpersonal influence once removed. When an experienced psychotherapist tells the neophyte therapist that a particular patient has a poor therapeutic prognosis, does this contribute to or even "cause" a poor prognosis by the neophyte? If the master teacher tells his apprentice that a pupil has the appearance of a slow learner, is this prediction reflected in the attitudes and interpersonal relationships of the apprentice and pupil?[14]

While there is evidence to indicate that a defined personality characteristic of the subjects interacts with a perceived characteristic of the experimenter, it is difficult to determine the specific effects of the experimenter, leading us to ask whether it is possible to eliminate him from the investigation. For some experiments in psychology completely automated devices have been developed and used successfully, as in running rats (with the subjects never exposed to a human experimenter), or with human subjects entering the experimental room and directed completely by taped instructions, thus removing all visual clues, olfactory stimuli, and other effects emanating from the experimenter. If the human experimenter should be replaced by automatic devices, is it possible that stimuli emanating from the devices may interact with the treatments under study? We do have at least three obligations in dealing with the experimenter as a stimulus object:[15]

1. Where one data collector is used in an experiment, the best that can be done is to attempt to hold constant his influence on the subjects.
2. Where more than one data collector is used: (a) techniques of control should be specified; (b) the data should be analyzed and reported as a function of experimenters; and (c) interactions between experimenters and treatments should be tested.
3. It is important to contribute to our relatively small fund of knowledge concerning the experimenter variable.

In summary, the personality and expectation of the experimenter are a source of bias in experimental work. Studies in experimenter bias have shown that experimenters are able to obtain from their human or animal subjects the data that the experimenters want, need, or expect to get. Therefore, we are challenged to learn more about the social psychology of the experimental situation and its focal unit, the experimenter-subject relationship; for example, certain "interpersonal" relationships or effects have been present in research on conditioning in animals. For the human experimental subject, the artificiality of the experimental setting and the student's knowledge that he is participating in an experiment may generate a higher-order problem-solving task in which the procedures and

14 Robert Rosenthal and Others, "The Role of the Research Assistant in the Mediation of Experimenter Bias." *Journal of Personality* 31: 313–35; September 1963.
15 F. J. McGuigan, "The Experimenter: A Neglected Stimulus Object." *Psychological Bulletin* 60: 421–28; July 1963.

experimental treatment are reacted to not only for their simple stimulus values, but also for clues in discovering the investigator's intent, with possible development of attitudes of play-acting, outguessing, or up-for-inspection (attitudes unrepresentative of the normal school setting).[16]

We should not overemphasize the familiar complaint, however, that the kind of control possible in the laboratory is impossible in the world at large. Human behavior is controlled in a number of ways. The genetic constitution of the individual and his personal history to date play a part in the determination of behavior, as does the social environment, which is man-made. There are many instances outside the laboratory in which independent variables may be freely manipulated with respect to human behavior; for example, the nursery, certain types of schools, and corrective and penal institutions, where the degree of control may be great, although there are certain legal and ethical restrictions. In such situations as education, industry, law, public affairs, and government the control is not so likely to be lodged in a single person or agency. Sometimes this control has been managed in such a way as to bring sorrow to the individual and to society.[17]

Factors Requiring Control. Among the factors, variables, or determiners of behavior requiring control in psychological and educational investigations are the following:[18]

Schooling: academic incentives, level of success in different areas of subjects, amount of training in different areas, curriculum likes and dislikes, speed and accuracy of work in different fields or subjects

Skills: sports, hobbies, musical instruments, mechanical; physical handicaps

Maturity: chronological, physiological, psychological, developmental experience in special areas

Culture: foreign language and ideologies, American, regional

Social activities and experiences: likes and dislikes, participation in activities (social, sports, hobbies)

Physiological factors: physiological development, emotional development, general physical well-being, specific physical impairments, susceptibility to particular diseases, level of energy output.

Control Through Physical Manipulation. In certain types of experimentation, particularly in psychology, control of variables may be effected through some form of physical manipulation:[19]

[16] Robert Rosenthal and Others, "Subjects' Perception of Their Experimenter under Conditions of Experimenter Bias," *Perceptual and Motor Skills.* Missoula, Montana: Southern Universities Press, 1960. p. 325–31.

[17] B. F. Skinner, *Cumulative Record.* New York: Appleton-Century-Crofts, 1959. p. 223–57.

[18] Clarence W. Brown and Edwin E. Ghiselli, *op. cit.,* p. 80–82.

[19] *Ibid.,* p. 82–83.

John C. Townsend, *op. cit.,* p. 64–67.

Mechanical means: insulating material for sound-proofing a room, a light-proof
   room, or a tachistoscope for exposing perceptual stimuli
Electrical means: generation of sounds for experiments in hearing, screening
   out a distracting noise, or use of telechron and other constant speed motors
   for driving apparatus, controlling relays, and measuring time intervals
Surgical means: surgical removal of glands, such as the thyroid or the adrenals
Pharmacological means: drugs, change of diet, or feeding of gland extracts,
   as illustrated by use of dilantin in the treatment of epilepsy.

Control Through Selection. Control of variables through selection
enables the experimenter to achieve results not possible through the
method of physical manipulation of the determining variables:[20]

Selection of materials: for example, in studying the relation between the
   amount of material to be learned and the time required for learning, to
   provide (select) a sufficiently large number of units of material which are
   comparable in terms of the ease of learning. Any difference in the difficulty
   of the material would introduce a spurious factor which might affect the
   speed of learning.
Selection of subjects: to consider such factors as experience, age, ability, interest, attitude.
Selection of data: as illustrated by such primary sources as the records of
   public institutions, collections of vital statistics, government census reports,
   and certain types of records for institutions where the behavior of the subjects could not be subjected to experimental control (as in a reform school or
   a state prison).

Control over Intraprocedural Factors. In psychological and educational
experimentation, determinant variable factors (intraprocedural factors)
sometimes are present within the experimental procedures themselves.
Certain techniques of control over potentially disturbing intraprocedural
factors, with examples of physical-response factors, are as follows:[21]

1. Equal exposure of the subject to the experimental conditions: equal time
   to work; or time required to complete the task and the nature and number
   of errors committed
2. Minimizing the contribution of the spatial arrangement of procedural
   factors: spatial relation of the apparatus to the subject, or the direction of
   the adjustive movement (right-left or left-right)
3. Minimizing the contribution of temporal factors within an experimental
   sitting: time intervals between trials in most conditioning experiments of
   a few seconds, and time intervals of a number of hours in some maze
   experiments
4. Minimizing the contribution of factors arising from the order of the experimental conditions: counterbalancing of the temporal order of condi-

[20] Clarence W. Brown and Edwin E. Ghiselli, *op. cit.,* p. 84–85.
[21] *Ibid.,* p. 280–86.

tions in experiments in memory and in work involving carrying forward practice or fatigue effects from one gradation or condition to another

5. Counterbalancing of the order of experimental conditions through their random assignment to subjects: similar to counterbalancing experimental conditions in time.

The importance of randomization may be illustrated simply. If the problem is to divide 30 pupils in a class into a control group of 15 and an experimental group of the same size, with 5 seats to a row, the experimenter might consider taking all pupils in the first three rows for one group and all pupils in the last three rows for the other group. However, if girls commonly sit near the front of the room and boys near the rear, possible sex interests and achievements in arithmetic might bias the experiment from the beginning.

Another procedure would be to place the 30 names in a hat or bowl, each on a separate slip, shuffle them thoroughly, and then draw out 15 names. Another less desirable plan is to alphabetize the 30 names, and place the odd-numbered pupils in one group and the even-numbered persons in the other group. The best method is to number the pupils from 1 through 30 (or from 0 through 29) and draw 15 numbers within this range from a table of random numbers.[22]

Development and Validity of Experimental Designs

HISTORICAL DEVELOPMENT OF EXPERIMENTAL DESIGNS

Helen Walker summarizes concisely the development of the literature of experimental design during a third of a century:[23]

From Thorndike on, many individual research workers were vividly aware of the danger of bias and took great precautions to keep extraneous factors from influencing the outcome of their work, but many others were not so careful. McCall's *How to Experiment in Education,* published in 1923, was probably the first book dealing explicitly with this important matter and apparently had a tonic effect upon educational research. Before the first issue of the *Review* at least 15 books on research methods in education appeared, most of them showing McCall's influence.[24]

Fisher's *Design of Experiments,* 1935, introduced novel ideas and patterns which made use of the technic of analysis of variance.[25] To the statistician,

[22] Julian C. Stanley, "Controlled Experimentation in the Classroom." *Journal of Experimental Education* 25: 195–201; March 1957.

[23] Quoted from Helen M. Walker, "Methods of Research," in "Twenty-five Years of Educational Research." *Review of Educational Research* 26: 323–43; June 1956.

[24] W. A. McCall, *How to Experiment in Education.* New York: The Macmillan Co., 1923. 282 p.

[25] R. A. Fisher, *The Design of Experiments.* Sixth Edition. New York: Hafner Publishing Co., Inc., 1951. xv + 244 p.

design means primarily the decision as to what subjects shall be employed, how many, and how distributed over the categories with which a study is concerned. Fisher showed how the design must control the analysis, and startled his readers by the statement, now generally accepted, that an "unfortunate consequence only ensues when a method of diminishing the real errors is adopted, unaccompanied by their elimination in the statistical analysis." This was a blow to research workers who had spent long hours in matching subjects but had not taken account of that matching in their statistical treatment of the data.

The first paper on research designs in the *Review,* by C. C. Peters,[26] appeared in December 1945. A very considerable development took place in the next three years, so that in the 1948 issue Lev was able to discuss randomized blocks, Latin squares, factorial designs, and split-plot designs and to quote 51 studies applying such designs to educational research.[27] In December 1951, a chapter of 15 pages by Norton and Lindquist had as its chief purpose "to draw attention to some of the more serious or more frequently recurring errors that are currently being made in experimental design and analysis in educational research," and commented that "on the whole, the authors have been none too favorably impressed with the general quality of contemporary educational research so far as experimental design and analysis are concerned."[28] In December 1954, there was a separate chapter by Kogan on applications of variance-covariance designs.[29]

The era of exhaustive person-to-person matching appears now to be over. The newer statistical methods at the same time facilitate more efficient use of data, make possible greater economy in design, and require that the statistician shall have a part in the initial planning of a study before the data are gathered.

Stanley's concise summary of the literature on experimental design, appearing during the middle 1950's, supplements Walker's review, indicates the complexity of the concepts, and emphasizes the extensive training needed to understand the rudiments of experimental design.

Many of the contributions to experimental design during the past three years should be incorporated rapidly into statistics textbooks designed for students in education and psychology. Authors of such books need the ability and willingness to translate into simpler but still accurate form relevant material published by mathematical statisticians. Then by studying for at least a year, and preferably longer, under a well-qualified instructor, graduate students

26 C. C. Peters and Others, "Research Methods and Designs." *Review of Educational Research* 15: 377–93; December 1945.

27 Joseph Lev, "Research Methods and Designs." *Review of Educational Research* 18: 410–23; December 1948.

28 Dee W. Norton and Everet F. Lindquist, "Applications of Experimental Design and Analysis." *Review of Educational Research* 21: 350–67; December 1951.

29 Leonard S. Kogan, "Applications of Variance-Covariance Designs in Educational Research," in "Statistical Methodology in Educational Research." *Review of Educational Research* 24: 439–47; December 1954.

may come to understand the rudiments of experimental design. To do less than this and still hope for properly designed experiments is asking for a miracle.[30]

VALIDITY OF EXPERIMENTAL DESIGNS

Certain factors jeopardize the validity of various experimental designs. As background for consideration of these factors, it is fundamental to distinguish between *internal* validity and *external* validity.[31]

Internal validity is the basic minimum without which any experiment is uninterpretable: did in fact the experimental treatments make a difference in this specific experimental instance? *External validity* asks the question of *generalizability:* to what populations, settings, treatment variables, and measurement variables can this effect be generalized? Both types of criteria are obviously important, even though they are frequently at odds in that features increasing one may jeopardize the other. While *internal validity* is the *sine qua non,* and while the question of *external validity,* like the question of inductive inference, is never completely answerable, the selection of designs strong in both types of validity is obviously our ideal. This is particularly the case for research in teaching, in which generalization to applied settings of known character is the desideratum.

Internal Validity. As to internal validity, certain classes of extraneous variables, if not controlled in the experimental design, might produce effects confounded with the effect of the experimental stimulus.

History: During the time span between the two observations or measurements, many events have occurred in addition to the experimental variable or event. Although experimental isolation, through the employment of experimental settings in which all extraneous stimuli are eliminated, may be approximated in physical and biological research, such control is difficult or even impossible in social psychology and in other social sciences.

Maturation: Certain effects are systematic with the passage of time and not, like history, a function of the specific events involved. Between the two observations the subjects may have grown older, hungrier, or tireder, and these conditions may have produced the difference between

---

[30] Quoted from Julian C. Stanley, "Research Methods: Experimental Design," in "Methodology of Educational Research." *Review of Educational Research* 27: 449–59; December 1957. Also see: Raymond O. Collier, Jr., and Donald L. Meyer, "Research Methods: Experimental Design and Analysis," in "The Methodology of Educational Research." *Review of Educational Research* 30: 430–39; December 1960.

Dee W. Norton, "Developments in Analysis of Variance and Design of Experiments," in "Statistical Methodology." *Review of Educational Research* 33: 490–500; December 1963.

[31] Quoted from Donald T. Campbell and Julian C. Stanley, *op. cit.,* Chapter 5.

the two observations or measurements, independently of the experimental variable. While maturation is unlikely to be a source of change in the typical brief experiment in the psychology laboratory, it has been a real problem in research in child development, social psychology, and education.

Testing: The effect of testing itself may explain the difference between the two observations, apart from the effect of the experimental variable. In many instances persons taking a test for the second time make scores systematically different from individuals taking a test for the first time; for example, a second mean for intelligence tests may run as much as 5 I.Q. points higher than the first one. In general, any measurement procedure which makes the subject self-conscious or aware of the fact of the experiment may introduce an effect other than the experimental variable or event; for example, measurement of weight, introduced into an experimental design involving adult American women, probably would stimulate weight reduction (through the mere process of noting weight) apart from any experimental variable involving food or nutrition.

Instrumentation and instrument decay: This variable may be illustrated by the fatiguing of spring scales. In educational and social psychology, education, and other social fields, fatiguing is an especially acute problem when human beings are part of the measuring apparatus or procedure, as in the case of judges, observers, raters, or coders. The two observations may differ because the raters have become more experienced, more fatigued, better adapted, or informed about the purpose of the experiment. Conditions are especially crude when observers or interviewers or coders are different for the two observations.

Statistical regression: Shifts toward the mean may occur owing to random imperfections of the measuring instrument or random instability within the population, as reflected in the test-retest reliability. Regression operates where groups have been selected on the basis of their extreme scores. In general, regression operates like maturation, in that the effects increase systematically with the time interval between the two observations or measurements. Failure to control this factor results in especially serious mistakes of interpretation in remedial research.

Differential selection of respondents: Biases may result in differential selection of respondents for the comparison groups.

Experimental mortality: Differential loss of respondents from the comparison groups may be confounded with the effect of the experimental variable. Even though the groups may have been equivalent at some prior time, differences between the two observations may result because individuals have dropped out, as illustrated in studies seeking to compare the attitudes of college freshmen and college seniors.

Selection-maturation interaction, which in certain of the multiple-group quasi-experimental designs is confounded with, i.e., might be mistaken for, the effect of the experimental variable.

External Validity. The factors jeopardizing external validity or representativeness are as follows:[32]

> The *reactive* or *interaction effect* of *testing,* in which a pretest might increase or decrease the respondent's sensitivity or responsiveness to the experimental variable and thus make the results obtained for a pretested population unrepresentative of the effects of the experimental variable for the unpretested universe from which the experimental respondents were selected.
>
> The *interaction* effects of *selection* biases and the *experimental variable.*
>
> *Reactive effects of experimental arrangements,* which would preclude generalization about the effect of the experimental variable upon persons being exposed to it in nonexperimental settings.
>
> *Multiple-treatment interference,* a problem wherever multiple treatments are applied to the same respondents, and a particular problem for one-group designs.

Pre-Experimental Designs[33]

ONE-SHOT CASE STUDY

Much research in social science has relied upon the *"one-shot" case study,* in which a single individual or group is studied in detail only once, subsequent to some agent or treatment presumed to cause change, and in which the observations are attributed to exposure to some prior situation. This design does not merit the title of an experiment, since the minimum of useful scientific information involves at least one formal comparison and therefore at least two careful observations. Such studies would be much more valuable if the one set of observations were reduced by half, with the saved time and effort directed to investigation in equal detail of an appropriate comparison instance. In these "one-shot" case studies, "standardized" tests provide very limited help, since the numerous rival sources of difference other than the so-called experimental variable render the "standard-test" reference group almost useless as a "control group." On the same grounds, comparison of a present case

---

[32] Quoted from Donald T. Campbell and Julian C. Stanley, *op. cit.,* Chapter 5.

[33] *Ibid.*

Donald T. Campbell, "Factors Relevant to the Validity of Experiments in Social Settings." *Psychological Bulletin* 54: 297–312; July 1957. This helpful analysis and the preceding reference are the basis for the review of pre-experimental, true experimental, and quasi-experimental designs on succeeding pages of this chapter. The *Handbook of Research on Teaching* includes a large number of examples of experimentation. It is recognized that the present summary of types of experiments in some instances serves chiefly to identify a form of experimentation by type and name.

study with potential future ones for experimental purposes would seem equally hopeless.

ONE-GROUP PRETEST-POSTTEST DESIGN

The *one-group pretest-posttest design* provides for one formal comparison of two observations and is still widely used. In this design, however, several confounded extraneous variables may be left uncontrolled so as to jeopardize internal validity and thus become rival explanations of any difference between the two observations or measurements, confounded with the possible effect of the experimental variable or event. These uncontrolled variables might include the effect of history, maturation, testing, instrumentation, and statistical regression, as described earlier in this chapter.

STATIC GROUP COMPARISON

Another pre-experimental design is the *static group comparison,* in which there is a comparison of a group which has experienced the experimental variable with a group which has not, for the purpose of establishing the effect of the variable or event. In this design, there is no means of certifying that the groups were equivalent at some prior time. The prevalence of this design in the social sciences and its weaknesses have been recognized. Any difference between the two observations might have come about through biased selection or recruitment of the persons making up the groups, or they might have differed without the effect of the experimental variable. Exposure to the experimental variable may have been voluntary, and therefore the two groups have an inevitable systematic difference on the factors determining the choice involved, a difference which no amount of matching can remove. Experimental mortality may have produced differences in the groups due to differential dropout of persons from the groups. Thus, two groups once identical may differ later because of selective dropout of subjects, as in seeking to determine the effects of a college education by comparing measures on freshmen (without the experimental variable) with seniors (who have encountered the experimental variable). If such a study should conclude that first-year women are more beautiful than seniors, we would inquire concerning the chances for a beautiful girl to finish college before marriage and recommend an experimental design in which the *same* girls are compared as freshmen and as seniors. Other examples of this type of comparison include: school systems requiring the bachelor's degree of teachers versus those not requiring it, students in classes given speed-reading training versus those not receiving it, and persons hearing a particular TV program versus those not hearing it.

True Experimental Designs[34]

PRETEST-POSTTEST CONTROL GROUP DESIGN

The difficulties of confounded extraneous variables in the pre-experimental designs led psychologists during the first quarter of the twentieth century to search for true experimental designs. The *pretest-posttest control group design* (the most widely used) was formed by adding a control group to the one-group pretest-posttest design. This experimental design seeks to control the main effects of history, matura-tion, testing, instrument decay, regression, selection, and mortality. If the differences between the two observations for the experimental group are due to intervening historical events, then they should also show up in the results for the control group, although there may be certain com-plications in achieving control. If the respondents operate as groups, with only one experimental session and one control session, then there is no control over the unique internal histories of the groups, possibly involv-ing a chance distracting factor appearing in one or the other group. If only one experimenter is involved, he ordinarily cannot make a simul-taneous initial observation or measurement for the two groups and like-wise cannot make a second or end measurement of the two groups at the same time. If two experimenters are available, one working with the experimental respondents, and the other with the control subjects, differences between the two experimenters probably introduce extraneous variable factors. Therefore, for a true experiment, the experimental and control groups should be tested and exposed individually or in small subgroups, with sessions of both types temporally and spatially inter-mixed.

If maturation or testing contributes to a difference between the two observations, this should appear also in the results of the control group. To make sure the design controls for instrument decay, it is necessary to use the same experimenter or a small-session approximation to the simultaneity needed for controlling historical events. Therefore, the running of the experimental group and the control group at different times is ruled out; otherwise the observers may have become more ex-perienced, more hurried, more careless, or the equipment or apparatus changed in some respect. When more than one experimenter or observer is used, counterbalancing the experimenter, time, and group is desirable, with the balanced Latin square frequently serving a useful purpose.

Although regression is controlled in the design as a whole, secondary

[34] Donald T. Campbell, *op. cit.*
Donald T. Campbell and Julian C. Stanley, *op. cit.*, Chapter 5.

analyses of effects may be made for extreme pretest scores in both experimental and control groups.

Selection is handled by the sampling equivalence insured through the randomization employed in assigning persons to groups, supplemented by matching procedures, with the initial observations of the experimental and control groups serving as a check on possible sampling differences.

With respect to experimental mortality, if the experimental and control groups do not differ in the number of lost cases or in their pretest scores, the experiment can be judged internally valid on this point. However, mortality reduces generalization of effects, as applied to the original population from which the groups were selected.

Although the pretest-posttest control group design was highly regarded in the social sciences for some thirty years, by 1940 serious criticism was voiced, in the form of an interaction effect of testing. The effects of history, maturation, and testing, in the language of analysis of variance, are main effects, manifesting themselves in mean differences independently of the presence of other variables, and capable of adding on to other effects, including the effect of the experimental variable. In contrast, interaction effect (a joint effect) may occur even when no main effects are present; for example, applied to the testing variable, the interaction effect might involve not a shift due solely or directly to the measurement process, but rather a sensitization of subjects to the experimental variable.

As a concrete example of interaction it is pertinent to cite the NORC study of a United Nations information campaign in Cincinnati, in which two equivalent samples of a thousand each were drawn from the city's population. After one of these samples was interviewed, Cincinnati was subjected to an intensive publicity campaign using the various mass media of communication, including special features in the newspapers and on the radio, bus cards, and public lectures. At the end of two months the second sample of 1,000 persons were interviewed and the results compared with the first 1,000. There were no differences between the two groups except that the second group was somewhat more pessimistic about the likelihood of Russia's co-operation for world peace, which could be attributed to history rather than to the publicity campaign in Cincinnati. As a result of the publicity campaign of two months, the second sample was no better informed than the first about the United Nations, nor had it been sensitive to the publicity campaign itself. The initial sample was reinterviewed, at the same time that the second sample was interviewed (after the publicity campaign), with the first group showing significant attitude changes, a high degree of awareness of the campaign, and important increases in information. The interaction effect was in the form of sensitizing the initial group (through the initial interview) to the topic of the United Nations, so as to make the subsequent publicity campaign effective for them.[35]

FOUR-GROUP DESIGN

A *four-group design* has been suggested by Solomon to control the problem of interaction effects.[36] This design involves adding to the traditional two-group experiment two groups that are not pretested. The design enables the experimenter to control and measure both the main and interaction effects of testing, and the main effects of a composite of maturation and history. These possibilities recommend the design highly to social scientists, with a deservedly higher prestige than the preceding design. It represents the first formal design consideration of external-validity factors.

POSTTEST-ONLY CONTROL GROUP DESIGN

The *posttest-only control group design* is disturbing to many investigators in education and psychology, because the concept of the pretest has become firmly fixed in the thinking of many such research workers, although the pretest is not actually essential to true experimental designs. For psychological reasons it is difficult to give up "knowing for sure" that the experimental and control groups were "equal" before the differential experimental treatment, whereas actually randomization without the pretest is the most adequate all-purpose assurance of lack of initial biases between groups. To cite an example, in research in the primary grades we frequently must experiment with methods for the initial introduction of entirely new subject matter, for which pretests in the ordinary sense do not exist and are impossible.

The *posttest-only control group design* is illustrated by Fisher's typical agricultural experiment,[37] which involves no pretest; equivalent plots of ground receive different experimental treatments, and the subsequent yields are measured. To cite an illustration in a social area, by way of testing the influence of a motion picture upon attitudes, two randomly assigned audiences would be selected, one exposed to the movie, and the attitudes of each audience measured subsequently for the first time. This design has been criticized as vulnerable to selection bias, especially where random assignment is not possible. Where naturally aggregated units such as classes are employed intact, these should be used in large numbers and assigned at random to the experimental and control conditions. If but one or two intact classrooms are available for each experi-

---

[35] Shirley A. Star and Helen M. Hughes, "Report on an Educational Campaign: The Cincinnati Plan for the United Nations." *American Journal of Sociology* 55: 389–400; January 1950.

[36] Richard L. Solomon, "An Extension of Control Group Design." *Psychological Bulletin* 46: 137–50; March 1949.

[37] R. A. Fisher, *op. cit.*

mental treatment, the pretest-posttest control group design is preferable. Other advantages of the pretest-posttest control group design over the posttest-only control group design are in terms of greater precision, dealing with experimental mortality (through comparing pretest scores of lost cases in both experimental and control groups), and studying the relationship of pretest attitudes to kind and amount of change. For the posttest-only control group design, there are certain social settings in which it is feasible; for example, whenever the social contact represented by the experimental variable is made to single individuals or to small groups, and where the response to that stimulus can be identified in terms of individuals or type of exposure to the experimental variable (as illustrated by direct mail and door-to-door-contacts).

It is traditional in discussions of experimental design in psychology, education, and such social fields as sociology to think of exposure to the experimental variable as opposed to absence of the experimental variable. While this condition may be possible in the stimulus-isolated laboratory in the physical sciences, it is difficult to think of a setting in the social scences as empty of potentially change-inducing stimuli. The experience of the control group, in social experimentation, may be described as another type of exposure to the experimental variable (a control experience) rather than complete absence of an experimental variable. Frequently, in the social areas, we are not so much interested in the qualitative fact of effect or no-effect as in the degree of effect for varying degrees of the experimental variable, which leads to designs in which multiple groups are used, each with a different degree of the experimental variable. When different degrees of the experimental variable are given to the same group, with different groups receiving the variable in different orders, the technique of counterbalancing is essential.

It is necessary to test for effects extended in time, since the longer-range effects of persuasive experimental variables may be qualitatively as well as quantitatively different from immediate effects. Experiments may be designed to measure the effect of the experimental variable at extended periods of time by adding two separate groups for each posttest period (including the additional control group). The additional control group is necessary; otherwise the effects of intervening history, maturation, instrument decay, regression, and mortality are confounded with the delayed effects of the experimental variable.

Quasi-Experimental Designs[38]

The investigator may introduce into many natural social settings something like experimental design in scheduling the data-collecting procedures, even though he lacks the full control over scheduling of

[38] Donald T. Campbell, *op. cit.* Donald T. Campbell and Julian C. Stanley, *op. cit.*, Chapter 5.

experimental stimuli that would make a true experiment possible. Such quasi-experimental designs in appropriate social settings may be encouraged, with full awareness of the specific variables not controlled in the particular design, even though there are serious risks by way of spurious confirmation of misdirection of subsequent research efforts and by waste of publication space. It is a question of using the tools we have for these natural social settings until more efficient designs are developed. We are cautioned that "quasi-experimental design" should not be so employed as to contend with "action research" for the nonrigorous aspects of experimentation.

SINGLE-GROUP EXPERIMENTAL DESIGNS

The *times-series design* involves the presence of a periodic measurement process on some group or individual and the introduction of an experimental change into this time series of measurements, the results of which are indicated by a discontinuity in the measurements recorded in the time-series.

The *equivalent time-samples design* is a form of the time-series experiment with the repeated introduction of the experimental variable, and is useful where the effect of the experimental variable is anticipated to be of transient or reversible character, as sometimes found in studies of learning, work production, conditioning, and physiological reaction.

The *equivalent-materials design* resembles the equivalent time-samples design, involving equivalence of samples of materials to which the experimental variables under comparison are applied; for example, massed versus distributed practice.

MULTI-GROUP EXPERIMENTAL DESIGNS

A common experimental design, the *nonequivalent control group design,* involves an experimental group and a control group both given a pretest and a posttest, but without pre-experimental sampling equivalence for the two groups. Examples are naturally assembled collectives such as classrooms, which are similar but yet require the pretest.

Counterbalanced designs (sometimes described by the terms "rotation," "crossover," or "switch-over") seek to achieve experimental control or precision by entering all respondents (or settings) into all treatments, with the Latin-square arrangement typically employed in counterbalancing.

The *separate-sample pretest-posttest design* may be used for large populations such as cities, factories, schools, and military units, where the investigator cannot randomly segregate subgroups for differential experimental treatment, but can exercise experimental control through random assignment procedures.

The *separate-sample pretest-posttest control group design* is possible when to the preceding design may be added a control group (comparable if not equivalent) from which the experimental variable can be withheld.

In the *multiple time-series design,* the investigator of major administrative change by use of time-series data may seek out a similar institution not undergoing the experimental variable, from which to collect a similar "control" time series (ideally with the experimental variable assigned randomly).

OTHER QUASI-EXPERIMENTAL DESIGNS

The *recurrent institutional cycle design* is labeled as "patched-up," in that the investigator in field research may start with an inadequate design and then add specific features to control for one or another of the recurrent sources of invalidity, often resulting in an inelegant accumulation of precautionary checks and lacking the intrinsic symmetry of the true experimental designs.

Regression-discontinuity analysis is a design developed in a situation where ex post facto designs were previously being used. To cite a possible example, if a foundation interested in improving higher education makes a large grant to a college to study the impact of the school on its students, what are the results ten years later?

Ex post facto design refers to efforts to simulate experimentation through certain procedures, especially as developed in the field of sociology, and represents one of the most extended efforts toward quasi-experimental design, although subject to grave errors in both sociology and education. To cite examples of such studies: the effect of high-school education on success and community adjustment ten years later, and the effect of housing on juvenile delinquency (tracing the earlier records of families before they became residents of a public-housing project, in order to compare the incidence of juvenile delinquency).

Another quasi-experimental design involves *correlation;* for example, between heavy smoking and lung cancer.

Panel studies in their simplest survey form represent observations at a single point in time, commonly offering to the respondent the opportunity to classify himself as having been exposed to the experimental variable or not so exposed, typically with correlations between "seeing the program" and "buying the product."

Other Classifications of Experimental Designs

The techniques of the more recent statistical approaches and forms of experimental design are beyond the scope of an introductory, descriptive account of research methodology, but these methods may be illustrated further by a list of the significant chapter headings[39] of a comprehensive textbook in this field. Study of such concepts usually is preceded by an introductory course in statistical method:

Completely Randomized, Randomized Block, and Latin Square Designs
Factorial Experiments
Confounding
Factorial Experiments in Fractional Replication
Factorial Experiments with Main Effects Confounded: Split-Plot Designs
Factorial Experiments Confounded in Quasi-Latin Squares
Methods for Study of Response Surfaces
Balanced and Partially Balanced Incomplete Block Designs
Lattice Designs
Incomplete Block Designs
Lattice Squares
Incomplete Latin Squares

To cite another approach, by way of classification of 1,000 experiments in education, dating from 1909 to 1952, and in many instances representing outmoded procedures, Shannon has identified seventeen headings or types:[40]

Groups of subjects
In single formation
1. Treated once, not in series (or in series with the same act repeated and no changing factor involved), and perhaps with comparison with earlier practice or with the mode of practice
2. Treated in series with a changing factor and with comparison from stage to stage
In parallel formation
3. Equivalent, with a single variable
4. Not known to be equivalent, with a single variable
5. Known not to be equivalent, usually with no variable factor, to determine the degree of nonequivalence in performance

[39] William G. Cochran and Gertrude M. Cox, *Experimental Designs*. Second Edition. New York: John Wiley & Sons, Inc., 1957. xiv + 611 p. Also see:

Walter T. Federer, *Experimental Design: Theory and Application*. New York: The Macmillan Co., 1955. xix + 544 + 47 p.

Oscar Kempthorne, *The Design and Analysis of Experiments*. New York: John Wiley & Sons, Inc., 1952. xix + 631 p.

E. F. Lindquist, *Design and Analysis of Experiments in Psychology and Education*. Boston: Houghton Mifflin Company, 1953. xix + 393 p.

Benjamin J. Winer, *Statistical Principles in Experimental Design*. New York: McGraw-Hill Book Company, 1962. v + 672 p.

[40] J. R. Shannon, "Experiments in Education: A New Pattern and Frequency of Types." *Journal of Educational Research* 48: 81–93; October 1954.

In reversed formation

6. Equivalent, with a single variable
7. Not known to be equivalent, with a single variable
8. Known not to be equivalent

Single subjects

In single formation

9. Treated once, not in series (or in series with the same act repeated and no changing factor involved), and perhaps with comparison with earlier practice or with the mode of practice
10. Treated in series with a changing factor and with comparison from stage to stage

In parallel formation

11. Equivalent, with a single variable
12. Not known to be equivalent, with a single variable
13. Known not to be equivalent, usually with no variable factor, to determine the degree of nonequivalence in performance

In reversed formation

14. Equivalent, with a single variable
15. Not known to be equivalent
16. Known not to be equivalent

Materials and instruments

17. Materials, material facilities, or instruments relating to schools or to formal instruction (inanimate objects or procedures rather than live subjects either as individuals or in groups).

Shannon found that the majority of the experiments in education had been in the area of teaching methods. The prevailing types of experimental procedure or technique were parallel groups, with the groups not known to be equivalent (but apparently presumed to be approximately so) or with the experimental factors so well controlled, according to Shannon, that the groups were known to be equivalent in the significant characteristics involved. The single-group type was second in frequency of use in educational experimentation.

To summarize the essential characteristics of a good experimental design: [41]

1. It will insure that the observed treatment effects are unbiased estimates of the true effects. (The term *treatment* refers to any induced or selected variation in the experimental procedures or conditions whose effect is to be observed and evaluated.)
2. It will permit a quantitative description of the precision of the observed treatment effects regarded as estimates of the "true" effects.
3. It will insure that the observed treatment effects will have whatever degree of precision is required by the broader purposes of the experiment.

[41] E. F. Lindquist, *op. cit.*, p. 1, 6–7.

4. It will make possible an objective test of a specific hypothesis concerning the true effects.
5. It will be efficient.

Inference and Generalization

Statisticians and experts in experimental design[42] frequently are asked for advice about making inferences from the results of experiments, sometimes after the investigation has been completed. Since the making of sound inferences depends on the way in which the experiment was carried out, the time to think about statistical inference and to seek advice is when the experiment is being planned. The statistician or expert in experimental design can make a valuable contribution beyond advice on some technical matter of statistical theory by getting the investigator to explain clearly why he is doing the experiment, to justify the experimental treatments whose effects he proposes to compare, and to defend his claim that the completed treatment will enable its objectives to be realized. The statement of objectives may assume the form of the questions to be answered, the hypotheses to be tested, or the effects to be estimated. (A general treatment of the formulation and testing of hypotheses has been presented in the chapter on the development of the problem.)

In experimentation, generalization beyond the specific group studied can be made only to other comparable groups; for example, if certain results are found when male college students are subjects, to what extent would this result hold true for female subjects, for high-school subjects, or for older subjects? If a specified amount of fertilizer applied to units of land in a section of Iowa results in greater production of corn than any other specified amount of fertilizer tested, to what extent could a generalization be made for land units in a different part of Iowa or in Nebraska? In this instance the varying amounts of fertilizer represent an independent variable, and the yield of corn a dependent variable. Soil differences may represent important independent variables in the sense that they are related to the results obtained from the applications of the different amounts of fertilizer; a particular amount of fertilizer may work well with certain kinds of land and have little or no effect when applied to other kinds.[43]

Evaluation of Educational Experimentation

Obstacles to controlled experimentation in the field of education and in the classroom include three factors: the limited training for experimentation offered in the field of education, as compared with prolonged

42 William G. Cochran and Gertrude M. Cox, *op. cit.*, p. 9–11.
43 Allen L. Edwards, *op. cit.*, p. 265.

exposure of doctoral candidates in psychology to experimental psychology, statistics, and measurement; the relatively small amount of experimentation done by professors of education; and the neutral or even negative attitude toward experimentation on the part of many school administrators and parents.

TRAINING FOR EXPERIMENTATION

It is essential for the graduate student or investigator interested in controlled experimentation to have the necessary training in statistics (especially the analysis of variance) and research methods before attempting to design an experiment, and to work closely from the beginning with a competent specialist. One answer is to take courses in statistics and experimental design usually offered in the psychology departments of major universities and relatively less frequently in graduate departments of education. It is common for experts in experimental design in education and psychology to consult each other and the mathematical statisticians. Although the specialist in experimental design may not know the investigator's subject-matter field thoroughly, he can point out logical flaws and methodological imperfections that might nullify otherwise commendable efforts. A number of the book-length treatises in the chapter bibliography are used as texts in experimental-design courses in psychology and education.

A critical comment on controlled experimentation in the classroom points out that we have neglected this technique to our great detriment; and we have made only limited advances in the 1960's.

> Most decisions about methods have been based upon colloquial, anecdotal, or administrative considerations rather than experimentation. Seldom are adequate control groups incorporated into classroom experiments. The necessity for long-rang experimental design is not usually appreciated by teachers and administrators. The principle of randomness is often misunderstood or ignored in favor of elaborate matching, which has several disadvantages. Worst of all, few teachers, including those with doctoral degrees, get even minimal training for modern experimentation. Our professional literature is virtually devoid of well controlled experimental studies in the classroom. We continue to pool ignorance via conferences, questionnaires, rating scales, opinionnaires, and ineffective correlational studies, all of which are valuable for certain purposes, but not sufficient in themselves.[44]

APPROPRIATE STANDARDS AND PROBLEMS FOR EXPERIMENTAL STUDY

Critical comments on the educational research of the second quarter of the present century, including experimentation, indicate the need for

[44] Quoted from Julian C. Stanley, "Controlled Experimentation in the Classroom." *Journal of Experimental Education* 25: 195–201; March 1957.

adequate standards of investigation and the overemphasis on purely local, trivial, or temporary problems. At times zeal for empiricism and experimentation may become a fetish, leading to expensive attempts to demonstrate experimentally certain hypotheses that could be tested more readily by other methods. It really does not require an experiment to conclude that an interested teacher has more time for individual instruction when class size is decreased. There is a place for the exercise of good judgment in attempting to bring about social and educational improvements, without seeking an answer through controlled experimentation, as illustrated by Andrew Carnegie's establishment of libraries and Abraham Flexner's reform of medical education. To provide teachers with a better knowledge of their subject matter is a worthwhile activity, but to secure and analyze such evaluative data as can be gathered may prove more costly than the results justify. A pertinent example of a project that does not lend itself to experimental evaluation is the program of the American Association for the Advancement of Science and the National Science Foundation, which has involved sending sets of books about science and scientists to more than 100 high schools, mainly to schools with meager library facilities of their own. An investigator could get records of how many times each book was withdrawn and could secure the opinions of teachers about the usefulness of the library materials, but the real purpose of the traveling libraries is to supplement the teaching resources of the schools and to stimulate some of the brightest students toward a career in science. The evaluation of such purposes lies primarily in the area of judgment rather than controlled experimentation.[45]

We must always remember, however, that experimentation is the only valid procedure for settling disputes concerning educational practice, for verifying educational improvements, and for establishing a tradition or setting in which improvements can be introduced without the danger of a "faddish discard of old wisdom in favor of inferior novelties." It is true that we need to avoid a recurrence of the pessimism concerning controlled experimentation, beginning in the latter part of the 1930's and following the overoptimism of the 1920's. We must increase our time-perspective to recognize that continuous, multiple experimentation is more typical of science than once-and-for-all definitive experiments; that experiments need replication and cross validation under other times and conditions; and that "crucial" experiments which pit opposing theories are not likely to have clearcut outcomes in the behavioral and social sciences.[46]

45 Dael Wolfle, "The Fetish of Experiment." *Science* 125: 177; February 1, 1957.
46 Donald T. Campbell and Julian C. Stanley, *op. cit.*, Chapter 5.

CLASSROOM EXPERIMENTATION AND THE TEACHER

Because of the nature of the strict controls necessary in experimental research, the operation of such variables outside the laboratory or experimental classroom must be field-tested in a variety of real school settings. After field testing, conclusions must be demonstrated and diffused to receptive practitioners before actual impact on practice. Therefore, the essential steps in a program of research leading to innovation include the cycle of basic research, field testing, demonstration and diffusion of results, as well as continuous planning and development, and training of research personnel.[47]

As a setting for experimentation the classroom is a complex human situation. The pupils in a classroom act not only as individuals, but together react as a social system. The school is a part of the political subdivision and of a community of educational institutions. The school itself is a system, of which the classroom is a part. Within the classroom many sources (sometimes unseen) are at work—a reference group to which each individual feels himself accountable, a pedagogical tradition that dictates subject matter and method, and a culture (societal needs, the peer culture, and the professional culture represented by the school and the teacher).[48]

Since experimentation is the most difficult and technically exacting research method for studying human and behavioral problems, if teachers do not understand the scientific spirit of inquiry and the requirements of controlled experimentation, they may make departures from the rules and design prescribed for the experiment. The teacher's values, attitudes, interests, motives, and sentiments may affect the procedure and results, since the natural inclination of the teacher is to try to "help" the pupils, the experiment, and investigator appear in the best possible light. Certainly it seems desirable for the classroom teacher to have a knowledge of the fundamentals of experimental methods and of illustrative investigations, but not to attempt formal experimental studies without the counsel of an appropriate expert in statistics and experimental design. Objective, impartial participation by teachers in appropriate experimentation should have a stimulating effect on both teachers and pupils and cultivate a spirit of exploration in the adventure of teaching (a personal value or by-product of the experiment).

[47] F. A. J. Ianni, "Research and Experimentation in Education." *Phi Delta Kappan* 46: 489–94; June 1965.

[48] Arthur W. Foshay and James A. Hall, *Research for Curriculum Improvement.* 1957 Yearbook. Washington: Association for Supervision and Curriculum Development, National Education Association, 1957. p. 8–11.

ETHICS

We must recognize that, as scientific inquiry pushes toward the limits of research on human behavior, some danger to the subjects and related legal and moral problems may be involved; for example, "Under what circumstances will integrated, rational behavior break down?" The answer can come only from placing experimental subjects under real stress, with some risk of personal damage from conditions of strain, fatigue, or other factors that induce abnormal mental states. The fact that the underlying legal and moral issues are being studied is evidence that scientific inquiry will prove increasingly powerful in knowing man himself.

[One legal analysis offers] a partial solution with the concept of "liability without fault." Under this concept, if a subject is damaged as a result of participation in a psychological experiment he would be entitled to be made whole, through treatment or rehabilitation, or to receive compensatory damages. Thus the subject would be protected. The experimenter would also be protected. He would not be considered to be at fault, but rather to have been acting in the interest of society. Thus society, through appropriate government channels, would assume the costs of rehabilitation or compensation just as society, also through government channels, supports most of the experimentation for which the concept of liability without fault would be appropriate.[49]

At times the experimenter balances his career and scientific interests against the best interests of his subjects, with a stated objective of doing the best possible job with the least possible harm to his subjects. The experimenter is indebted to his subjects, however, even when the reason for volunteering may be course credit or monetary gain. Most experimental conditions cause no pain or indignity and hold a certain interest or challenge, thus presenting no problem of ethics. In volunteering, the subject agrees to assume a posture of trust and obedience, and assumes that this security and self-esteem will be protected. Procedures that involve loss of dignity, self-esteem, and trust in rational authority are likely to prove harmful in the long run to all concerned.[50]

The question of ethics in relation to deception has been forcefully stated by an anthropologist:

The question can be stated simply: Is it scientifically and ethically permissible to deceive the subjects of research by disguising oneself as a "participant observer," or by introducing stooges into an experiment, or by making use of long-distance television or hidden microphones or other devices for concealed

[49] Quoted from Dael Wolfle, "Research with Human Subjects." *Science* 132: 989; October 14, 1960. Reprinted from *Science* by permission.

[50] Diana Baumrind, "Some Thoughts on Ethics of Research." *American Psychologist* 19: 421–23; June 1964.

observation? When a human being is introduced who is consciously distorting his position, the material of the research is inevitably jeopardized, and the results always are put in question as the "participant"—introduced as a "psychotic" into a mental ward or as a "fanatic" into a flying-saucer cult group —gives his subjects false clues of a nonverbal nature and produces distortions which cannot be traced in his results. Concealed instruments of observation may not distort the subjects' course of action, but the subsequent revelation of their presence—as in the jury room that was tapped for sociological purposes—damages the trust both of the original participants and of all others who come to know about it. The deception violates the conventions of privacy and human dignity and casts scientists in the role of spies, intelligence agents, Peeping Toms, and versions of Big Brother. Furthermore, it damages science by cutting short attempts to construct methods of research that would responsibly enhance, rather than destroy, human trust.[51]

Small-group experiments especially may involve deceptions of some kind—"stooges" who pretend to be subjects, messages purportedly coming from other group members, or instructions about whether the rest of the group will be compatible. In evaluating the moral acceptability of such procedures, it is suggested that the consequences of the act be given more weight than the nature of the act itself, with careful consideration of both the immediate consequences to the subjects and the more remote scientific results. It may be argued that, when subjects have volunteered for a psychological experiment, a certain amount of deception may be expected, provided the subjects do not suffer undue annoyance or embarrassment at the time and are not adversely affected later by the experiment. From this point of view, experiments dealing with such variables as frustration and stress involve important questions of ethics.[52]

To cite other examples from the behavioral sciences, we have noted that many of the techniques for manipulation of variables involve deception, prevarication, and misdirection of the subject and that, in working with human subjects, the experimenter is obligated to keep in mind his responsibilities to the subject and the ethics of experimentation. One of the difficulties in classroom experimentation is that the subjects are children, who for ethical reasons must not be subjected to conditions that may harm them. The investigator may be handicapped by the popular attitude of "no experimenting with children." The experimenter should perform some service for the subjects in exchange for their help; for example, to give the subjects (if mature enough to comprehend) a full explanation at the conclusion of the experiment, even though it may require more time for explanation and discussion than it took to do the

[51] Quoted from Margaret Mead, "The Human Study of Human Beings." *Science* 133: 163; January 20, 1961. Reprinted from *Science* by permission.

[52] Michael Argyle, "Experimental Studies of Small Social Groups," *Society: Problems and Methods of Study*. London: Routledge & Kegan Paul, 1962. p. 86.

experiment. If this explanation is well done, the subjects will feel that they have learned something and have not wasted their time.[53]

A more comprehensive enumeration of the obligations and ethics involved in the "human" study of human beings includes: the need for consent to the research by both observer and subject, control of the individual and cultural bias of the observer or experimenter, protection of both the subject and experimenter from the effects of cruelty (and safeguarding from ill effects other human beings not directly involved in the observations), effect of the research methods on the behavior observed, and protection of science itself from any possible loss of confidence or respect. To single out the issue of cruelty toward an animal, it has been recognized that adequate protection of the experimental subject is essential, but less often have we recognized that callousness toward the suffering of a living thing may produce moral deterioration in the experimenter. As to the effect of deception on public confidence in science and research, scientists do not yet have a satisfactory answer.

To cite a specific example in the area of testing, the Houston, Texas, School Board ordered certain answer sheets for tests destroyed, because of complaints from parents about the intimate nature of some test items. This action precipitated a controversy concerning freedom of investigation and the ethics of invading the privacy of the individual. Even though the tester, in effect, says that he is studying the subject for his own good, the child through his parents may reply that intrusion of his privacy is not desired. As in most such conflicts in the area of ethics and values, the actual facts and consequences became involved with emotional states and attitudes.[54]

Questions of ethics arise in dealing with the institutions that supervise the children sought for experimental study. While many of the institutes or agencies devoted to study of the child maintain child populations and facilities for research purposes, it is frequently necessary to seek access to the children and resources of other agencies—schools, hospitals, and institutions for the disturbed, handicapped, or retarded. Although the public school rarely has been under any mandate or obligation to cooperate with the university investigator, the response usually has been favorable to the student of child-related research interests. However, in order to avoid complications, many of the larger school systems have assigned to an administrative officer the task of reviewing research proposals and providing the necessary contacts with principals, teachers, and children, thus making certain that the proposed study is compatible with

[53] Leon Festinger and Daniel Katz, *Research Methods in the Behavioral Sciences.* New York: Holt, Rinehart and Winston, Inc., 1953. p. 170.

[54] Gwynn Nettler, "Test Burning in Texas." *American Psychologist* 14: 682–83; November 1959.

the routine, regulations, practices, and responsibilities of the particular school system. A comparable reciprocating arrangement in the university has been less frequent.[55]

Experimentation in Relation to Other Techniques

PSYCHOMETRIC AND STATISTICAL RESEARCH

Some investigators differentiate between experimental research and psychometric research (studies in which psychometric techniques are used to investigate relations between variables, but excluding such procedures in assessing individuals for clinical or other applied psychological work). Since experimental and psychometric techniques are basically similar in purpose, they can be combined in areas traditionally restricted to one or the other.

In an investigation of the relation between, let us say, reaction time and alcoholic content of blood, variations in alcoholic content of blood are likely to be produced experimentally by feeding comparable groups of subjects different amounts of alcohol. The groups are treated in different ways, subjected to different conditions. On the other hand, in studying the relation between memory and intelligence, for example, variations in intelligence are obtained psychometrically by selecting individuals who vary with respect to scores on an intelligence test. In both cases we vary each of at least two variables in order to determine the relation between them, but the method of producing variation is different. In experimental investigations the investigator produces variation by changing the external environment, or internal state, or both, of his subjects. In psychometric research no attempt is made to produce any change in the individual subject. Rather, the subject is assumed to stay put with respect to the property (e.g., intelligence) in which the investigator is interested, and variation in that property is obtained by selecting individuals who differ with respect to it. The experimentalist obtains variation by subjecting a given group of subjects to different experimental conditions, the psychometric researcher achieves it by moving from individual to individual.[56]

Expressed in other terms, it is not enough for the two disciplines of correlational psychology and experimental psychology to borrow from each other. Although correlational psychology studies only variance among organisms, and experimental psychology investigates only variance among treatments, a united discipline will study both of these and

55 Alfred Castaneda and Leila S. Fahel, "The Relationship Between the Psychological Investigator and the Public Schools." *American Psychologist* 16: 201–3; April 1961.

56 Quoted from Dalbir Bindra and Ivan H. Scheier, "The Relation Between Psychometric and Experimental Research in Psychology." *American Psychologist* 9: 69–71; February 1954.

will also be concerned with the otherwise neglected interactions between organismic and treatment variables.[57]

> There was a time when experimental psychologists concerned themselves wholly with general, nonindividual constructs, and correlational psychologists sought laws wholly within developmental variables. More and more, nowadays, their investigations are coming to bear on the same targets. One psychologist measures ego involvement by a personality test and compares the behavior of high- and low-scoring subjects. Another psychologist heightens ego involvement experimentally in one of two equated groups and studies the consequent differences in behavior. Both investigators can test the same theoretical propositions, and to the extent that their results agree they may regard both procedures as embodiments of the same construct. . . .

We are reminded that statistical and experimental methods represent one approach to problems but not the only scientific method, although the prestige of statistics and experimentation is great, in part deriving from the high repute of mathematics and logic. Strong professional societies are devoted to the advancement of mathematics and statistics, and hundreds of technical books and journals in the fields of statistics and experimentation are published annually. We must keep in mind, however, that important parts of the scientific process do not now lend themselves to mathematical, logical, or any other formal treatment, as illustrated particularly by certain of the studies cited in the chapter on case and clinical techniques.[58] All statistical techniques are tools, to be fitted to the experimenter's requirements, and the "statistical tail" should never be permitted to wag the "experimental dog." Formal statistical training of graduate students should not be such as to obscure the possibility and desirability of simple procedures and direct experimental control wherever feasible. In the interest of fertility of invention and flexibility of thinking, the young investigator must find and use the methods appropriate to his problem rather than to limit his choice to techniques with which he may be familiar or overly impressed.[59]

A caricature of the preparation of a hypothetical thesis with an experimental approach and certain statistical aspects is biting in its humor, but is well worth our attention:

1. Skim through the paragraph headings and summaries of articles in the last couple of issues of the *Journal of Abnormal and Social Psychology, Journal*

57 Quoted from Lee J. Cronbach, "The Two Disciplines of Scientific Psychology." *American Psychologist* 12: 671–84; November 1957.

58 B. F. Skinner, "A Case History in Scientific Method." *American Psychologist* 11: 221–33; May 1956.

59 Donald W. Taylor and Others, "Education for Research in Psychology." *American Psychologist* 14: 167–79; April 1959.

of Consulting Psychology, the *Journal of Projective Techniques,* and *Journal of Personality.* This is known as *surveying the literature.*

2. Select the measurement device most frequently used in recent work (preferably one that is self-administering and requires no effort to score or interpret, like the Taylor Manifest Anxiety Scale). This assures your study of *timeliness, topical relevance, and publishability.*

3. Find some other fashionable instrument or procedure with which the first has never been correlated, also preferably one that gives a quantitative, objectively derived score. State that this score will be adopted as a measure of *self-actualization,* or some other fine sounding and not too easily defined concept, and note that, when you say "self-actualization," you mean it only in the restricted sense of your test's score. This puts your work on a sound *operational basis.*

4. Get a group of subjects—any old subjects who happen to be available. Divide them into an experimental and a control group, taking elaborate precautions to match them for mean age and years of schooling, whether these variables have anything to do with your problem or not. This procedure solves all of the problems of *experimental design.*

5. Give the two tests to both groups, scaring hell out of the experimental group by solemnly assuring them that your dependent variable is a test of intelligence, leadership, innate decency, and sexual potency and that they have all scored below second percentile and you are sorry but you feel honor bound to report them to the dean. This process, called *exprimentally manipulating the independent variable,* is really good clean fun because after the papers are handed in you tell them that it was just a little trick, all for science.

6. Then you correlate X with Y under your experimental and control conditions, reporting the coefficient and its *PE* to four decimal places. This shows you to be a *rigorous, mathematically* exact sort of scientist.

7. If your correlations are not quite different enough, rescrutinize the data to make sure that you have not inadvertently included subjects who were *insufficiently motivated,* and eliminate the ones who were fouling up the results.

8. Now write it all up, predicting whatever finding you happen to get, which makes it permissible for you to use one-tailed tests of significance throughout. Make it as long, ponderous, and dull as possible; dedicate it jointly to your spouse and your advisor, "without whose help this work could not have been completed," and you are in.[60]

THE EXPERIMENTAL CLINICIAN OR
FLIGHT FROM THE LABORATORY

Many graduate students in psychology (and some in education) have experienced frustration in attempting to mold themselves in the image of

[60] Quoted from Robert R. Holt, "Researchmanship or How to Write a Dissertation in Clinical Psychology Without Really Trying." *American Psychologist* 14: 151; March 1959.

the "experimental clinician." The graduate student seeks to find some appropriate middle ground in his training and profession between the goal of research as the pursuit of understanding and the ideal of service as the welfare of the client.[61] On the one hand is the rather rigid, controlled methodology of the experimentalist and, on the other hand, the flexible, eclectic approach of the clinician. It is the difference between a data- and research-centered approach versus a client- and service-centered attitude or orientation (frequently relying on clinical intuition and qualitative insight). (The relationship of the clinical and statistical approaches to problem-solving has been discussed in the chapter on clinical and case studies.) The student's predicament is shared by the profession of psychology as a whole. Psychologists have yet to learn how to test in the laboratory the induced hypotheses of the therapy room, and to develop a theoretical framework which will deductively support both clinical insight and experimental inquiry.[62]

Some doubts concerning experimental psychology became apparent near the middle of the present century when many graduate students and some professors were turning to social, personal, clinical, and applied psychology. Movements competing with experimental psychology for the attention of professors and graduate students, or even encouraging "flight from the laboratory," included statistical specialization and machine tabulation, mathematical models, case histories, psychoanalysis and the organization of personality, and over-popularization of psychological concepts and language. At that time there was a familiar caricature of the experimental psychologist which runs something like this:

He is first of all an apparatus man, who spends a good share of his time tinkering with sundry pieces of equipment which never quite work to his satisfaction. He investigates only problems which he calls appropriate to the laboratory. He cannot study learning as part of the complex and subtle interplay of behavior and environment in everyday life, so he confines himself to the memorizing of meaningless words presented with clocklike regularity in a standard aperture. He cannot bring love or hate or envy into the laboratory, so he investigates reactions to garter snakes and pistol shots. The only strong motives he knows are his own, for his subjects perform merely to oblige him or because they are required to do so as part of a course they are taking. (In an exceptional case, if he "has a grant," they may be paid seventy-five cents an hour.) He remains an experimental psychologist only so long as his problems have no practical value; that is how he stays pure. If his field suddenly becomes important for industry or the public weal, then he becomes an industrial or applied psychologist and does the whole thing over again in no time at all with better and more expensive apparatus. He works only with amena-

61 Lawrence N. Solomon, "The Paradox of the Experimental Clinician." *American Psychologist* 10: 170–71; April 1955.
62 George A. Kelly, "I Itch Too." *American Psychologist* 10: 172–73; April 1955.

ble subjects—that is to say, with subjects in whom no one is really interested: white rats or dogs or human beings who have stepped out of their normal lives and into a laboratory frame as standard organisms.[63]

This picture of the experimental psychologist is not amusing to the thoughtful student of education and psychology. Until past the middle of the twentieth century, parts of it were perhaps too close to the truth to be funny. Psychologists with a broader interest in the affairs of men have sometimes grown impatient with their experimental associates and often have resented the historical seniority and prestige of the experimental field. Experimental psychologists themselves in increasing numbers have become uncertain of their scientific position and in some numbers have turned to other fields of psychological endeavor. However, the entire field of scholarship and research should place in high priority the survival of experimental psychology as a field of investigation and should assure its ultimate position with respect to other branches of psychology, even though certain factors have contributed to our doubts concerning experimental psychology. In defining or delimiting the scope of experimental psychology there is no reason to suppose that this field is concerned chiefly with such limited areas as sensory processes, reaction times, and certain limited learning situations; as a matter of fact, experimentation is now common in every field of human behavior. The experimental psychologist is no longer distinguished by the fact that he uses apparatus; use of apparatus may improve an experiment, but must not be confused with experimentation itself. Since the experimental psychologist is no longer distinguished by a special field of research, by technical equipment, or by laboratory simplification of conditions, his statements or conclusions must not necessarily be considered any more reliable than those of other research specialists and scholars.[64]

There are signs that educational psychology will attract a relatively large number of the new research workers in psychology during the years ahead, just as clinical psychology did in the 1940's and 1950's.

OBSERVATIONAL OR DESCRIPTIVE-SURVEY STUDIES

For certain purposes direct observation of a descriptive-survey type may prove more rewarding than controlled experimentation, as in noting the particular stimuli in a complex social setting to which the individual child reacts, consistency of reaction for an individual, and variability in response between the different members of the group. From this point of view, controlled experiments in laboratories and in many classrooms

[63] Quoted from B. F. Skinner, *Cumulative Record*. New York: Appleton-Century-Crofts, 1959. p. 223.

[64] *Ibid.*

are regarded as artificial or unnatural. Some observational studies may even satisfy the requirements of controlled observation, in that certain controls are used in selecting the room, equipment, children, stimuli, and observers. The simpler technique of observation of behavior, as compared with controlled experimentation, is useful in securing accurate running accounts of what happens from day to day in teaching a group of children some complex skill, generalization, or attitude.

On the other hand, if the experimenter succeeds in controlling the conditions under which an event occurs, he has certain advantages over an observer who simply watches the course of events without exercising any control: the experimenter can make the event occur when he wishes; he can repeat his observation under the same conditions for verification; and he can vary the conditions systematically and note the variation in results.

Psychologists sometimes have used the term *qualitative* in contrast to *quantitative* in discussing experimentation. Woodworth points out that certain important variables are qualitative rather than quantitative: the role of the different senses in revealing the environment as an important psychological problem; training with "understanding" differs from routine drill; an animal will approach one object and avoid another; and a human subject likes one odor and dislikes another. "How could chemistry ever have become quantitative without first being interested in the various kinds of elements and compounds? A qualitative survey is often necessary to show up the important problems and suggest hypotheses for more exact testing."[65]

Examples may be cited of other investigational techniques used in conjunction with experimentation, actually as part of the experimental design. Use of eye-movement photography, for the purpose of establishing central tendencies, is descriptive-survey in character, but may become a first step in experimentation when reading content is varied (from prose to poetry to written problems in arithmetic). As a co-twin control technique, using identical twins, one infant may be taught to climb the stairs, while the other waits until he has reached a stage of stair-climbing "readiness." This study may be so analyzed and reported as to possess the characteristics of case-study and genetic procedures, as well as experimentation.

Instrumentation

Instruments may be thought of as unifying elements which help self-centered disciplines shed their isolationism. The scientist who produces

---

[65] Robert S. Woodworth and Harold Schlosberg, *Experimental Psychology*. Revised Edition. New York: Holt, Rinehart and Winston, Inc., 1954. p. 6–7.

instruments for research is recognized among his fellows, especially in the cooperative efforts of interdisciplinary research. An instrument for scientific use is a physical means for observation and experimentation directed to securing and utilizing information, and may be one of several types:[66]

1. A device in which known physical principles are applied to increase one's perceptivity of natural phenomena, or to render observable otherwise completely elusive phenomena. It is an amplifier for sensory perception.
2. Means for measuring whatever attributes of a physical entity are susceptible of quantitative treatment. It provides numbers which uniquely describe the characteristics observed.
3. Means by which response to a condition may be recorded, or applied to the condition which elicits the response. It makes possible the automatic control of a condition, as in a servomechanism.
4. Means by which recorded information may be treated and processed to make it accessible to evaluation, thereby vastly decreasing the drudgery of manipulating data, or, indeed, making their evelution feasible.

Instruments play an important part in modern science, technology, and business organization, and also in the design of controlled experimentation (with relatively greater use in psychological research than in educational experiments). Achievements made possible by modern instruments include the development of sensing devices capable of operating under extreme conditions and sensitive to physical changes far beyond the range of human sense organs, computing machines of extreme rapidity, and devices for automatic control of machining and assembling operations. Many current discoveries would have been impossible without the aid of the specially designed instruments made possible by modern technology, and improved instruments are essential for research progress in the future. Scientists can expect and even demand more assistance from machines in handling scientific data, including the processes or techniques of integrated and electronic data-processing.[67] (The numerous instruments for mechanical recording and for data-gathering, as described in the chapter on descriptive-survey studies, are available for use in controlled experimentation.)

In recent years increased funds available through government support of research would not have been so useful except for this revolution in instrumentation, especially in radio and radar astronomy, space research, nuclear physics, chemistry, biochemistry, molecular biology, and the be-

[66] Quoted from Paul E. Klopsteg, "The Indispensable Tools of Science." *Science* 132: 1913–22; December 30, 1960. Reprinted from *Science* by permission.

[67] Graham DuShane, "Instruments and Man." *Science* 124: 771; October 26, 1956. Karl F. Heumann, "Data Processing for Scientists." *Science* 124: 773–77; October 26, 1956.

havioral sciences (including psychology). There is danger in misuse of powerful new gadgets, however, if some investigators treat them as new toys or chiefly for amassing vast amounts of data.[68] Although generous financial backing and inventive skill have brought this increasing growth in complexity, number, and cost of instruments, there is a haunting fear that too many such instruments, together with an increased number of technicians, may reduce seriously the creativeness and originality of the young investigator. A research environment is needed in which, first of all, originality thrives and where technicians, equipment, and money are contributing factors to the creative mind rather than an end in themselves. The primary usefulness of instrumentation is in opening new research frontiers and in finding thoughtful answers to meaningful questions.[69]

To comment more specifically on the processes of automation, here we have a functional agent essential to man's usefulness and even his very survival, as he seeks to cope with the ever increasing knowledge of his environment and the universe. Mechanized solution of routine problems may well continue at an accelerated rate, but there is real danger that the computer may be given responsibilities with which it is less able to cope than man is. The computer should not be called on to act for man in areas where he cannot define his own ability to perform or feels uneasy about his own performance. For example, problems in the area of decision-making commonly involve values: one programmer may value cheap, efficient roads and ask the computer to provide the specifications, whereas another programmer may value beautiful, expensive roads (with difficult questions of what is beautiful, and of how much money for how much beauty). We must analyze carefully all automation used in systems of which man is a part, to make sure that man reflects upon his own reaction to, and use of, mechanization. Long ago (1872) Samuel Butler asked: "May not man himself become a sort of parasite upon the machines; an affectionate machine tickling aphid?" We must always be able to answer, "No."[70]

One form of instrumentation in educational research is found in the relatively new devices commonly known as teaching machines, including a multiple-choice machine (with an automated learning graph), a machine for discrimination training, a disk machine (commonly intended to increase rate of learning), an automatic random-access recording micro-

68 Philip H. Abelson, "Instrumentation Creates New Opportunities." *Science* 142: 161; October 11, 1963.

69 Irvine H. Page, "Technicians, Equipment, and Originality." *Science* 140: 451; May 3, 1963.

70 Samuel Butler, *Erewhon*. New York: Doubleday & Company, Inc., 1872.

David L. Johnson and Arthur L. Kobler, "The Man-Computer Relationship." *Science* 138: 873–79; November 23, 1962.

film and motion-picture projector to present frames in any order, computers, language-laboratory equipment, and a relatively simple write-in machine. The more traditional forms of instrumentation developed in experimental psychology include:

(a) Behavior recording systems (polygraph), (b) timing and counting (clock, electronic counter), (c) audition (audio oscillator), (d) vision (light meter, color plate), (e) other senses (anasthesiometer), (f) human learning and perception (memory drum, stereoscope), and (g) bioelectricity (electroencephalogram and galvanic skin response).[71]

As suggested earlier, the electronic computer has greatly advanced the procedures of automation in data processing and calculation, making possible new methods in many areas of research, although detailed discussion of these techniques is beyond the scope of this book. Selected references on computers, data-processing, automation, teaching machines, and programmed instruction and learning are listed in the chapter bibliography.

To cite a relatively early illustration of great skill in instrumentation, Edward W. Scripture of Yale was a brilliant technician, who devised a number of pieces of apparatus in the area of psychology and phonetics. He required all of the students specializing in experimental psychology to pursue a shop course, where they manufactured various pieces of apparatus.

In these latter days of relatively generous appropriations for laboratories and instrumentation, it is interesting to note the budgets with which the psychological laboratories began at the following universities:[72] Iowa, $175; Chicago, $500; Minnesota, $500; Pennsylvania State, $1000 for two years; Maine, $150; Missouri, 500; and Wyoming, $50.

To return to our recurring theme concerning the proper use of instruments, it was early recognized by some psychologists, including Helmholtz, that elaborate instrumentation was not so important as the human mind and the insight of the teacher or investigator.

As a teacher, he [Helmholtz] seems to have rather disdained the current trend toward spectacular methods in the teaching of science. According to contemporary writers, the custom of the time was for each scientist to try to outdo all other scientists in this respect: they used huge charts that could be raised and lowered mechanically, a darkened auditorium for showing slides, large models of the eye and the ear, and "hundreds of animals, large and small . . .

[71] Quoted from Edward B. Fry, "Research Tools: Instrumentation in Educational Research," in "The Methodology of Educational Research." *Review of Educational Research* 30: 513–21; December 1960.

[72] J. E. W. Wallin, "Reminiscences from Pioneering Days in Psychology, with a Few Personality Portraits." *Journal of General Psychology* 67: 121–40; July 1962.

sacrificed, and in one case even a horse . . . introduced to show heart action." Textbooks were "almost useless . . . except for review"; the trend was all toward demonstration, and several assistants were kept continually occupied by each lecturer in preparing for the next day's lecture. One chemistry laboratory —that of Kolbe—was decorated with the motto: "God made the world according to number, weight, and measure."

Helmholtz apparently left these elaborate demonstrations to his assistants and taught a small group of advanced students with no other aid than a blackboard. On this he would work out complicated equations, sometimes finding errors in his calculations, and always preferring to work out problems as he went along rather than to prepare every lecture beforehand. According to Hall, he had a habit of thinking out loud in lecture room and laboratory, and he used to spend some hours each day discussing experiments with his student assistants. But all these attributes, which might seem progressive today, apparently could not eradicate the impression—at least as far as Hall was concerned—that Helmholtz was a man "far more gifted in discovery than in teaching."[73]

Concluding Statement

In experimentation the investigator controls (manipulates or changes) certain independent variables and observes the changes that take place in the form of dependent variables. The "rule of the single variable" is now considered a narrow and mechanical theory of causation. The efficient statistical methods and experimental designs of today make it possible to handle several independent variables in the same design and to have as many dependent variables as may seem necessary. These true experimental designs have been developed by psychologists and others who sought to overcome the difficulties of confounded extraneous variables in the pre-experimental designs widely used during the first quarter of the twentieth century and even later.

We should not overemphasize the familiar complaint that the kind of control possible in the laboratory is impossible in the world at large. Human behavior is controlled in a number of ways. The genetic constitution of the individual and his personal history to date play a part in the determination of behavior, as does the social environment, which is man-made. There are many instances outside the laboratory in which independent variables may be freely manipulated with respect to human behavior; for example, the nursery, certain types of schools, corrective and penal institutions, where the degree of control may be great, although there are certain legal and ethical restrictions. In such situations as educa-

73 Quoted from Howard Gruber and Valmai Gruber, "Hermann von Helmholtz: Nineteenth-Century Polymorph." *Scientific Monthly* 83: 92–99; August 1956.

G. S. Hall, *Founders of Modern Psychology*. New York: Appleton-Century-Crofts, 1924. vii + 470 p.

tion, industry, law, public affairs, and government the control is not so likely to be lodged in a single person or agency, but at times has brought sorrow to the individual and to society.

The influence of social and psychological forces or factors other than the independent variable has come to be known as the "Hawthorne effect." The active participation and response of the subject may involve a special form of social interaction known as the "social psychology of the experiment."

Obstacles to controlled experimentation in the field of education and in the classroom involve three factors: limited graduate training for experimentation in the field of education, relatively little experimentation by professors of education, and a neutral or even negative attitude toward experimentation on the part of many school administrators and parents. It is essential that the graduate student or investigator interested in controlled experimentation have the necessary training in statistics (especially the analysis of variance) and in research methods before attempting to design an experiment, and that he work closely from the beginning with a competent specialist. It has been emphasized in the literature that all statistical techniques are tools which should be fitted to the experimenter's requirements, and that the statistical tail should never be permitted to wag the experimental dog.

At times, zeal for experimentation has become a fetish. There is a place for the exercise of good judgment and logic in attempting to bring about social and educational improvements, without insisting on an answer through controlled experimentation. Near the middle of the present century many graduate students and some professors were turning to social, personal, clinical, and applied psychology for answers to their questions. Movements competing with experimental psychology for the attention of professors and graduate students or even encouraging "flight from the laboratory" included statistical specialization and computer techniques, mathematical models, case histories, psychoanalysis and the organization of personality, and over-popularization of psychological concepts and language.

If teachers do not understand the scientific spirit of inquiry and the requirements of controlled experimentation, they may invalidate an investigation as the result of departures from the rules and design prescribed for the experiment. Objective, impartial participation by teachers in appropriate experimentation should have a stimulating effect on both teachers and pupils as a personal value or byproduct of the experiment.

We must recognize that, as scientific inquiry pushes toward the limits of research on human behavior, some danger to the subjects and related legal and moral problems may be involved. Sometimes parents and others complain about the intimate nature of some items in experimentation and testing, resulting in controversy concerning freedom of investigation and the ethics of invading the privacy of the individual.

Instruments are physical means for observation and experimentation directed to securing and utilizing information and may be thought of as unifying elements which help self-centered disciplines shed their isolationism. The scientist who produces instruments for research and experimentation is recognized among his fellows, especially in the cooperative efforts of interdisciplinary research. We may be reminded again, however, that the most important instrument for research is the mind of man, with automation and instrumentation serving as aids in opening new research frontiers and in finding thoughtful answers to meaningful questions.

SELECTED REFERENCES

ALT, Franz L., Editor. *Advances in Computers*. Vol. 1. New York: Academic Press, 1960. x + 316 p.

BERKELEY, Edmund C. *The Computer Revolution*. Garden City, New York: Doubleday & Company, Inc., 1962. xi + 249 p.

BIJOU, Sidney W., and BAER, Donald M. "The Laboratory-Experimental Study of Child Behavior," *Handbook of Research Methods in Child Development*. Edited by Paul H. Mussen. New York: John Wiley & Sons, Inc., 1960. Chapter 4.

BOOTH, Andrew D., Editor. *Progress in Automation*. Vol. 1. New York: Academic Press, Inc., 1960. viii + 231 p.

BORING, Edwin G. *A History of Experimental Psychology*. Second Edition. New York: Appleton-Century-Crofts, 1950. xxi + 777 p.

BORKO, Harold, Editor. *Computer Application in the Behavioral Sciences*. Englewood Cliffs, N.J.: Prentice-Hall, Inc., 1962. 633 p.

CHAPIN, F. Stuart. *Experimental Designs in Sociological Research*. Revised Edition. New York: Harper & Row, Publishers, Inc., 1955. xxii + 295 p.

COCHRAN, William G., and COX, Gertrude M. *Experimental Designs*. Second Edition. New York: John Wiley & Sons, Inc., 1957. xiv + 611 p.

COLLIER, Raymond O., Jr., and ELAM, S. M., Editors. *Research Design and Analysis*. Second Anual Phi Delta Kappa Symposium on Educational Research. Bloomington, Ind.: Phi Delta Kappa, 1961. viii + 208 p.

COLLIER, Raymond O., Jr. and MEYER, Donald L. "Research Methods: Experimental Design and Analysis," in "The Methodology of Educational Research." *Review of Educational Research* 30: 430–39; December 1960.

COX, D. R. *Planning of Experiments*. New York: John Wiley & Sons, Inc., 1958. viii + 308 p.

DAVIDSON, John F. *Programming for Digital Computers*. New York: Gordon and Breach, 1961. xi + 175 p.

EDWARDS, Allen L. *Experimental Design in Psychological Research*. Revised Edition. New York: Holt, Rinehart and Winston, Inc., 1960. xvi + 398 p.

FEDERER, Walter T. *Experimental Design: Theory and Application*. New York: The Macmillan Co., 1955. xix + 544 + 47 p.

FEIGENBAUM, Edward A., and FELDMAN, Julian, Editors. *Computers and Thought.* New York: McGraw-Hill Book Co., 1964. xiv + 535 p.

FINNEY, D. J. *An Introduction to the Theory of Experimental Design.* Chicago: The University of Chicago Press, 1960. 232 p.

FRY, Edward B. *Teaching Machines and Programed Instruction: An Introduction.* New York: McGraw-Hill Book Co., 1963. vii + 244 p.

GAGE, N. L., Editor. *Handbook of Research on Teaching.* Chicago: Rand McNally & Co., 1963. xiv + 1218 p.

GARRETT, Henry E. *Great Experiments in Psychology.* Third Edition. New York: Appleton-Century-Crofts, 1951. 400 p.

GOOD, Carter V. *Introduction to Educational Research: Methodology of Design in the Behavioral and Social Sciences.* Second Edition. New York: Appleton-Century-Crofts, 1963. Chapter 8.

GREEN, Bert F., Jr. *Digital Computers in Research: An Introduction for Behavioral and Social Scientists.* New York: McGraw-Hill Book Co., 1963. xii + 333 p.

GREENBERGER, Martin, Editor. *Management and the Computer of the Future.* New York: John Wiley & Sons, Inc., 1962. xvi + 340 p.

GREGORY, Robert H., and VAN HORN, Richard L. *Automatic Data-Processing Systems: Principles and Procedures.* San Francisco: Wadsworth Publishing Co., 1960. xii + 705 p.

KEMPTHORNE, Oscar. *The Design and Analysis of Experiments.* New York: John Wiley & Sons, Inc., 1952. xix + 631 p.

KESSEN, William. "Research Design in the Study of Developmental Problems," *Handbook of Research Methods in Child Development.* Edited by Paul H. Mussen. New York: John Wiley & Sons, Inc., 1960. Chapter 2.

LINDQUIST, E. F. *Design and Analysis of Experiments in Psychology and Education.* Boston: Houghton Mifflin Company, 1953. xix + 393 p.

NORTON, Dee W. "Developments in Analysis of Variance and Design of Experiments," in "Statistical Methodology." *Review of Educational Research* 33: 490–500; December 1963.

RAY, William S. *An Introduction to Experimental Design.* New York: The Macmillan Co., 1960. xii + 254 p.

SMITH, Wendell I., and MOORE, J. W. *Programed Learning: Theory and Research.* Princeton, N.J.: D. Van Nostrand Co., Inc., 1962. iii + 240 p.

STEVENS, S. S., Editor. *Handbook of Experimental Psychology.* New York: John Wiley & Sons, Inc., 1951. xi + 1436 p.

TIEDEMAN, David V. "Experimental Method," *Encyclopedia of Educational Research.* Edited by Chester W. Harris. Third Edition. New York: The Macmillan Co., 1960. p. 486–90.

WHITLOCK, James W. *Automatic Data Processing in Education.* New York: The Macmillan Co., 1964. ix + 144 p.

9

Reporting and Communication

THE MESSAGE

This chapter discusses the technical or research report in relation to communication and implementation of findings, dissemination and public understanding of research, effective use of
language, major parts of the report (development of the problem, presentation of evidence, summary and conclusions), bibliographical technique, documentation, style, readability, and
shortcomings in technical reporting.

Communication, Implementation, Dissemination[1]

THE TECHNICAL OR RESEARCH REPORT IS AN EXPOSITION TYPE OF COMPO-
sition, with emphasis on communication of ideas and evidence in such
form as to be readily understood by the reader.

EFFECTIVE USE OF WORDS

In trying to make our meanings clear, without regard for experience,
it is often useless to explain words with other words, because these in
turn require more words. There is no meaning beyond experience, and
no two individuals can share an identical significance for an experience.
Tennyson has Ulysses say:

I am a part of all that I have met;
Yet all experience is an arch wherethro'
Gleams that untravell'd world, whose margin fades
Forever and forever when I move.
And so, to be understood, if one could keep silent and only point![2]

---

1 Claire Selltiz and Others, "The Application of Social Research," *Research Methods
in Social Relations*. Revised One-Volume Edition. New York: Holt, Rinehart and
Winston, Inc., 1959. Chapter 13.
2 Harlan C. Koch, " 'Words' and the NCA." *North Central Association Quarterly* 33:
209–10; January 1959.

When Polonius asked Hamlet, "What do you read, my lord?" he replied: "Words, words, words." Shakespeare also used such expressions as "mere words," "words that are no deeds," which "pay no debts." He tells us about "harsh words," "the power of the word of Caesar." He suggests that we "give sorrow words" and thus assuage "the grief that does not speak."

But whether words are good or bad, sincere or insincere, empty or full, powerful or weak, lead to deeds or do not, they are ever-present. Each day we read and speak thousands of words all combined in simple or complex patterns. Indeed the depth and breadth of our daily vocabulary furnish the best single index of our mental ability.[3]

In discussing reporting as a process of communication, it is pertinent to note Whitehead's answer when he was asked whether facts or ideas are more important; he replied: "Ideas *about* facts." In illustrating the difficulty of communication in words, Whitehead pointed out that something could be said about one's personality, but much would remain that could not be put into words. He believed that a marked limitation of philosophy is the supposition that language is an exact medium and that a verbalized philosophical idea is stated for all time; to overcome this difficulty, when ordinary verbal methods failed Plato, he came nearer to the truth by giving us a myth. When Whitehead was collaborating on a book with Bertrand Russell, the latter satisfied his craving for expression by composing directly in words and thus satisfying his ideas of things, whereas Whitehead composed in concepts and then tried to find words into which the concepts could be translated.[4]

To cite an example from science, for description of certain recently discovered phenomena the existing language is totally inadequate. Modern physics says that the density within the nucleus of an atom is of the order of ten thousand million tons per cubic inch. Such a statement is simply meaningless, and this collapse of meaning has resulted from trying to use "man-sized" language where totally inapplicable.[5]

Samuel Taylor Coleridge says that plain terms are close to eloquence.

"The source of bad writing is the desire to be something more than a man of sense—the straining to be thought a genius; and it is just the same in speech-making. If men would only say what they have to say in plain terms, how much more eloquent they would be!"

COMMUNICATION IN SCHOLARLY WORKS

In the technical report the soundness of the data and insight in interpretation are the important considerations rather than form and style

3 Quoted from Edgar Dale, "Words, Words, Words." *News Letter* (The Ohio State University) 25: 1–4; April 1960.

4 *Dialogues of Alfred North Whitehead*. As Recorded by Lucien Price. New York: New American Library of World Literature, Inc., 1954. p. 149–50, 271–72, 295–96.

5 Warren Weaver, "Scientific Explanation." *Science* 143: 1297–1300; March 20, 1964.

as such, although commonly there is a relationship between careful organization of materials, sound interpretation of data, and effective style. To make it possible for the reader to give undivided attention to content and interpretation, it is essential to meet standards of usage with respect to certain details of form, style, and readability. Many examples of the time requirements and other essential conditions for effective research and technical reporting are included in the chapters on formulation of the problem and on historical writing.

Darwin's treatises on evolution and natural selection are unusual examples of the time, labor, revision, and rewriting necessary, when he shifted from his original plan of a detailed two-volume work with full documentation for an audience of specialists in order to communicate his ideas to a wider public.[6] Darwin's "big book" is still generally unknown, except for what he called "my abstract," *On the Origin of Species*, involving both a reduced scale and a simplified, more popular treatment. Darwin's long manuscript, entitled "Natural Selection," is really version 3 of his book on species. Early in the summer of 1842 he wrote out, in pencil, a sketch of his species theory in 35 pages, as version 1, and by July, 1844, he had expanded the first document to a draft of 230 manuscript pages, as version 2. It is interesting to speculate on whether Darwin's theory would have appealed to the general public, as it did so widely, had he published only a detailed two-volume work with full documentation, as originally planned.

On the other hand, the writings of Herbert Spencer, formerly so influential, now line the back shelves of second-hand bookstores, while the chief books of Darwin are frequently republished and are so much read that their author's name is virtually a synonym among ordinary folk for "evolution," and among sophisticates for "natural selection."[7] In his own day, however, Spencer was regarded as a giant, based substantially on his *Principles of Biology*, although neither Darwin nor Spencer was a first-class stylist, but must have depended on content and general arrangement for their following among readers.

John Lubbock wrote books that sold by the hundred thousand, edition after edition, published in many languages. His success is not really surprising, for he had hit on a technique then quite new and rarely copied successfully since that time, for he took the whole reading public into his confidence and never wrote down to it.[8] Lubbock's books could be suitably read to the family before bedtime and at the same time were

---

[6] Robert C. Stauffer, " 'On the Origin of Species': An Unpublished Version." *Science* 130: 1449–52; November 27, 1959.

[7] George K. Plochmann, "Darwin or Spencer?" *Science* 130: 1452–56; November 27, 1959.

[8] R. J. Pumphrey, "The Forgotten Man: Sir John Lubbock." *Science* 129: 1087–92; April 24, 1959.

informative to the expert in the field represented, thus possessing the qualities of readability and substantial scientific value.

John Dewey is another of the comparatively rare instances in which a man achieves greatness in spite of a generally ineffective style of writing. Most of his books are unorganized and repetitious, but he was a visionary with an original mind and a spokesman for the best hopes of his generation, helping us see farther and move more freely.[9]

As many graduate advisers and research workers know, even great ability in general does not guarantee talent and facility in either oral or written expression. After thirty years of acquaintance, and at times close association, Thomas Jefferson said of George Washington:

> Although in the circle of his friends, where he might be unreserved with safety, he took a free share in conversation, his colloquial talents were not above mediocrity, possessing neither copiousness of ideas, nor fluency of words.
>
> In public, when called on for a sudden opinion, he was unready, short and embarrassed. Yet he wrote readily, rather diffusely, in an easy and correct style. This he had acquired by conversation with the world, for his education was merely reading, writing and common arithmetic, to which he added surveying at a later day.
>
> His time was employed in action chiefly, reading little, and that only in agriculture and English history.
>
> His correspondence became necessarily extensive, and, with journalizing his agricultural proceedings, occupied most of his leisure hours within doors.

DISSEMINATION AND PUBLIC UNDERSTANDING OF RESEARCH

By the middle 1960's, the National Science Foundation had increased only slightly its 1959 budget for furthering public understanding of science, during a six-year period when the total budget increased some 600 per cent. In view of the fact that scientific knowledge approximately doubles every ten years, and that the time between discovery and application is decreasing, this low budget figure for promoting public understanding of science indicates a gap in national thinking and planning.

It has been maintained that information and research are "blood relatives" rather than "in-laws" and that dissemination of the results of experimentation or scientific investigation is an integral part of the total research process. When an organization has some part of a research budget designated for dissemination, there are difficult questions to answer:

1. How should such funds be spread among primary publication, abstracting and indexing, dissemination through other media, and research aimed at

[9] Charles Frankel, "John Dewey: Where He Stands." *Teacher Education Quarterly* 17: 84–94; Spring 1960.

developing new and improved techniques for making scientific information available?

2. With respect to primary journal publication, which periodicals should receive support, how much should they receive, and how can this support be given within the present framework of scientific journal management?

3. How should the questions just raised for primary publications be answered for abstracting and indexing services?

4. With respect to study and research on techniques for information control and dissemination, should the organization conduct such investigations itself, should it join with other such projects, or should it ignore this area?[10]

Possible approaches to the problem of dissemination and implementation involve the federal government and private enterprise. Since two-thirds of the scientific investigation and development in the United States is supported directly or indirectly by the government, an obvious solution might appear to be creation of a mammoth federal agency to take over all scientific and technical publishing, abstracting, indexing, and associated activities.

On the other hand, however, the existing U.S. system for disseminating scientific information is extensive, long-established, scientifically accepted, and in large part privately sponsored and operated by scientific societies, commercial publishers, and universities. In this connection, the role of private enterprise in our system seems important in avoiding increased governmental control. One time-tested technique of dissemination is the so called "page charge," adopted by an increasing number of research periodicals, with the cost levied against the organization supporting the research (not the author) as a fair charge against a research budget. There still remains the question of an additional charge per article to assure adequate abstracting and indexing of the paper.

COMMUNICATIVE ACCURACY AND SCIENCE NEWS WRITING

Scientists are cautioned against attempting, in a "popular" description of their efforts, the same precision and detail as would be appropriate in communicating with colleagues, although in communicating with the public they should be generally understandable and properly informative. For such purposes scientists and scholars do not need all the cautionary qualifications, supporting details, and footnotes that would be appropriate in a technical report written for their colleagues. "Communicative accuracy," or the effective accuracy of a written statement, depends primarily upon the reader's interpretation. An effective report takes the audi-

[10] Dwight E. Gray, "Information and Research—Blood Relatives or In-Laws?" *Science* 137: 263–66; July 27, 1962. Also see:
E. G. Sherburne, "Public Understanding of Science." *Science* 149: 381; July 23, 1965.

ence closer to a correct understanding of the problem and must not interfere with subsequent and further progress toward the truth.[11]

Many science news writers and reporters say that communication would be greatly improved if the scientist would behave or act as follows:[12]

1. Be willing to cooperate with the press and society.
2. Have a better concept of the public that is to be informed. Scientists work with things. Reporters know about and write for people. The reporter's reader cannot be told what to read. If a science writer can convey the excitement of science he will get and hold the attention of the reader. The excitement factor is most important since newspapers, to be successful, must be read, and therefore a newspaper must appeal to both intellect and emotion.
3. Be willing to interpret his subject for the layman.
4. Realize that a reporter works with a deadline, not only on straight news stories but also on feature stories.
5. Recognize that newspapers contribute to civic projects, and that they need more help from scientists than they are getting at the present time. In the opinion of the science news writers this is particularly true with regard to crusades to raise teaching standards and teachers' salaries, wherein scientists, both as individuals and as groups, could work with the press better than they now do. Scientists appear not to accept enough public responsibility.
6. Realize that newspapers must crusade for 200 different things, of which science is only one.
7. Recognize a common tie between scientists and reporters; both are curious and both are skeptical.

COMMUNICATION AND EDUCATIONAL RESEARCH

The importance of communication in the field of educational research has been stressed by the American Educational Research Association in cooperation with UNESCO. Adequate communication will contribute to the development of research and to applications of its findings in improvement of education at the personal, community, national, and international levels. Many of the sources of information and media of communication are listed in the chapter on library guides and techniques. Progress has been made in such areas as technical terminology and summaries of research. Procedures for extending and improving communication, especially at the national and international levels, are as follows:[13]

1. Compilation and publication of a list of primary sources of information about educational research.

[11] Warren Weaver, "Communicative Accuracy." *Science* 127: 499; March 7, 1958.

[12] Quoted from David M. Gates and John M. Parker, "Science News Writing." *Science* 133: 211–14; January 20, 1961. Reprinted from *Science* by permission.

[13] Ben S. Morris and Others, "Communication in the Field of Educational Research," *Report of the First International Conference on Educational Research.* Educational Studies and Documents, No. 20. Paris: UNESCO, 1958. p. 10–15.

2. Preparation and publication of abstracts of the more important studies in certain fields of research selected because they are considered to be of international concern.
3. Compilation and publication of sources of information about research methods.
4. Clarification of technical terminology.
5. Compilation and publication of a list for all countries of sources of information about agencies of educational research, especially those which produce or publish the various types of instruments required for evaluation and measurement.
6. Greater international utilization of existing national periodicals carrying reports of research.
7. Development, where they do not already exist, of national centers for the collection, dissemination, and co-ordination of information about educational research and, in those national centers which already exist, a re-examination of their functions and responsibilities with respect to communication.
8. Expansion of the personal mailing list of individual research workers.
9. Widening the coverage of related studies that are reviewed before a piece of contemplated research is undertaken.
10. Use of ephemeral publications to reduce the time lag in communication.
11. More frequent movement of research workers from one country to another.
12. Greater recognition by research workers of their professional responsibility for improving the utilization of the results of research.

The foregoing procedures for extending and improving communication cover most of the techniques sometimes discussed under the topic of implementation of the results of research. The opening chapter of this book presents a related discussion of the social responsibility of the scholar and scientist in making certain that the discoveries of research are used for the benefit of society. Scientific communication and improved relations between science and society will be advanced greatly if every practicing scientist assists in representing to the public the way in which science advances, the need for tests of the validity of conclusions, the logical processes of science, the demands for objectivity, the need for adequate and valid data, and the difference between claims and proved results (with his own research reports so written as to be models of objectivity and clarity).[14]

Structure of the Report

Standards of technical reporting and publication have taken form in a series of parts or sections that should be generally observed. These

[14] Fred W. Decker, "Scientific Communications Should Be Improved." *Science* 125: 101–5; January 18, 1957.

items of mechanical make-up are known as *format*. While the manuals and handbooks in the chapter bibliography are generally helpful, many publishing houses, editors of journals, and graduate schools or departments have their own sample pages, style sheets, or outlines for preparation of the book, thesis, or technical report.

Relatively short reports of less than forty or fifty pages usually do not lend themselves to a chapter form of organization, but can be divided into sections, with appropriate headings and subheadings. The parts of the longer technical report or thesis and the usual sequence are commonly as listed below. The several sections or subdivisions of this book may serve as examples of the different parts of the research report:

Title Page
Acknowledgment (if any)
 (The terms *Preface* or *Foreword* ordinarily are used in printed books, and
 sometimes an *Editor's Introduction* is included.)
Table of Contents
List of Tables (if any)
List of Figures (if any)
Formulation and Definition of the Problem
 (One or more chapters dealing with such items as the problem, sources,
 procedure, and related literature)
Presentation and Interpretation of Data
 (Commonly divided into several chapters)
Summary and Conclusions
 (Restatement of problem, sources, and procedure; conclusions and their
 limitations; application and recommendations; needed research)
Bibliography
Appendix (if any)
Index (if any)
 (Customary only in printed volumes)

Preparation of the research or technical report is an aspect of the investigation that may move shuttle-like in relation to the various stages of formulation of the problem, development of the data-gathering procedure, gathering of evidence, and analysis and interpretation of data. In preference to waiting until the end of the investigation before preparing the report, first drafts of sections relating to formulation of the problem and the related literature may be prepared early in the project, and helpful notes at different stages of the study will simplify greatly preparation of the complete report.

Certain skills of outlining, briefing, and note-taking are basic to preparation of an adequate report. While the outline should be prepared before the report is written, in order to serve as a framework of organization, revision of the outline takes place as the study progresses and even as the report is being written. The brief, a more advanced stage than outlining, expresses concisely the principal statements under each topic. From the outline and brief may be phrased the appropriate headings and subheadings for the report. It is helpful to place the headings and subheadings of the outline and the different statements of the brief on separate slips of paper, in the interest of revision or rearrangement of the outline and brief.

As an example of difficulties encountered and overcome by the American literary historians, Parkman and Prescott, for long periods they were almost blind and could not refer constantly to notes and printed sources, which made it imperative for them to master their materials completely before beginning to compose the narrative. Both historians had to have most of their materials read aloud by assistants. Both men had retentive memories, great constructive skill, and vivid imaginations, which permitted them to compose mentally and hold in mind long passages before dictating the narrative. Prescott frequently kept in his memory for several days the equivalent of sixty printed pages, going over in his mind the whole mass five or six times and revising as he deemed appropriate. Few authors have such retentive memories or the power to compose in such fashion. The beginner who thinks that he is above the drudgery of a painstaking preliminary outline believes himself better than the English historian, Macaulay, who carefully outlined his best historical works, even though he possessed an unusually retentive memory and a lucid mind.[15]

Few men have had Winston Churchill's resources by way of a phenomenal memory, concentration, organization of large bodies of historical materials, command of language, and research and secretarial assistants. He employed research assistants to assemble the detailed information from historical records, then later strode up and down his study, smoking the inevitable cigar, dictating rapidly to a team of secretaries.

The chapters of this book may serve as illustrations of outlining and of headings. Note-taking has been discussed in some detail in the chapter on the related literature. The pages of this chapter in particular and of this book as a whole include many illustrations of form with respect to formulation of the problem, presentation of evidence, summarizing, conclusions, headings, footnotes, bibliographies, quotations, and other matters of format.

Title of the Report

The title of an investigation should be concise and as adequately descriptive as preferably two lines of space will permit. Certain forms of

---

15 Allan Nevins, *The Gateway to History*. Second Edition. Garden City, New York: Doubleday & Co., Inc., 1962. p. 373–76.

expression and phrasing are either redundant or superfluous; for example, aspects of, comments on, study of, investigation of, inquiry into, analysis of. Exceptions to this statement are helpful attempts to indicate the research procedure involved; for example, experimental investigation of, developmental study of, case study of. Many of the titles in the references of this book, in the *Review of Educational Research,* and in the *Encyclopedia of Educational Research* are suggestive. The particular graduate school or department usually has its own style sheet for the title page of the thesis or dissertation.

Acknowledgment

The terms *acknowledgment, preface,* and *foreword* are commonly used as synonyms in the preparation of graduate studies and similar typed reports, although the printed book frequently makes distinctions between these expressions. The usual designation for this preliminary part of the thesis or dissertation is acknowledgment. It is appropriate to recognize substantial assistance and cooperation in concise and temperate language, although tributes to the graduate advisory committee, librarians, typists, and clerks seem out of order.

Table of Contents

If the working outline and brief are logical and well organized, the design or structural pattern of the report should be clearly apparent, with the table of contents serving as a synopsis or headline display. Since the typed report or thesis usually has no index, a reasonably complete table of contents is essential for the guidance of the reader. It is advantageous for a heading in the body of the report and in the table of contents to keep within one line of space. The table of contents and the index of this book may serve illustrative purposes.

Tables and Figures

Titles of tables and figures should be listed accurately on separate pages in the front matter or section of the report, numbered consecutively in one list for tables and in another list for figures. Figures may include all types of graphic representation or illustrations, whether called graphs, charts, diagrams, maps, or photographs. Titles of tables and figures should include information concerning who, what, when, where, and how many. It is advantageous to phrase the titles concisely within two lines, avoiding such wording as "showing," "table showing," or "graph showing." Titles or legends are placed above tables and below figures.

A table is appropriate for any series of items that involve frequencies.

For purposes of interpretation, it is well to confine each table to a single page, sometimes breaking up unwieldly tables into smaller tables, and placing each table in the manuscript as near the point of first reference as possible. Sometimes an especially lengthy or complex table of several or more pages can be placed to advantage in the appendix, with a shorter summary table in the body of the thesis for purposes of discussion and interpretation. A practical test of the effectiveness of a table or figure is whether it is understandable apart from the text or discussion of the technical report.

Figures should be used only when they make a real contribution to interpretation of the data or tables, never to impress the reader. The general arrangement of a figure is from left to right, and the lettering is placed so as to be easily read from the base as the bottom or sometimes from the right-hand edge of the figure as the bottom. The horizontal scale for curves usually reads from left to right, and the vertical scale from bottom to top.

The details of tabular and graphic representation are such that an adequate treatment is not possible within the limits of this chapter. Therefore, the writer of a technical report that includes tables or figures is referred to the available handbooks or manuals, some of which are listed in the chapter bibliography.

Formulation of the Problem

The formulation and development of the problem may require one or more chapters to present an analysis of the problem into its constituent elements, limits or scope of the study, related literature, sources of data, method or technique, technical terminology, initial assumptions, and hypotheses. Since these details have been presented at some length in the chapter on the development of the problem, only brief comment will be made at this time. If the sequence in a well-organized report is to tell the reader where he is going, take him there, and then tell him where he has been, the first purpose should be accomplished in the section devoted to formulation and development of the problem. In this sense, the introductory chapter looks forward, and also looks backward through the medium of the related literature and historical background. The opening chapter may well begin with a direct statement of the purpose of the study. This overview section of the research report may be prepared to advantage early in the investigation, with necessary revisions as the study progresses. A functional test of the effectiveness of the introductory chapter is to ask whether one who has never heard of the investigation could secure, through the statement of the problem, a satisfactory understanding of the purpose, sources of data, and technique.

Body of the Report

The body of the research report presents the evidence. The inexperienced writer frequently leaves gaps in his report, partly because he is so familiar with the investigation that he overlooks the importance of certain details and of a unified organization for the reader. A careful outline, meaningful headings, and a brief of key statements will aid materially in developing a unified report. The body of the report varies in keeping with the content and research method represented. The historical narrative usually is presented in a series of chronological or topical chapters. The case-clinical report may have a series of chapters dealing with the different types of cases, or a number of sections on the several steps in case study and case work, or some combination of these two forms of organization of content. Unity can be promoted within a chapter and within the report as a whole through introductory, transitional, and summary statements; appropriate cross references; placement of lengthy tables, questionnaires, tests, and other exhibits in the appendix; skill in handling quotations; and avoidance of overloading of the text with statistical details.

Summary and Conclusions

The chapter of summarization and conclusions looks backward, and also forward through consideration of applications, recommendations, and needed research. The final chapter should be an illustration of the adage that the whole is greater than the sum of the parts. Although chapter summaries are helpful in preparing the closing chapter, the mere process of adding these details together falls short of the synthesis or integration expected at the end of the report. The summarizing chapter is especially valuable to many readers, particularly in business and industry, who may not go outside the closing chapter (sometimes the summary is the opening section in business reports) for information concerning problem, sources of evidence, method or technique, conclusions and their limitations, applications and implementation, recommendations, and needed research. The final chapter should recapitulate the answer to the opening question or hypothesis of the study. The investigator should plainly label all instances where he has depended on his own judgment rather than directly on the data in presenting limitations, applications, recommendations, and problems for future research.

Bibliography and Documentation

Adequate bibliographical and summarizing work as a phase of the investigation has been characterized as the "pilot" of research. This view has been emphasized in the chapters on formulation of the problem and on the library guides. The rules of professional ethics require adequate documentation of ideas and quotations from other sources. Appropriation of ideas from another author, without proper recognition, is a type of intellectual dishonesty known as plagiarism. The ethical standards of psychologists, as characterized in the chapter on case-clinical studies, include principles relating to professional relationships, research, writing, and publishing. Specific examples of plagiarism or literary piracy include theft of ideas without documentation, use of figures or drawings without credit lines, direct or indirect quotations without proper documentation, and sometimes reproduction for class use of large portions of copyrighted works without permission from the publisher or author. As a general rule, permission to quote is not necessary in an unpublished thesis or typewritten report. In writing for publication, however, when quoting more than a few lines from a published source it is wise to secure permission from the copyright holder. Extremes of documentation are to be avoided; there is a common body of knowledge in each field which belongs to the discipline itself rather than to an individual author. A major purpose of direct quotations is to portray accurately the language and thought of the particular author. This book includes numerous illustrations of direct and indirect quotations and documentation (in footnotes):

> Direct quotations of more than a few lines in smaller type (single space in a typed manuscript)
> Shorter direct quotations within double quotation marks as part of the paragraph of discussion
> Indirect quotations (paraphrasing or borrowing of ideas) without quotation marks but with appropriate documentation in footnotes.

Footnotes have several valid purposes:[16]

1. To indicate to the reader where he may find the source of a quotation or a more extended account of some subject mentioned in the text
2. To cite authority—not just any old source—in support of a statement, an opinion, or contention in the text that might be questioned by the skeptical reader
3. To direct the attention of the reader to opinions on controversial issues contrary to those expressed in the text.

Criteria for evaluating footnotes include:

1. The accuracy and precision by which the footnote guides the reader to the source

[16] William D. Mallam, "A Focus on Footnotes." *Journal of Higher Education* 31: 99–102; February 1960.

2. The reliability of the source
3. The extent to which the source satisfies and fulfills the intention of the citation.

While the following characterization of footnotes was written in humorous vein, it has considerable value for wise use of documentation:[17]

The *coy* footnote says, in effect, "I could tell you a lot more if you were really interested."

The *decoy* footnote is usually written, *"vide infra*—read on and you will know."

The *hidden ball* footnote says, in effect, "If I snow you with enough references you won't bother to ask what I'm trying to say."

The *play-your-aces* footnote: "Now I have to mention this somewhere, but I don't know where to get it in." Don't go to bed with a piece of information that you haven't got out somewhere.

The *false modesty* footnote: "I don't want to parade my learning, but I've read a lot of books."

The *Madison Avenue* footnote: "Please read my other books" or "See my essay on. . . ."

The *I-know-more-than-you-do* footnote: Use a lot of foreign languages in these. It's terribly learned—and besides, there's a good chance the reader won't be able to translate them anyway.

The *looking-down-your-nose* footnote: "I don't like to get into this, but I can't let it pass."

The *bet-you-forgot* footnote: *"vide supra*—I have mentioned this before, although you may not recall it."

The *snob* or *little-brother-of-the-great* footnote: "As Mr. Y (Miss X), the celebrated writer (actress) once remarked to the author. . . ."

The *"I'm-no-fool"* footnote: "Yes, I've read Professor Z's book too."

The *strategic retreat* footnote: "In earlier days I held the view that . . . ., but I have now come about." You don't have to say how.

The *let's-forget-about-it* footnote: "I still adhere to my earlier view, but I don't want to discuss it."

The *I'll-take-credit-for-this* (even though it may not be entirely original) footnote: "With apologies to Professor A. . . . ." (You don't really have to know what A said, or whether he said it or not.)

And finally, the *flattery* footnote: "The reader will naturally recall. . . ." (If he does, he's pleased; if he doesn't, he's pleased that you thought he might.)

In technical or research reports, it is common practice to place a complete bibliography of all pertinent references immediately after the summary chapter, arranged alphabetically by authors, although chapter bibliographies sometimes are listed, as illustrated in the *Review of Edu-*

[17] Philip H. Rhinelander, "Furtive and Frivolous Functions of Footnotes." *Phi Delta Kappan* 44: 458; June 1963.

cational Research. The references in the bibliography must be numbered consecutively, if a cross-reference system of citation from the body of the report to the bibliography is preferred to footnotes. In the interest of uniformity and completeness of information, it is necessary to translate references of different styles from a variety of sources into the form adopted by the particular graduate school or publisher. In this chapter and book are hundreds of illustrations of bibliographical form for the several types of references: books not identified with a series, publications (monographs, yearbooks, and certain books) identified with a series, journals or periodicals, and unpublished studies (including theses and dissertations).

In this book the reader will find hundreds of illustrations of footnote usage, relating to such items as: consecutive numbering throughout each chapter or section of the report, listing of the author's name in normal order (rather than surname first), use of *ibid.* and *op. cit.,* and the system of cross reference to a consecutively numbered chapter bibliography. *Ibid.* is an abbreviation of *ibidem,* meaning "in the same place"; it is used when succeeding uninterrupted citations of a work occur on the same page or within the space of a few pages. *Op. cit.* is the abbreviation of *opere citato,* meaning "in the work cited"; it is used (following the author's name) when other references intervene between different citations of a particular work or when a number of pages have intervened since the work was cited in full. Some writers prefer a system of cross reference to a consecutively numbered bibliography, rather than numerous footnotes, as illustrated in the *Review of Educational Research* and *Encyclopedia of Educational Research.* John Brown's report (12: 80–90) would mean that pages 80–90 of item 12 in the bibliography contain the quotation or material cited.

Appendix

The appendix serves a useful purpose in providing a place for cumbersome or voluminous materials which tend to break the continuity of discussion and interpretation for the reader (in the body of the report). However, the appendix should not be made a convenient dumping ground for irrelevant materials, sometimes placed there in an attempt to impress the reader or to swell the volume of the report. The pertinent materials assigned to the appendix should be grouped in homogeneous parts, provided with appropriate numbers and headings, and listed in the table of contents. Cross references in the body of the report may be made to the appendix in connection with such materials as lengthy tables, raw data, questionnaires, schedules, interview forms, standard tests, form letters, formulas, and lengthy quotations from documents (for example, constitutions, laws, and court decisions).

Style and Readability

The details of style, usage, and readability cannot be discussed within the scope of this chapter and must be left to the manuals, handbooks, and dictionaries listed in the chapter bibliography. The dictionaries of education, psychology, and sociology are also listed in the chapter dealing with the related literature and library guides. A number of illustrations of style are presented in the chapter on historical writing.

The manuals may be consulted for assistance in diction (the choice and use of words), phraseology (the arrangement of words in groups), and style, which is concerned with certain more general characteristics of writing, especially individuality of expression. The graduate student and others may turn to selected manuals and handbooks listed in the chapter bibliography for many other details of form and usage which cannot be presented within the limited scope and space of the present chapter.

Skill in proofreading of manuscripts and printer's proof is an important asset, as appropriately expressed in the following anonymous verses, probably written by some harried proofreader:

> The typographical error is a slippery thing and sly,
> You can hunt till you are dizzy, but it somehow
> will get by;
> Till the forms are off the presses it is strange how
> still it keeps;
> It shrinks down in a corner, and it never stirs or
> peeps.
> That typographical error, too small for human
> eyes,
> Till the ink is on the paper, when it grows to
> mountain size.
> The boss he stares with horror, then he grabs his
> hair and moans,
> The copyreader drops his head upon his hands
> and groans,
> The remainder of the issues may be clean as clean
> can be,
> But that typographical error is the only thing you
> see.

EXAMPLES OF STYLE

There are too many indications that good practices are being disregarded or abused in scientific and technical writing.[18] What would have

[18] J. R. Porter, "Challenges to Editors of Scientific Journals." *Science* 141: 1014–17; September 13, 1963.

been considered illiteracy a half century ago has come to be labeled by many as homespun American. Although language is alive and evolving, we should not adopt or accredit new words and phrasings merely because they are used by substantial numbers of careless or ignorant persons. We probably would not use our great historical documents as models for the design of a scientific or technical report today, but let us recall what a few well chosen words can say: The Gettysburg Address, 266 words; the Declaration of Independence, 300; and the first scientific article in an English serial publication, 341.

We learn from the *Confessions of St. Augustine* that truth may be uttered in either eloquent or plain language.

> Already, therefore, I had learned from you that nothing should be held true merely because it is eloquently expressed, nor false because its signs sound harsh upon the lips. Again, I learned that a thing is not true merely because rudely uttered, nor is it false because its utterance is splendid. I learned that wisdom is like wholesome food and folly like unwholesome foods: they can be set forth in language ornate or plain, just as both kinds of food can be served on rich dishes or on peasant ware.

The young author may be reminded that certain rules of good sentence structure and word choice sometimes have been broken in order to express ideas simply and effectively, as witnessed by Lincoln's Gettysburg Address. The "corrected theme" reproduced on the next page was intended to poke a little fun at the teacher who would have writing done strictly "by rule."[19]

Scientists and research workers at times are accused of being inarticulate and at other times are charged with writing in a language that few persons can understand. A technical or research report may well use a style that is simple, direct, and effective, without ornateness or literary embellishments, but with whatever skills in language the reporter possesses. Formality in reporting should not be permitted to stifle an effective individual style of writing, although there is something about technical or research reporting which sometimes freezes the pen of an author. As illustrated in the chapter on historical writing, able scholars have varied greatly in style. Ebbinghaus and William James wrote with sufficient scientific rigor, yet in a lucid and interesting manner, with glimpses of the author as a human personality, whereas Wundt almost overwhelmed the reader with a mass of facts, arguments, and dicta. Gibbon experimented extensively before he could find a middle ground between a dull chronicle and a rhetorical declamation.

[19] R. Hugh Schrain, "Think English Is Easy Here?" *Michigan Education Journal* 34: 250; February 1, 1957.
Stanley Elam, "Think English Is Easy Here?" *Phi Delta Kappan* 41: 330–31; May 1960.

THINK ENGLISH IS EASY HERE?

Bad start- be explicit say "eighty-seven"   *"fathers"?*

repetition of sounds

Fourscore and **seven** years ago, <u>our fathers</u> brought

<u>forth</u> upon this continent a new nation, conceived in lib-

erty, and <u>dedicated</u> to the <u>proposition</u> that all men are

created equal. *not a good word* *"gigantic" would be better*

Now we are engaged in a great civil war, testing

whether that nation, or any nation so <u>conceived</u> and so

Tr - rule 194, p.6 dedicated, can long endure. We are met on a great battle-
you used these words before

too many monosyllabic words field of that war. We have come to dedicate a portion of

that field as a final resting place for those who here

gave their lives that that nation might live. [It is alto-

gether fitting and proper that we should do this.] *trite sentence*

meaning?? But in a <u>larger</u> sense we cannot <u>dedicate</u>, we cannot
use another word

consecrate, we cannot <u>hallow</u> this ground. The brave men,
spelling!

living and dead, who struggled here, have consecrated it.
Don't you mean "subtract"?

far above our poor power to add or <u>detract</u>. The world will *awkward*

Rule 194 p.6 little note nor long remember what we say here; but it can

never forget what they did here. It is for us, the living, *make up your mind!*

awkward rather, to be <u>dedicated</u> here to the unfinished work which

they who fought here have thus far so nobly advanced. It *Too many "here's"*

Tr. is rather for us to be here dedicated to the great task *trite word, use "tremendous"*

Too many small words. Eliminate remaining before us: that from these honored dead we take *Rule 74, p.89*

increased devotion to that cause for which they gave the

last full measure of devotion; that we here highly resolve

that these dead shall not have died in vain; that this

nation under God, shall have a new <u>birth</u> of freedom; and
spelling!

that government of the <u>people</u>, by the <u>people</u>, and for the

<u>people</u>, shall not perish from the earth.

This theme is fair, but there is too much repetition in it. There are six "That's" in the last sentence alone. Need more variety in word choice, and your words are too simple. Try again — you are improving. C—

In his teaching William James was vivacious and humorous, with picturesque language and vivid imagery, although the lectures were considered by some listeners as lacking in organization. However, for both speaking and writing James carefully worked through the evidence and arguments, with a resulting clarity and brilliance unexcelled in the literature of psychology. Comparison of the style of the James brothers often has been made. The most frequently repeated comparison states that Henry was a novelist who wrote like a psychologist, while William was a psychologist who wrote like a novelist.

> With a bit more awareness and a little less sententiousness one would today have to ask: What kind of psychologist? Our contemporary to-do over the clandestine rendezvous of experimental and clinical psychologies makes one swallow precociously before accepting this dubiously balanced verbal bait. In the light of fuller knowledge of both Henry and William, it would be more tenable to assert that Henry was essentially a clinical psychologist who worked professionally as a novelist, while William was essentially a philosopher who worked for a time professionally as a clinical psychologist. The pretty paradox, alas, vanishes, but in compensation we see the brothers re-emerge, more alive than before, from the word magician's vanishing box.[20]

Carl Becker's advice was to take care of the thought and the style will take care of itself. Becker did not wish to be known in his later years simply as a stylist among historians, and took the position that good style is good thought, with organic structure or logical arrangement and continuity running through the entire work or narrative. This means thorough mastery of every part of the content, with emphasis on ideas rather than on style as a matter of felicity or decoration, toward the goal of truthfulness of substance rather than vivacity of style as such. However, through his dual interest in the works of novelists and in careful historical research, Becker was able to achieve harmony of form and substance.[21]

In spite of his style, John Dewey was our greatest educational philosopher. His written statements have been labeled as flat and involved, "lumbering and bumbling." His style provoked Justice Holmes to the famous comment: "So, methought, God would have spoken had He been inarticulate, but keenly desirous to tell you how it was." Dewey's published books, articles, and pamphlets represent a pile more than twelve feet high, but one critic declared that, if he ever wrote one quotable sentence, it got permanently lost in the pile. As of the middle of the

---

[20] Quoted from review by Saul Rosenzweig, "The Jameses' Stream of Consciousness." *Contemporary Psychology* 3: 250–57; September 1958, of Frederick W. Dupée, Editor, *Henry James: Autobiography.* New York: Criterion Books, 1956. xiv + 622.

[21] Burleigh T. Wilkins, *Carl Becker: A Biographical Study in American Intellectual History.* Cambridge, Mass.: M.I.T. Press and Harvard University Press, 1961. p. 19–35.

present century, none of the standard books of quotations contained a single Dewey entry, yet in personal conversation and sometimes in the classroom the Vermont Yankee's native wit and shrewdness became evident. The secret of Dewey's extraordinary power to stimulate his students in the remaking of their minds probably is found in the statement of Ralph Barton Perry: "He does not feel obliged to live up to his reputation: to be impressive, witty, eloquent, or even interesting; he simply says what he thinks."[22]

Kettering's exceptional ability as a public speaker was one of his great gifts. But so unconventional was his platform manner that the reasons for his singular success are not easy to analyze. He made no pretense of being an orator nor did he have any of the mannerisms or tricks of one. His talks are like an informal chat with his audience, full of wit and wisdom. However, his thoughts and expression are stimulating, involving a knack of putting things in direct and simple terms, of using imagery and apt analogy, and of injecting illustrations, anecdotes, and humor which give his talks vividness and vigor. Many of his epigrams have been widely quoted. In the transcript of one of his addresses on the serious subject of research, parentheses occur forty-two times to indicate laughter. "Some technical reports are so dry and dusty," he would say, "that if you put a pile of them in a hydraulic press and apply millions of pounds pressure to it, not a drop of juice will run out."[23]

Greenstein's interests were broad and ranged far beyond the sciences. He was a prolific reader and in his Harvard days delighted in Dickens, especially in *Pickwick Papers*. He read widely in philosophy, theology, and biography and was something of an expert on the history of the Civil War—its battles, issues, and great men. His breadth of reading and appreciation of literature must have contributed to the high quality of his own writing.[24]

Style and Effective Writing in Psychology and Education

An apparently anonymous report of a conversation between a graduate student and his professorial adviser includes humorous illustrations of the simple language in the student's draft of his manuscript and the ornate language supposedly suggested by the professor.

STUDENT: "It will be hard to provide enough schools for the children entering in 1966."

22 Harold A. Larrabee, "John Dewey as Teacher." *School and Society* 87: 378–81; October 10, 1959.

23 T. A. Boyd, *Professional Amateur: The Biography of Charles Franklin Kettering.* New York: E. P. Dutton and Co., 1957. p. 215.

24 John T. Edsall, "J. P. Greenstein, Biochemist and Investigator of Cancer." *Science* 130: 83–85; July 10, 1959.

PROFESSOR: "The phenomenon of fecundity has confronted American education with a challenge of Herculean proportions. An evaluation of the implication to the tax structure of state governments in providing adequate educational facilities is a difficult and complex task."

STUDENT: "Professor Blank's scheme of teaching reading was tried, but it did not work."

PROFESSOR: "The writer does not choose to disparage the efficacy of Professor Blank's method of teaching reading. It is not inappropriate, however, to point out that careful scrutiny of the method shows it to be what might be called ineffective."

STUDENT: "The federal government has no control over local schools."

PROFESSOR: "The federal government has no plenary jurisdiction over local school matters. Moreover, since government in the United States is administered at federal, state, and local levels, the implications to government are several, rather than single, and affect each of these three levels of government in separate and differing fashion."

STUDENT: " 'Early to bed and early to rise, makes a man healthy, wealthy, and wise,' strikes me as an effective form of expression."

PROFESSOR: "It is better to say: 'Early retirement is a significant factor in one's physical development, pecuniary success, and intellectual stature.' "

Certain principles of readability in reporting research may be summarized as follows:[25]

1. Appeal and interest increase readability.
2. Personalization means putting human interest into the report: through a review of previous investigations as a story of other persons' successes and failures, an account of how the author collected and treated the data, illustrative cases, and deviations from central tendencies.
3. Pattern or design should be made plain to the reader.
4. Through appropriate emphasis the reader should get the important points.
5. Too great density or concentration of ideas may make reading difficult, requiring some expansion or dilution.
6. Plain words are important in making a report readable.

Elimination of carelessness and individual peculiarities from seminar reports and theses is important training for graduate students, and is at the same time good training for preparation of articles for publication. Many graduate students and some professors, however, regard the requirements of style manuals and of scholarly journals as representing rigidity and severity in form, even a strait jacket to insure conformity and to extinguish the creative spark of individuality. We should remember that the advantages of exact standards in professional writing and of reason-

[25] Ruth Strang, "Principles of Readability Applied to Reporting Research," *Improving Educational Research*. Washington: American Educational Research Association, 1948. p. 41–43.

able uniformity in style for technical reporting have a long history of testing by scholars and the public. On the other hand, we should not squelch flexibility and individuality of style by way of effective communication to the reader, when wisdom and good judgment dictate a particular variation in the speaking and writing of English. As long as young scientists and scholars write accurately, clearly, and attractively, their differences in expression may render science a happier way of life for them and for the reader.[26]

Shortcomings in Technical Reporting

Examination of almost 18,000 reports in the several areas of business education reveals certain shortcomings, which are common in other fields of research and technical reporting; the list may indeed serve as a partial summary of this chapter:[27]

THE TITLE OF THE RESEARCH REPORT

Overly long. Does not reflect accurately the problem solved; that is, it is broader or narrower than the problem stated.

THE PROBLEM

Statement and analysis of the problem, delimitations, definitions, and purpose/s of the study are omitted.

Statement and analysis of the problem, delimitations, definitions, and purpose/s of the study are treated so lightly or are so widely scattered in the report that it is extremely difficult to determine what problem the researcher set out to solve.

Statement and analysis of the problem, delimitations, definitions, and purpose/s of the study are reported in organized form but serious shortcomings are observable:

The problem is too big to permit solution by one person with limited resources.

The merit of the problem is nil or negligible (the impression is that the person was interested only in meeting a degree requirement, not in having a worthwhile professional experience).

Statement of the problem is ambiguous, wordy, too long and involved (carries items that might well be included in the delimitations), or not in keeping with the findings reported.

Analysis fails to round out concept of problem; the bodies of data necessary as the basis for the solution of the problem are not identified or are

26 Edwin G. Boring, "On Eschewing Teleology." *Science* 129: 608–10; March 6, 1959.
Dell Lebo, "Uniformity of Style in Professional Writing During the First Century." *American Psychologist* 14: 151–52; March 1959.
27 Earl A. Dvorak, "Shortcomings of Graduate Research in Business Education." *Ohio Business Teacher* 23: 19–22; April 1963.

not clearly indicated. Explanation of a problem rather difficult to grasp is poorly written or omitted.

Major delimitations necessary to setting clearly the boundaries of the study are omitted, are not placed where they will do the reader the most good, or are poorly stated. Related delimitations are not placed in proximity to one another.

Definitions of terms necessary to a clear understanding of the study are omitted.

RELATED LITERATURE

Related literature is omitted.

Related literature is reported but certain shortcomings are observable:

Some of the items reported as related actually are not related or are remotely so. One gets the impression that this section of the report is "padded."

The relationships of the items to the study undertaken are not reported.

Little more than a list of summaries is presented; that is, no sound pattern of organization is discernible. In other words, even though classification is possible, no attempt is made to do so.

The volume and the pertinency of the literature are not indicated at the outset; one has to read all of the related literature and then judge for himself.

Something less than the original of a related item is used even though the original may be relatively easy to obtain.

Complete bibliographical information for each of the related items is omitted.

METHODS OF RESEARCH AND THE PROCEDURE

The methods of research and the procedure followed are not reported.

The methods of research and the procedure followed are so sketchily or ambiguously reported that the worthwhileness of the completed research is difficult to discern.

The methods of research and the procedure followed are reported but serious shortcomings are observable:

The appropriateness of the methods of research used is open to question.

The methods of research used are incorrectly identified.

The procedure followed is badly scattered; that is, a lack of organization prevents easy comprehension of the total plan followed.

The nature of the data used in the solution of the problem is not described, or the description is merely a repetition of the elements of the problem.

The sources of data are not identified, or they are inadequate in terms of the problem set out to be solved. Dates of published materials are not revealed.

Bases for preparation of data-collection devices are not indicated; copies of the devices are not included in the report. Poorly prepared devices are used, devices which have not had the benefit of a trial run. The devices are inappropriate for collection of the types of data desired.

Bases for selection of cases are not indicated. The number of cases is too small or unnecessarily large.

Tests for amount, validity, and reliability of data are not undertaken; or indefensible ones are used.

Unnecessary detail is included—that is, the unimportant is not weeded out from the important—making reading of the procedure laborious and difficult to detect the major steps taken.

The steps taken in processing and interpreting the data and in making generalizations are omitted or are so poorly developed that it is difficult to determine what the researcher did.

Statistical devices are used incorrectly.

In experimental studies, factors are not controlled carefully.

FINDINGS

Findings are reported based on data which are not accounted for in the statement and analysis of the problem and in the procedure followed.

Unprocessed data are presented, the form used being too rough for the reader to gain the maximum benefit from the results of the study. It may be said that "data" are not distinguished from "findings."

Findings are incomplete; that is, data from some of the cases included in the study are not accounted for.

Bias of the researcher is obvious.

Findings of a secondary nature are overemphasized; that is, they are not placed in proper perspective.

Findings by subgroups are not revealed.

The format for presentation of the findings blocks insight.

Interpretation of findings is confused with summarization of findings.

Summarization is lacking at strategic points.

GENERALIZATIONS

A distinction is not made between findings and generalizations. Summaries of findings are called "conclusions," for example.

No generalizations are made, though the basis for them is clear.

Generalizations beyond the data collected are made.

The premises for drawing the generalization are questionable.

Bias of the researcher is obvious.

Generalizations are based on the related literature rather than on the findings of the study.

A distinction is not made between conclusions and recommendations.

Concluding Statement

As an exposition type of composition, the major purpose of the technical report is communication of ideas and evidence, with the emphasis of the interpretation on ideas about facts. In trying to make our meanings clear, without regard for experience and examples, it is often useless to explain words with other words, because these in turn require more words. There is no meaning beyond experience and example.

Effective communication will contribute to the development of educational investigation and to the application of research findings to improvement of education at personal, community, national, and international levels. Research budgets should provide for dissemination and public understanding of research.

Preparation of the report is an integral part of the total research project which may move shuttle-like in relation to the several stages of development of the problem, gathering evidence, and analysis and interpretation of data, rather than waiting until the end of the investigation before starting the writing of the report.

In the interest of readability and communication, the technical report should have a style that is simple and direct, without rhetorical flourishes, but with every bit of language skill the reporter possesses. It is true that greatness sometimes has been achieved in spite of a generally ineffective style of writing. The young author may be reminded that certain rules of good sentence structure and word choice sometimes have been broken in order to express ideas simply and effectively. Elimination of carelessness and individual peculiarities from seminar reports and theses is important training for graduate students, and is at the same time good training for preparation of articles for publication.

To comment on a special type of creative writing, translators sometimes have been described as the forgotten men of literature, especially in technical fields, although normally authors receive considerable attention. In a technical translation there is little opportunity for the kind of re-creation enjoyed by the translator of a literary work in prose or poetry. There are special difficulties of translation in dealing with quotations and footnotes from a language other than that used in the book; for example, English quotations in a French book. The unrewarding returns from technical translations are such that the best-qualified persons probably will not engage in this specialized and difficult work, with the result that poor translations frequently lead to misunderstanding of the original concepts.[28]

To close by returning to a major emphasis of the opening chapter and of this book, educational research may be used:

1. To provide answers to operational questions
2. To assess educational programs, practices, and materials
3. To build up a body of information about educational enterprises

[28] "The Travails of Translators." *Contemporary Psychology* 10: 396–97; September 1965.

4. To provide the outlook, stimulation, and guidance for educational innovation
5. To develop more adequate theory about educational processes.[29]

SELECTED REFERENCES

ALEXANDER, Carter, and BURKE, Arvid J. *How to Locate Educational Information and Data.* Fourth Edition. New York: Bureau of Publications, Teachers College, Columbia University, 1958. p. xvii + 419.

CROUCH, W. G., and ZETLER, R. L. *A Guide to Technical Writing.* Third Edition. New York: The Ronald Press Company, 1964. 447 p.

DUGDALE, Kathleen. *A Manual of Form for Theses and Term Reports.* Bloomington, Ind.: Indiana University Bookstore, 1962. 58 p.

DUGDALE, Kathleen. *A Manual on Writing Research.* Bloomington, Ind.: Indiana University Bookstore, 1962. 50 p.

ENGLISH, Horace B., and ENGLISH, Ava C. *Comprehensive Dictionary of Psychological and Psychoanalytical Terms.* New York: Longmans, Green and Co., 1958. xiv + 594 p.

FOSTER, John, Jr. *Science Writer's Guide.* New York: Columbia University Press, 1963. 271 p.

GOLDHAMMER, Keith, and ELAM, Stanley, Editors. *Dissemination and Implementation.* Third Annual Phi Delta Kappa Symposium on Educational Research. Bloomington, Ind.: Phi Delta Kappa, 1962. xi + 200 p.

GOOD, Carter V. *Introduction to Educational Research: Methodology of Design in the Behavioral and Social Sciences.* Second Edition. New York: Appleton-Century-Crofts, 1963. Chapter 9.

GOOD, Carter V., Editor. *Dictionary of Education.* Second Edition. New York: McGraw-Hill Book Company, 1959. xxx + 676 p.

HARWELL, George C. *Technical Communication.* New York: The Macmillan Co., 1960. 342 p.

HICKS, Tyler G. *Successful Technical Writing: Technical Articles, Papers, Reports, Instruction and Training Manuals, and Books.* New York: McGraw-Hill Book Company, 1959. 305 p.

HUBER, Jack T. *Report Writing in Psychology and Psychiatry.* New York: Harper & Row, Publishers, Inc., 1961. xii + 114 p.

KIERZEK, John M., and GILISON, Walker. *The Macmillan Handbook of English.* Fourth Edition. New York: The Macmillan Co., 1960. xxi + 489 p.

KLOPFER, W. G. *The Psychological Report: Use and Communication of Psychological Findings.* New York: Grune & Stratton, 1960. x + 146 p.

LEGGETT, Glenn, MEAD, C. David, and CHARVAT, William. *Prentice-Hall Handbook for Writers.* Third Edition. Englewood Cliffs, N.J.: Prentice-Hall, Inc., 1960. 524 p.

LIPSON, Shirley, and ABRAMS, Anne W. *The College of Education Style Manual.*

[29] Ralph W. Tyler, "The Field of Educational Research," *The Training and Nurture of Educational Researchers.* Bloomington, Indiana: Phi Delta Kappa, 1965. p. 1–12.

Revised Edition. Columbus, Ohio: College of Education, The Ohio State University, 1960. v + 18 p.

A Manual of Style. Revised and Enlarged. Chicago: The University of Chicago Press, 1949. x + 498 p.

MARDER, Daniel. *The Craft of Technical Writing.* New York: The Macmillan Co., 1960. 414 p.

MENZEL, Donald H., JONES, Howard M., and BOYD, Lyle G. *Writing a Technical Paper.* New York: McGraw-Hill Book Company, 1961. 141 p.

Publication Manual of the American Psychological Association. 1957 Revision. Washington: The Association, 1957. 70 p.

PUGH, Griffin T. *Guide to Research Writing.* Second Edition. Boston: Houghton Mifflin Company, 1963. iii + 64 p.

RHODES, Fred H. *Technical Report Writing.* Second Edition. New York: McGraw-Hill Book Company, 1961. 175 p.

ROGERS, Anna C. *Graphic Charts Handbook.* Washington: Public Affairs Press, 1961. iv + 189 p.

TUTTLE, Robert E., and BROWN, C. A. *Writing Useful Reports: Principles and Applications.* New York: Appleton-Century-Crofts, 1956. xiv + 635 p.

ULMAN, Joseph N., Jr. *Technical Reporting.* Revised Edition. New York: Holt, Rinehart and Winston, Inc., 1959. 382 p.

VAN HAGAN, Charles E. *Report Writers' Handbook.* Englewood Cliffs, N.J.: Prentice-Hall, Inc., 1961. 287 p.

WELD, Walter E. *How to Chart: Facts from Figures with Graphs.* Norwood, Mass.: Codex Book Co., 1959. xiv + 218 p.

WOOLLEY, Edwin C., SCOTT, Franklin W., and BRACHER, Frederick. *College Handbook of Composition.* Sixth Edition. Boston: D. C. Heath & Company, 1958. 474 p.

ZEISEL, Hans. *Say It with Figures: How to Make Figures Make Sense—a Guide for Those Who Use and Read Statistics.* Fourth Revised Edition. New York: Harper & Row, Publishers, Inc., 1957. xviii + 257 p.

ZETLER, Robert L., and CROUCH, W. George. *Successful Communication in Science and Industry: Writing, Reading, and Speaking.* New York: McGraw-Hill Book Company, 1961. 296 p.

INDEX OF NAMES

INDEX OF SUBJECTS